The Detective's Handbook

The Detective's Handbook

Edited by
John A. Eterno
Molloy College
Rockville Centre
New York, USA

Cliff Roberson
Emeritus Professor of Criminal Justice
Washburn University
Topeka, Kansas, USA

CRC Press
Taylor & Francis Group
Boca Raton London New York

CRC Press is an imprint of the
Taylor & Francis Group, an **informa** business

CRC Press
Taylor & Francis Group
6000 Broken Sound Parkway NW, Suite 300
Boca Raton, FL 33487-2742

© 2015 by John A. Eterno and Cliff Roberson
CRC Press is an imprint of Taylor & Francis Group, an Informa business

No claim to original U.S. Government works

Printed on acid-free paper
Version Date: 20150420

International Standard Book Number-13: 978-1-4822-6004-5 (Paperback)

Visit the Taylor & Francis Web site at
http://www.taylorandfrancis.com

and the CRC Press Web site at
http://www.crcpress.com

Contents

Preface   ix
Editors   xi
Contributors   xiii

Section I
INVESTIGATIONS INVOLVING PERSONAL VIOLENCE

1 Homicide Investigations   3
JOHN A. ETERNO

2 What Detectives Should Know about Sexual Predators   19
RON RUFO

3 Special Victims Investigations   35
DANA GALANTE

4 Arson Investigation   51
JOHN BOAL

Section II
INVESTIGATIONS INVOLVING PROPERTY

5 Investigation of Insurance Fraud   67
PETER C. KRATCOSKI AND MAG. MAXIMILIAN EDELBACHER

6 Burglary Investigations   87
HARRISON WATTS

7 Investigation of Health-Care Fraud   99
STEPHEN A. MORREALE

8 White-Collar and Financial Fraud Investigations   117
FRANK DIMARINO

Section III
INVESTIGATIONS INVOLVING COMPUTERS AND ANALYSIS

9 **Collection and Preservation of Digital Evidence**   135
MARK MCCOY AND RACHAEL ELLIOTT

10 **Cybercrime Investigation: An International Perspective**   147
SZDE YU

11 **Use of Crime Analysis in Criminal Investigations**   163
DENIESE KENNEDY-KOLLAR

Section IV
SPECIALIZED INVESTIGATIONS

12 **Gang Investigations**   179
JOHN P. MCLAUGHIN

13 **Handling Informers**   193
DAVID LOWE

14 **Investigations by Police of Police**   211
ROCCO DEBENEDETTO

15 **Investigation of Occult Groups**   227
GORDON A. CREWS

Section V
ALL-PURPOSE PRACTICES AND LESSONS FOR INVESTIGATIONS

16 **Practical Aspects of Interviewing and Interrogating Witnesses and Suspects**   255
MATHEW O'DEANE

17 **Detectives and the Criminal Investigation Process**   277
CASILDA E. ROPER-SIMPSON

18   **Interviewing and Communicating with**
        Special Populations, Including Nonverbal
        Individuals, Persons with Mental Disabilities
        or Illness, and the d/Deaf   297
        LAUREN M. BARROW

19   **Fourth Amendment**   315
        ROBERT WINTERS

20   **How to Get That Warrant Every Time**   337
        MATHEW O'DEANE

Index   357

Preface

The Detective's Handbook was developed with the goal of providing a one-volume text that contains vital information to assist law enforcement officers to become better detectives. The work of detectives is involved and complex. Accordingly, not all essential aspects of the work can be covered in a one-volume work, so the editor attempted to select 20 of the most critical issues and present them in 20 separate chapters.

Each of the 19 contributors to this text presents key issues involved in the aspects covered by their chapters. The style and format of the chapters differ. We allowed the expert contributors latitude in presenting the material in a manner they were most comfortable with, rather than requesting that they follow strict guidelines and formats.

What is a detective? In this text, we refer to the position as if it is a detective in a law enforcement agency. While this text is probably valuable to a private detective, it is directed toward the public law enforcement officer. We use the concept of law enforcement departments to refer to police, sheriffs, and other government agencies that are responsible for protecting the public.

While detectives have a wide variety of techniques available in conducting their investigations, for the most part the majority of cases are solved by the interrogation of suspects and the interviewing of witnesses. Detectives frequently rely on informants that they have cultivated over the years. Informants generally often have connections with persons a detective would not be able to approach formally. Evidence collection and preservation is also a significant aspect of a detective's work.

The qualifications to become a detective in a law enforcement agency vary. In small departments, the detective work may be informally assigned to the more experienced officers. In larger agencies, the officer may need to take specialized education courses and pass an examination before being formally appointed as a detective. While the qualifications may vary, the nature of the work is generally the same.

During the probationary period, the officer is assigned to look for evidence. During this time, the officer is supervised and mentored by an experienced sergeant. Some officers further their college education by attending a two-year or four-year college or university, attaining a degree in criminal justice or administration of criminal justice. Colleges have options for a concentration or certificate in a specialized field of criminal investigation.

The editors thank the 19 contributors who provided the chapters for this book. They encourage comments and suggestions for improvement for subsequent editions from the readers who read and use this material. Those comments and suggestions may be e-mailed to John Eterno or Cliff Roberson at cliff.roberson@washburn.edu.

Editors

John A. Eterno is a professor, associate dean, and director of graduate studies in criminal justice at Molloy College in Rockville Centre, New York. He is also a retired captain of the New York City Police Department (NYPD). He has won awards for his research and teaching, including a Police Foundation Award for his research on physical standards for the NYPD, an Enterprise Initiative Award from the mayor of the City of New York for his work on mapping, a Molloy College Faculty Research Award for his research in the field of criminal justice, and two teaching awards from graduate students. Dr. Eterno has penned numerous books, book chapters, articles, and editorials on various topics: democratic policing, human trafficking, data-driven policy, police management, policing within the law, investigations, combatting terrorism in democracies, global policing, and many other police-related topics. Some of his most recent publications include an op-ed in *The New York Times* titled "Policing by the Numbers," a peer-reviewed article in the *International Journal of Police Science and Management* with Eli Silverman (professor emeritus at John Jay College) called "Compstat: Compare Statistics or Compose Statistics," and two books titled *The Crime Numbers Game: Management by Manipulation* (with Eli Silverman) and *The New York City Police Department: The Impact of Its Policies and Practices.*

Cliff Roberson is a professor emeritus of criminal justice at Washburn University, Topeka, Kansas. He is also a retired professor of criminology from California State University, Fresno. He is the former editor in chief of the *Professional Issues in Criminal Justice* journal and former managing editor of *Police Practice and Research*. He has also authored or coauthored more than 60 books and texts on legal and criminal justice subjects. His previous academic experiences include associate vice president for academic affairs, Arkansas Tech University; dean of arts and sciences, University of Houston, Victoria; director of programs, National College of District Attorneys; professor of criminology and director of justice center, California State University, Fresno; and assistant professor of criminal justice, St. Edwards University. His nonacademic experience includes U.S. Marine Corps service as an infantry officer, trial and defense counsel and military judge as a marine judge advocate, and director of the Military Law Branch, U.S. Marine Corps. Other legal employment experiences include trial supervisor, Office of State Counsel for Offenders, Texas Board of Criminal Justice, and judge pro tem in the California courts. Cliff is admitted to practice before the U.S. Supreme Court, U.S. Court of Military Appeals, U.S. Tax Court, Federal Courts in California and Texas, Supreme Court of Texas, and Supreme Court of California. His educational background includes PhD in human behavior, U.S. International University; LLM in criminal law, criminology, and psychiatry, George Washington University; JD, American University; BA in political science, University of Missouri; and one year of postgraduate study at the University of Virginia School of Law.

Contributors

John Boal served as a military advisor in Vietnam prior to becoming a police officer in the city of Barberton, Ohio in 1975. After retirement from the police department, John has become a tenured faculty member at the University of Akron specializing in criminal and forensic investigation. As a police officer, John has received specialized training in a number of areas and completed two of the top police management schools in the country, graduating from the Southern Police Institute 82nd session of the Administrative Officers course at the University of Louisville and the FBI National Academy 152 session in Quantico Virginia. At the time of retirement, John was second in command of the department in charge of the patrol division, central dispatch, and the five-day jail facility.

John has taught criminal justice and security courses at the University of Akron since 1990, part time and full time since 1997. He founded and directed the University of Akron Law Enforcement Training Center while directing the two-year associate degree program.

John is a certified fraud examiner, certified protection professional, physical security professional, and professional certified investigator through ASIS International. He is a crime prevention specialist with the Ohio Crime Prevention Association and is an assessor with Quality Matters for online course construction and has also served as an assessor for CALEA.

Lauren M. Barrow is an assistant professor of criminal justice at Chestnut Hill College in Philadelphia, Pennsylvania. She has over 15 years' experience in research and teaching. As a generalist, Dr. Barrow teaches a wide range of criminal justice courses, including research methods, victimology, and police ethics. She began her career at the National Victim Center, Arlington, Virginia, and moved on to graduate studies in criminal justice at CUNY Graduate Center, John Jay College of Criminal Justice in New York City. Her research interests lie in exploring the question of equal justice for vulnerable persons. She has previously published books titled *Criminal Victimization of the Deaf* (2007) and *Police and Profiling in the US: Applying Theory to Investigations* (2014).

Gordon A. Crews is a professor of criminal justice and criminology at Marshall University, Huntington, West Virginia. He is also the president of a private consulting firm entitled The Veritas Group, based out of Huntington, West Virginia. Dr. Crews has over 25 years of education and training experience after 10 years of working in the field. Prior to teaching, he worked in law enforcement (in South Carolina at Richland Country Sheriff's Department and University of South Carolina Police Department and in Rome, Georgia, at Floyd Country Sheriff's Department/Mount Berry College Police Department) as a bloodhound/narcotics k-9 officer and trainer, field-training officer, and criminal investigator; in corrections as a training and accreditation manager; and in insurance fraud as a private-licensed investigator. He earned a PhD in education/criminal justice, a graduate certificate in alcohol and drug studies, a bachelor of science in criminal justice, and a master's in criminal justice from the University of South Carolina. His publications include referred works dealing with juvenile and school violence, occult/satanic involvement and youth, and various law enforcement and correctional issues. Since 2000, he has conducted extensive field research in these areas across the United States, the United Kingdom, Middle East, the Netherlands, Central Europe, Scandinavia, Turkey, Ghana, and Central and Eastern Europe (Greece, Macedonia, Bulgaria, Romania, Hungary, Slovakia, Austria, Czech Republic, Slovenia, Serbia, and Croatia). His most recent research was conducted in Brazil (2010), Japan (2011), and the United Kingdom and the Republic of Ireland (2012). Dr. Crews has also appeared as a consultant on national and international programs such as CNN, MSNBC, *Good Morning America*, *Anderson Cooper 360°*, The Abrams Report, Nancy Grace, Gloria Van Susteren, Ghana, African National Television, and Due Diligence on Voice of Russia Radio Network.

Rocco DeBenedetto began his professional career as a police officer with the New York City Police Department (NYPD), New York City, New York. His last assignment was serving as the commanding officer of Brooklyn's 84th precinct, where he was promoted to deputy inspector and later designated the Downtown Brooklyn Incident Commander and placed in charge of all police operations during and after the events of September 11, 2001. As a lieutenant, he led a team of internal investigators assigned to the Brooklyn North Investigations Unit. In addition to investigating acts of police misconduct, he led a team that investigated more than 60 police-involved shootings and he has conducted more than 350 internal or "Garrity warning" interviews and interrogations. In 2002, DeBenedetto left the NYPD to become the director of security at the Securities Industry Automation Corporation (SIAC), which is a wholly owned subsidiary of the New York Stock Exchange. In addition to serving as an adjunct professor within Molloy's Criminal Justice Department, he teaches graduate-level courses on workplace safety, corporate compliance, and other management-related topics at Long Island University's School of Business, Public Administration and Information Sciences. DeBenedetto presently serves as a senior consultant with T&M Protection Resources, a global security solutions firm located in New York City.

Frank DiMarino served as an assistant U.S. attorney for more than 18 years in Florida and Georgia. He has specialized litigation experience in prosecuting financial institution fraud, money laundering, procurement fraud, labor embezzlement, access device fraud, tax fraud, public corruption, and other economic and public integrity offenses. He served as a senior trial attorney with the Commodity Futures Trading Commission, litigating multidistrict fraud cases. He served as an attorney in the U.S. Army Judge Advocate General's Corps prosecuting cases involving fraud and embezzlement. He retired as a field grade officer. He coauthored *An Introduction to Corporate and White Collar Crime* (Taylor & Francis, 2013) and *American Criminal Courts* (Pearson, 2014) with Cliff Roberson.

Mag. Maximillian Edelbacher was born in Vienna. He served as the chief of police during 1972–2006 and as chief of major crime bureau, Vienna, Austria. Prior to that, he was a lecturer at the Vienna University of Economics and Danube University. From 2000 to 2009, he was a lecturer at Kent State University and Turku University. He has served since 1995 as an international expert of United Nations Organization (UNO), Organization for Security and Co-Operation in Europe (OSCE), Council of Europe, and European Union;

since 2007 as a special investigator of General Office for Insurances, Accidents, Claim Regulation and Loangiving (AVUS Group),* an international claim regulator; since 2008 as lecturer at Vienna University, Department of Sociology; since 2008 as member of the Academic Council on the United Nations System (ACUNS), specializing in organized crime, white-collar crime, and corruption; since 2011 as representative of International Police Executive Symposium (IPES), to the United Nations in Vienna; since 2012 as member of the European Academy of Sciences and Arts; and since February 2014 as vice-president of ACUNS, Vienna Liaison Office. He is the author of several books, book chapters, and articles.

Rachael Elliott is a computer forensic examiner for the University of Central Oklahoma Police Department, Edmond, Oklahoma. She has been a Certified Forensic Computer Examiner (CFCE) since 2013 and has a BSc degree in mathematics education and a MSc in forensic science both from the University of Central Oklahoma. Before becoming a computer forensic examiner, she taught high school mathematics for six years in the public school setting and two years for a company offering online education.

Dana Galante holds a BSc degree from Molloy College, Rockville Centre, New York, where she was a member of the Criminal Justice Honor Society. She was appointed to New York City Police Department in 2006. In 2009, while working full time, She earned a master of arts in criminal justice from John Jay College, NYC. First as a beat cop and then as a domestic violence officer, She performed public safety and critical emergency duties serving victims of violence. She is currently a detective in the elite Special Victims' Squad and is often cross assigned to the Hate Crimes Task Force. She has received certifications from the FBI National Academy for Behavioral Analysis Training, the New York State National Children's Justice Task Force for Forensic Interviewing, as well as NYPD Homicide Investigators Course, Criminal Investigators Course, and Sex Crimes Course. Additionally, Dana designed a college-level criminal justice course to be instituted in September 2014.

Deniese Kennedy-Kollar earned her PhD in criminal justice in 2008 from the City University of New York Graduate Center, New York City, New York. She also holds an MA in forensic psychology from John Jay College of Criminal Justice and a BA in psychology from SUNY Stonybrook. Before joining the faculty at Molloy, she taught at Monroe College, Adelphi University, and John Jay College of Criminal Justice. In addition, she spent several years conducting research with a forensic psychiatric population at Kirby Forensic Psychiatric Hospital and with the Nathan Kline Institute for Psychiatric Research at Manhattan Psychiatric Center. Her areas of academic and research interest include technology and crime analysis, crime theory, psychology and the law, and capital punishment.

Peter C. Kratcoski is an emeritus professor of justice studies, Kent State University, and adjunct professor of justice studies at Kent State University's regional campuses and served as chairperson of the Department of Criminal Justice Studies at Kent State, Kent, Ohio. He completed research and served as a consultant for numerous juvenile justice and social

---

* AVUS is the English translation of the German terms used to designate the title of the organization.

service agencies. He has authored a number of books, written numerous book chapters and articles for professional journals, and presented many papers at national and international professional conferences. He served as editor of the *Journal of Crime and Justice* and is currently a North American editor of *Police Practice and Research*. He is the official recorder for the International Police Executive Symposium and has authored a number of articles and book chapters based on the topics that were the focuses of the IPES meetings. He is the coeditor (with Dilip K. Das) of *Meeting the Challenges of Global Terrorism* (2003), *Police Education and Training in a Global Society* (2007), and *Financial Crimes: A Threat to Global Security*, with Maximillian Edelbacher and Michael Theil (2012), and author of *Juvenile Justice Administration* (2012).

His current research and writing focuses on juvenile justice, school violence, international policing, insurance fraud, preventing financial crimes, and terrorism.

Work in progress includes *The Relationship of the Informal Economy to Corruption, Fraud and Organized Crime* (edited by Edelbacher, M., Kratcoski, P. and B. Dobovsek, CRC Press/Taylor & Francis Group; tentative publication, 2015) and *Collaborative Policing: Police, Academics, Professionals and Communities Working Together for Education, Training Research and Program Implementation* (edited by Kratcoski, P. and M. Edelbacher, CRC Press/Taylor & Francis Group; tentative publication, 2015).

David Lowe is a principal lecturer at Liverpool John Moores University's law school, Liverpool, United Kingdom. Prior to becoming an academic, he was a police officer for 27 years in the United Kingdom. A detective for most of his service investigating most types of criminal activity, most of his detective service was in the United Kingdom's Special Branch Counter-Terrorism Unit. His academic work in the area of policing, terrorism, and security has been published in books and journals, his latest work being *Examining Political Violence: Studies in Terrorism, Counterterrorism and Internal War*. Following the Edward Snowden revelations, his research into surveillance and intelligence exchange and balancing the interests of national security with individual liberties is being published in *Terrorism and Political Violence*. David is regularly used by the television, radio, and print media (particularly the BBC) in the United Kingdom and the rest of Europe and the United States for commentary in his research areas.

Mark McCoy is a professor in the Forensic Science Institute and the School of Criminal Justice at the University of Central Oklahoma (UCO), Edmond, Oklahoma. He joined the faculty at UCO following retirement from his position as deputy inspector with the Oklahoma State Bureau of Investigation, where he was the first supervisor of the OSBI Computer Crime Unit. Prior to his career at the OSBI, he worked as a police officer for the Tulsa Police Department and was an officer in the U.S. Marine Corps. Dr. McCoy serves as the Forensic Science Institute's Digital Evidence Program Administrator, and he has been a Certified Forensic Computer Examiner (CFCE) since 1996. He was selected as a Fulbright Senior Specialist in digital forensics in 2012. His research interests include the application of technology in law enforcement, digital forensics, computer crime, and law enforcement education and training.

John P. McLaughlin received his BSc degree from St. John's University, Queens, New York, and master's degree in public administration from C.W. Post College, Long Island, New York. He has been a sworn member of the Nassau County Police

Department since 1987. In 1994, he was assigned to narcotics bureau and promoted to detective. McLaughlin worked 10 years as an undercover detective. In 2003, he was selected to work with the FBI Violent Gang Task Force on Long Island, where he is currently a member. McLaughlin is also an adjunct professor in the Department of Criminal Justice at Molloy College, where he has been teaching since 1998. McLaughlin has received numerous awards for police service and performance in the line of duty as well as awards for distinction at Molloy College. He is married to Maryellen and father to Kaitlin, Taylor, and Jack.

Stephen A. Morreale currently serves as an associate professor and chair of the Criminal Justice Department at Worcester State University, Worcester, Massachusetts. He is also affiliated with Walden University and Roger Williams University—Justice System Training and Research Institute. Dr. Morreale served in law enforcement for 30 years, having retired as assistant special agent in charge for U.S. Department of Health and Human Services, Office of Investigations, Inspector General. For nearly 20 years, he served with the Drug Enforcement Administration, serving as a special agent and managing agent as well as serving with the Dover, New Hampshire Police Department, and the U.S. Army Military Police Corps. Dr. Morreale serves as the lead consultant and major case coordinator for a Medicare Program Safeguard Contractor in both Florida and California. While at HHS-Investigations, Steve supervised and coordinated complex and far-reaching investigations focusing on health-care fraud, which included pharmaceutical, PDMA, and pricing fraud. He also oversaw investigations into false reporting, schemes to defraud various health-care programs, grant and research fraud, obstruction of audits, obstruction of justice, contract fraud, contractor and provider fraud, conflicts of interest, and substandard quality of care leading to serious harm or death.

Mathew O'Deane currently serves as a supervising investigator with the San Diego County District Attorney's Office Bureau of Investigation. He is also affiliated with the University of Phoenix, National University, and Kaplan University. Dr. O'Deane has served in law enforcement since 1991, working the first 10 years of his career with the National City Police Department in California, and with San Diego County since 2002. He has also authored several books and dozens of articles in the area of street gang investigations.

Casilda E. Roper-Simpson was born in Panama (Central America) and was raised in Brooklyn, New York. She received her bachelor of arts degree from Baruch College (CUNY) and her juris doctorate degree from Brooklyn Law School, 1994. As an accomplished trial attorney for many years, Casilda is admitted to practice in federal and state courts and has garnered an astounding trial record in both criminal and civil cases. Known as a tough, tenacious, but creative litigator, Casilda was a part of the original legal team in the land-mark case of Abner Louima, 1997. Professor Roper-Simpson is presently an adjunct at Molloy College in the Criminal Justice Department and hosts her own talk radio show "Know Your Rights." Amidst all her accomplishments, Casilda considers her biggest and proudest accomplishment to be the raising of her three children—Coreen, Camille, and Conroy, Jr. She refers to her children as her "diamonds." Casilda also has two grandsons—Rashaun and Jayden. Her parents Ralph and Norma Roper raised Casilda with the adage "to whom much is given, much is expected." Even after her parents' passing, she continues to live her life according to such adage and instills it in her children. Casilda writes this chapter in memory of her mother Norma Roper and offers a special thank you to her niece Norma A. Roper Webster, Esq.

Ron Rufo has been a Chicago police officer for 20 years and is currently in the 18th police district. He was a crime prevention speaker in the Preventive Programs unit for over 13 years. He also teaches criminal social justice online in the master's program at Kaplan University for the last six years. He received his bachelor of arts degree in criminal social justice from Lewis University, graduating with highest honors and a scholar of the university in 2000. His master of arts degree in organizational leadership was from Lewis University in 2002. Ron received his doctorate degree in organizational leadership from Argosy University in 2007. His dissertation was An Investigation of On-Line Sexual Predation of Convicted Male Offenders. His first book, *Sexual Predators Amongst Us*, was recently released on December 7, 2011. He coauthored a second book on criminal profiling that was released in July 2013. Ron is currently finishing up his third book on police culture and police suicide that will be released in 2015. He has also contributed a chapter to a book on terrorism and property management, regarding building safety. He has three beautiful daughters, Rita, Laura, and Cara, from his previous marriage and is married to a wonderful woman named Debbie. His hobby is antique cars, and he is proud to own two classic convertibles.

Harrison Watts is an associate professor of criminal justice at Our Lady of the Lake University in San Antonio, Texas. His former faculty appointments include positions at Washburn University (Kansas), Cameron University (Oklahoma), and Vernon College (Texas). Harrison is a former police detective and Criminal Investigation Division commander and holds a Master Peace Officer license through the Texas Commission on Law Enforcement. He is a graduate of the Bill Blackwood Law Enforcement Management Institute's Leadership and Command College. Harrison also served two terms as a city commissioner for Vernon, Texas. He earned both bachelor's and master's degrees from Midwestern State University. He earned a second master's degree from Sam Houston State University and his PhD from North Central University. His research interests are in policing and law. His most recent publication is a book coauthored with Cliff Roberson, *Law and Society: An Introduction*, published by Taylor & Francis Group. He is a frequent lecturer in police in-service training sessions across the county and specializes in police custody deaths.

Robert Winters holds a JD and is a professor at Kaplan University. He is also a member of the National Criminal Justice Association and serves as a Western Regional Representative and a member of the National Advisory Board and their National Elections Committee. Robert has taught courses at both the graduate and undergraduate levels in a wide range of areas of criminal justice, including criminal evidence, criminal procedure, constitutional law, criminology, ethics, terrorism, cyber crime, domestic violence, and criminal law. In addition to being a serial entrepreneur from the age of 7, Robert has held management positions in the aerospace, international logistics, and legal industries in Southern California. Robert resides in the southwest with his wife and son. He can be reached at RCWinters01@gmail.com. He is the leading author of a 2014 text published by Taylor & Francis Group, *Introduction to Crime and Crime Causation*.

Szde Yu is currently teaching criminal justice at Wichita State University, Wichita, Kansas. Prior to that, he used to teach at Brockport College, State University of New York, and served on the College Information Security Oversight Committee. He formerly served as a unit chief information security officer and lieutenant crime inspector in the military for the Coast Guard of the Republic of China (Taiwan). He holds a BSc in computer science and information engineering, an MS in criminal justice and criminology, and a PhD in criminology. His research interests involve cyber crime and digital evidence. He has also been developing the use of cyber profiling in criminal investigations. His research publications can be found in numerous journals, such as *International Criminal Justice Review*, *Computers in Human Behavior*, *International Journal of Cyber Criminology*, *Journal of Mixed Methods Research*, *International Journal of Digital Crime and Forensics*, *Defendology*, *Journal of Behavioral Profiling*, *International Journal of Criminal Justice*, and *Policing: An International Journal of Police Strategies and Management*.

Investigations
Involving Personal
Violence

I

Homicide Investigations

1

JOHN A. ETERNO

Contents

Chapter Objectives 3
Chapter Outline 3
Introduction 4
  Definition of Homicide 4
  Background Information 5
Basics of Homicide Investigation 6
  Crime Scene 7
  Types of Evidence 8
    Testimonial 8
    Documentary 10
    Physical 10
  Other Important Facets of Homicide Investigations 11
    Estimating the Time of Death 11
    Interpreting Wounds 12
    Autopsy 13
    Understand the Law 13
    Lineups and Identifications 14
    Motive, Method, and Opportunity 14
    Rivalry among Police 14
    Others 15
Experienced Homicide Detectives 15
References 17

Chapter Objectives

After studying this chapter, you should understand

1. What constitutes a homicide
2. How a homicide investigation is conducted
3. The types of evidence used in homicide investigations
4. How a crime scene is examined
5. The essential elements of a homicide investigation
6. The importance of using experienced officers to investigate homicides

Chapter Outline

Introduction
Definition of Homicide

Background Information
Basics of Homicide Investigation
Crime Scene
Types of Evidence
Other Important Facts of Homicide Investigations
Experienced Homicide Detectives
References

Introduction

This chapter will cover the basics of homicide investigations. It will focus on what typical officers and detectives need to accomplish to properly handle homicides. There is no magic involved but an established approach that needs to be meticulously followed by all involved. From the discovery of the body to the arrest and conviction of a suspect, there are basic procedures and tasks that need to be properly completed. Additionally, if tasks are not done correctly from the beginning, the detectives, no matter how good, may not have the evidence or ability to make up for sloppiness and mistakes that occur before they arrive. Every action and/or inaction by law enforcement is critical for a good homicide investigation to take place. This short chapter cannot cover the range of investigative techniques and information needed to become a seasoned investigator; rather, it is meant as an overview or general guide that both neophyte and seasoned investigator may find helpful (see references for further information). I like to think of this chapter as a roadmap guiding someone to the right places to go but not covering every nuance of those places.

Definition of Homicide

There are different types of homicides recognized under the law. The New York State Penal Law, for example, has statutes for various degrees of murder, manslaughter, criminally negligent homicide, vehicular homicide, and more. At its most basic level, a homicide

> …refers to any killing of a person. Such a killing may be a violation of criminal law, or it may be excusable or justifiable. Because criminal law exists to identify, prevent, and punish harms that persons cause one another, and because killing is, by general consensus, the greatest harm that can befall a person, every system of criminal law takes homicide seriously. It is almost always among the most severely punished of crimes. Unintended killings, as well as intended killings, are often punished. Because of the finality of death, legal prohibitions extend not only to intentionally taking life but to unusually risky and careless conduct that puts lives unjustifiably in jeopardy. (Hall, 2004, para. 1)

In determining the type of homicide, the mental state of the offender at the time of the commission of the homicide is important. Having intent to kill and doing the act is most serious and is termed murder. Other culpable mental states include reckless or negligent. Reckless conduct is defined as when a person is "aware of and consciously disregards a substantial and unjustifiable risk…" (NYS Penal Law §15.05 [3]). Criminal negligence is when a person "fails to perceive a substantial and unjustifiable risk…" (NYS Penal Law §15.05 [4]).

Who was killed (e.g., a police officer, firefighter), how many, and other aggravating factors can influence what is charged. Mitigating factors such as extreme emotional disturbance can lower the charge to a manslaughter.

Making matters more complicated, the taking of a human life is not always a crime. For example, a police officer can take a life lawfully in the performance of his or her duty. This is justifiable homicide. Other examples are the insanity defense or self-defense. The investigator is responsible for uncovering the truth of what occurred.

Detectives must have a good understanding of the law to properly conduct their investigation. At a minimum, there are several reasons for this. First, detectives as law enforcement officers need to know what the possibilities are under the law so that suspects can properly be charged (or not charged) with criminal acts. Second, detectives need to help build a case for the prosecutor or, conversely, to unearth a lack of wrongdoing. A death that appears criminal, for example, may actually be a suicide. Investigators must be open to all possibilities. Detectives need to understand the law so that they can offer appropriate testimony and evidence in court. In this chapter, we are going to focus on the practical aspects of the investigation. Therefore, the definitions given will suffice. However, in advanced investigations' courses, investigators must be made familiar with every nuance in the law in their jurisdiction applicable to their expertise. Indeed, this will not only involve the criminal law but the procedure law as well (e.g., law of arrest; stop, question, and frisk; interrogations; search warrants).

Beyond knowing the law and basics of investigations, detectives need field experience and training. Reading about concepts in a book is far different than street experience. There is absolutely no substitute for experiencing real-life situations. A typical career path begins with internships and some college courses. The next step, as with all law enforcement, is becoming a good patrol officer—the more active (making arrests, stops, etc.), the better. After patrol, the next steps generally involve advancing to plain clothes, doing other types of investigations, and then progressing to homicide. Taking as much training as possible and networking with others throughout the path is also highly advised.

Background Information

According to the FBI in 2012, there were approximately 14,827 persons murdered in the United States. This represents approximately a 1.1% increase from the previous year (FBI, 2013). However, homicides in the United States have decreased markedly from their highs in the 1970s through the 1990s (see Figure 1.1). Even with this marked decrease, the United States still has one of the highest homicide rates in the industrialized world (Fox et al., 2012).

Recent statistics reveal that the vast majority of murders in the United States are accomplished with a firearm (67%), followed by knife or cutting instrument (13.4%), unknown or dangerous weapon (13.1%), and personal weapons (hands, fists, etc.) (5.8%) (University at Albany, 2011, Table 3.118.2011). Yet, the homicide rate for the United States even without firearms is still very high compared to other western countries (Fox et al., 2012). Thus, guns appear to only be part of the problem for Americans.

The situation with respect to the correlation between guns and violence is complicated. For example, some of the worst killers are less likely to use a gun. Organized serial killers—the most common type—are an excellent example. The most widely accepted definition of serial killing is "the unlawful homicide of at least two people, carried out in a series

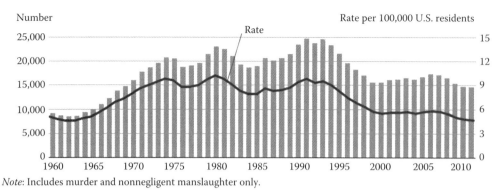

Number   Rate per 100,000 U.S. residents

Note: Includes murder and nonnegligent manslaughter only.

Figure 1.1 Number and rate of homicides in the United States, 1960–2011. (From Bureau of Justice Statistics (BJS), Homicide in the U.S. known to law enforcement, 2011. Retrieved from http://www.bjs.gov/content/pub/pdf/hus11.pdf.)

over a period of time" (Serial Murder, 2014). It is differentiated from mass killing in that with serial killers there is a cooling off period in between the killings. Serial killers generally commit homicide "because they like to kill" (Geberth, 2006). Organized serial killers "engage in purposeful postmortem mutilation of the corpse as opposed to the disorganized offender who engages in sexual or exploratory mutilation…[both] commit lust murders" (Geberth, 2006, pp. 481–482). Overall, these organized serial killers are exercising power and control. They prefer to use methods of killing in which they can feel the death such as strangulation or stabbing. A gun is far too impersonal.

There are many different types of homicides and the seasoned detective must familiarize himself or herself with each. It is beyond the scope of this chapter to discuss each and every nuance of these various homicides. However, a brief listing of some of these specialized homicides includes family homicide; hate homicide; mass murder, including, but not limited to, school shootings; narcotic-related homicides; medical homicide; terror-related homicide; cult homicide; serial killing; and gang-related homicide.

Basics of Homicide Investigation

A homicide investigation begins at the crime scene (Geberth, 2006). However, much will happen before the detective arrives. The first officer on the scene has important duties such as assisting any injured, making any arrests, detaining witnesses, securing the crime scene, and calling additional officers and the supervisor. If the perpetrator got away, then getting a good description of the suspect and any other relevant information should, as soon as practical, be given to the dispatcher so that a search can be started. The 911 operator should be aware that the initial caller is very important (and may actually be the perpetrator). Every 911 call should be audio recorded. Regardless of how the homicide is reported (911, in person, text message), as much information about who is reporting must be taken.

Usually, a patrol officer will be the first to arrive at the scene. There are key actions that the first responding officers must do: take necessary action with respect to protecting life (if the victim is still alive, all necessary care must be given and called in; if the situation is volatile, it must be controlled), apprehend the perpetrator or send out an alert with a description (if known), to the extent possible detain witnesses (at least get contact information if they must leave), make appropriate notifications such as the patrol supervisor, and safeguard the crime scene.

It is possible that the officer, or later the detective, will have to take what is known as a dying declaration. That is, the person is certain to die and wants to say something.

Specifically, a dying declaration is

> A declaration by the victim of a homicide …More precisely, a statement made by the victim of a homicide while about to die, and without any hope of recovery, concerning the facts and circumstances under which the fatal injury was inflicted, and offered in evidence on the trial of the person charged with having caused the death of the declarant. (Dying Declaration, 2014)

If at all possible, record the statement. These days, a cell phone or other device might be readily available. Also try to get a witness who is not an officer. If it is possible, the following information should elicited: the victim's name, where he or she lives, the victim's belief that he or she will die with no hope of recovery, and that the victim is making a truthful statement (Geberth, 2006).

Crime Scene

Every officer who responds should be cognizant of the crime scene. The initial situation may be volatile and dangerous; all necessary police action should be taken (i.e., arrests, safety of all, medical assistance rendered). Nevertheless, to the extent possible, officers should consider the crime scene and not purposefully damage it without justification (e.g., it is proper to safeguard a gun that is clearly exposed to a perpetrator). It is impossible to discuss every nuance. However, I have seen officers needlessly walking through crime scenes just to "see what happened" or to take their own personal photographs. Such unprofessional behaviors must never be allowed. The first officers and later the patrol supervisor must ensure that the scene stays as pristine as humanly possible. Officers should be assigned to guard entry into the scene, and generally speaking, the crime scene should initially be made larger than one might think (you can always scale back but it is far more difficult to make it bigger after the area was exposed to the public, unnecessary emergency responders, and/or the media).

There are many tasks that investigators, sometimes with the help of other personnel, need to accomplish. Interviewing the first officers on the scene and witnesses will be done by detectives. Detectives will generally go door to door and ask if anyone saw anything. If the perpetrator is still at large, sweeps of the area in a coordinated search may be done. This may involve a large number of officers including aviation (if available), specialized units with equipment (e.g., lights for night searches), boats, and whatever else may be required. Small agencies often call larger ones to assist when they do not have the expertise or personnel. Of course, this can get very complicated and the need for coordination and teamwork is essential.

At the crime scene, evidence comes in many forms. Detectives must be the ones who work the scene—no one else except the medical examiner (ME) and perhaps a knowledgeable district attorney. Detectives have the expertise to recognize, properly collect, and understand the meaning of what is contained at the crime scene. Crime scene sketches and official photographs will also be taken at the appropriate time. Detectives will also have procedures to protect the chain of custody of the evidence, that is, documenting who had control of the evidence from the time it was collected until the time it is presented in court. This is very important to the court case. Specifically, chain of custody is defined as

> the witnessed, unbroken, written chronological record of everyone who had an item of evidence, and when each person had it; also accounts for any changes in the evidence. (Swanson et al., 2006, p. 777)

An example of major mistakes in this area where numerous hard lessons were learned is the O. J. Simpson trial. Among the mistakes were socks that had bloodstains on them but were not noticed until months later. Even more to the point are two key mistakes with respect to the chain of custody of the evidence,

> …Henry Lee, the defense forensic expert during the trial, said that although there was lots of evidence, the source of evidence wasn't always explained and it wasn't closely tracked… Another criticism during the trial dealt with a vial of blood taken from Simpson. Police Detective Philip Vannatter drew Simpson's blood at the LAPD on June 13, the day after the killings. But instead of booking it into evidence, Vannatter put the blood vial in his pocket and went to Simpson's home where criminalists were collecting evidence. Jurors questioned why he would have carried it around for hours rather than booking it and the defense argued it may have been used to plant evidence such as blood drops on Simpson's front walkway. (Abdollah, 2014)

By not following specific procedures, prosecutors, law enforcement, and others attempting to try the case are greatly hindered.

Types of Evidence

Rodivich (2012) describes three categories of evidence: testimonial, documentary, and physical. Testimonial evidence includes statements made by witnesses and suspects. Interviewing techniques are different for witnesses versus suspects. Only trained investigators should be interviewing witnesses or interrogating suspects. Documentary evidence is that which documents the people, places, and things the detective comes across in the investigation. Photographs, sketching, and notes are the primary methods used for documenting. The term physical includes any tangible evidence (not necessarily visible) that will be subject to examination, analysis, and presentation.

Testimonial

There are very specific ways to interview and interrogate someone. As a start, the terms interview and interrogation are often used interchangeably. However, in modern police science, they should be considered separate and distinct categories with very different techniques. According to Inbau et al. (2004), an interview is nonaccusatory; its purpose is to gather information; it may be conducted early during an investigation, is conducted in a variety of environments, and is relatively unstructured; and written notes are taken. Conversely, an interrogation is accusatory, involves active persuasion, is conducted in a controlled environment, and is only conducted when the investigator is reasonably certain of the suspect's guilt, and no notes are taken until the suspect is fully committed.

Most interrogations occur when the investigator does not have enough evidence, and there is a need to get that evidence. In general, investigators should interview those suspects who are not likely to be guilty and then, as the investigation progresses, focus on more likely suspects. Interviewing and interrogating require special skill sets. Only those with expertise in this area should be doing this work.

Witnesses   All contact information needs to be taken from witnesses. Further contact may be necessary and without this vital information the investigation will be hampered. An eyewitness is very valuable but each and every witness may have important information. Witnesses need to be interviewed separately (Geberth, 2006). For basic questions of a person not in custody, no rights need be read. The U.S. Supreme Court case *Miranda v. Arizona* (1966) means that rights have to be read if a custodial interrogation is to take place (although there are some exceptions to this). When interviewing a nonsuspect, the person is not in custody nor is an interrogation taking place. The situation may change if the person becomes a suspect and the detective should be aware that the perpetrator may still be on the scene and, in fact, one of the witnesses being interviewed. However, at this point the persons being interviewed are only witnesses.

Witnesses may later be sought out for another interview, which can be either formal or informal. A formal interview is conducted in a controlled environment. That environment should be noncustodial. If it becomes custodial, *Miranda* may become an issue. If the interview is to be formal, much preparation should be done before it takes place. Questions should not be written out but the topics to be covered need to be clear and concise. How the investigator gets the person to agree to a formal interview is important.

Suspects   Suspects, especially primary suspects, should generally not be told that they are being interviewed to determine their culpability. After a person becomes a primary suspect in a homicide, the situation will likely progress into an interrogation. Inbau et al. (2004) discuss the characteristics of an interrogation. Before it starts, the investigator must be reasonably sure the suspect is the guilty party. It will take place in a controlled environment—not in the field—and the investigator should not take notes until the party has committed to the truth. It is an accusatory method of getting information. The investigator must be confident in telling the suspect that it is certain that that person is the guilty party. The interrogator uses active persuasion techniques making statements rather than asking questions. The main objective of the interrogation is to get at the truth. It is not to get a confession. If during the interrogation the suspect is actually found not to have done the homicide, this is a success and the investigation can go forward with the new information.

Videotaping of confessions is a more controversial topic. One major concern is that the suspect is less likely to talk if the entire interrogation is taped (assuming it is overtly done). While defense attorneys might not agree, a middle ground option is that after the truth is obtained, then do the videotape. Inbau et al. (2004, p. 397) advise that there could be consequences to taping the entire interrogation: "...[we] have stressed the importance of privacy during interrogation and the confession..." However, others argue that videotaping is a good alternative: "making a videotape of an interrogation can be extremely helpful, particularly if a suspect confesses or makes incriminating statements. Often later, regretting having said anything suspects will deny having said anything... a videotape to play at the trial can quickly deflate these types of exchanges" (Snow, 2005, p. 101).

The decision to videotape and when will have to be made on a case-by-case basis depending on many factors such as the legal restrictions of the jurisdiction, the suspect's demeanor, the investigator's expertise, the type of evidence, and the scientific study on the issue. The federal government and many states, however, are now moving toward video recording of the entire interrogation (Schmidt, 2014).

Documentary

Photographs, sketches, and notes are the primary methods of documenting (Birzer and Roberson, 2012). Photographs of the crime scene, in as pristine a condition as possible, must be taken. These photographs may become critical to the investigation and offered as evidence in the trial. Only an experienced crime scene photographer should take these pictures. Specialized cameras that will allow the photographs to be expanded (blown up) are important. Everything needs to be photographed as you never know what might later be important. This means even areas that may seem somewhat tangential need to be photographed. There are legal requirements so it is best if an official who is a police photographer with this type of expertise does the work. Most larger departments have such a person on staff. Smaller departments often call in larger ones when they do not have the expertise. The photographer should take pictures from the general to more specific items to give an idea of perspective (Geberth, 2006). Crime scene photographers must work closely with investigators to do as thorough a job as possible.

At times, it is difficult to get a full understanding of perspective with photographs only. The crime scene sketch fills this gap. Again, only an experienced crime scene sketch artist should be doing the work. Sometimes, photographs do not capture the distances or evidence very well. The sketch rendering can also simplify a case especially for a jury. Photographs can overwhelm the viewer with information, while the sketch simplifies and clarifies the crime scene. Certain information needs to be included in the sketch, and it can get complicated for one not initiated into the job. All objects of importance need to be included (e.g., evidence, doors, and windows). Again, working with the detective investigator is critical so that nothing is missed. There needs to be excellent communication among those at the scene. Measurements and distances are very important. A good legend and a compass point showing north are also critical. Additionally, I have seen both basic sketches and more detailed ones. Capturing as much detail as possible is important although a rough sketch is generally done first and then a more detailed one. Nevertheless, the rendering can always be simplified later on.

Physical

The identification, collection, and analysis of physical evidence is one of the most important aspects of the investigation. Physical evidence, properly collected and analyzed, is very powerful. It is tangible and objective. There is less subjectivity with physical evidence. Such evidence needs to be properly collected and handled. For example, blood evidence should not be placed in a plastic bag since the blood can chemically react with the plastic.

Most larger police departments have very specific policies on the handling of physical evidence. As an example, I will use the New York City Police Department's policy contained in their Patrol Guide. The evidence at the scene will be collected by a member of the crime scene unit—a detective with special skills. The property is properly invoiced at the local precinct. For evidence that needs analysis, that will usually be sent to the police laboratory.

When collecting evidence, certain important qualifications about packaging and other concerns are clearly explained in the guide. For example, note in the following procedure how plastic is never used for blood, DNA, and other biological evidences. Also note how carefully the evidence must be handled: the use of biohazard stickers, when the evidence must be taken to the police laboratory, prevents crushing and similar procedures.

BLOODSTAIN, DNA, SEROLOGY, OR OTHER BIOLOGICAL EVIDENCE AND ANY OTHER BODY FLUID/BIOLOGICAL EVIDENCE SHOULD BE PACKAGED IN PAPER BAGS OR BOXES. Do not seal in a plastic security envelope. Additionally, an orange bio-hazard sticker must be affixed to the package. Bloodstain, DNA, serology, or other biological evidence must be refrigerated, therefore, it must be delivered to the Police Laboratory IMMEDIATELY.

QUESTIONED DOCUMENTS
Any piece of paper, where the authenticity of the writing or the source of the writing must be determined, will be submitted to the Document Fraud Squad. These items include, but are not limited to, checks, bank robbery notes, and harassing letters. The evidence may be secured in a PLASTIC SECURITY ENVELOPE. DO NOT write on the security envelope when the evidence is inside. Cardboard inserts should be used in the security envelope to prevent the evidence from bending or folding.

HAIR AND FIBER
Evidence that contains possible hair and/or fiber evidence should be handled carefully to prevent the loss of any evidence. If the evidence is wet or bloodstained, or has other serological or biological evidence thereon, it should not be packaged in plastic; instead it should be placed in a sealed paper bag. If the evidence is dry, and it does not have bloodstain, serological, DNA or other biological evidence thereon, it should be packaged in a plastic security envelope or any bag/container that will prevent the hair or fiber evidence from being lost.

LATENT FINGERPRINTS
Items that must be processed for latent prints should be handled carefully. Latex gloves should be worn when handling. Members of the service handling such evidence should prevent the item(s) from being crushed, bent, folded, etc. Items being delivered to the Police Laboratory for fingerprint analysis should be placed in a plastic bag, not a paper bag. However, if an item must be analyzed for BOTH fingerprint and bloodstain/serological/DNA/other biological evidence, then it should NOT be placed in a plastic bag; it should be placed in a paper bag. (Source: NYPD Patrol Guide Section 218-09)

Other Important Facets of Homicide Investigations

Estimating the Time of Death

There are many methods to estimate the time of death depending on the circumstances of the case. Generally, the greater the length of time since the death, the more the estimate of time of death is likely to be off. Additionally, environmental conditions of where the body has been will also greatly affect the estimate. There are, however, typical methods that are used to estimate the time of death.

One way to estimate the time of death is the temperature of the body (algor mortis). This is generally most effective in the first 10 h after death (Swanson et al., 2006). Usually, the body cools at 1.5° per hour but this will depend on many factors such as the temperature where the body is located, if the deceased had a higher than normal or lower than normal temperature initially, among other factors. There are mathematical formulas to help determine this, which factor in environmental conditions and other variables (Fox et al., 2012).

Another way to estimate time of death is through rigor mortis or the level of rigidity in the muscles. The body will stay rigid for 24–36 h after death. Different muscles become stiff at different time. Further, if the body is moved, rigor can be broken. Thus, rigor mortis can help determine the time of death and whether the body was moved.

Since the heart stops beating at the time of death, blood will begin to collect according to gravity. Fox et al. (2012, p. 231) describe the process of livor mortis: "A purplish discoloration of the skin at the low points sets in within thirty minutes and becomes fixed in about eight hours. Furthermore, the shade of discoloration can help to indicate the cause of death."

Other ways to determine the time of death include decomposition, forensic entomology, stomach contents, and supplemental evidence such as eyewitnesses, a final cell phone call, or anything else that might help. Decomposition is when the body undergoes natural deterioration due to the elements. Environmental factors will play a major role in this. Entomology is the study of insects. Entomologists can determine a range of days or times of death by examining insect life on the body. The ME will examine the stomach contents, and using digestive rates may be able to come up with a time of death as well.

Usually, there is no single factor that goes into determining the time of death but a number of factors that will coincide. Determining the time and method of death is critical to the investigation. For example, it helps detectives determine what suspects could have physically been at the seen (those without an alibi). The ME and detectives may have to piece together the available evidence to ultimately determine a time or range of time and days that the homicide occurred.

Interpreting Wounds

In a homicide investigation, a basic understanding of evidence from wounds is essential. The most common types of wounds that police deal with are "firearm wounds, incised wounds, stab wounds, puncture wounds and lacerations" (Swanson et al., 2006, p. 293).

Bullet wounds can be very difficult to interpret. Sometimes, it is hard to tell entry from exit wound (assuming there is an exit wound). A bullet may not travel in a straight line through a person. An autopsy must be completed to determine trajectory and other critical information. Any recovered bullets can be sent for ballistic examination. Powder and other marks should also be examined if they are discernable. They can help determine distance and other information. Residue on the hands of the victim can, for example, help determine whether the case is actually a suicide.

An incision is usually accomplished with a knife or other very sharp instrument. The size of the wound has little to do with the size of the instrument. Death is more likely based on the organs or location of the incision. Puncture wounds usually occur with a screwdriver or similar instrument. They have a very small mark. At one homicide that I responded to, the puncture was very small but directly over the heart of the victim. The victim bled quickly and died at that location. Lacerations occur with more irregularly shaped objects. These wounds bleed a lot and leave bruising. Lacerations can occur accidently (such as a drunk). Defensive wounds are also important. These usually occur to the arms and forearms. I have noted at homicides that crime scene investigators often place paper bags over the hands to protect such evidence especially before a body is moved. Signs of strangulation are also of various types. They can be manual (death generally occurs due to a lack of blood to the brain) and ligature strangulation by a constricting band, which is usually a homicide (Swanson et al., 2006).

Autopsy

The autopsy or examination of the body after death should be conducted by a qualified medical doctor who is also a certified pathologist. Swanson (2006, p. 633) defines an autopsy "...to establish the cause of death and make a medical determination of all the other factors which may be involved in the death." This will start at the scene and eventually be completed in the ME's office. Detectives might be able to assist with information, but unlike what I have seen on many television programs, if present, they should not interfere with the examination. The certified ME is the ultimate authority. Sometimes, the death cannot be categorized as a homicide, suicide, and accidental or natural death without further investigation. These deaths are usually termed undetermined. The autopsy can greatly assist the detective with the investigation. A good investigator should familiarize himself or herself with basic human anatomy as well as medical terminology. The autopsy report will reflect the entire examination. According to Geberth (2006, p. 663), it contains the following:

1. External examination:
   a. Description of the clothing
   b. Description of the body
2. Evidence of injury:
   a. External
   b. Internal
3. Central nervous system (head and brain)
4. Internal examination—cardiovascular system, pulmonary system, gastrointestinal system, stomach, small and large intestines, etc.
5. Anatomical findings
6. Toxicological findings
7. Opinion

Understand the Law

All court cases pertinent to your jurisdiction must be understood. Every investigator must have a practical understanding of the power that he or she has or, conversely, does not have. Modern media often portrays police as having powers that they simply do not have in democratic society. All evidence in a case must be obtained legally or it will not be admissible in court. Here are some examples of basic questions that officers should know in their jurisdictions:

1. What powers officers have to hold suspects?
2. How to go about holding witnesses?
3. When should I get a search warrant?
4. How do I get a search warrant?
5. When can I search a cell phone?
6. How do I get records from various government agencies?

7. How do I get records from private agencies?
8. Know exigent circumstances to the need for warrants—consent, emergency, etc.
9. Be prepared beforehand. Do not wait until the situation arises.

Lineups and Identifications

Investigators need to be familiar with procedures for lineups, showups, photo arrays, the use of computer peripherals to assist in the investigation (e.g., a tablet to show photographs to a witness), forcible stops, frisks, and much more. Again, each jurisdiction will have its own procedures and laws. In general, the key to successful identification is being fair. It is essential to be fair. For example, if a suspect is white, do not have fillers in a lineup who are all black. Distinctive features should be covered. For example, if the suspect has a distinctive tattoo on the arm, then all arms in the lineup should be covered. This general rule holds for all types of identifications. Also, as a general rule, try to show a witness/victim more than one person at a time—that is a suspect with other people (NYPD recommends at least five fillers in a lineup) (Patrol Guide Section 208-24). There are exceptions such as when the victim is at the hospital and in grievous condition, the suspect could be brought there. However, care needs to be exercised to be as fair as possible in all situations.

Motive, Method, and Opportunity

The three pillars upon which the homicide investigation rests are motive, method, and opportunity. Motive is the underlying reason why the perpetrator killed the victim(s). Snow (2005, p. 131), for example, writes:

> …when looking to develop a suspect, always search for a motive… Most murderers kill their victims for very clear reasons. For example, whenever we have an adult female murdered, we first look to a relationship motive because so many female murder victims are killed by the husbands, ex-husbands, boyfriends and ex-boyfriends…Even in cases not as clearcut as relationship murders, the police can often establish a motive by looking extensively into the background of the victim, a discipline called victimology.

Method is how the person was killed. The way a victim is killed can help lead to a killer as well. Was there evidence of a struggle? Was it particularly violent? What type of weapon was used? The way a killing is done can be helpful to identifying a suspect as well as other murders that were done by the same suspect. The last pillar is opportunity. Does the suspect have an alibi? Could the suspect have done it? Does the suspect have the requisite knowledge to commit the murder in the way that it was done? Determining motive, method, and opportunity can help solve a murder.

Rivalry among Police

One of the dark secrets of law enforcement is that there is often some rivalry between agencies and, at times, between different bureaus within the same agency. Inbau et al. (2004, p. 17) discuss this in terms of evaluating information from an interview: "Consider the possibility of rivalry between two or more investigative agencies (for example, a local police department and a sheriff's office)." As unprofessional as this is, investigators must be made aware of such possibilities. Overall, professional investigators must be willing to share information such that the truth can ultimately be revealed. It should not be about the glory or the headline.

Others

There are many other aspects to an investigation. Importantly, investigators should always keep an open mind. A good example of this is the case of Dr. Bruce Ivans. He was likely guilty of anthrax poisonings right after the 9/11 attack. The FBI went to him initially to assist in the investigation since he was a renowned microbiologist. He later turned out to be the likely culprit.

Experienced Homicide Detectives

One of the most important aspects to this chapter on homicide investigations is input from the homicide detectives themselves. I contacted three well-known homicide detectives and asked them about their experiences. They were very seasoned with a range between 100 and 500 homicide investigations. Two became supervisors and one was a detective supervisor for over 20 years. These are what they reported to me.

All of them felt that field experience is very important if not critical. The amount of formal training tended to be quite limited. As one of the detectives wrote, "It is typical for most new investigators to receive minimal structured training. Most investigators learn 'on the fly.'" Another suggested that new detectives be teamed with a senior investigator.

They all felt that how the first officers on the scene handled the situation can make or break a case. Essentially, the first officers need to keep witnesses at the scene, try to keep them separated, preserve the crime scene, get detectives as soon as possible, and check the scene for unusual and/or suspicious persons. They had much concern over the integrity of the crime scene especially from other officers, the media, and curious onlookers.

The detectives tended to get called to the scene by a supervisor. However, at times, if on the street, the detectives could get to the scene more quickly when they were monitoring the radio. Before arriving at the scene, there were some actions the investigators would take. For example, conduct a history of the location, get information on the victim (if possible), get any materials needed for the scene (pens, pads), evaluate how much personnel might be needed, notify the boss, and assign detectives to all locations as necessary (e.g., hospital, crime scene, canvass area).

Once on the scene the detectives tended to conduct basic duties. They would make sure the scene is secure. They would also check to be sure witnesses were separated. Suspects should also be separated from each other and witnesses. This is exceedingly important. They also report to the supervisor. Finding and talking to the first officers on the scene was also very important.

As the incident progressed, allow the crime scene specialists to handle the scene. However, a walk-through of the scene should be done before they collect evidence. A homicide detective should stay with the crime scene personnel during the evidence collection process. Only detectives, not patrol officers, should be interviewing witnesses. If interviewing at the station house, one detective suggested listening the first two times the witness went through the account of what happened. The third time around, it was suggested you then record the statements. Use of audio- and videotaping was also suggested when feasible.

It was suggested you work with the ME (sometimes called the coroner) at the scene after the crime scene has been fully explored and recorded. By the time the ME arrives, you generally could create a timeline of events (although this can be difficult in some cases such as bodies that were killed at another location and dumped at the scene you are now at). The ME is very important and can help identify gender, use identifying marks, and determine a more exact time of death, signs of sexual abuse, and defensive wounds, if the body was transported and much more. The ME's report is critical. Additionally, detectives should be present during the autopsy.

Work closely with other agencies but this can be challenging. Always be respectful as you never know when you might need their assistance. Sometimes, there is a lack of trust between agencies and detectives will "size each other up." If there is a lack of trust, sometimes, information is not given freely. In the background of a multiagency investigation, there is a concern about who will get credit. However, in general, when a trusting relationship is built, information will flow freely and aid both agencies. This is also true of officers within a larger agency as well where several detective units may be involved.

The very next day (after the homicide is discovered), a team meeting of detectives should be called. At the meeting, a plan should be developed after going over all the details. A detective needs to be sent to the autopsy and investigators need to stay in contact to share new information. Evidence from the crime scene should be checked to ensure it is properly safeguarded and, where applicable, being sent for analysis or testing. All paperwork needs to be properly completed and everything properly documented.

In terms of suspects, not jumping to conclusions was seen as very important. Investigators need to proceed methodically based on the evidence, getting all reports from the ME and other analyses. In short, everything depends on the evidence. All motives should be explored, leaving nothing to chance—gangs, domestic, drugs, etc. Going over interviews conducting additional interviews is important. The background of the deceased, interviewing friends, family members, and witnesses should be completed.

The detectives gave their views on some tactics that can be critical to solving homicides. One very important action is to assign a detective to conduct an audio/visual canvass of the scene looking for cameras, plate readers, traffic cameras, phone records, and the like. Another is focusing on the importance of the modus operandi ([MO] the way the crime is committed). It is, according to one detective, the criminal's "signature." The method of death, the method of entry, posing of the body, and similar clues related to the MO are invaluable in the homicide case.

All of the detectives recommended videotaping. It was very powerful at trial. One suggested hiding the camera behind a two-way mirror to help prevent the suspect from being intimidated by it. In fact, one of them mentioned that many suspects would not talk with a camera in the room but would if the camera was not there.

Having the court case in mind when doing the investigation was important. What is admissible and what is not should always be considered by a good detective. Additionally, properly documenting all activities and evidence is essential. The investigation must take a step-by-step approach.

Some common mistakes by investigators are

1. Missing evidence at the scene
2. Giving crime scene to others too quickly
3. Not verifying what witnesses say
4. Talking too much

5. Not confirming information before applying or conducting surveillance
6. Appearing unsympathetic to family by acting as if it is just another case
7. Not following up
8. Not asking for help
9. Sloppy paperwork
10. Not being patient
11. Not being prepared

Investigators should take note of these common mistakes and learn from the good practices suggested in this chapter.

In conclusion, investigating a homicide can be challenging. There are many do's and don'ts. In this chapter I have shared with you those practices that are known to be successful. But as the seasoned detectives indicated, it is not a simple matter of reading a book and following the steps. Rather, experience is the most critical component of becoming a successful investigator. As one of the detectives wrote, "A homicide detective is the best job in law enforcement. You are the only person who can help the deceased receive any justice."

References

Abdollah, T. (2014, June 8). OJ Simpson taught police what not to do. ABC News/Associated Press. Retrieved from http://abcnews.go.com/US/wireStory/oj-simpson-case-taught-police-24045077. Accessed on June 12, 2014.

Birzer, M. L. and Roberson, C. (2012). *Introduction to Criminal Investigation*. Boca Raton, FL: CRC Press/Taylor & Francis Group.

Bureau of Justice Statistics (BJS). (2011). Homicide in the U.S. known to law enforcement, 2011. Retrieved from http://www.bjs.gov/content/pub/pdf/hus11.pdf. Accessed on June 12, 2014.

Dying Declaration. (2014). *Ballentine's Law Dictionary*, 3rd edn. Retrieved from Lexis Nexus (2014). http://www.lexisnexis.com/hottopics/lnacademic/. Accessed on June 12, 2014.

Federal Bureau of Investigation (FBI). (2013). Crime in the United States 2012. Retrieved from http://www.fbi.gov/about-us/cjis/ucr/crime-in-the-u.s/2012/crime-in-the-u.s.-2012/violent-crime/murder. Accessed on June 12, 2014.

Fox, J. A., Levin, J., and Quinet, K. (2012). *The Will to Kill: Making Sense of Senseless Murder*, 4th edn. Upper Saddle River, NJ: Pearson.

Geberth, V. J. (2006). *Practical Homicide Investigation: Tactics, Procedures, and Forensic Techniques*, 4th edn. Boca Raton, FL: CRC Press/Taylor & Francis Group.

Hall, K. L. (2004). *The Oxford Companion to American Law*. Oxford, U.K.: Oxford University Press. Retrieved from http://www.oxfordreference.com/view/10.1093/acref/9780195088786.001.0001/acref-9780195088786-e-0418?rskey=nTCfje&result=4. Accessed on June 12, 2014.

Inbau, F. E., Reid, J. E., Buckley, J. P., and Jayne, B. C. (2004). *Criminal Interrogation and Confessions*, 4th edn. Sudbury, MA: Jones and Bartlett.

New York City Police Department (NYPD). (2014). *Patrol Guide*. New York City Government Document. New York.

New York State Penal Law §15.05. Culpability: Definitions of culpable mental states.

Rodivich, C. (2012). Evidence. In M. L. Birzer and C. Roberson (eds.), *Introduction to Criminal Investigation*. Boca Raton, FL: CRC Press/Taylor & Francis Group. pp. 81–98.

Schmidt, M. S. (2014, May 22). In policy change, justice dept. to require recording of interrogations. *The New York Times*. Retrieved from http://www.nytimes.com/2014/05/23/us/politics/justice-dept-to-reverse-ban-on-recording-interrogations.html?_r=0. Accessed on June 12, 2014.

Serial Murder. (2014). *Encyclopaedia Britannica*. Retrieved from http://www.britannica.com/EBchecked/topic/863836/serial-murder. Accessed on June 12, 2014.

Snow, R. L. (2005). *Murder 101: Homicide and Its Investigation.* Westport, CT: Praeger.

Swanson, C. R., Chamelin, N. C., Territo, L., and Taylor, R. W. (2006). *Criminal Investigation* (9th ed.). New York: McGraw-Hill.

University at Albany, Hindelang Criminal Justice Research Center. (2011). *Sourcebook of Criminal Justice Statistics.* Table 3.118.2011. Retrieved from http://www.albany.edu/sourcebook/pdf/t31182011.pdf. Accessed on June 12, 2014.

What Detectives Should Know about Sexual Predators

2

RON RUFO

Contents

Chapter Objectives   19
Chapter Outline   19
Characteristics and Patterns of Sexual Predators   21
Grooming a Child   21
10 Ps of Sexual Predation   22
Law Enforcement Involvement and the Internet   27
Entrapment Defense   28
Meeting the Victim   29
Interviewing a Child That Has Been Sexually Abused   29
Crime Scene Processing of Sex Offenders   29
Fourth Amendment and the Collection Computer Evidence   30
Police Evidence Technicians and the Crime Lab   31
Special Victims Crime Units   31
National Sex Offender Public Registry   32
Conclusion   33
Discussion Questions   34
References   34

Chapter Objectives

After reading this chapter you should be able to do the following:

1. Identify a few characteristics associated with sexual predators.
2. Know exactly how a sexual predator grooms his/her victim.
3. Know in what way law enforcement uses the Internet to nab sexual predators.
4. Know in what manner sexual predators try to use the entrapment defense in court.
5. Know how specialized units in law enforcement are important in catching a sexual predator.
6. Understanding why the National Sex Offender Public Registry exists.
7. Know possible solutions to combat the sexual predation problem.

Chapter Outline

Characteristics and Patterns of Sexual Predators
Grooming a Child

10 Ps of Sexual Predation
Law Enforcement Involvement and the Internet
Entrapment Defense
Meeting the Victim
Interviewing a Child That Has Been Sexually Abused
Crime Scene Processing of Sex Offenders
Police Evidence Technicians and the Crime Lab
Special Victims Crime Unit
National Sex Offender Public Registry
Conclusion

Sexual predation has been and will continue to be a problem in society. My goal is to educate and enlighten criminal justice professionals, students, and the public to the cloak of deception involving sexual predation and the Internet. Most police officers and detectives are well aware of the individuals in their community that exhibit signs of criminal behavior in the commission of a crime. An example is a shoplifter running down the street with a bundle of clothes in his or her arms as they are trying to get away. An officer stops a van with a few suspicious people that have been reported at the scene of a few burglaries in the area. When the officer stops the vehicle, he or she discovers burglary tools and proceeds stolen from recent burglaries. A killer leaves his or her fingerprints at a murder scene again, valuable information needed to find the criminal and motive. When it comes to sexual predators, police and detectives often have no indication that the person they are talking to is a sexual predator. An officer cannot tell he or she is dealing with a sex offender unless they have been previously arrested. A sexual predator can be anyone the police encounter; they can be the wealthiest individual or a homeless person. Occupation does not necessarily matter, so long as they have access to children. That access can be a family member or an unsuspecting stranger meeting a sexual predator over the Internet. Many sex offenders choose an occupation that deals with young people, for example, a dance instructor, teacher, Boy Scout or Girl Scout leader, and priest. Research has shown that 95%–96% of sexual predators are men and 4%–5% are women.

Detectives enter a chat room with the hope of enticing a sexual predator or sex offender into speaking about sexual desires. According to many detectives, that often does not take long. Many sexual predators will casually begin a conversation innocently enough and, within a few minutes, may ask the naive child or teenager about their sexual experiences. They are hoping for a curious youngster to reply in a positive and encouraging manner. The entire conversation may last just a few minutes or hours. All the while, the sexual predator is doing his best to meet the young child. The sexual predator may try talking to a few unsuspecting teens at the same time. He is taking his chances that he will eventually get lucky in his attempt to control the situation. Even though thousands of e-mails are sent soliciting boys and girls alike over the Internet by sexual predators at any given minute, law enforcement officers have barely "scratched the surface" of catching the hundreds of thousands of sexual predators out there. For every one sexual predator that is revealed, caught, convicted, and imprisoned, there are 1000 enjoying lurking and scouring the social media networks who will never be caught. They want their victim to be young and innocent—they prefer girls in their early teens who are virgins.

Characteristics and Patterns of Sexual Predators

Every race, nationality, and religion has its share of sexual offenders and child sexual predators who often seem to act out solely to achieve their own sexual gratification. Rufo (2007) confirmed that many sexual offenders and sexual predators come from dysfunctional families. Growing up in a dysfunctional family may be a precursor to a sexual predator's need to seek love, affection, and comfort from children. Sexual predator's feelings of inadequacy may cause them to use force or threatening behavior against their victims. The same inadequacies may often show themselves in a dominant position of control and power toward their victims.

Sexual predators move methodically in their evaluation and approach toward their intended victim(s), often employing a cautious, low-risk strategy that they hope will keep them from getting caught. Rufo (2007) reiterated that there are two types of sexual offenders: one who likes to groom his victim and the other who acts on impulse. Both types of sexual offenders have little or no regard for the consequences of their actions or the effects on their victims and often rationalize their behavior and why the child resisted their advances. Sex offenders feel safe and more comfortable with children because children are naïve, gullible, innocent, and trusting. They often lure or entice a child through affection, attention, gifts, or money and will use this strategy to exploit and demand gratification from the child. Such offenders view the child as a willing participant as they take advantage of their victim in a casual and comfortable environment with which the child is familiar.

Grooming a Child

The child will tell the true account of a story or incidence; the sexual predators will make up the story as he goes along. Rufo (2012) noted that the art of sexual grooming is a common characteristic displayed by almost all sexual predators. Grooming can be compared to a master chess player waiting to make the ultimate move to take control: the sexual predator knows what the child needs and what he or she is missing or lacking in his or her life. Researchers are beginning to understand the communication process by which sexual predators lure their victims into a web of entrapment and how a child's innocence and vulnerability present an immense opportunity of abusive behavior by the sexual predator, who is very disciplined, calculating, and patient in attaining the ultimate goal of seducing a young child.

Our kids know what a stranger means in real life, but it is important for children to realize the danger sexual predators on the Internet pose. Very few kids see them as trouble or a problem. For example, if a stranger in a car calls out to a youngster, that youngster has been taught to run away and report the incident. If a stranger asks a child to help him find his dog or cat, the child is taught to again run away. A child at the computer gets asked the question, "Where is your computer located" or "who else uses your computer?" These questions should get the same reaction as in the other two scenarios... let someone know that something is wrong.

Access to the child is pivotal in the relationship in controlling the situation and focusing on the goal to sexually exploit their victim. Often the sexual predator seeks out the opportunity to sexually mistreat the child through continuous planning and manipulation.

In his attempt to satisfy his sexual desires, the sexual predator will patiently draw upon natural activity the child is familiar with and that he or she understands. He may change his plan or course of action, depending on the situation. He will wait for the right moment to get the child alone, getting the victim to believe he is harmless and poses no risk. Children inherently view adults as protectors, not offenders.

The sexual predator oftentimes is a relative, family friend, member of the clergy, neighbor, caregiver, babysitter, coach, or mentor and uses the innocent fondness and affection of his prey to initiate his routine of control. Sexual predators do not want their actions to seem suspicious and out of the ordinary. They will attempt to use seemingly acceptable forms of touching, depending on whom they plan to seduce. If it is a girl, they may use playful tickling, bathing, back rubs, or made-up games. In his attempt to seduce a young boy, the predator may use wrestling, playful fighting, horsing around, or different physical or sports activities to break down the barriers. Gifts, money, or favors are often used to quiet a victim about the sexual abuse that may take place or that has already taken place. The predator's deliberate, scheming, and opportunistic approach will often test the child to see how far they can go before being stopped, caught, or until the child complies with the sexual abuse. In an adult–child relationship, children are often too young to realize what is occurring and naïve to the fact that an adult would ever do harm to them. The sexual predator is considering the following:

- Is the intended victim a loner?
- Will adults believe that any abuse took place?
- What is the possibility of the victim being believed?

Grooming may include other activities, such as sitting on a child's bed and watching him or her get into their bedclothes, accidentally touching, showing the child pornography, and making contact with implicit sexual suggestions. Sexual predators prey on innocent children to satisfy their sexual desires. I have found that most sexual predators integrate what I like to call the 10 Ps of the predation process when forming a relationship with a child. This is a 10-step progression in the sexual predator's quest to groom and maintain their connection with the child they intend to pursue and exploit.

10 Ps of Sexual Predation

Proficiency: Anyone who does something for an extended period of time becomes proficient at what they do. The Internet has brought an entirely new medium for sexual predators to develop their skills. A sexual predator, just by sheer volume of the Internet chat rooms, can practice his routine. He will develop, apply, and use what works and disregard what doesn't. I like to compare their actions to a fisherman casting his lure and fishing hook into a river with thousands and thousands of fish even the poorest fisherman will get lucky with those odds. They throw out that hook for a particular type of victim who intensifies their lust and excitement. Even a blind squirrel will find a nut once in a while that is the same attitude they incorporate. If they are not lucky in their first few attempts to lure a victim in their trap, there is always tomorrow. Sexual predators are good at what they do. The sexual predator will continue to molest children until they stop on their own (which is very rare) or until they are caught by police. One problem is that sex offenders and sexual predators, even when convicted and sentenced to prison, are still dangerous. They will take the chance to reoffend again. If the urge and the resources are there, they will continue to sexually abuse as often as they can, possibly becoming more cautious so as not to get caught again.

Prefer: Sexual predators most likely have been abused themselves. Sexual predators prefer a specific age group and rarely deviate from that preference. If a sexual offender was molested at a certain age, he is likely to target the same age group as an offender. Many studies have indicated that individuals who have been molested at a certain age are more likely to search for the same age victim when they become older. For example, a young boy who is 12 years old is raped by his next-door neighbor. The young man who was raped is living with this humility and shame for the rest of his life. The young man grows up and has the same desire for 12-year-old boys or someone near that age. It is a continuous circle of abuse; the young person who was being abused is now the abuser. Researchers have found this throughout their studies. It is fairly common for a grandfather, father, and then son to all be abused and turn out to all become the abuser in future relationships. The cycle has to stop somewhere.

Puberty: Sexual predators will generally be interested in a child near the age of puberty or a child who is sexually inexperienced or curious. Sexual predators using the Internet often target young female teens that are going through a rebellious stage in their formative years. The sexual predator will often go on the Internet and enter a chat room where he or she will hunt for a victim that has a "sexy" moniker. Chat rooms are online, real-time sites where anyone can communicate interactively. The transmission is immediate, with the person on the computer at the other end receiving the message. Once two people meet in a chat room, they can quickly move the conversation to yet another private chat room. Online predators are out there lurking and scanning chat rooms, waiting for the opportunity to join a conversation. They are looking for someone independent, adventurous, looking to explore the world, confused, and inexperienced or possibly someone who has been arrested and is seeking help. The sexual predator will look for naïve teenagers who have obvious issues that they cannot handle. A perfect scenario is a troubled teen who has been arrested and has nowhere to turn. The sexual predator has a perfect excuse even if he is caught. Who would authorities believe: a respected, esteemed, and distinguished citizen of the community or a young, troubled teen who is confused and problematic? Sad to say, many people in our culture would believe and take the side of the community leader over the distressed teen.

Any teen expressing problems and issues over the Internet will be targeted by sexual predators. This gives them a great opportunity and a chance to open the door to begin a conversation and communication. It gives the predator the opportunity to come to the teens' rescue. It will not take long for the sexual predator to become a trusted friend and confidante. His tactics are deliberate, often knowing when the victim is comfortable and relaxed. Some predators take their time introducing their sexual wants and desires; others may display their true intentions early in the Internet chat. Like a piranha, he latches on to the moment and begins an intimate and soothing approach in his advances, with the ultimate goal of meeting the teen in his effort to attain sexual gratification. If the girl or boy becomes alarmed or suspicious, they take a step back, possibly changing the subject or saying that they were misunderstood.

Listed are a few issues that a sexual predator watches for as he reads conversation in his search for his next victim:

- A few provocative monikers: "Bikini Party Girl 69" or "Sexy Girl 2001." The 2001 in the last moniker most likely reflects the year the teen was born. She would be 13 years old at this writing, a most sought-after age by sexual predators because the teens are young, naïve, inexperienced, and adventurous. Like getting four aces in a card game, there is a great chance to walk away a winner in their mind.
- Control issues with the teens' parents.
- The teen comes from an abusive setting.
- The teens' parents are going through a divorce.
- Not being understood, rebellious.
- Teen who has a troubled life and has few or no friends.
- Communication problems; no one understands them.
- Staying out all night, having no curfew.
- Leaving home or running away, looking for somewhere to stay.
- Mostly home alone, or alone most often.

Plan: One thing sexual predators are good at is planning their next course of action. They use different techniques and methods that work for them and that they have used before. The predator will cautiously and carefully scrutinize the child's behavior and activities and attempt to find out what the child is good at, their likes and dislikes, and what he or she enjoys doing. They refine their approach and skills as often as necessary, often seeking the path of least resistance. A sexual predator's goal is for their intended victim to be comfortable, relaxed, and content. They take the opportunity to be a friend and companion as they are very good at being an active listener. This could take several hours, several days, or several months. Sexual predators often gamble by moving forward, especially if their confidence level is high. The sexual predator will plan each step to gratification with the ultimate goal of fulfilling their desires by enticing their intended victim into a sexual tryst.

Patience: Many sexual predators are very patient and "laid back" in their approach to dealing with their intended target. This is a skill that the sexual predator develops and acquires over time. It is subtle yet deliberate behavior. He slowly breaks down any resistance their intended victim initially responds to. The sexual predator has an answer for everything, blaming others for any negative reaction that the victim experiences. The sexual predator uses time to his advantage and is careful not to send up red flags to anyone that is interested in the victim's well-being. He does not want anyone to become suspicious of the behavior that would indicate his true objective and intent.

The next scenario is based on a true story. A young couple named Bill and Mary and their 4-year-old son Matt moved to the Scottsdale, Arizona, area from New York City. Bill and Mary found a quaint little home that needed some repairs, is reasonable for the area, and is in a good school district. The kitchen was their first priority and they asked neighbors if they knew of any local carpenters or handymen in the area that were both affordable and reliable. A retired neighbor recommended Jeff, a 35-year-old handyman that did work for her. Jeff came to the house and provided some very good ideas at a reasonable price.

Bill and Mary hired Jeff to start on their kitchen in a few days. He estimated that the job would take 3–4 weeks to complete. Bill and Mary were unsuspecting of the handyman's background or criminal past. Jeff sodomized his two young nephews and was arrested, convicted, and served 5 years in prison. It did not take long for Bill and Mary to become comfortable with their new carpenter. Bill left for work when Jeff arrived each morning. Jeff soon became very attentive to their son, but never gave any other indication of misconduct. The boy's parents did not seem concerned that their handyman was spending more and more time with their son, always managing to be alone at some point with their son.

Mary would often run errands when Matt took a nap in the late morning, leaving Jeff alone in the house with Matt. One day when Mary came home from shopping, she heard Matt crying. Jeff said he just started crying. Jeff said he needed additional material at the lumber yard. When Mary went to check on Matt, she found him crying uncontrollably. That was not like him; he was visibly shaken and complained that his butt hurt. When Mary looked, she found blood coming from Matt's rectum. She immediately called 911. The paramedics indicated that Matt may have been sodomized, but the doctors would verify that fact. The police soon arrived and Mary told them the only person that was home alone with Matt was Jeff, their handyman. Mary said that Jeff left soon after she arrived and that he needed additional material for the kitchen. Mary was in disbelief that Jeff would do such a thing; he was always patient and caring for her son. Matt was transported to the hospital and the emergency room doctors did confirm that Matt was sodomized and his rectum was torn. Matt was prepared for immediate surgery to stop the bleeding. The officers investigated the handyman's identity and found that Jeff was a convicted sex offender. Jeff was nowhere to be found, and a warrant for Jeff's arrest was issued. Matt recovered from his injury but the trauma will be with him the rest of his life. Jeff was caught and arrested 10 days later when he was stopped for a traffic violation. Jeff admitted sodomizing the young boy and was eventually charged and sentenced to 10 years in prison.

Praise: It is human nature to want to be accepted and praised, especially for teens that are seeking someone to compliment them and acknowledge their accomplishments. Adolescents and preteens thrive on praise. Teens need to know that people believe in them, especially by hearing positive and reaffirming messages from time to time. The sexual predator always finds the right words to say and will have little trouble building the child's self-esteem. This may be something the child is not used to, especially if he or she comes from a dysfunctional or abusive family. Some teenagers may become suspicious if someone is praising them all of the time, but positive reinforcement is a powerful tool that usually works to the advantage of the sexual predator, especially if it seems genuine and sincere.

Persuasion: A sexual predator has the uncanny ability to coax a child into doing what he or she wants the child to do. One way that a predator uses persuasion is by coaxing the young and inexperienced victim into believing that the nature of their sexual encounter is normally acceptable and appropriate. Persuasion often is used in the process of grooming a victim. Children inherently view adults as protectors and people they trust, not as those that are going to harm them. The grooming process is a common characteristic of most, if not all, sexual predators. The power of persuasion is a powerful tool. The predator listens intently, taking in information about what the child is lacking in his or her life. It could be emotional support from his/her family or friends; it could be money for school or clothes. Whatever the need, the sexual predator uses this need to take advantage. With the power comes leverage and control. The sexual predator will take advantage of any opportunity and often wait for the right moment to take advantage of the child. If he is successful in his attempt to gain sexual satisfaction, he or she will try and try again until he or she meets resistance and knows further actions can be risky. The sexual predator could be a relative, family friend, member of the clergy, neighbor, caregiver, babysitter, coach, or mentor and will use the innocent fondness and affection of his prey to initiate domination. In regard to girls being sexually seduced, the tactic of persuasion and grooming can be acceptable forms of touching, back rubs, and tickling. For boys, it could come in the form of playful fighting or wrestling.

The sexual predator will do whatever it takes to break down any barrier or resistance that he or she encounters in their attempt to control their victim. The offender will attempt to keep his actions discreet and will try to keep the child silent through a variety of strategies. They will attempt to continue to exploit the child, especially if the act is gentle and pleasurable and the child does not believe that what had occurred is wrong or harmful. One persuasive strategy is to involve the child in sexual escapade. Swearing a child to secrecy by threatening them or a family member, a friend, or a pet is another way to persuade them to be careful not to reveal anything. It is this fear that will ultimately allow the sexual predator to persevere in his efforts to control and mask the situation.

Privacy: This is the ultimate goal for the sexual predator: encouraging a one-on-one meeting or to be alone with the child. The sexual predator looks for ideal status conditions, such as a child living in a single-parent home or where the parents are going through a divorce. This allows the predator ample time to be with the child usually when Mom is at work or running errands. These conditions offer the predator various opportunities to take advantage of the situation. The predator will find emotional opportunities such as a young adolescent who has been bullied, is needy, seems unhappy, and is a loner, with lack of supervision. It is the sexual predator's intention to incorporate intimacy and any type of sexual contact while they try to make the child feel special and that the gratification is consensual. Drugs and alcohol may sometimes be used in an attempt to make the victim more compliant.

Power: The predator will intimidate the child to keep their secret and not reveal it to anyone. This is the power the sexual predator has over the child. The predator will say, "We will get in trouble if you tell," which puts the blame on the child before the exploitation starts or if there is any resistance by the child. This is a way that the predator knowingly involves the victim to accept the blame and share the consequences. It also inevitably helps prevent the child from coming forward revealing any improprieties. The predator wants the victim to be afraid to if they reveal anything about their secret relationship. The young adolescent is put into a predicament; he or she will be dammed if they do or dammed if they don't tell. Either way, the child being abused is vulnerable and confused and is constantly being controlled. In revealing any wrongdoing that has happened, the sexual predators want the victim to believe that the victim is just as accountable as they are.

Sexual predators use guilt, fear, and manipulation to keep the child quiet. This is seen most often in cases of incest with a child by a family member. Incest is defined as a sexual relationship that may also include sexual abuse or sexual intimacy with a child by a family member or relative in a position of authority. An incestuous relationship jeopardizes not only a child's physical safety but also his or her emotional and psychological well-being, sense of trust, and self-esteem. A child may often feel that he or she will be punished or blamed if the sexual abuse is revealed and the child will also believe that no one will believe their story anyway. A relative of the victim, most often the victim's parent, will skillfully manipulate the child into believing that if anyone were to find out about the sexual abuse, their family unit would be in jeopardy of breaking up. The blame and the guilt weigh so heavy on the child that most incest cases are never discovered until after other allegations have been revealed or when the abuser died. Therapists have acknowledged that many victims of incestal abuse have come forward with the pain and heartache of being abused by a parent or relative in counseling sessions long after the incidents have occurred.

Law Enforcement Involvement and the Internet

Law enforcement officers are faced with two separate dilemmas: The first difficulty is trying to control and diffuse the growing number of sexual predators using the Internet, and the second struggle is alerting and teaching adolescents and their parents about the dangers of the Internet and how to safeguard against the likelihood of being contacted by a sexual predator. Sexual predators feel that the Internet is a safe medium to contact children, with a very good chance of not getting caught or arrested for their behavior. The Internet has given sexual predators an abundance of opportunities in their search for victims.

The Internet has brought about the increased distribution of child pornography. Child pornography is not just a naked picture of a child but a picture of a child that exposes his or her genitals, rape or sodomy of a child, and masturbation or simulation of sex with a child. Mike Sullivan,* Deputy Chief of Investigations for the Illinois Attorney General's Office and author of the book *Online Predators*, had this to say regarding sexual predation on the Internet. The attorney general's office is proactive in their approach toward child pornography. They have handled hundreds of cases of child pornography from infants to children who are 6 years old. Juries are shown actual photos depicting horrific acts of child abuse. The realization is that these kids have suffered tremendously. The attorney general's office is worried about the specific makeup of the images, not necessarily the amount in the collection. The volume of pictures does not correlate to the dangers the pedophile is to the community. There are a few factors that the attorney general may look at when profiling a pedophile:

1. How dangerous is this pedophile?
2. How soon can law enforcement get to the pedophile?
3. How much of a threat is the pedophile to the community?
4. How much access does the pedophile have to a child or children?

Many pedophiles share illegal photographic images of minors everyday on the Internet, often sharing only with people that they know and trust. Rarely will pedophiles let someone new into their tight-knit inner circle of Internet friends and associates. A pedophile sending out child pornography is always in danger of being reported to, or possibly intercepted by, law enforcement posing as sex offenders interested in trading or buying child pornography over the Internet. Undercover law enforcement officers impersonate eager sex offenders who want to collect, trade, and sell child pornography. A problem that many law enforcement officers face in trying to apprehend, arrest, and convict sex offenders and pedophiles using the Internet is that the process incorporates additional time, resources, and manpower that many police departments are already lacking. When a pedophile is arrested, their computer is often confiscated and held for evidence of the crime. In an attempt to avoid getting arrested, many pedophiles will store their child pornographic pictures in files that are not easily accessed. Police department computer technicians are often used to decipher intricate passcodes and passwords in order to gain access to hidden files that contain the illegal pictures.

Drew Donofrio, owner of Cyberology Consultants, a company that provides investigative tools and services to curtail activities of sexual predators, said that children today

---

* Sullivan, M., Deputy Chief of Investigation, Illinois Attorney General's Office, ICAC Task Force Commander, 69 W. Washington, 18th floor, 60601. Personal interview.

are exposed to sexual material at an early age. Many children are not shocked when a sexual predator uses brazen language when they are conversing over the Internet. The combination of children who are not put off by discussions of sex and the availability of the Internet in their lives makes for a target-rich environment for sexual predators. Donofrio feels that sex offenders will try to justify their actions when caught with child pornography. He stated they frequently claim that the interest in child pornography started by accidental exposure. Donofrio expresses concern that an offender who views child pornography will be fueled to act out against a vulnerable child and that fantasy will not sustain the sex offender for too long. A few sex offenders may be satisfied masturbating to child pornography, but if presented with access to sex with a child, planned or not, they would most likely act out to achieve sexual gratification. Donofrio insisted that sex is a powerful form of motivator.

The FBI has a program that deals specifically with child pornography. The program is called the Innocent Images National Initiative. This program deals with cybercrimes that involve child solicitation and child exploitation. The mission of this unit is to reduce the vulnerability of children that use Internet chat rooms, to investigate and prosecute sexual predators that exploit children, and to identify and rescue child victims. Not all pedophiles physically molest children and not all molesters of children collect child pornography, but often child pornography is the common dominator.

Law enforcement officers will pose as young teens trying to attract sexual predators into an online conversation. It often does not take very long for a sexual predator to initiate a conversation with overtones of sexual questions and innuendos. The officers posing as teens are instructed to let the sexual predator initiate any sexual conversation or encounter. They can use the defense they were enticed into a sexual conversation (or entrapped), but it is very clear that the sexual predator initiated any inference of sexual demeanor, behavior, or performance.

Entrapment Defense

The entrapment defense is based on the belief that someone should not be held accountable and convicted of a crime derived from communication that the government originally instigated. There is no entrapment by police officers using the Internet, if they provide an opportunity for a crime or offer to engage in any illegal activity and the sexual predator is willing to violate the law by continued conduct. The U.S. Supreme Court has recognized that when investigating certain criminal behavior, law enforcement may lawfully use an array of undercover techniques. There are two foundations to the current entrapment defense:

1. *The government inducement of the crime*: The government's behavior or performance would instigate or induce a law-abiding citizen into crossing the line and breaking the law. The government actions of inducement may include promises, persuasion, threats, or harassment.
2. *Willingness to commit the crime*: One of the main components in the entrapment defense is the defendant's inclination or predisposition to engage in illegal activity or criminal conduct. The person is willing to commit the crime.

Meeting the Victim

Most sexual predators on the Internet are trying to meet and have sex with their intended targets. These predators will go to any length to meet the young naïve victims, even traveling across the United States to do so. Law enforcement personnel have coined the term "traveler" to describe the sexual predator who will cross state lines to have sex with the teen they have met through the Internet. Law enforcement personnel will send in a young decoy to meet at a desired location near or at the victim's house. It is not uncommon for the sexual predators to deny their true intentions for meeting the "decoy." Their intent was to fulfill their sexual fantasy of having sex with an adolescent or teen that was clearly too young, knowing that their actions and intent were clearly against the law. It is not unusual for the sexual predator to find out everything there is to know about his victim. They particularly prey upon a child who is obviously troubled, timid, vulnerable, shy, withdrawn, and weak, possibly coming from a divorced home and living with a single parent. The sexual predator will often make the excuse they just wanted to talk or take the teen out to lunch, dinner, or shopping at the mall. The undercover officers have often caught the sexual predator with condoms, sex toys, alcohol, and other items that may be used for their sexual pleasure. What is important to make the arrest of the sexual predator that travels is the Internet transcripts that the law enforcement agency has as evidence of their true intentions. When questioned with the evidence, many will still deny any wrongdoing.

Interviewing a Child That Has Been Sexually Abused

When a child is a victim of a sex crime, the abused child is interviewed, but it is not a normal interview that many TV viewers associate with. Children are spoken to in a friendly, comfortable setting that also is in front of a two-way mirror. A person doing the interview is trained to ask nonleading questions; the well-being of the sexually abused child is taken into account. Normally, there is a two-way glass room that is for anyone involved in the case. The two-way mirror is there so the child is not intimidated by the number of people in the room or those involved in the case. Behind the two-way glass mirror is normally a police detective who is responsible for writing down what the child said about the alleged crime and abuse, a person from the Department of Children and Family Services or a similar agency, someone from the state's attorney or prosecutor's office, police officers or sheriff's deputies, and any other personnel essential to the case. The police will take into account the testimony of the child but will often charge the offender based on his own confession. Many times the offender is a relative or family member of the child that is charged with incest or child abuse.

Crime Scene Processing of Sex Offenders

Like any crime scene, investigators or detectives must first try to locate evidence that was left behind by the offender. Crime scene processing is an important part of the investigation. Detectives collect any evidence associated with the crime, which may include condoms, semen samples, and any other items that were discarded, all of which is significant to the case. Deoxyribonucleic acid (DNA) is contained in virtually every cell in the human body and is considered the building blocks of the body. An important feature about DNA is that it may be able to be extracted at the scene of the crime. A trained evidence technician (ET) can collect DNA evidence from many different sources at the crime scene. If the crime is a sexual assault, DNA can be collected from the offender's sweat, saliva, blood, hair, cigarettes, condoms, clothing, or any other pertinent articles that are in the offender's possession. A judge would have to issue a warrant to extract DNA from an offender by swabbing his mouth of the offender if he refuses to give a DNA sample. The collection of DNA evidence and how it was obtained are critical in identifying the possible offender and proving who was and was not at the scene, with a greater likelihood of solving the crime.

When a child needs to be examined for sexual abuse, the medical exam is an essential part of the investigation. The doctor who examines the child uses a machine that takes detailed pictures of the affected area, which are often used at trial. This collected and documented evidence often leads to a conviction of the offender. The combination of DNA evidence and medical evidence often leads to a successful arrest.

Fourth Amendment and the Collection Computer Evidence

The Fourth Amendment states that people have the right to be secure in their homes and on their persons, their papers, and their personal effects against any unreasonable searches and seizures by the government. The Fourth Amendment is not a guarantee against all searches and seizures but all of those deemed unreasonable under the law. The Fourth Amendment states that no warrants shall be issued without probable cause. Whether a particular search or seizure is considered reasonable depends on two specific factors:

1. Is the intrusion on an individual's rights warranted? Many sexual predators use this in their defense in that their rights are being violated by law enforcement agencies when it comes to removing computers or items from their home (most often for child pornography or for chat room conversations). Sex offenders and sexual predators deem their home computers, child pornographic pictures, and other such items their private property. Their contention is that they are not hurting anyone. Searches and seizures inside a home without a warrant would be considered unreasonable.
2. The government, through law enforcement and their agencies, has the explicit duty of public safety, most often issuing a warrant to collect evidence and seize their property against a person who has exhibited behavior that indicates that he or she will endanger a child through sexual exploitation. Many law enforcement agencies monitor the Internet looking for unusual sexual behavior and may issue a warrant against a person that may be considered dangerous to the public, especially children who are at risk.

Rufo (2007) noted that according to the FBI, Division of Criminal Justice Services, and all digital investigations especially the Internet, facilitated child sex crimes rely on forensic analysis to secure evidence needed to obtain a conviction in a court of law. What is important to an investigation is duplicating the image of evidence, which can be found on hard drives, cell phones, and other external media. Forensic analysis is an effective means of leading to the identification of sexual offenders that create and distribute child pornography. Data and records obtained from digital media and Internet usage can yield important investigative leads. Digital evidence of exploitive images that are seized from computers and other electronic files needs to be analyzed to establish the production, possession, transport, and distribution of child pornography. This collection of digital evidence is critical for prosecution.

Police Evidence Technicians and the Crime Lab

One of the more important jobs in apprehending any criminal is the collection of evidence left and discovered at a crime scene. There are many television programs that encourage young people to pursue this specific area of criminal justice. The Crime Scene Investigation (CSI) show promotes the collection of crime scene evidence with new modern technology. In the real world, it is unrealistic to expect to solve a crime so quickly; realistically, a crime may take many months, possibly years to solve.

ETs are dispatched to a crime scene shortly after the crime has occurred. The police officer assigned to a crime in progress or one that has taken place is the preliminary investigator. When an officer first pulls up to the scene of the crime or disturbance, he or she will determine if an ET should be called to the scene. The officer's first priority is to set up a perimeter of yellow tape (outer perimeter) and the red tape (inner perimeter). The tape initially preserves the crime scene by not allowing anyone to disturb the crime scene and maintain needed evidence that could possibly help solve the crime and catch the offender (s). The ETs and detectives are often the only law enforcement officers allowed inside the secured area.

At a crime that involves a sex offender, the ET would approach the crime scene with an open mind, first observing what he or she initially saw outside of the yellow tape, looking for any obvious signs of a struggle or sexual assault. The ET would not only note that on paper, but possibly by an audio recording. Next, the ET would take pictures of the crime scene from every possible angle and note the direction he or she was shooting the camera from. An important collection of evidence is any physical evidence left at the crime scene of the sexual assault that includes hair, clothing, fibers, and bodily fluids. The ET may proceed to the hospital where the victim was taken to collect evidence from him or her. The evidence is also called a rape kit. After taking photographs and collecting evidence, it is important for the ET to complete a written report and document the evidence collected and how it will be preserved. Many lawyers will summon ETs to court to explain not only the collection and preservation of evidence but the chain of custody that followed where and how it was stored. Trials may take years to travel through the court system, and preservation of evidence is an important component if the offender arrested did commit the sexual assault and if he is convicted of the crime.

Special Victims Crime Units

Many police jurisdictions have detectives that deal with sex offenders. Many departments have named these units the special victims units (SVUs). Many detectives that are assigned to the SVU also investigate sexual assaults, criminal sexual assault (rape), child abuse, and any other sex offenses, especially if children are involved. The detectives often keep track of registered sex offenders and check to see if their current addresses are correct and up to date. Detectives in the SVU investigate all citizen complaints about known sex offenders and any suspicious people that someone has complained about. The SVU provides educational and safety presentations for youngsters, teens, and adults that inform everyone of the dangers of the Internet. SVU detectives are dedicated to thwarting sexual predators from continuing their online enticement of children, exploitation of children, and online child pornography. Many local law enforcement agencies are trying to increase their undercover capabilities that would more than likely increase their apprehension of sexual predators that frequent the Internet. Detectives are often called into court to testify for the prosecution on the reports that were taken at the crime scene. These reports may include any oral or written statements made by the victim, any suspects that were near or at the scene of the crime, and especially any suspects or offenders. It is not unusual for SVU detectives to request search and possibly arrest warrants.

National Sex Offender Public Registry

The National Sex Offender Registry allows society to know what sexual offenders have done and where they live. According to the U.S. Department of Justice,* the National Sex Offender Public Registry was first established in 2005. Sex offenders convicted of a crime were mandated to register where they lived with local police authorities. Rufo (2012) wrote that President George W. Bush signed into law the Adam Walsh Protection and Safety Act on July 27, 2006, in a ceremony in the White House's Rose Garden. The Adam Walsh Protection Act is intended to track sex offenders nationwide and provide stricter registration for offenders. Sex offenders can register through the National Sex Offender Registry, which is an online service that links all state offender websites. Sex offenders will also receive tougher penalties especially if they prey on children over the Internet. If an offender fails to register, he or she could face a 10-year maximum term or a 5-year consecutive mandatory minimum sentence for committing a crime while failing to register. The Adam Walsh Act not only gives sex offenders a mandatory 10-year prison sentence if they assault any child under the age of 18, the act also prohibits them from showing or sending child pornography or any obscene material.

The U.S. government initiated the Dru Sjodin National Sex Offender Public Website (NSOPW) that was named after Dru Sjodin, a young woman who was kidnapped and murdered by a sex offender who was registered in Minnesota. This website is a public safety resource that provides public access to sex offender data nationwide and links public state, territorial, and tribal sex offender registries from one national search site. Up-to-date information is provided and hosted by each jurisdiction, not by NSOPW or the federal government. There are a number of search options and tools about sex offenders that can be utilized by the NSOPW website. They are

- Search by name nationally
- Search by name from an individual jurisdiction
- Search by address (if provided by jurisdiction)

* U.S. Department of Justice. NSOPW, 950 Pennsylvania Avenue, NW, Washington DC 20530.

- Search by zip code
- Search by county (if provided by jurisdiction)
- Search by city or town (if provided by jurisdiction)

Conclusion

Although counseling and therapy have educated and helped many sexual offenders, most sex offenders believe they still would not be totally rehabilitated upon their return to society. Sexual predators live and work in all social, economic, and educational levels of society. Growing up in a dysfunctional family is often the norm for most sex offenders. A majority of sex offenders come from families that have had encounters with law enforcement. Many sex offenders also have problems that include alcoholism, drug addiction, mental illness, medical issues, and self-abuse. Studies have indicated that an overwhelming number of sexual predators have felt empathy for their victims, but it was not until counseling that they were able to realize the extent of the damage they caused.

The importance of researching this topic was to better understand the behavior of a person's deliberate attempt to sexually exploit a vulnerable child using technology that children favor. Sexual predators often use the Internet to view and distribute child pornography, to meet and befriend young victims, and to manipulate their victims into meeting them for sexual encounters. In today's society, statistics show that the rapidly growing number of sexual predators that have been acting out their criminal intent using the Internet has increased at a progressively alarming rate.

Many law enforcement agencies have implemented strategies to combat online predation. I feel that we have only touched the surface of the problem. The Internet has introduced a new venue that allows sexual predators a greater opportunity to reach their victims. The U.S. Department of Justice (2008) discussed the "Think Before You Post" campaign, which was a public service announcement that stressed to teenagers, mainly teenage girls, that "anything you post online, anyone can see family, friends, and even not-so-friendly people." The goal of this campaign was to open teenagers' eyes to potential dangers on the Internet and to warn them to be careful about what information they give out about themselves.

Law enforcement often does not have the manpower or resources to handle the magnitude of sex offenders and sexual predators that infiltrate chat rooms on the Internet. The success rate is very small and limited. The Internet predators will often portray themselves as caring and trusting individuals. The sexual predator is often thrilled to step into the new role of friend, mentor, and confidante. It will not take long for the predator to win the child over by listening to what he or she needs.

There are a number of suggestions and recommendations that a parent or guardian can initiate that would help deter their child from dangerous Internet activity. Parents should share e-mail accounts with their children. This would enable a parent to see all correspondence, not only coming in to their home computer but also sent out. Many criminal justice system officials suggested that parents scrutinize a child's e-mail and be aware of the Internet locations their child is visiting. Law enforcement agencies in each city throughout the United States need to develop programs to combat the use of the Internet by sexual predators to attract young victims. We have seen many federal efforts that have collaborated with state and local agencies to help with this problem, but more needs to be done. In my opinion, additional changes are necessary to safeguard children.

Discussion Questions

2.1 Describe a few reasons why sexual predators go undetected while committing sexual crimes.

2.2 Name a few dimensions of human behavior intrinsic to sexual crimes.

2.3 Explain deceptive trust development.

2.4 What tools does a sexual predator use to groom his intended victim?

2.5 Define manipulation and explain how it ties into the way a sexual offender operates.

2.6 Explain how a sexual predator uses persuasion.

2.7 Explain denial as it relates to a sex offender.

2.8 Explain how a sexual predator entraps a victim.

2.9 What are some symptoms or indicators that a child has been sexually abused?

2.10 What is one way for a parent to prevent or stop their child from becoming a victim of a sexual offender?

2.11 Define child pornography.

2.12 Explain how crime scene processing is an important factor in the investigation.

References

Rufo, R. (2007). An investigation of online sexual predation of minors by convicted male offenders. Dissertation. Argosy University, Chicago, Illinois.

Rufo, R. (2012). *Sexual Predators amongst Us*. Boca Raton, FL: Taylor Francis Group/CRC Press.

U.S. Department of Justice. (2008). Fact sheet: Project safe childhood. From www.ojp.usdoj.gov/newsroom/pressreleases/2008/doj08845.htm.

Special Victims Investigations

DANA GALANTE

3

Contents

Chapter Objectives	35
Chapter Outline	36
Introduction	36
Special Victims	36
Interviews	37
Victim Interview	37
Interview of a Child Victim	38
Forensic Interview	38
Interview of a Subject	39
Confessions	40
Investigations	40
False Reporting	41
Witnesses	41
Canvass	41
Corroboration	42
Resources	42
DNA Evidence	42
Warrants/Subpoenas	43
Identification Process	44
Media	45
Conclusion	45
Case Study #1	46
Case Study #2	46
Case Study #3	47
Case Study #4	48
Case Study #5	49
Questions for Discussion	49
References	49

Chapter Objectives

After reading this chapter you should be able to do the following:

1. Identify the crimes investigated by a special victims squad.
2. Establish guidelines for interviews—victim or subject.
3. Explain the forensic interview process in regard to a child victim.
4. Describe different techniques used to gain corroboration.
5. Identify the steps in an identification process.

Chapter Outline

Overview of a Special Victims Squad
Interviews
Investigations
Corroboration
Identification Process

Introduction

> Murder is a crime. Describing murder is not. Sex is not a crime. Describing sex is.
>
> **—Gershon Legman**

Welcome to the world of "Fifty Shades of Grey" relative to criminal investigations: sex crimes. Aside from homicide, sex crimes are of the most heinous, yet bizarre, nature. And the investigations prove to be exhilarating but nonetheless tedious. These investigations continue to be, and will be for years to come, the hype of media, movies, and television series. Why? Because there is something about sex crime investigations that stimulates societal interest. Perhaps it is the nature of the crime that arouses attention or perhaps it is the even more enticing investigation process. Either way, people become completely invested in the investigation. So much so that the outcome tends to become more of a "need to know" basis rather than a "want to know." However interesting, television shows, or series, provide a common misconception regarding these cases. Likewise, society is poisoned with a fallacy that the cases are quickly and easily solved. What people fail to recognize is the lengths investigators go through to identify and prosecute these perpetrators. This chapter will discuss, in grave detail, the investigation process. Keep in mind that the investigative steps identified will provide the investigator with knowledge of available resources; however, the use of the resources should be assessed on a case-by-case basis. Additionally, case studies will be provided to exemplify the process. The case studies provided are based on factual cases investigated by special victims squads.

Special Victims

The special victims squad is an elite unit within some law enforcement organizations that investigate adult sexual assault, child physical abuse, and child sexual assault allegations. Although case criteria may vary by jurisdiction, the core sex crimes investigated remain the same, that is, rape, criminal sexual act/sodomy, and sexual abuse. Consequently, some departments have separate adult and child abuse squads that allow for the investigator to attain an expertise in specific areas. This helps ensure that each victim will receive the most qualified member(s) assigned to their case. Moreover, this enables the investigators to build a relationship with the prosecutor's office. Maintaining open lines of communication assists in the overall outcome of the investigation.

Special victims squads typically comprise seasoned investigators that receive extensive training in regard to sex crime investigations. Trainings are usually provided by the respective department; however, some are offered by outside agencies. Likewise there are annual nationwide conferences in which investigators may attend. These trainings and conferences arm the investigator with a plethora of tools from interview techniques to investigative strategies.

Interviews

As an investigator, it is your job to obtain the details of the incident. What a victim considers relative to the investigation often differs from that of the investigator. The most obscure detail can quickly become the most prominent. If the victim seems embarrassed or reserved, make it a point to explain how crucial every little detail is to the investigation. Reassure the victim that he or she will not be judged by what happened. Approach the victim with sensitivity but do not allow the victim to take your kindness for weakness. The goal here is to get the victim comfortable enough to provide extensive detail about the incident but not too comfortable whereby he or she may embellish the truth.

Prior to an interview, the investigator should conduct a "victimology." The victimology provides insight as to who the victim is. The purpose for this is to see if the victim is a chronic reporter. To conduct a victimology, the investigator performs basic computer checks, which include the victim's history pertaining to arrests, complaint reports, domestic incidents, associated persons, previous addresses, and phone numbers. Additionally, when responding to a location, commercial or residential, the investigator should conduct an address check. This is for the safety of the investigator. Not only do you want to know who you will be interviewing, you want to know what you will be walking into. There are times when you will be responding to a building with multiple apartments; it would behoove you to know whether firearm arrests were related to anyone in that building as well as if search warrants were executed in the building. This is not like patrol where there is no time to conduct these checks prior to response. Use this to your advantage.

Victim Interview

The victim should be interviewed alone in a private location. There should be no outside support present in the room during the victim interview. From experience, the victim typically reveals more detail when one on one with the investigator(s). This is for a number of reasons. One reason would be that the victim may withhold information to protect loved ones from the truth. Remember, most sex crimes are quite heinous in nature. The victim may not want their loved ones to know the extent of the incident. Another reason would be that the person present may interrupt or get involved in the interview. Therefore, to avoid both scenarios, the interview is conducted alone.

In all interviews, ask for pedigree information. Although you already did your homework, ask the victim for his or her name, address, date of birth, phone number, e-mail address, marital status, current/previous employment, and amount of time at current/ previous employment. Try to ascertain drug/alcohol history as well as psychological history; find out if they are currently on medication, if so, the reason for the medication. If applicable, obtain the same for the subject. Be sure to question what, if any, the relationship is to the victim/subject. More often than not, the subject is known to the victim.

Now, the most important part of the investigation: the victim's account of the incident. Give the victim free narrative to describe the incident. Avoid interruptions and questions during this time but keep note of what you want to question further. Do not allow the victim to be vague with their account of the incident. It is imperative to get as much detail as possible. Do not be concerned with long pauses. Some victims are not as forthcoming as others.

Before exploring the victims account, make sure the victim understands that the questioning is for clarification. Explain that you want to be able to refer the incident as if you were the victim. Avoid negative questions that would make the victim feel as if the blame is being shifted toward him or her. You want to keep the victim on board with the investigation. Also, be cautious of your body language and facial expressions; both speak volumes.

Additionally, drugs and alcohol are most often conveniently left out of the equation. The victim usually does not want to admit to drug/alcohol use in fear of being shunned by the investigator. Explain that the use of drugs or alcohol does not justify the crime; however, it is important information for the investigator. For instance, the combination of the details provided as well as the knowledge of drug/alcohol use may lead the investigator to request a drug-facilitated sexual assault kit. Again, stress the importance of details.

The conclusion of the victim interview will set the tone for the remainder of the investigation. Using the details provided, the investigator should have an investigative strategy session to analyze and evaluate which steps should follow. During this time, do not become overly concerned when inconsistencies arise. There is plenty of time to question the validity of the incident. In the end, the truth will unveil itself as the investigation progresses.

Note: It is important to find out what, if any, the underlying factors for the report are, that is, late for curfew, married, and boyfriend/girlfriend.

Interview of a Child Victim

There is a completely different protocol in regard to interviewing a child victim. Here, a multidisciplinary approach is typically used to minimize trauma to the victim. This is a collaborative effort among law enforcement, the prosecutor's office, social workers, and medical staff. Likewise, these interviews should be conducted in child-friendly environments by qualified person(s). A child-friendly environment is one that is welcoming to the child. It tends to be light and colorful; it may even have toys and games. The most commonly used child-friendly environments are child advocacy centers (CACs) and schools.

The way the CAC works is as follows: An interview is conducted by a qualified forensic interview specialist. The interview is observed by members of the multidisciplinary team from another room within the CAC. This enables the interviewer to confer with those members throughout the interview. Depending on the disclosure of the victim, the investigator can request a medical examination for the victim. The said medical examination is conducted on sight by the medical staff associated with the CAC. The medical staff consists of experts in the field of child abuse who can identify and distinguish the injuries of a victim. Upon conclusion of the examination, the medical staff will confer with the investigator and prosecutor.

Note: Each interview room in a CAC is equipped with a camera, usually for observation only.

Forensic Interview

Rapport is huge in child interviews. The first contact the investigator has with the child victim should not be in the interview room. When practical, the investigator should try to spend a few minutes with the child prior to the interview. This allows the child to become comfortable with the investigator, which, in essence, helps to build trust. Informally, on first-name basis, introduce yourself to the child. Take interest and participate in what the child is doing. Make mental note of consistency in colors or activities the child seems to favor. Attempt to discuss commonalities (sports/television shows/favorite colors). The information gathered here will become useful during the interview. For instance, children often become shy and introverted when confronted with the actual abuse. At this time, the investigator should revert back to a commonality identified during the initial contact. By diverting off topic, the child becomes relaxed again. Revisit the topic when appropriate.

Begin the interview with a developmental assessment. This is used to determine the competency of the child. Some techniques include but are not limited to truth/lie; good/bad touches; difference between inside of, on top of, and underneath; and identification of body parts with use of anatomical drawings. Continue with the interview once it becomes evident that the child is capable of understanding and answering questions.

When the focus is shifted to the actual abuse, attempt to occupy the child by use of drawing, play dough, and/or coloring. This helps to ease the child into disclosure. Because the child is completely enthralled in the activity, he or she will likely disclose information pertaining to the incident without thought. Oftentimes, the child will look up in shock after realizing a disclosure was made. Subsequently, if the child becomes talkative, do not interrupt. Allow the child to go at his or her own pace.

Note: Thoroughly explore the disclosure for consistency and clarity. Address potential issues that may arise.

Interview of a Subject

Why do subjects make admissions? There is no correct answer; however, there are plenty of theories. In the end, it will always depend on the subject. The goal of the subject interview is to obtain an oral, written, or video admission. You will come across all types of subjects. Some will confess easily, some will take time and effort, and others will never give it up. For the purpose of this section, the focus will be on the subjects that take time and effort.

Begin with a self-introduction and indicate the reason for the interview. Inform that the premise of the interview is to gather all facts of the incident before drawing a conclusion. Explain that you are conducting a thorough, impartial investigation to be fair to all parties involved. After covering the basis, the hardest hurdle for the investigator to overcome is the reading of the Miranda warnings. This can be the most nerve-wracking part for the investigator. Why? Because you do not know how the subject will respond. A cooperative subject may quickly become uncooperative. Innocent or not, the Miranda warning often makes the subject think twice before speaking with investigators. Once the subject waives his or her Miranda, it's on. For all those baseball fans, it's the bottom of the ninth, down by one with two outs and a runner on third. It's all on you!

The fate of the case sometimes lies with the outcome of the subject interview. Ultimately, the investigator should go to all lengths to obtain a confession. The four basic steps to aid in this process are as follows:

- Connection—foundation of the interview; this is paramount to everything else. Here, patience is truly a virtue.

- Fact gathering—it is important to gather as much facts and background information about the incident as possible. Oftentimes, the subject will test you as to how much information you know. The trick here is to arm yourself with enough knowledge to stay a few steps ahead of the subject. Ask questions you already know the answer to. At the same time, lead the subject to believe that he or she convinced you otherwise.
- Strategize—the cliché: good cop/bad cop.
- Tactics—different techniques work on different subjects. Figure out which approach will work best on your subject. Some subjects may require several techniques before the actual confession. Some techniques include, but are not limited to,
  - Befriend the subject.
  - Play them as the victim—question the possibility that the victim was the one that led them on.
  - Use props—photos of the victim and/or their injury, drawings made by the victim, and religious artifacts/texts for those that are religious.
  - Express concern—tell them you want to get them help.

There is another type of subject interview that can be conducted. Prior to police custody, the investigator can conduct a noncustodial interview with the subject. Noncustodial interviews can be conducted anywhere. Some investigators may even conduct these interviews in public places. Here, the investigator can arrange to meet the subject on common grounds. This is done as more of a nonaccusatory conversation about the incident rather than as an interrogation. All aspects of the conversation are to be documented. This will aid the investigator later on in the investigation.

   Note: Subject interviews can last hours, sometimes days. Be sure to document when, and if, food and drinks are provided to the subject. Also, indicate the use of the bathroom or cigarette break. This may come up at trial.

Confessions

There are three types of confessions: verbal, written, and video. Clearly, obtaining all three would give advantage to the prosecution. This is not always as easy as it may sound. After a successful interview, where an admission is made, question the subject if he or she will provide a written statement containing the facts that were disclosed. Furthermore, if available, ask the subject if he or she will be willing to give a video confession. Explain that it may behoove him or her because it is not just words on paper; it enables the jury to see the sincerity/remorse of the subject. This may help at the time of sentencing because jurors may empathize more after viewing a video confession. And no, it is not that you are trying to "help" the subject; it is that you are solidifying the case by having a video confession.

Investigations

…Skepticism and doubt lead to study and investigation,
and investigation is the beginning of wisdom.

—**Clarence Darrow**

To state that it is important to follow the proper steps when investigating sex crime cases is an understatement. It is absolutely crucial because the results of your investigation can be the difference between a conviction and an acquittal at trial. There is no better feeling than knowing that your investigation led to the conviction of a deviant human being.

There are two basic types of sex crime cases: stranger and acquaintance. A stranger case is when the subject is unknown to the victim; he or she is a complete stranger. On the other hand, an acquaintance case is when the subject is known to the victim. He or she may be a friend, family member, significant other, etc. A vast majority of sex crime investigations are acquaintance cases. As previously stated, in both cases, the fundamental steps of the investigation will remain the same, but the additional steps will differ greatly. Remember: No victim is the same, no subject is the same, and no investigation is the same. Yes, there may be some similarities in all categories, but ultimately each is unique. Keep an open mind and develop distinctive approaches to conquer issues that arise.

False Reporting

Sex crime investigations are extremely convoluted. An allegation may not always be based on truth. It is up to you, as the investigator, to find the underlying truth. Cases that seem legitimate may end up with conflicting evidence and vice versa. There are several factors to consider in regard to false allegations, such as inconsistent statements, conflicting witness statements, lack of substantiating evidence, and lack of plausibility in description of the crime.

Reasons for false reporting vary. Some primary motivations include seeking attention/sympathy, mental illness/depression, revenge, and blackmail. Yes, blackmail. Although this is highly unlikely, it has happened in the past (refer to Case Study #2).

Note: Do not become overly concerned with the possibility of false reporting. A case can be easily disproved while proceeding with your usual investigative steps.

Witnesses

The investigator should immediately identify the outcry and, if applicable, an eye witness. An outcry is a person in which the victim confided in immediately after the incident *or* the person whom the victim first disclosed to. An eye witness is a person that witnesses the incident firsthand. An eye witness can account for the incident without doubt. Each should be interviewed separately from each other and the victim. The interview should be as thorough, and detailed, as the victim interview. This is done to verify the victim's account of the incident. Remember back to the false reporting section. Justified or not, oftentimes, victims will fabricate an incident. Be sure to explore conflicting accounts of the incident.

Note: Be aware that there is a chance to uncover additional witnesses during the canvass.

Canvass

When possible, conduct a cognitive reenactment of the crime scene with the victim. In this step, the investigator will walk the exact route with the victim: prior to the initial encounter of the subject, during the incident, and after the incident. Again, question the victim as to incident. Have the victim indicate the events that lead up to the incident. This may help recollect additional details. Take note of debris and possible items left behind by the subject. Recover any item identified as that of the subjects.

Return to the location of occurrence without the victim. At this time, conduct an extensive canvass in the vicinity of the crime scene. Identify surveillance cameras in the area. Ascertain if the video is of value to the investigation; recover video if necessary. In addition, conduct a door-to-door canvass in attempt to identify potential witnesses. Ascertain whether neighbors were home at the time of the incident. If so, question if he or she heard any commotion or witnessed anyone leaving the location. Follow up on any leads obtained from the canvass.

Corroboration

Sex crime investigations often require some type of corroboration in order to effectively prosecute the case. There is not always visible injury or DNA evidence; however, there are other ways to corroborate a victim's account of the incident. This portion will discuss the available options/resources to gain the sometimes necessary corroboration. It will also touch upon the recovery and submission of DNA evidence.

Note: The idea is to avoid complications: the typical "he said/she said" accusations.

Resources

When there is no witness, the investigator can conduct a controlled call or a controlled meet. Again, this will depend on the situation: age, relationship, and capability. The idea is to have the victim (or a stand-in for the victim, i.e., parent/guardian) confront the subject with the allegation in hope that the subject will make an admission. At this time, the subject is not to have any knowledge of police involvement. This is extremely beneficial to the investigation. Therefore, when apprehended, if the subject invokes his or her right to counsel, the investigator already has (obtained) a statement/enough evidence for a successful prosecution. Remember as long as one party is aware that the conversation is being recorded, this is completely legal. And the victim will always be the knowing party.

To provide a better understanding of the two, a controlled call is a phone call in which the victim calls the alleged subject and confronts him or her about the incident. The call is conducted in the presence of the investigator. A device is used to record the conversation as well as enable the investigator to actively listen through an earpiece. The investigator will likely assist the victim with the conversation. A controlled meet is when the victim meets with the alleged subject in a controlled environment. The victim will have a nondescript device that will record the conversation. Depending on the device used, the investigator will have live feed of the conversation. In this step, there is no coaching by the investigator. The location of the meet is usually in a public place, for instance a diner, coffee shop, or mall. This allows the investigator, along with other undercover officers, to set up in the location prior to the meet. The investigator is to maintain a visual of the victim and subject at all times throughout the meeting. If necessary, the investigator and other officers will intervene.

DNA Evidence

Victims of sexual assaults are walking crime scenes, especially directly after an incident. Their body tends to become the most prominent place to recover evidence. This is because of the physical contact between the victim and the subject. Have the victim immediately transported to the hospital. Advise the victim not to shower or use the bathroom. Once at the hospital, ascertain the areas in which DNA evidence could be recovered. Decipher the way in which to recover the said evidence: kit(s), swab(s), or article(s) of clothing. That which is recovered is to be sent to the forensic lab and processed for DNA analysis.

In rape cases, where the victim is female, probative evidence, such as semen, will likely be found in the vagina. Such evidence is recovered by the use of a sexual offense evidence collection kit (SOECK), also known as the rape kit. This is an intrusive examination conducted by qualified sexual assault response team (SART) nurses at the hospital. Keep in mind that most sexual assaults are not immediately reported; therefore, the use of a rape kit may not be feasible. The SOECK is available up to 96 h post assault. Furthermore, if the victim made mention that drugs may have been used to facilitate the assault, the investigator should request a drug-facilitated sexual assault kit. Utilizing the same SART nurse, blood and urine are taken from the victim to detect specific narcotics known to mentally and physically impair the victim.

Note: If the victim consents to a SOECK, the hospital provides the victim with a "cocktail" to avoid pregnancy and disease. This tends to make the victim sick (nausea); therefore, some steps may be put on hold, that is, cognitive reenactment and identification of subject via computer application(s)/photo array/lineup.

Not every sexual assault is a rape. In incidents of sodomy/criminal sexual act, where the encounter is anal or oral, swabs become useful. There are two types of swabs: buccal and perianal. The buccal swab is collected from inside the victim's mouth, whereas a perianal swab is collected from the area around the anus. This is a way to collect DNA from the cells inside a person's cheek or around the anus. Likewise, where oral sex was performed on the victim (mouth to penis/vagina), the investigator should request a swab of that area. Also, be mindful to question other forms of intimacy, that is, kissed/licked an area on the victim's body (face, neck, breasts) and have a swab taken from that area. These swabs will be tested for saliva.

Although investigators may receive positive results from the evidence submitted, there may not be a match in the DNA database. How do we know? The DNA profile found among the evidence is automatically entered into the local, state, and national database: CODIS. It is then up to the investigator to obtain DNA for an alleged subject, if in fact, the person was identified. DNA can be received from a subject with consent *or* with an abandonment sample. An abandonment sample is something left behind by the subject in which DNA can be recovered, that is, cigarette butt, bottle, and Styrofoam cup. The recovery of an abandonment sample is sometimes difficult, leading investigators to think on their toes. Oftentimes, investigators have to become extremely creative in obtaining an abandonment sample.

The aforementioned steps do not lessen the importance of the actual crime scene. Although DNA evidence may be recovered from the victim, the investigator should respond to the crime scene to canvass for additional evidence. At the crime scene, identify articles that seem misplaced; it may have been touched by the subject. Recall the victim interview. The victim may have indicated that the subject left something behind, that is, shirt/hat/rag/glasses. Attempt to locate and recover those item(s). Furthermore, the victim should have provided the exact location the incident took place. If the incident occurred on a bed, take the sheets. The recovery of any articles pertaining to the crime should be submitted for DNA analysis (skin cells, hair, and fiber).

Warrants/Subpoenas

Warrants can be issued anywhere, but there is an expectation of privacy within. There is the typical search warrants regarding phone, computer, vehicle, and residence, but in

The true beauty in investigations is the continuous learning curve. Investigations are timeless; however, there is a constant development of new ideas and techniques as cases continue to be investigated. As an investigator, it is important to find your niche and become a contributor to these developments. Do not be scared to fail. For there is no success without failure. There will be much trial and tribulation before excelling in any particular area of investigations. Learn from others and allow others to learn from you. Albert Einstein said it best: "The only source of knowledge is experience."

Case Study #1

The case details are as follows:

- Female/11 years of age
  - Indicated criminal sexual act
  - Subject unknown
- Interview revealed
  The victim stated that an unknown male entered the elevator with her. As the elevator door closed, the subject displayed a silver firearm. He ordered the victim to turn around and take her pants off. She complied. He then inserted his penis inside the victim's anus whereby he ejaculated inside the victim's anus. The subject then forced the victim to perform oral sex on him. After the incident, the subject threatened the victim not to tell anyone and fled the location.

Results
- Positive results
  - 911 call immediately after the incident
  - Swabs recovered
    - Perianal—swab taken from area around the anus
    - Buccal—swab taken from inside of the victim's mouth
  - Sketch
    - No leads of value were developed from the sketch.

Note: A DNA profile was developed from the semen found on the evidence recovered. There was a match to the DNA and the subject was apprehended.

Case Study #2

The case details are as follows:

- Male/21 years of age
  - Indicated robbery/criminal sexual act
  - Possible blackmail
- Interview revealed
  The victim met the female subject (S1) via online website. The two agreed to meet in person. The subject invited the victim in for sexual pleasure in exchange for money. Upon entering the upstairs room, the victim was confronted by a male

subject (S2) with a firearm. The victim attempted to leave whereby S2 struck the victim twice with a closed fist. S2 proceeded to remove money and an ATM card from the victim's pocket. S2 forced the victim to provide the PIN number to the said card. At this time, the card and PIN number were given to another female subject (S3). Additional money was withdrawn by S3 at an unknown ATM. While waiting for S3 to return, the victim was told to put a condom on. S1 performed oral sex on the victim until ejaculation. The victim was advised that the condom containing his semen will be saved. The victim was further warned that if he goes to the police, S1 or S3 will use the semen-filled condom as proof of rape.

Results

- Positive results
  - Computer check—the victim had a phone number for S1.
  - Video canvass—image of possible subject(s) was retrieved.
  - Controlled call—the victim called S1 and set up a meeting to exchange the condom for money.
  - Controlled meet—while en route, S1 called to change the agreed upon location. Undercover detectives were able to set up at the new location prior to the arrival of the victim and S1. During the meet, S1 provided the victim with the condom from the initial incident.
    - The said evidence was recovered by the detective.
  - Subpoena from the prosecutor's office for
    - Website
    - Trap/trace of cell phone number
  - Photo array
    - The victim was able to positively identify all three subjects.
  - Lineup
    - Positive identification made by the subject
  - Subject interviews
    - Oral/written statements made by the subject(s)

Case Study #3

The case details are as follows:

- Female/8 years of age
  - Indicated possible sexual abuse
  - Subject: family member
- The details of the forensic interview are as follows:
  That the last time the victim was with the subject, he did something bad to her and hurt her. She was in the subject's bed watching *SpongeBob SquarePants* on television when he came in and locked the door behind him. He took off her pants and her underwear and then his pants and underwear. First, he sat beside her on the bed and put his fingers inside her vagina. Then he began pushing his fingers inside her vagina at which time she stated that it hurt really bad and she asked him to stop. The victim moved her hand in a back and forth motion. She then stated that the subject got on top of her and put his penis in her vagina. The victim describes his

penis to be very, very hard and that it hurt inside of her. At which point, the victim gets up from her chair and lies on the floor to demonstrate the subject on top of her and his rocking back and forth motion on her. The victim stated that when the subject got up, his penis was drooling and white stuff was coming out. He wiped it, wiped the bed, and then wiped her vagina. The subject told her not to tell anyone what had happened. The victim stated that she told her mom because her mom asked her why her vagina hurt. The victim stated that the inside of her vagina felt like it was scratched and hurt.

Results

- Positive results
  - Outcry—the victim disclosed to her mother
  - Forensic interview
    - Anatomical drawing
  - Medical examination
    - The victim had a complete transected hymen.
- Some things are out of the investigators' hands:
  - The subject was confronted with the allegation prior to police involvement. Upon apprehension, the subject immediately requested a lawyer. There is no chance to obtain a confession.
- Was the multidisciplinary approach used?
  - Yes, all members of the multidisciplinary team were involved throughout this investigation.

Note: Despite the fact that the investigator was unable to speak to the subject, enough evidence was provided for a successful prosecution.

Case Study #4

The case details are as follows:

- Female/29 years of age
  - No crime established
  - Subject: known acquaintance
- Interview revealed
  The victim stated that a known male acquaintance began massaging her. Shortly after, the victim fell asleep. She woke up several hours later and felt a discharge from her vagina. Although she could not establish a sexual assault, she requested a SOECK.

Results

- Positive results
  - Controlled call
    - The subject made an admission—stating he inserted his penis into her vagina while she was asleep
  - Subject interview
    - Oral/written statement made by the subject

Case Study #5

The case details are as follows:

- Female/20 years of age
  - Indicated criminal sexual act
  - Subject unknown
- Interview revealed

  She was approached from behind by an unknown male. He covered her mouth with his hand, displayed a silver firearm, and forced her inside the front passenger seat of a four-door sedan. He then drove to a location and ordered the victim into the backseat. While the victim was climbing into the backseat, her earphones came out of her ears and were left behind in the front seat of the vehicle. The subject proceeded into the backseat and forcibly penetrated his penis to her vagina. After the incident, the subject ordered the victim out of the vehicle and drove off.

Results

- Positive results
  - 911 call immediately after the incident
  - The victim was extremely detailed:
    - Provided the make/model of the vehicle as well as the license plate number.
    - She informed that her headphones remained in the car.
  - DNA evidence
    - SOECK
- Later on in the investigation
  - Vehicle recovered
    - Headphones were inside; matched DNA from the victim.
  - Lineup
    - Positively identified the subject

Questions for Discussion

3.1 Discuss the most common interview tactics.
3.2 Discuss the various techniques of corroboration.
3.3 Why is a media release a useful investigative tool?

References

Howell, D. (2010). *Sex Crimes Interviews Simplified*. San Clemente, CA: Lawtech Publishing Company.
Jordan, F.D. (1996). *Sex Crimes Investigations: The Complete Investigator's Handbook*. Boulder, CO: Paladin Press.
New York State Children's Justice Task Force. (2004). *Forensic Interviewing Best Practices*. Rensselaer, NY: New York State Office of Children and Family Services.

Arson Investigation

4

JOHN BOAL

Contents

Chapter Objectives   51
Chapter Outline   51
Introduction   51
Arson Defined   52
Legal Considerations   53
Preliminary Investigation   55
Documenting the Fire Scene   58
Follow-Up Investigation   62
Prosecution   63
Questions for Discussion   63
References   63

Chapter Objectives

After reading this chapter, you should be able to do the following:

1. Explain the elements of the crime of arson.
2. Relate the differences between an administrative warrant and a search warrant.
3. Conduct a preliminary arson investigation.
4. Document the point of origin.
5. Conduct follow-up interviews.
6. Form an arson investigation team.

Chapter Outline

Introduction to Arson Investigation
Arson Defined
Legal Considerations
Preliminary Investigation
Documenting the Fire Scene
Follow-Up Investigation
Prosecution

Introduction

Arson investigation can be one of the most complex investigations an investigator can encounter. The investigative skills required for an arson investigation encompass normal investigative skills in addition to skills in the understanding of fire dynamics. During a fire, much of the evidence is destroyed or damaged, and special skills in locating the point of origin and the location of other evidences are the key components to solving the crime and proving the case. It is best to use the team approach in investigating arson fires because of the multitude of skills required.

Many departments use a combination of fire and police investigators to investigate arson cases. The two investigators can be mutually supportive in the investigation. The fire investigator can provide the technical skills of understanding the fire dynamics, while the police investigator can provide the needed expertise in maneuvering through the criminal investigative process. Both skills are necessary for the successful resolution of an arson investigation.

Most criminal investigations require that the investigator prove something occurred as a result of criminal activity. In an arson fire investigation, the investigation must show that the fire was not the result of an accident or a natural event. This has to be done by eliminating all possible causes of the fire other than arson. Arson crimes are unique in that the investigator must prove arson by eliminating any possible accidental or natural causes.

In most criminal codes, arson is the willful destruction or damage to property by means of fire or explosion. The seriousness of the offense is judged by the danger to persons or the amount of property damage. If a person is present or likely to be present at the time of the arson fire, then the crime takes on aggravated specifications. All aggravated arsons and arsons causing a large amount of property damage are considered felonies. The amount of damage required to qualify for a felony is defined by individual state statutes.

Normal investigative skills in an arson investigation would include the ability to recognize and collect evidence to prove the fire or explosion was an intentional act, to develop a suspect or suspects through interviews and evidence examination, to read the crime scene by discovering the point of origin and analyzing the conduct of the fire, and to determine possible motives through interviews with owners, employees, witnesses, and all stakeholders in the property damaged.

According to the Uniform Crime Reporting (UCR) Program (2014) compiled by the Federal Bureau of Investigation (FBI), the crime of arson has shown a slight decrease in reporting in the preliminary assessment for the first half of 2013. This is a slight change in the gradual increasing numbers each year over the last several years.

Arson Defined

According to the FBI's UCR Program (2013a), arson is defined as "any willful or malicious burning or attempting to burn, with or without intent to defraud, a dwelling house, public building, motor vehicle or aircraft, personal property of another" (Para. 1). Fires that are labeled as suspicious or of unknown origin are excluded from the UCR reported data.

According to the UCR (2013a) for 2012, over the last few years, the crime of arson has been trending upward slightly. Arson offenses increased less than 1/10th of 1% in 2012 from 2011. Close to half of all arsons involved a structure of some sort. Mobile property fires such as vehicles accounted for 23.1% of all arson fires in 2012. The average loss for each arson fire was found to be about $12,796 with the arsons of industrial structures accounting for the highest average loss. In 2012, there were 18.7 arson offenses for every 100,000 inhabitants.

Also according to the UCR (2013b), the arson table 2 for 2012, of the 45,926 reported arson offenses in 2012, only 9,477 or 20.6% of the offenses were cleared by arrest or exceptional circumstances. About a third of the clearances involved offenders under the age of 18. The low solvability rate of just over 20% is good evidence of the difficulty in investigating such a complex destructive crime as arson. It also indicates a need for improved investigations and better-trained investigators. Improved investigation skills begin with an understanding of the legal requirements in conducting an investigation.

Legal Considerations

The investigation and prosecution of an arson case requires that the investigator prove the individual elements of the crime. According to 29 Ohio Rev. Code (2011), these elements must be committed knowingly and by means of fire or explosion. The arson crime must cause or create a substantial risk of physical harm to property of another without their consent. The crime of arson can also be committed by causing or creating a substantial risk of physical harm to property of the offender or another with intent to defraud; can be committed by causing or creating a substantial risk of physical harm to government buildings used for public purpose; can cause or create a substantial risk of harm to property through offer or acceptance of agreement to hire to any property without the consent of the owner or by the owner with intent to defraud; and can cause or create a substantial risk of harm to any park, preserve, well, and/or other real property.

Any criminal arson investigation must be conducted with the rights guaranteed by the fourth, fifth, and sixth amendments to the U.S. Constitution in mind. The fourth amendment guarantees the right to be free from unreasonable or illegal search or seizure. As an investigator, we must make sure that we conduct all searches within the context outlined by the Constitution and interpreted by the U.S. Supreme Court and that any suspect seized is seized based on probable cause. The fifth amendment provides arson suspects with the right not to be a witness against themselves. They also will not be deprived of life, liberty, or property without due process of law. The sixth amendment guarantees an accused the right to a speedy and public trial and the right to an impartial jury and to confront the witnesses against them.

The fourth amendment guarantees the right to be secure in one's person, houses, papers, and effects against unreasonable searches and seizures. No warrant shall be issued unless based on probable cause. The warrant requirement was impractical in all situations, and the courts through judicial decisions in various criminal cases recognized certain exceptions to the warrant requirement. Emergency or exigent circumstance is one exception to the search warrant requirement. This exception recognizes that not all situations are conducive to getting a warrant such as when someone is in danger, hot pursuit, escape, or the destruction of evidence. Officers, based on their ability to articulate the emergency situation and the compelling need to take action without a warrant, may take official action until a warrant may be obtained. It is important to note that the ability to take official action without a warrant exists only as long as the emergency is present. Once the emergency or exigent circumstances are quelled, the warrant requirement returns to conduct the search.

Another exception to the search warrant requirement is consent. The owner or person authorized to give consent may grant investigators permission to search for evidence at a crime scene. There are a couple of things to note when receiving permission to conduct a consent search. You need to be certain that the person granting permission for a search has the authority to grant permission, specifically in the area you are going to be conducting the search. The real backbone of the consent search is that the consent was freely given and no coercion was applied to gain consent. It is also important to note about consent searches that consent can be withdrawn at any time, even if the consent was given in writing.

Another exception to the search warrant requirement is the automobile exception. In cases where officers have probable cause to believe evidence or contraband may be found in an automobile, a search may be conducted without a warrant, but the officers conducting the search must be able to articulate their probable cause for conducting the search. This mobile exception to the search warrant requirement was created by Carroll v. United States (1925). Another exception to the search warrant requirement that sometimes involves the automobile exception to the search warrant requirement is the search incident to a lawful arrest. Basically, an officer is allowed to search the "person" of a person arrested and the immediate surrounding area of the arrest. Recently, the Supreme Court has placed some restrictions for searches of vehicles incident to a lawful arrest in Arizona v. Gant (2009).

Plain view seizures are permitted without a warrant by law enforcement officials if the evidence or contraband is in plain view to the officer and the officer has a legal right to be in the place to make the observation. A qualifying statement here is that the evidence or contraband must be immediately apparent as contraband or evidence. This has to be apparent without any manipulation of the item or items. Evidence is to be immediately apparent as evidence located by firefighters, while extinguishing the fire, must be immediately recognizable as evidence before it can be seized as being in plain view. Once the fire is extinguished and the fire investigators need to conduct further searches to determine the cause or causes of the fire, an administrative warrant is going to be necessary.

Searches at fire scenes present unique problems for investigators. The fire department as part of their function of protecting the community may search the fire scene for the cause of the fire. The amount of time fire investigators may remain on the scene, after extinguishing the fire to search for the cause of the fire, was determined to be a "reasonable period of time." This "reasonable period of time" standard was established in the Michigan v. Tyler (1978) decision. If the investigator is in doubt of what a reasonable period of time is, legal advice should be obtained from the prosecuting attorney, or an administrative warrant should be obtained.

The administrative search warrant is obtained from the court that has jurisdiction of the fire location by showing that access to the fire location has been denied or consent not granted. The issuance of the administrative warrant is not based on probable cause but on a valid and reasonable government interest in determining the cause of the fire. If, during the process of conducting the search for the cause of the fire, investigators discover evidence that the fire was the result of a criminal act, then the investigators must obtain a search warrant to continue the search for evidence to be used in a criminal trial. The court with jurisdiction over the matter will then issue a criminal search warrant based on the articulation of probable cause that the fire was the result of a criminal act. The criminal search warrant must contain the identification of the items sought, specific description of the person or places to be searched, and the probable cause that the items to be sought will be present at the location of the person or place to be searched.

The fifth amendment protects persons from self-incrimination and guarantees the right of due process of law. As part of the guarantee against self-incrimination, a suspect has the right to representation by an attorney before any questioning occurs if the suspect requests an attorney. Interrogation of the suspect falls under the protection against self-incrimination afforded by the fifth amendment. The suspect is guaranteed certain rights that are enumerated in what has become known as their rights under Miranda. Under these Miranda rights, the suspect has a right to remain silent. They are advised that any statement made will be used against them in a court of law. They have the right to have an attorney present before any questioning occurs. They are advised that if they cannot afford an attorney one will be provided by the court before any questioning occurs. The suspect has the right to exercise these rights at any time during the interrogation.

The rights under Miranda were guaranteed in the court decision of Miranda v. Arizona (1966). Miranda rights are not guaranteed to everyone arrested. The suspect is required to be advised under the Miranda ruling when two conditions are present. The two conditions that apply the Miranda ruling to a police interrogation are custody and questioning. The suspect must be in custody or at least in a position that they are not free to leave. Many factors must be considered to determine if the suspect felt they were free to leave the interrogation including the suspect's perception that they were not free to leave. When the suspect is in custody, they must be asked questions. When both conditions are present, then Miranda would apply.

Other applicable sections of the fifth amendment are that no person shall be subject to double jeopardy in any criminal offenses and suspect must be provided their due process of law. These constitutional rights guarantee that the government agents will honor their commitment to the judicial process and not seek to bring charges against someone previously released by the court once the judicial process is started. This requirement requires that the investigator get the facts right the first time and present a case fully documented and respectful of a suspect's constitutional rights.

The sixth amendment guarantees the suspect the right to a speedy trial and the ability to confront the witnesses against them. These rights are important in arson cases in that a hasty arrest may put the prosecution under some unfortunate time constraints in trying to meet the time requirement in bringing the suspect to court after their arrest. In many arson cases, the crime is committed without witnesses. The main witnesses in arson cases are going to be the investigators and the forensic examiners that examined the collected evidence. Through the process of discovery the suspect has the right to the information in the prosecution's case and the evidence that could be presented at a trial. This preview of the evidence and witnesses is important in allowing the defense to prepare their defense by questioning the testing, collection, or preservation process and challenging the legality through motions to the court.

Preliminary Investigation

Any criminal investigation begins with the discovery of the crime. Many times, the crime is the discovery of a crime scene by persons not affiliated with law enforcement. A fire or explosion scene is located, and emergency personnel are notified. The fire can be discovered in various stages of progress. Since fires and explosions are not ordinary everyday occurrences, it is important for firefighters to determine the cause of the fire and whether there are continuing threats or dangers to the rest of the community. The very first consideration in responding to the scene of the fire or explosion is to protect life and then to save further property damage or spread of the fire.

Once the fire is extinguished and the scene stabilized, the important task of determining the cause of the fire begins. It is important that the scene be made safe for investigators to complete their tasks. The fire may have damaged portions of a structure to render them unsafe for investigators to operate. Once the fire has been extinguished, the scene made reasonably safe, and a reasonable period of time has expired, it is important to obtain consent from the owner or person authorized to give consent to examine the fire scene to determine the cause. If consent cannot be obtained, an administrative warrant needs to be obtained to conduct further investigation into the cause of the fire. If conducting the investigation into the cause of the fire evidence of a criminal act is uncovered, the investigation continues to investigate the cause of the fire and collects evidence important to any criminal investigation. Once the evidence of criminal activity is found, the investigators must obtain a criminal search warrant because the administrative warrant would not cover evidence recovered since it is not based on probable cause.

Evidence discovered during the administrative search would be admissible under the plain view doctrine in that investigators come upon the evidence while working a legitimate administrative warrant. They are allowed to be where they found the evidence. Once the evidence is found and the criminal search warrant is necessary, it changes the focus of the investigation. To continue the search for criminal evidence, a criminal search warrant based on probable cause would have to be obtained. The evidence found during the administrative search would apply to establishing probable cause required for the criminal warrant.

The most important evidence in determining the cause of the fire and related criminal activity will more than likely be located at the point of origin. It is the focal point of the investigation once the fire is out. The point of origin can yield the best evidence of the heat and duration of the fire. A good indicator of the point of origin is the signs of the lowest and deepest charring. Much fire evidence will be located at the lower levels of the scene. The very location of the point of origin can be indicative of possible arson in some fires. An accidental fire typically has one point of origin, and multiple points of origin are indicative of a suspicious fire.

According to the National Fire Protection Association (NFPA) (2004), the location of the fire's origin requires the coordination of information from a number of sources: the physical marks of the fire, observations of witnesses, analysis of physics, fire chemistry, initiation and development of the fire, and location of electrical arcing. The careful examination of the fire burn patterns can provide key direction in locating the point of origin. Recognition of these physical marks requires a keen eye and training in fire dynamics. These burn patterns can provide an arrow to the point of origin.

Another source of information in determining the point of origin is the observations of witnesses or people familiar with the conditions and contents of the area damaged by fire. These witnesses can provide information on what was present that could have contributed to the start of the fire or its acceleration. Witnesses can provide valuable testimony on the behavior of the fire. These people should be noted and interviewed because they could become key contributors in understanding the path and intensity of the fire. Some of the interviews that would be important are witnesses that observed the fire at the start and noted how fast it did or did not spread. They may have also noted the color of the flames that would indicate the nature of the material being burned. Any witnesses including news crews could be a valuable resource of video or photos of the fire behavior. Any video or pictures of the scene could also be important in developing a possible suspect. A source that is often overlooked as a resource for witnesses is the public first responders. Firefighters and police officers can provide valuable first responder evidence as to the starting of the fire and how it behaved.

The point of origin can be located with the careful analysis of the laws of physics and chemistry and what the fire can be expected to do and what actually occurred. This could be considered profiling of the fire and breaking down fire behavior based on commonly accepted laws of physics and principles of chemistry. This analysis of the fire will also help in determining the cause. Determination of the cause is accomplished by examining all the materials and factors that were present and caused the fire to occur.

Sometimes, the cause of the fire can be determined by the process of elimination. Ideally, if the cause is to be determined, it is important to base that conclusion on evidence found at the scene. It is sometimes possible to determine the cause at the point of origin by eliminating all other sources of ignition. Determination of the cause in a fire requires that all circumstances and factors necessary for the fire to have occurred are identified (NFPA, 2004).

According to the NFPA (2004) standards, the causes of damage and casualties in an arson investigation used for the assignment of responsibility are generally divided into four categories. Causes of fires are classified as accidental, natural, incendiary, or undetermined. For purposes of classification, suspicious is not a very accurate description of a cause, and it is recommended that it not be used to describe the cause. A key component in establishing the cause of a fire is to remain objective and not make assumptions not based on evidence at the scene.

To find that a fire should be listed as due to accidental causes, it is necessary to show that the fire did not involve some type of intentional human act causing ignition and the resulting burning was intentional. If the fire shows signs of being spread by human action to other areas that would not be included in the original fire, it cannot be classified as accidental. If the fire is caused by a human act, the intent of the human must be determined, and if the intent is not clear or cannot be established with reasonable certainty, then the fire should be classified as undetermined causes. An example of this might be a campfire started in the vicinity of a barn. During the cooking of hotdogs and marshmallows, the fire spread to the barn. The campfire was intentionally set, but there was no intention to burn the barn, and even though the fire was started by humans, it was still accidental. It would also involve such things as baling of wet hay, and through the chemical reaction and spontaneous combustion, the hay catches fire and burns down the storage facility. The fire would be an accidental cause because it would be difficult to show that someone intentionally baled wet hay and knew that the fermentation process would cause the hay to catch fire and burn down the storage facility.

Natural fire causes are fires that are the result of acts of nature or without any intentional human involvement. This would include things like lightning strikes. Any naturally caused fire creates circumstances that cannot be controlled by humans. An earthquake that causes a ruptured gas line that results in fire or explosion could not be controlled or predicted by humans, and the resulting damage would be a natural event.

Incendiary fire causes are fires that are intentionally started by humans for the purposes of burning in circumstances where the fire should not be ignited. If a fire is started on the basement floor to cook dinner, it would be an incendiary fire. If the real intention of the fire starter cannot be determined with a reasonable degree of certainty, then the fire would be classified as undetermined causes. If an incendiary fire is started in a fireplace on a cold night and that fireplace had not been cleaned in years, it resulted in a chimney fire that burned down the house. Through investigation, it appears that the intent in starting the fire was to keep warm. This fire in all likelihood would be ruled an accidental fire. The basement floor fire would be a little more difficult to establish the intent with reasonable certainty and that fire in all likelihood would be listed as undetermined causes.

While these are broad definitions of causes of fires, they should be looked at in terms of local jurisdictional definitions. The importance of assigning causes for the fire comes into play when attempting to assign responsibility for the fire. Establishing the cause of a fire is one particular aspect of an arson investigation that highlights the difficulties in prosecuting arson cases. If the intention of the fire starter is difficult to establish, the location of some physical evidence can hold the key to the assignment of cause. One piece of physical evidence that can contribute to the finding of an arson incendiary fire is the use of an accelerant. Another item of evidence would be the use of trailers to move the fire from place to place over and above the natural progression of the fire. This type of evidence would preclude the finding of accidental or underdetermined cause.

After determining the origin and cause of the fire, it is important to conduct a failure analysis to determine the responsibility of the fire. Responsibility could be the result of act or the omission of something that caused the fire. The failure analysis of the fire is more important in understanding and documenting the nature and behavior of the fire and future criminal prosecution. This failure analysis also gives investigators areas of the investigation that need further information or development. The complexity of the fire and the responsibility links for the fire can result in a complex failure analysis.

According to the NFPA (2004), the failure analysis can consist of a variety of tools with differing degree of skill requirements. One tool is the development of the time line. The time line should include a chronological list of events, before, during, and after the event. The systems analysis tool would have such things as a fault tree. Mathematical modeling provides tools for testing hypothesis of the origin and cause. Fire testing is a tool that can be used to complement evidence found at the fire scene and is also used to test hypotheses. Another tool requires the identification of fuel present at the fire scene and the total release of heat and fire growth. It is noted that a vertical configuration of fuel will burn faster than a horizontal configuration.

Documenting the Fire Scene

The proper documentation of the fire scene will be important not only to assist the future investigation but also to assist in any future prosecution of the arsonist. A thorough documentation of the crime scene will help the investigators with their interviews and development or leads. It is also very helpful when and if the case is prosecuted. Being able to explain and show the jurors what the scene looked like at the time of the incident is beneficial. Potential jurors because of forensic television programming believe they are very well informed on what type of evidence can be found at a crime scene, what type of tests can be conducted, and hypothetically what type of information can be obtained from the evidence. If there is one thing television is short on, then that is the documentation process. Particularly, the scene of a fire is challenging because of the damage done by the fire and debris piles from trying to extinguish the fire.

The most common methods of documenting the crime scene are through videos, photographs, diagrams, recordings, notes, and reports. One particular tool that has the ability to capture a variety of information is the notes taken by first responders. Anything taken in through the five senses should be noted for further reference such as people present upon arrival, the progress of the fire, the location and degree of fire if seen, and color of the smoke. If there is any peculiar smell in the air that would indicate the presence of an accelerant, it should be noted. Any interviews with people at the scene should be included in the notes. Information about what they noticed when they got there or whether there was any change in the fire since that time should be noted. This information could be critical since third parties are often the first ones to discover the fire.

The condition of fire safety equipment should be noted whether or not the fire equipment operated the way it should have. The fire equipment should have been present and properly maintained, and any information, such as missing fire equipment, should be included in the notes. If there were valuables removed from the scene before the fire, this should also be noted. Building conditions that help the spread of the fire should be noted, such as open windows and doors.

A key method of documenting the crime scene is going to be the use of photographs. Digital cameras are the best and most economical method for recording the scene through photographs. The scene should be photographed from general to specific. In the case of fire scenes, the photos should go from the least amount of damage to the area of greatest damage. What that means is that overall shots of the locale of fire with sequential photos down to the evidence and point of origin. When taking photographs, a photograph log should be kept. This log will keep track of each individual photo by recording the type of camera, the person taking the photos, what the photograph represents, the date and time the photo was taken, name of the photographer, and case number.

All photographs should be taken in the crime scene as it appears before any addition of evidence markers. After the items of evidence have been located and location marked, another set of photos need to be taken. These photos should include individual close-ups of individual pieces of evidence. The area of the fire origin should be photographed at least twice both before the rubble is disturbed and then after debris has been cleared away. Other areas that should be photographed are the burn patterns, since burn patterns can suggest direction of the fire and the possible use of accelerants. Multiple photo shots of the scene that can be linked together to present a panoramic view of the fire scene can be helpful in understanding what has occurred. In cases where small items of evidence need to be photographed, it is very beneficial to place a marker, in most cases a ruler, next to the small item so that when photographed the item will be given perspective and the viewer will better be able to understand the size comparison.

Videotaping of the fire scene can also be helpful if the case goes to court for prosecution. Videotaping presents the jury with a journey through the crime scene as the investigator saw it. A couple of things that should be remembered when videotaping a crime scene are as follows: A brief introduction at the beginning of the tape to help the viewer orient themselves to the scene they will be viewing is a good practice. Once the introduction information has been added to the tape, the microphone should be turned off. This will prevent comments or unwanted conversation from making its way onto the tape. It is important to keep the tape running to prevent any gaps that have to be explained. The most common mistake in videotaping the crime scene is to move through the scene at a fast clip and the viewer loses the perspective you are trying to offer.

An often missed source of photographs of the fire is the bystanders. Today, many people from all walks of life carry some type of cell phone, and most have the ability to take photographs and videos. It is important to check the crowd for people that are photographing the fire. Another valuable resource for pictures and videos of the fire are the news media. A request should be made to the media for any and all photos and videos taken by their people while covering the fire. Any photo of the crowd at a fire not only has the potential to identify possible witnesses that were not interviewed but also could record the suspect or someone that seems to be present at more than one fire scene.

Another means of documenting the crime scene is through the use of sketches. Sketches are diagrams of the crime scene and represent the scene to scale. Sketches should be made of the crime scene with the measured location of key pieces of evidence. One purpose of the sketch is to orient the location of physical evidence precisely on the diagram to aid in reconstruction of the crime at some future time. At the fire scene, a rough sketch is completed with all the measurements of key pieces of evidence. With this information gathered from the forensic mapping, a finished sketch to scale can be prepared for presentation later in court. The sketch is usually drawn with one of three viewpoints. The most common viewpoint for the sketch is going to be the overhead view. The cross-projection view is going to be used to show damage or evidence located on the walls of the crime scene. The third viewpoint for the sketch is going to be the elevated view that shows heights.

According to Swanson et al. (2012), forensic mapping is the collection and recording of precise measurements of items of evidence. A number of methods are used to record the measurement information for transfer to the sketch. The best method to use is to depend on the crime scene itself and any unique characteristics. The methods commonly used are the rectangular coordinates, triangulation, baseline coordinates, polar coordinates, and grid system.

After the point of origin and evidence has been located and the crime scene thoroughly documented, the collection and preservation of evidence becomes a priority. Evidence that is susceptible to destruction or is perishable should be collected as soon as possible. Accelerant residue is susceptible to evaporation, so it needs to be an item documented and collected quickly. Since accelerant residue is so fragile and subject to evaporation, it should be collected and placed in a vapor-tight container to preserve it until it can be tested. A clean unused paint can work best for preserving material containing traces of accelerant. Other evidence containers acceptable for evidence that could contain accelerant residue are glass jars and airtight special evidence bags.

When collecting evidence, it is important the investigator avoid contamination and spoliation of the evidence to make it unreliable in later court proceedings. The collection process should be tightly controlled and care taken to preserve evidence in the condition found. Especially at fire scenes, equipment that uses fuel is a possible source of contamination of the scene. Clean tools and personal protection clothing are necessary to maintain evidence integrity. The investigator should be familiar with the safety standards in evidence collection. Adherence to collection standards and packaging requirements of the laboratory that will be doing the forensic testing is very important in maintaining evidence integrity.

Burn patterns are another source of evidence. There are basically two types of burn patterns, and these are movement patterns and intensity patterns. According to Swanson et al. (2012), burn indicators are the effects of heat and partial burning. These burn indicators are indicative of points of origin, rate of fire development, temperature, the duration of the fire, and the use of flammable liquids. It is commonly believed that the large shiny blisters seen in alligator charring were indicative of an accelerant being used. There is no scientific evidence to indicate that this is the case. Evaluating the depth of charring is reliable in tracking the fire spread. It can sometimes be used to determine the duration of the fire but must be evaluated based on many variables.

Glass breakage at the scene of the fire can be caused by a number of factors. Glass in a frame with protected edges will crack at a lower temperature difference between the center of the glass and the protected edges. Fewer cracks in the glass are found in glass with unprotected edges. Crazing of glass can be straight or crescent-shaped cracks that research indicates is the result of rapid cooling like the application of water in a hot environment (Swanson et al., 2012).

Also according to Swanson et al. (2012), spalling is defined by the breakdown in the surface strength of such things as masonry, brick, and concrete and is believed to be caused by high temperatures. It was long believed that spalling is the result of the use of an accelerant because of the high temperature. A rapid cooling of the heated concrete by the application of water can result in spalling. Spalling comes into play at a fire scene in the documentation and analysis of the heat source. Other factors besides heat can cause spalling.

According to the NFPA (2004), oxidation is the chemical process associated with combustion. The amount of oxidation of some materials that did not burn can establish a clear line of demarcation and fire patterns. Higher temperatures and extended lengths of exposure will produce the more pronounced effects of oxidation. The melting temperature of various materials can be used as baseline to determine the temperature of the fire. Typically, accelerant-driven fires burn hotter than regular combustibles. Most accelerants burn at about 3000°C that is about twice the temperature of ordinary combustibles.

Another piece of evidence to be on the lookout is an incendiary device. A number of things can be used to ignite the fire. The incendiary mechanism can be chemical or mechanical, and the most common scenes involving explosions are mechanical and chemical explosions. The arsonist needs to use an ignition device to start the fire. The more experienced arsonist is going to use some type of timing device. It is common that the ignition device be surrounded by material to boost the initial ignition. This material used to feed the fire initially is called a "plant." In searching the crime scene, look for signs of one or more "trailers" that are used by the arsonist to spread the fire to different parts of the scene. When a chemical ignition system is used, it usually leaves some kind of residue or odor. Chemical ignition is usually beyond the scope of knowledge of most arsonists.

We had an arsonist that would walk around the neighborhood in the early morning hours after the bars closed. During his walk, he would smoke cigarettes. As he headed for home, he found car doors unlocked in driveways and would toss the cigarette onto the front seat and close the door. The next morning when the vehicle owner went to get into the vehicle and opened the door, the influx of oxygen ignited the simmering fire and destroyed the inside of the vehicle.

It is critical to the investigation that an evidence log sheet is kept for the collection of all pieces of evidence. The log sheet should contain the location, case number, and officer's name recording the evidence. Proper packaging and chain of custody of the evidence should be maintained through the collection process. Volatile evidence should be transported to the crime lab without delay.

According to Swanson et al. (2012), the investigator has several tools at their disposal to attempt to locate accelerant residue at the scene. The human olfactory abilities are limited, and a better tool is the olfactory abilities of canines trained to identify the smells of accelerants. Chemical color test detectors can be used to detect accelerant and vapors. These color test detectors can interfere with additional lab tests. The advantage of color test detectors is they are simple to use and inexpensive. The catalytic combustion detector is the most common flammable vapor detector. The flame ionization detector burns a mixture of hydrogen and the sample gas. Probably, the most common detector used in an arson investigation to detect accelerant is the gas–liquid chromatography. Others are the highly sensitive infrared spectrophotometer and the ultraviolet fluorescence.

Follow-Up Investigation

The most successful arson investigations are conducted using the team approach. A team has the ability to maximize the skills of all team members. Arson investigation teams should be made up of a variety of specialties to increase perspectives. Police investigators, firefighters, laboratory technicians, prosecutors, and, in the case of death, a forensic pathologist are all possible members of an arson investigation team.

Once the fire scene has been processed and documented, the in-depth continuation of the investigation to determine if it is a criminal act is conducted. In arson cases, there are a variety of possible motives. The establishment of a motive is very important to the successful investigation. Often the primary motive for an arson financial. Through the commission of some type of fraud by burning property, the owner of the property can gain some type of financial relief from financial stress. Financial stress can be caused by debt from bad business decisions, debt from gambling or drug addiction, or a need to upgrade the physical or technological assets of the business.

Some of the most common arson frauds are the real estate and redevelopment money that are collected from federal programs and then razed through arson for a profit. Overinsurance on property that is destroyed by arson where the owner collects the insurance payment is suspicious. This is also probably the most lucrative scheme. These insurance-based arsons can be performed in a number of different scenarios.

Some arson fires are set by someone other than the owner. These types of arsons are little more difficult to investigate. There are a variety of reasons for these third-party motives such as a means to extort money from the property owner. Different unresolved grievances and as a business moves to eliminate the competition are sometimes motives. Other types of motives for arsons would be the arsons committed for revenge of some type of perceived wrong or in retaliation against the property owner.

While some interviews are done at the scene of the fire, they become much more in-depth in the follow-up investigation. Interviews should be done with as many people as possible that were present at the scene including the first responders. Employees of the insurance company that were involved in mitigating the risk to the owner are interview candidates. Individual personal contacts of the property owner in regard to any financial problems the owner may have been having. Anyone that can help determine who would have the most to profit from the fire should be interviewed. The news media personnel covering the fire are important interviews in what they observed or what someone at the scene may have told them. Any suspect can be a valuable information source and is an important interview. The investigator will want to be the best prepared with known information when conducting the interview with the suspect.

The evidence found at the fire scene is transported to the forensic laboratory. Before the evidence is transported to the lab, the investigator needs to make sure the correct tests have been requested on the correct pieces of evidence. Maintenance of the proper chain of custody from the fire scene to court must be maintained. Once the tests have been completed, the investigator must evaluate the results and determine how the information can best be utilized in the investigation.

Prosecution

Since arson investigations are very complex, it is important that members of the team are all informed on the progress and decisions throughout the investigation. Arson cases and forensic examination rely primarily on circumstantial evidence with little or no direct evidence. It is important that the investigator not rely on assumptions not supported by scientific proof. Decisions that are based on sound scientific principles will strengthen not only the testimony of the investigators but also the importance of the evidence.

Another key point in the prosecution of the case is going to be working very closely with the prosecuting attorney. The prosecutor can serve as an independent reviewer of the case and provide meaningful suggestions for further investigation that could make the case stronger. Meetings with the prosecutor should not be a one-time event that only occurs at the end of the investigation. Consultation with the prosecutor should be an ongoing process. It is good practice to ask the prosecutor, or their representative, to be a member of the arson investigation team.

Questions for Discussion

4.1 Discuss the complexities of investigating an arson case.
4.2 Discuss the type of evidence typically looked for at an arson scene.
4.3 Why is it important to document an arson scene?
4.4 What is the difference between an administrative warrant and a search warrant?
4.5 Why is it important to understand case law?
4.6 Discuss the most important method for documenting the crime scene.
4.7 Discuss what makes up of an arson investigation team.
4.8 What are the steps in conducting a preliminary investigation?
4.9 Discuss various motives for committing the crime of arson.
4.10 Discuss the types of questions commonly asked in an interview or witnesses.

References

29 Ohio Rev. Code. § 2909.03 (2011). Available at: http://codes.ohio.gov/orc/2909.03. Accessed on April 2014.
Arizona v. Gant, 129, S. CT. 1210 (2009).
Carroll v. United States, 267 U.S. 132 (1925).
Crime in the United States 2013. (2014). Uniform Crime Reports. Retrieved from http://www.fbi.gov/about-us/cjis/ucr/crime-in-the-u.s/2013/preliminary-semiannual-uniform crime-report-january-june-2013. Accessed on April 2014.

Crime in the United States 2012. (2013a). Uniform Crime Reports. Retrieved from http://www.fbi.
    gov/about-us/cjis/ucr/crime-in-the-u.s/2012/crime-in-the-u.s.-2012/property-crime/arson.
    Accessed on April 2014.

Crime in the United States 2012. (2013b). Uniform Crime Reports: Arson table 2. Retrieved from
    http://www.fbi.gov/about-us/cjis/ucr/crime-in-the-u.s/2012/crime-in-the-u.s.-2012/tables/
    arson_table_2_arson_by_type_of_property_2012.xls. Accessed on April 2014.

Michigan v. Tyler, 436 U.S. 499 (1978).

Miranda v. Arizona, 384 U.S. 436 (1966).

National Fire Protection Association. (2004). Guide for fire and explosion investigations, NFPA 921,
    Quincy, MA.

Swanson, C.R., Chamelin, N.C., Territo, L., Taylor, R.W. (2012). *Criminal Investigation*, 11th edn.
    New York: McGraw Hill.

Investigations Involving Property

II

Investigation of Insurance Fraud

5

PETER C. KRATCOSKI AND MAG. MAXIMILIAN EDELBACHER

Contents

Chapter Objectives	67
Chapter Outline	68
Introduction: Development of Insurance	68
Insurance Fraud: Elements and Types	69
Insurance Fraud	69
Cost of Insurance Fraud in the United States, Europe, and Other Non-European Countries	71
Insurance Fraud Crimes in Austria	72
Understanding the Psychological Aspect of Insurance Fraud Motivation	73
Profiles of Insurance Fraud Offenders	74
Initial Investigation of Insurance Fraud by Insurance Companies	75
Criminal Investigation of Insurance Fraud	76
Indicators of Insurance Fraud	76
Types of Information Investigators Review for Possible Fraud	78
Credentials and Training Needed for Insurance Fraud Investigation Positions	78
Workman Compensation Fraud Investigators	79
Police Strategies for Investigating Insurance Fraud	80
Cooperation in the National and International Investigation of Insurance Fraud	81
Prevention of Insurance Fraud	83
Summary	83
Discussion Questions	84
References	85

Chapter Objectives

After reading this chapter you should be able to do the following:

1. Describe the development of insurance.
2. Define and explain insurance fraud.
3. Explain the motivations of insurance fraud.
4. Explain how to investigate insurance fraud.
5. List and explain the credentials of investigators.
6. Explain the global aspects of insurance fraud.

Chapter Outline

Introduction: Development of Insurance
Insurance Fraud: Elements and Types
Costs of Insurance Fraud in the United States, Europe and Other Continents
Motivation for Committing Insurance Fraud: Psychological Aspects
Profiles of Insurance Fraud Offenders
Initial Investigation of Insurance Fraud by Insurance Companies
Criminal Investigation of Insurance Fraud
Credentials and Training to Prepare for Insurance Fraud Investigation
Workers Compensation Fraud
Police Strategies for Investigating Insurance Fraud
National and International Cooperation in Insurance Fraud Detection and Prevention
Summary
Discussion Questions
Notes and References

Introduction: Development of Insurance

Theil (2012) notes that while the taking of risk is a principal characteristic of all enterprise, those who head most enterprises do not want to assume the amount of risk in their planning and operations of the enterprise that would lead to great uncertainty of its future.

Survival is a basic human instinct, and ever since the histories of civilizations have been recorded, we find reports of various ways humans developed to protect themselves and provide security for their property. In societies where the basis of the economy was hunting, fishing, and agriculture, an individual's economic security was always uncertain since unpredictable changes in natural elements, such as changes in climate, drought, floods, fires, and diseases, could completely eliminate a society's source of food. Even as late as the nineteenth century, the destruction of the potato crop and overpopulation in Ireland resulted in millions of people starving and millions of others migrating to other countries (Haywood, 1987: 213).

The idea of insurance was originally developed to protect human beings against the effects of natural disasters, which would ruin their lives if there was not some means to compensate victims for their losses. The insurance principle is based on the idea of solidarity, that is, "a sorrow shared is a sorrow halved" or "one for all, and all for one." (1) However, the solidarity between the insurer and the insured presupposes mutual trust, that is, the notion of "uberrimae fidei." (2) However, in addition to mutual trust, insurance policies are based on mathematical principles, that is, the principles of probability. If the precalculated mathematical assumptions are upset, the system will be out of balance. Crimes affecting the insurance industry, such as fraud, may be a factor that seriously endangers the system.

Theil (2012: 270) noted: "The taking of risks is one of the principal characteristics of enterprise. The concept is most valid for insurance companies whose main purpose is to assume risks that other economic entities do not want to bear and whose principal factor of production is equalization of risks by forming a suitable portfolio of insured risks over time."

Insurance Fraud: Elements and Types

Insurance fraud is not a new problem. Geerds (1984: 96) noted that insurance fraud has been committed ever since insurance has been available in the market. It is committed by all classes of individuals, by businesses and corporation heads, and even by government officials. The specific nature of insurance fraud is due to the insurance contract, which makes the obligation of the insurance company to indemnify the insured contingent on an uncertain future event. In the case of insurance fraud, the event is either brought about on purpose, pretended to have occurred, or an actual loss is exploited by increasing the amount lost beyond that which occurred.

Insurance companies are profit-making enterprises that must operate on a profit and loss formula. In order to assure relative security, they distribute the risks (Dorfman, 1994; Trowbridge, 1975) by making contracts with a large number of parties and operate on the basis of the mathematical law of large numbers. Thus, the determination of the amount paid for the premium by the insurance premium holder is determined by five elements (Theil, 2012: 271):

1. A net risk premium calculated on the basis of the individual loss exposure
2. A security loading to absorb variance
3. A loading to cover costs that are not directly risk related
4. A profit margin
5. Taxes

The crime of fraud is directly related to element number three. Although the insurance corporations are aware that there will be some claims made by those insured that do not have a legitimate basis, the exact number and dollar amounts of the claims can be estimated but not determined with a high degree of accuracy.

Insurance Fraud

Fraud occurs when someone knowingly lies to obtain some benefits or advantage to which they are not otherwise entitled or someone knowingly denies some benefit that is due and to which someone is entitled (California Department of Insurance, 2014: 1.2). Insurance fraud may be committed by the insurers as well as by those who are insured. Although the majority of the insurance fraudulent claims are made by those holding insurance policies, legal providers of services and insurance companies also commit fraud by inflating billing or deliberately misrepresenting the facts of a policy, not paying appropriate worker's compensation deductions to the government, and even embezzling funds collected from policyholders. The Insurance Information Institute (2014b: 6) makes a distinction between "hard and soft" fraud. Hard fraud occurs when there is deliberate fabrication or faking of the matter that relates to the claim, whereas as "soft" fraud is more related to opportunistic situations in which a legitimate claim is made, but the claimants pad the amount of loss or inflate the costs of services rendered to their businesses.

The following are the most common types of fraud schemes known to be committed by the administrators of insurance agencies or insurance agents (FBI-Insurance Fraud, 2014: 1):

- Premium diversion, that is, an insurance agent fails to send premiums to the underwriter and keeps the money for personal use or sells premiums without a license and keeps the money collected for the premiums.
- Fee churning, that is, a number of intermediaries take commissions through insurance agreements and eventually there is no longer sufficient money available to pay the claims.
- Asset diversion involves the theft of insurance company assets.
- Worker's compensation fraud involves entities purporting to provide worker's compensation at a reduced cost who misappropriate the premium funds without providing insurance.

The number of fraudulent insurance claims related to natural disasters, such as Hurricane Katrina, is extensive and costly. For example, the Hurricane Katrina storm caused approximately $100 billion in damages. The U.S. government appropriated $80 billion for reconstruction, and insurance fraud may have accounted for 6 billion of the $100 billion appropriated (FBI-Insurance Fraud: 1).

Another type of insurance fraud that can result in billions of dollars of losses is health insurance fraud. Health insurance fraud can involve insured individuals or group insurance. Fraud occurs when an individual or group conceals information, misrepresents information, or provides false information. For example, the FBI (2015: 1) reports that the amount of health care fraud exceeds tens of billions of dollars a year. The FBI investigates and exposes fraud in the health care profession. It has jurisdiction over both federal and private insurance programs. The FBI has developed partnerships with federal, state and local agencies and with private insurance associations to pursue investigations against large scale health insurance fraudsters. Individuals commit fraud when they alter policy forms, conceal preexisting health conditions, file claims for work-related injuries that are not covered by the policies, fake disability, and falsify drug prescriptions.

The California Government Health Fraud Enforcement Division (2014: 1, 2) lists several types of insurance fraud other than those mentioned earlier. Perhaps the most widespread type is fraud related to automobiles. Automobile collision–related frauds include schemes pertaining to moving vehicles such as right of way, hit and run, sudden stops, phantom vehicle causing an accident, falsely claiming injuries, and organized criminal groups staging auto accidents. Automobile property frauds include faked damages, vehicle theft, automobile vandalism, inflated damages, vehicle arson, and agent and broker collusion on settlements of claims.

Property fraud, other than automobile fraud, pertains to residential and commercial structures and includes theft, vandalism, fire and water damage, mold-related claims, and fraud related to accidents that allegedly occurred on the home or business property of the insured. Other forms of fraud pertaining to insurance are claims made for loss or theft of valuable items such as jewelry, paintings, or antiques (Edelbacher, 2004-2006).

Cost of Insurance Fraud in the United States, Europe, and Other Non-European Countries

According to an FBI report (FBI Reports and Publications, 2014: 1), in the United States, "the insurance industry consists of more than 7,000 companies that contribute over $1 trillion in premiums each year." The massive size of many of these insurance companies and the fact that so much of the insurance business involves international transactions lead to tremendous opportunities to commit fraud. Again referring to the FBI report on insurance fraud sited earlier, "the total cost of insurance fraud (non-health insurance) is estimated to be more than $40 billion per year." Since the insurance companies are likely to recoup their losses by passing them on to their customers, it is estimated that the average insurance holder may pay hundreds of dollars each year in increased premiums to offset the losses from fraud. The Insurance Information Institute (Insurance Fraud, 2014: 1) reports that "insurance industry estimates put fraud at about 10 percent of the property/causality insurance industry's incurred losses and loss adjustment expenses each year, although the figure can fluctuate, based on line of business, economic conditions and other factors."

A coalition against insurance fraud (CAIF, 2014: 1) report indicates that "workers comp fraud is a large crime in America today. Tens of billions of dollars in false claims and unpaid premiums are stolen every year. Scams are forcing premiums higher, draining business profits, and costing honest workers their pay and jobs."

Exact statistics on the cost of insurance fraud in Europe are not available. Thus, we must rely on estimates. The amounts estimated are no doubt quite low, since much of the fraud is not likely to ever be detected, and even if detected, the evidence needed to bring those who had committed the fraud to justice is just not available. According to Pscheidl and Edelbacher (2013: 12), the cost of crimes relating to insurances is

- €75 billion for all of Europe
- €500 million for Austria
- 12 billion for Germany
- $2000 billion worldwide

The Association of Austrian Insurance Companies (2005) registers 88 member insurance companies with 26,300 employees. The volume of premiums increased by 9.5%, with about €15.32 by the end of 2005. During the year 2006, a more than 10% growth is expected. This expected growth is the result of the expansion of the Austrian insurance corporations to the eastern part of Europe, Bulgaria, and Rumania, countries in which insurance fraud is prevalent. It is ironic that the amount of overall crime is declining, while the amount of crime relating to insurance is increasing. For example, the amount of crime against insurance increased by 10% for the European Union countries in 2013 (Pscheidl and Edelbacher, 2013: 11). It is estimated that 5%–10% of the 3.2 million damage claims reported to Austrian insurance companies may be fraudulent reports. This would indicate that the amount of insurance fraud in Austria may reach nearly 1 billion Euro each year (Pscheidl and Edelbacher, 2013: 11). It is estimated that about 15% of the fraudulent cases can be detected and stopped by insurance specialists and the police who investigate suspected cases of fraud.

The types of crime, as covered by the Austrian Criminal Code pertaining to insurance fraud Seiko (1979: 9), include

- Homicide, bodily injury, robbery, traffic accidents
- Property offenses, such as burglary, theft of motor vehicles, embezzlement, check and credit card fraud, arson, white-collar crime, industrial crime
- Drug-related crime

In regard to such crimes as homicides, bodily injuries, and traffic accidents, no reliable statements can be made on the economic loss that is entailed resulting from fraud. In the case of homicides, the assumed loss of productivity is a factor that should be considered when estimating loss. In the case of bodily injuries due to negligence, the cost of treatment and therapy of those injured in relation to the number of cases reported can provide a basis for making estimates.

The economic impact of crimes against property is easier to quantify. An attempt to establish the cost of crime for the national economy of Austria resulted in a total economic loss of ATS 4.4 billion due to robberies, burglaries, and high-tech crime. For example, in 1993, there were 15,214 reports of burglary of dwellings and 13,424 reports of burglary of shops in Austria, and it is estimated that a total of €0.573 billion was paid out by insurance companies for burglary claims in 1993. If indemnification paid for fire, household, accident, and motor-all-risk insurance policies is added, the total loss amount was ATS 9 billion equaling €0.0678 billion in 1993 and nearly twice that amount in 2006 (Pscheidl and Edelbacher, 2013: 12–13).

The costs of drug-related crimes are not to be underestimated. According to current estimates, there are about 7,000 heroin addicts, 7,000 cocaine users, and more than 40,000 users of cannabis in Vienna and more than 2 billion ATS spent on heroin consumption alone Geerds (1984: 96).

Insurance Fraud Crimes in Austria

All types of crimes relating to insurance fraud appear to be on the increase in Austria. Murder cases, violent crimes, burglary, theft of cars, arson, and a great number of accidents are the "modi operandi" of criminals that commit crimes that have a direct effect on insurance companies. As the number of stolen cars, burglaries, and robberies has increased dramatically in the last 5 years in Austria, insurance companies are confronted with enormous losses not only by the costs of paying the insurance policyholders for their losses but also for the suspected increases in the numbers of cases involving insurance fraud. There is evidence that many of the insurance fraud cases are committed by organized criminal organizations, particularly those relating to drug trafficking, identity theft, and various other types of crimes that perpetrated through the Internet such as the theft of securities, antiques, art, and even internationally controlled auto theft organizations. Pscheidl and Edelbacher (2013: 10) note that criminal organizations are using very sophisticated and efficient methods to commit crimes, the international borders are less controlled, and the government and law enforcement organizations do not have the laws and resources to protect the nations affected by transnational crime.

Understanding the Psychological Aspect of Insurance Fraud Motivation

The financial and emotional strain insurance fraud puts on both the insurance companies that sell the policies and those who purchase the policies has gradually become recognized, and as a result, nations throughout the world have tried to respond to the threat through the passage of legislation. In the past, insurance fraud was not considered a real serious problem, and even those policyholders who would never consider cheating or engaging in some form of deception when filing a claim still could somewhat side with those policyholders who in some way practiced some form of fraud, particularly those individuals holding small policies. Schwarz (1987: 45) collected some of the most often stated rationales given by people who do commit insurance fraud:

- No one is personally affected.
- They have been regularly paying into the insurance policies and they want some of their money back.
- A loss was not covered by the policy.
- They were in financial trouble.
- Someone else recommended that they commit fraud.
- The "big ones" are all doing it; why shouldn't I do it?
- They wanted to "trick" the powerful insurance company.
- They wanted to help friends.
- Everyone else is doing it.
- The treatment they received from the insurance company was too impersonal.
- Fraud is part of the business.
- Insurance is a bit like the lottery or gambling.
- It is a risk-free way to do something illegal; it is money you do not have to work for.
- It boosts your ego.
- It is a cavalier thing to do.

A survey completed in 2013 on attitudes toward insurance fraud (Insurance Research Council, 2013) revealed that 24% of the respondents thought it acceptable to pad an insurance claim to make up for the deductible on the policy and 18% of the respondents believed it acceptable to pad a claim to make up for the money paid on their premium. In this survey, it was found "that 86% of the Americans think that insurance fraud leads to higher rates for everyone."

Psychologically, those who hold various types of insurance policies, such as health, property, accident, and automobile, expect to receive a payment when something happens such as an accident, personal injury, or destruction of property, even if the matter is not covered by the insurance policy. Hence, taking out insurance is perceived as a way of "making the damage undone." Moreover, many policyholders, particularly those involved in major accidents, expect more than just indemnification. They want someone who cares and understands, they long for human support and assistance, and they need someone to talk with them about their fears and anxieties. Given the fact that insurers are neither confessors nor psychotherapists, many people who are seriously harmed, either physically or financially, as a result of some catastrophic event, feel alone and abandoned. They feel that the insurance company has failed to respond to their longing for care, recognition, a feeling of community support, and security in their lives. They find that rather than receiving psychological support from the insurance representatives, the insurance holders perceive the service they receive from the insurance representatives as being materialistic and formalistic. Policyholders in general and particularly those who have been paying their premiums for a long period of time become aware of two things. First, the loss has occurred despite payment of the premium; the accident cannot be undone and claims adjustment and indemnification agents, while being experienced in material financial matters, are generally lacking in personal care and attention; and in the event of a loss, the policyholder will never get what was expected. The second factor relating to the potential for fraud is that some policyholders realize that they have been paying for their insurance for many years and never received anything in return. When something does happen, the holders feel they should get back from the company everything they deserve and even more. The whole concept of the insurance principle and the notion of financial solidarity underlying the insurance system are rather hard for the typical insurance holder to grasp. Some people are not made sufficiently aware of the fact that "a sorrow shared is a sorrow halved." This is probably due in part to the fact that the tactic taken by many insurance companies is to underline the savings idea and the "waste not, want not" approach.

Profiles of Insurance Fraud Offenders

Derrig (2002: 271) notes that although the insurance fraud concept implies that criminal behavior is involved, the reality is that the concept covers a number of "opportunistic manipulations of the system" by either the insurers or those who are insured that fall short of criminal behavior. He proposed that those actions that border on but do not meet all of the elements of criminal behavior should be handled through either civil action or through legislation. The term fraud "… should be reserved for criminal acts, provable beyond a reasonable doubt, that violate statutes making the willful act of obtaining money or value from an insurer under false pretenses or material misrepresentations of a crime" (273). The Insurance Information Institute (2014: 1) notes that "fraud may be committed by different parties involved in insurance transactions: applicants for insurance, policy holders, third-party claimants and professionals who provide services and equipment to claimants." Thus, it is not possible to categorize the typical offender. Based on more than 30 years of experience as a police officer who investigated hundreds of criminal cases relating to insurance fraud, Edelbacher (2007) concluded that approximately 3% of the cases were related to organized crime or terrorist activity, 12% were committed by professional criminals, and 85% were committed by nonprofessional people, generally average citizens who were motivated by one or more of the psychological factors mentioned earlier in this chapter (Edelbacher, 2007).

A study of white-collar criminals completed by Price Waterhouse Coopers (2014) presented a profile of white-collar criminals engaged in insurance fraud to be predominately men, older than 35, and established in high-rank leadership positions in corporations or firms. However, as noted earlier, the majority of the fraud cases are individual policyholders. In these cases, the offender is an anonymous person to the insurance company and there is no existing personal relationship between the offender and the victim. This type of relationship makes it easier to commit insurance fraud because there is no criminal energy needed to be active against a congregate person or victim. To commit robbery or burglary, for example, there always has to exist aggregated criminal energy against a person. The criminal always has to be aware of the potential of the victim to fight back. With insurance fraud, the risk of personal harm is minimal.

Initial Investigation of Insurance Fraud by Insurance Companies

Generally, the investigative process for insurance fraud involves many steps and can include a variety of agents who have specialized training relating to the investigative process. In the United States, the federal government and the majority of the states enacted legislation pertaining to insurance fraud, and all states and the District of Columbia have set up one or more fraud bureaus to investigate and process the different types of insurance fraud such as worker's compensation, health care, arson, and property-related fraud that affect the state governments (Insurance Information Institute, 2014: 5). The matter of insurance fraud is covered in a number of federal legislative acts, including the Affordable Health Care Act of 2010, the Health Insurance Portability and Accountability Act of 1996, and the Violent Crime Control and Law Enforcement Act of 1994 (Insurance Information Institute, 2014: 11). In addition, all of the major insurance firms employ special investigators who screen claims and try to determine if a claim is fraudulent. There are several private national organizations that are dedicated to the investigation and curtailing of insurance fraud. For example, "the National Insurance Crime Bureau (NICB), is a non-profit organization that partners with the insurance companies and law enforcement to help identify, detect, and prosecute insurance criminals," and "the Coalition Against Insurance Fraud (CAIF) is a national alliance of consumer groups, public interest organizations, government agencies, and insurers dedicated to preventing insurance fraud" (FBI-Insurance Fraud, 2014: 2).

A large number of countries located throughout the world have enacted legislation pertaining to insurance fraud. For example, Canada founded the Insurance Crime Prevention Bureau in 1973, and in the United Kingdom, the Serious Fraud Office, set up under the Criminal Justice Act, was established in 1987 (Wikipedia, the free encyclopedia, 2014: 8). The Austrian Criminal Code of 1975 defines insurance fraud and special sections of the code define the punishments pertaining to specific types of crimes. Section 161 contains the provision on allowing fraud perpetrators to make voluntary amends and thus avoid criminal prosecution (Austrian Criminal Code, Sections, 146, 298, 161, 1975). The police and law enforcement agencies apply the general provisions of the criminal code regarding fraud that is found in Section 146 of the code. Since Section 161 provision allows perpetrators of some forms of insurance fraud to make voluntary amends, while Section 146 states that the police and insurance fraud investigators are expected to pursue insurance fraud as a crime just as any other crime, there is often a problem between the insurance organizations and the police on how to handle insurance fraud cases. The police have taken the approach based on the "contingency principle," which means the case is assessed according to the effects and consequences of the event.

In the investigation of insurance fraud, there are many unknowns that hamper the investigation and many decisions that have to be made before the cases are brought to a closure. Derrig (2002: 276) states that the top 10 defenses against insurance fraud and abuse are the adjusters, computer technologists, criminal investigators, data and information sources, experts, judges, lawyers, legislators, prosecutors, and special investigators. The large majority of the cases of suspected fraud never reach the prosecution stage for several reasons, even if some evidence of fraud or abuse was found. Once a claim has been filed, much of the original work is completed by the claims adjuster. The claims adjuster is provided with the basic information and facts surrounding the case and generally, based on the information provided, makes a determination on whether or not the facts are true and thus the claim is legitimate or that there are some doubts and the case needs additional investigation before a decision to pay the claimant or deny the claim can be made. Those claims in which there are no questions can be paid out immediately, while those in which there are some questions may be sorted for additional fact-finding. There are several red flags that the experienced adjuster uses to assist in the decision making. For example, in a personal injury automobile accident claim, the adjuster might discover that the claimant has filed several previous claims or has filed for medical expenses based on the reports of questionable doctors.

The use of new technology and data processing systems has led to a reduction in the cost of sorting out of cases, as well as an improvement in the efficiency of case processing, since the sorting process can be completed in less time than in the past and the claimants whose cases only need routine adjusting can be paid immediately after the case is settled. Data mining, the process of sorting out information on cases and placing the cases in categories ranging from those that should be immediately paid because there is no indication of fraud to those cases in which fraud is highly suspected, is a useful tool for the adjuster or a special investigator. The ISOClaimSearch is an example of a data-mining system. It is the world's largest comprehensive database for insurance claims (Insurance Information Institute, Insurance Fraud: 10). In the United States, the member insurance companies of the National Insurance Criminal Bureau send questionable claims to the bureau for review and additional investigation, if there is some suspicion of fraud (Insurance Information Institute, Insurance Fraud, 2014: 2).

Criminal Investigation of Insurance Fraud

The methods applied to the detection and prosecution of insurance fraud are based on criminalistics. Criminalistics involves the investigation and solution of criminal cases. It is defined as the science of crime control through detection and crime prevention. Those who are considered criminalists should not be confused with criminologists. The criminologist studies the underlying causes of criminal behavior, whereas the goal of the criminalist is to detect crimes, investigate and arrest the perpetrators, and "clear up" the crimes. In regard to insurance fraud, methods of recognizing fraud cases are initially based on criminological theories. Having knowledge of psychological and sociological theories of human behavior is very important for the understanding of criminal behavior, and the experienced investigator of insurance fraud should have acquired such knowledge during the course of training or through on-the-job experiences.

Indicators of Insurance Fraud

The methods used by those officials investigating fraud are based on principles developed in the field of criminology. Generally, those who investigate insurance fraud will follow a three-step procedure. The first step involves the creation of suspicion that something is wrong after the initial information provided by the policyholder is reviewed. The second step involves collecting more information on the case. However, much of the additional information is gathered from sources other than the policyholder. The third step involves gathering evidence that indicates fraud and having sufficient evidence that will hold up in criminal proceedings if the claimant is charged with a crime. The "golden rules" followed for the gathering of information are used during the evidence gathering and establishing proof that the person is in the guilty phase of the investigation. These six rules require that the investigator establish the following (Schwind, 1993: 9):

- Who has committed a crime?
- What was done to confirm that the act was criminal?
- When did the crime occur?
- Where was the crime committed?
- How was the crime committed?
- Why was the crime committed?

Establishing the information needed to answer the questions posed earlier is obtained through gathering of evidence that can be obtained from many sources, such as documents, physical evidence, and witnesses to the crime, and through interviewing the people who are suspected of being involved in the crime. As previously mentioned, the use of high-tech electronic equipment in the compiling and analysis of information has provided valuable assistance to the investigator trying to find answers to the questions posed earlier.

Insurance companies have a huge problem in recognizing fraud because of the enormous number of cases that come into their companies each day. Although the large majority of the claims are legitimate, there is still a need to complete some sort of initial investigation to determine if the claim is legitimate or needs more investigation. The insurance companies are confronted with a situation where the number of claims increases each year and the resources, including the personnel, either do not increase or decline. Very often experienced investigators will retire or move to other fields of employment, leaving the company management with the problem of processing an increasing number of cases with fewer numbers of experienced investigators to work on the case. One method used to handle the problem is for the companies to collaborate on the investigations by creating a team of investigative experts who serve all of the companies participating in the cooperative venture. For example, in Austria the Board of Insurance Fighters (experts) was founded in 1968. The underlying idea for the forum is to gather knowledge about the latest developments in insurance fraud and to find answers on what and how to combat insurance fraud. Each of the participating insurance companies selects one or more investigators who then receive the most advanced training available on how to deal with insurance fraud. These experts cooperate at the board of experts, which is housed in the Austrian Board of Insurance Companies (2005). The board has regular meetings at which information is exchanged and cooperation is established with prosecutors and judges. Standardized fraud indicator instruments were developed and are used at the initial stages of the investigation of an insurance claim. The board of experts reports to the authorities of their companies and the Austrian Board Organization of Insurance (Klaus, 1996).

The central information system (ZIS–Austria) (Klaus, 1996) was created by the Association of Austrian Insurance Companies in the early 1990s. It was developed similar to the Dutch model. Since the Austrian insurance companies processed more than three million claims of losses each year, it was impossible for claims managers to identify every case of fraud. Thus, the insurance companies created a central file of cases of policyholders

On the other side of the coin, the employers have been known to engage in various types of fraud relating to worker's compensation. The most common is illegally reducing the amount of worker's compensation premiums they owe and trying to cover it up with fake accounting, tax records, and creating dummy companies. Other professionals who have engaged in worker's compensation scams include doctors and clinic directors, who inflate the extent of injuries and take kickbacks, and attorneys who file bogus law suits against the insurance providers.

The curtailment of worker's compensation fraud requires a multifaceted strategy. The employer can do a great deal to prevent fraud (Coalition Against Insurance Fraud, 2014: 5) by

- Building partnerships with the workers and developing a safety plan in which workers are rewarded for following safety rules
- Establishing zero tolerance policies for fraud
- Checking job applications carefully
- Reporting accidents immediately and insisting the person hurt receive medical treatment
- Reporting suspected fraud
- Alerting insurers on suspicious claims
- Rewarding fraud tips, knowing the warning signals about suspicious claims, and making sure the worker's compensation insurer is licensed in the state

Who completes the investigation of the worker's compensation fraud is determined by the nature of the fraud and the type of claim submitted. Many of the states in the United States, including California, have set up special agencies for the investigation of worker's compensation. The California Workers' Compensation Insurance Fraud Program was set up in 1991 and Senate Bill 1218 established the Fraud Assessment Commission. Recognizing that some worker's compensation fraud schemes can be very complex, particularly those that include white-collar criminals such as doctors, lawyers, and business executives, those selected for fraud inspector's positions must have a high and wide range of knowledge on many subjects, including law, medicine, law enforcement, and insurance (California Department of Insurance, 2014:1).

Police Strategies for Investigating Insurance Fraud

Law enforcement authorities depend on the information they receive from insurance managers as the starting point for fraud investigations. Of course, they have other sources of information, such as their own internal records on suspects. These records may contain information on past infractions and on other types of crimes for which the person was charged and convicted. Other sources of information helpful in the investigation might come from the public prosecutors' offices, courts and financial institutions, queries addressed to insurance companies, credit card companies, car rental companies, gambling casinos, and registration offices, such as the bureau of motor vehicles, postal authorities, and even international data sources such as the Interpol. The purpose of the exhaustive search is to determine if the suspect has a history of committing fraud-related crimes and, if so, if there is a pattern in the methods used to commit the fraud.

After the police investigator is assured that all of the sources of useful information on the suspect have been exhausted, the next steps in the investigation are completed:

- A description of the facts surrounding the current charge is complete.
- Coordination of the components and the involved personnel in the investigation within the police agency is completed.
- Coordination with other agencies is established.
- An analysis of the current state of the case and additional planning is completed.
- Cooperative investigations with other authorities are completed.
- Ongoing participation in working groups such as special commissions is completed.
- Fraud control strategies are constantly being developed, implemented, and evaluated.
- Once the evidence is sufficient, the suspect is arrested and questioned.
- The case to the public prosecutor's office where the suspect will be charged and be tried in the court.

The process presented earlier indicates the most frequently used procedures followed by public policing agencies as well as other investigative agencies. However, not all cases of suspected insurance fraud will be handled in the same manner. There are a number of factors that must be considered in the decision to vigorously pursue the case or to let it slide, including the cost of the investigation and the likelihood of success. If the insurance fraud claim is being perpetrated by a career criminal or by an organized crime group, such as art theft and identity theft, the investigation becomes very complex and may take months or even years of investigation before a closure of the case is finalized. The criminal quickly becomes aware of the tactics followed by the police in their investigations. They exchange knowledge and practical experience and easily adapt and develop new methods to avoid detection.

Cooperation in the National and International Investigation of Insurance Fraud

As the insurance industry expands internationally, the problem of insurance fraud also becomes an international concern. For example, the European Union now includes a number of wealthy countries as well as several countries that are relatively poor. The new framework of the European Union makes it easier for criminals to use the opportunity of a free market and the advantage of unrestricted mobility between countries to develop international insurance fraud schemes. There is evidence that organized crime groups are much more active in various insurance fraud schemes than in the past. Since there are no country borders for the European Union member nations, there are no controls, and this creates a great advantage for the criminal. Criminals have expanded their knowledge of criminal techniques to include insurance fraud. It is imperative that insurance companies, particularly those that operate internationally, communicate and cooperate in fighting against insurance fraud. In the past, insurance company administrators were only concerned with the success of their own company. Focusing on short-range goals, particularly making a profit, these insurance companies reduced their funding for the personnel and equipment needed to curtail the criminal activities of the internationally organized criminal groups. By doing so, they failed to understand the long-range effects of insurance fraud, such as the need to raise premiums and the loss of confidence in the company by policyholders.

The cooperative efforts used by insurance companies both on a national scale and also on an international scale, to prevent and detect insurance fraud, have been enhanced by the use of computerized analyses of insurance claims. The Association of Certified Fraud Examiners (ACFE) and the American Institute of Certified Public Accountants have detailed how the use of the most advanced methods can be used by insurance companies, if they are willing to share their information on suspected fraud cases by putting it in an information data file that all of the participating insurance companies can access.

Transactional analysis is one of the most powerful ways of detecting fraud within an organization. To maximize its effectiveness as a fraud detection system, the analysis works with a comprehensive set of indicators of potential fraud, taking into account the most common fraud schemes as well as those that relate specifically to the unique risks faced by a particular organization. The system includes all transactions of participating companies within a given area and tests these transactions against the parameters that highlight indicators of fraud. The analyses and tests are completed as close to the time of the transaction as possible, ideally even before the transaction has been finalized. In addition, there is a continuous monitoring of the transaction. The methods used by the participating companies to access the database in order to compare data and transactions generally are easily assessable to all participating companies. The matter of being assessable is particularly important. Many suspicious transactions only come to light after transactional data from one company are compared to that of another. For example, the addresses of paid vendors with employee addresses can be used to detect potential "phantom vendor" schemes. Individuals intent on fraud seek out organizational "soft spots" where there is little regular cross-system data validation, thus providing a golden opportunity for the fraud schemes to remain undetected.

The access control list (ACL) system adopted by many insurance companies enables timely fraud detection and often the prevention of fraud. ACL provides business assurance that complements and completes business intelligence. By giving organizations access to all of their data, the participating organizations are able to analyze and independently validate data and transactions for integrity, in a fraction of the time that it would have taken before the system was implemented, because of the powerful analytics and robust capabilities of the system. The system enables tens of thousands of organizations around the world to make decisions on transactions with speed and confidence. It helps to reduce risk, to minimize loss, to increase profits, and to assure that other companies are in compliance with the rules and regulations governing the insurance industry. ACL has proven its worth by the fact that it has clients from the largest and wealthy corporations throughout the world: 176 countries and more than 500 national, state, and local governments on 6 continents are represented.

In summary, a well-designed and well-implemented fraud detection system, based on transactional analysis of operational systems, can significantly reduce the chances of fraud being attempted and, if attempted, reduce the chances that it will not be detected. If the indicators of fraud are detected early in a transaction, there is a much greater chance that the fraud can be prevented and, if not prevented, detected and the losses experienced by the company can be recovered. In addition, any weaknesses in the system can be addressed and possibly corrected. The bottom line is that effective detection techniques serve as a deterrent mechanism, since they may persuade potential fraudsters, who know that experts are keeping a close watch of all transactions and have the ability to detect abnormalities, from even attempting to commit fraud.

Prevention of Insurance Fraud

Traditionally, organizations have tried to prevent and detect fraud by implementing appropriate internal controls such as internal audits. The transactions of the company are regularly audited, and when potential fraud is detected, an investigation is started. Other methods for detecting fraud come from tips or by accident. While strong internal controls and audits play a significant role in preventing and detecting fraud, it is unrealistic to assume that they are completely effective. A study by the ACFE (Schwalb, 2007a,b) found that 46% of the fraud that occurred was the result of insufficient controls to prevent the opportunity for committing the fraud. An additional 40% of the exploitation occurred when the controls were ignored. For many of the organizations, there is a strong possibility that a large amount of fraud is never detected. Even after frauds do come to light, it is some time after the fraud had occurred and the chances of recovering the loss have diminished.

The ACFE (2002) estimates that 6% of insurance organizations' revenue will be lost each year as a result of occupational fraud. Worldwide, this translates into hundreds of billions of dollars. More than half of the cases of fraud exceeded $100,000 and almost one-sixth of the cases exceeded $1 million. The indirect costs of fraud, such as damage to the reputation of the company, loss of customer confidence, lower employee morale, and the resignation of important personnel, and other costs are hard to measure, but they all have an impact on the organization's productivity and its ability to increase its revenue.

Summary

The basis in the quest for survival is the desire to be able to protect oneself and significant others from danger, the want of food or clothing, as well as the desire to make one's life as comfortable as possible. With the development of commerce, those who could pay for the security protection hired someone else to take the risk. The principle of insurance developed when those who could afford it paid someone else to protect their goods, transactions, property, and themselves.

The insurance companies provide some reasonable guarantee that the goods, property, and person of the insured are secured, and in those cases in which the insured experiences a loss, the insurance holder will be compensated. Insurance companies are profit motivated and are willing to take the risk of losing money if the amount of money given to those who have claims exceeds the amount of revenue taken in by the company. At times, the losses do exceed the revenue.

Most criminals engage in criminal activity because there is some type of gain or profit to be made from their acts. Criminals must take a risk whenever they engage in criminal behavior. Generally, the greater the risk taken, for example, the possibility of getting caught or being personally attacked by the victim, the greater the reward or profit expected. However, for a variety of reasons, those who engage in insurance fraud often receive very high rewards but have very low risk.

Surveys of policyholders reveal that many insurance company executives are much more concerned about making a profit that they are about the welfare of their policy-holders. Such attitudes toward the insurance industry and the industry's failure to address some of the major complaints of policyholders, such as claims not being handled quickly, customers not getting personal service and advice, deceptive presentations of the services offered, and a lack of transparency in the management of the company, can foster an attitude among many that it is acceptable to commit fraud against the insurance companies that are "ripping off the customers." Without having the cooperation and assistance of the policyholders, the efforts to detect and prevent insurance fraud will not succeed, even though the fraud investigators have all of the latest technological equipment and employ complex strategies for detection and prevention of fraud.

The statistics available on the amount of insurance fraud reveal that it is increasing throughout the world. As insurance companies develop world markets, many criminal organizations find that hundreds of millions can be made by implementing various types of insurance fraud schemes. The detection and prevention of insurance fraud requires concerted efforts from many sources, including private enterprise, public law enforcement agencies, and the people who hold insurance policies. Regardless of the difficulty, all concerned parties will benefit if they are successful in their efforts.

Discussion Questions

5.1 Discuss the factors that account for the drastic increase in the amount of international fraud schemes.

5.2 Contrast the methods used by insurance companies to investigate fraud with those used by police agencies.

5.3 Discuss the differences between "soft" insurance fraud and "hard" insurance fraud. What factors might influence insurance companies to not prosecute those who have detected as being involved in insurance fraud schemes?

5.4 Discuss the steps/procedures followed by the police in the investigation of insurance fraud. Why is it necessary for police investigators of insurance fraud to have specialized training?

5.5 Transactional analysis has proved to be an effective method for the prevention and detection of insurance fraud schemes. Discuss the characteristics of transactional analysis and the conditions that insurance companies must adhere to in order for transactional analysis to be effective.

5.6 Discuss the reasons and rationalizations used by those who engage in insurance fraud to justify their behavior.

5.7 Discuss the duties of an insurance fraud investigator. Why is it essential for insurance fraud investigators to have broad-based knowledge in a variety of fields?

5.8 Contrast the types of insurance fraud schemes that have been used by the providers of insurance (insurance companies) with those schemes typically used by the holders of insurance policies.

5.9 Worker's compensation insurance fraud is found to have been perpetrated by employees, employers, and various types of professionals such as doctors and lawyers. Discuss the types of fraud typically employed by workers, by employers, and by professionals.

5.10   Define fraud, identify the major types of insurance fraud, and discuss the effect insurance fraud has on individuals holding insurance policies, on the companies selling insurance policies, and on the national economy.

Notes:

1. Roman law, "pacta sunt servanda"—"treaties have to be fulfilled."
2. Roman law, "uberrimae fidei"—"you have to trust each other."

References

Association of the Austrian Insurance Companies (2005). Training manual, Salzburg, Austria.

Austrian Criminal Code, sections 146, 161, 298 (1975).

California Department of Insurance (2014). Fraud: Workers' compensation fraud and convictions. Workers, Compensation, Insurance. http://www.ca.gov/0300-fraud-division-overview/0500-fraud-division-programs/workers-comp-fraud/. Accessed April 21, 2014.

Coalition Against Insurance Fraud (2014). Workers compensation scams. http://www.insurancefraud.org/scam-alerts-workers-compensation.htm#UO2LRJufmv0. Accessed April 15, 2014.

Derrig, R. (September 2002). Insurance fraud. *Journal of Risk and Insurance*, 69(3):271–287.

Dorfman, M. (1994). *Introduction to Risk Management and Insurance*, 5th edn. Englewood Cliffs, NJ: Prentice-Hall.

Edelbacher, M. (2004–2006). Notes on insurance fraud. Completed while chair of the Austrian Insurance Fraud Control Office, 2004–2006.

Edelbacher, M. (2007). Strategies to fight insurance fraud. Document constructed for the education and training at the Vienna University of Economy and Business Administration, Financial Department, Vienna, Austria.

FBI (2014). Insurance fraud reports and publications. http://www.fbi.gov/stats-services/publications/insurance-fraud. Accessed March 10, 2014.

FBI (2015). Rooting out health care fraud is central to the well-being of both our citizens and the overall economy. *Health Care Fraud*. http://www.fbi.gov/about-us/investigate/white_collar/health-care-fraud. Accessed February 4, 2015.

Geerds, F. (April 1984). Zur sozialen problematic des versicherungmissbrauches-Die kriminellen praktikenund ihre folge fur das versicherungswesen. *Die Versicherungsrundschau* 39(3–4): 96.

Haywood, J. (1987). *The Great Migrations*. London, U.K.: QuercusBooks.

Indeed (2014). Insurance fraud investigator. http://www.com/jobs?q=Insurance+FraudInvestigator &I=Find Jobs. Accessed April 22, 2014.

Insurance Information Institute (March 2014a). Insurance fraud. http://www.iii.org/issue_updates/insurance/fraud.html. Accessed April 15, 2014.

Insurance Information Institute (2014b). Identity theft and cyber security. http://www.iii.org/facts_statistics/identity-thefyt-and-cyber-security.html. Accessed April 15, 2014.

Insurance Research Council (2013). Insurance fraud: A public view. http:www.insurance-research.org. Accessed March 22, 2014.

Klaus, P. (1996). Dachverband der Osterreichischen versicherungen. Interview completed by Maximilian Edelbacher in 1996.

Price Waterhouse Coopers (2014). Global economic crime survey 2014. Retrieved from http://www.pwc.com/en_GX/9X/economic-crime-survey/pdf/global-economic-crime-survey-2014. Accessed January 4, 2015.

Pscheidl, D. and M. Edelbacher (2013). Crime against insurances: A kind of organized economic crime. Paper at *the Meeting of AVUS*, Vienna, Austria, November 2013.

Schwalb, T. (2007a). Insurance applications. Accessed April 26, 2014.

Schwalb, T. (2007b). White Paper: Fraud detection and prevention: Transactional analysis for effective fraud detection. Accessed April 26, 2014.

Schwind, H.E. (1993). *Praxisorientierte einfuhrung mit beispielen*, 6th edn., Vol. 28. Heidlbarg, Germany: Kriminalsitik Verlag, p. 9.

Seiko, T. Austrian Criminal Code, Sections 146,161,298 (1979). *Vernehmungskunde* Graz, Leykam, Verlag fur recht, Stat und Wirtschaft: 92.

Theil, M. (2012). Dealing with insurance: What can be learned. In *Financial Crimes: A Threat to Global Security*, M. Edelbacher, P. Kratcoski, and M. Theil (Eds.). Boca Raton, FL: CRC/Taylor & Francis Group, pp. 269–288.

Trowbridge, C. (1975). Insurance as a transfer mechanism, *Journal of Risk and Insurance*, 42:1–15.

Burglary Investigations

HARRISON WATTS

6

Contents

Chapter Objectives	87
Chapter Outline	87
Law of Burglary	88
Types of Burglary	88
Scope of Burglary in the United States	89
Proactive Preventative Measures	90
Investigative Techniques	92
Residential Burglaries	92
Investigating the Point of Entry	92
Evidence Collection at the Scene	93
Commercial Burglaries	94
Burglary of Vehicles	95
Summary	96
Questions for Discussion	96
References	96

Chapter Objectives

After reading this chapter you should be able to do the following:

1. Identify the elements of the crime of burglary.
2. Distinguish between the various types of burglary.
3. Depict the scope and trends of burglary in the United States.
4. Identify proactive measures that prevent burglary.
5. Describe the different investigative techniques for the various types of burglary.

Chapter Outline

Law of Burglary
Types of Burglary
Scope of Burglary in the United States
Proactive Preventative Measures
Investigative Techniques
Summary

Law of Burglary

Many burglary calls start off with a call to the police department with a scared victim who reports that they have been "robbed." The police dispatcher ascertains that the victim was away from their home, and when they returned, they found that someone had entered their residence and taken valuables. The suspects in this type of call are not actually in the residence when the victims return home. Consequently, this is a case of residential burglary rather than robbery. Many victims get these two types of crimes confused when reporting them (Figure 6.1).

Burglary is defined as entering a habitation or building without the effective consent of the owner with the intent to commit a felony, theft, or assault. Some states call burglary by another term, breaking and entering. For example, Massachusetts identifies the crime of breaking and entering at night where the elements of the crime are the same as the Texas statute apart from that they include vehicles and boats in addition to residences and buildings.

Many states address a person remaining concealed in a building with the intent to commit a theft or felony crime. This type of burglary does not require a breaking into a building because the suspect enters when a building is open and remains hidden in a bathroom, for example, until the business closes. After all of the employees have left, the suspect commits a theft. This type of burglary is not to be confused with criminal trespassing. A person commits criminal trespassing if the person enters or remains on or in a property of another, without the effective consent of the owner and the person had notice that the entry was forbidden or received notice to depart but failed to do so. Now the "notice" part should be explained. Of course if a person is told that they must leave and then they remain, they would meet the notice element. In addition, if there is signage that no trespassing is allowed or a fence that would indicate no entry to the general public, this serves as notice. The principle difference between criminal trespassing and burglary is that no other crime is contemplated by the suspect other than to remain when not authorized by the owner or by law.

Types of Burglary

Defining burglary is a complicated matter as there are different types of burglary to include aggravated burglary or burglary in the first degree. In Washington State, for example, if a person commits a burglary and is armed with a deadly weapon or assaults any other person

---

(a) A person commits an offense if, without the effective consent of the owner, the person
  (1) Enters a habitation, or a building (or any portion of a building), not then open to the public, with intent to commit a felony, theft, or an assault
  (2) Remains concealed, with intent to commit a felony, theft, or an assault, in a building or habitation
  (3) Enters a building or habitation and commits or attempts to commit a felony, theft, or an assault
(b) For purposes of this section, "enter" means to intrude
  (1) Any part of the body
  (2) Any physical object connected with the body

Figure 6.1 Texas Penal Code 30.02, Burglary.

during the commission of a burglary, it is a burglary of the first degree. Consequently, burglary is a crime that can be enhanced by degree or title (aggravated burglary) if a weapon is used in the commission of the crime. The penalty for this type of burglary is generally of the highest type of felony crime. In Texas, for example, a burglary of a habitation is a first-degree felony punishable of up to 99 years or life in prison.

Many states differentiate the severity of punishment by the various types of places that are burglarized. For example, a residence carries a more severe punishment than a burglary of a business. Burglary of a vehicle carries less severe punishment than a burglary of a business. Generally speaking, burglary of a residence or a building is a felony crime. Knowing that all state laws are quite unique in and of themselves, a generalization can be made that burglary of vehicles and/or coin-operated machines are high misdemeanors rather than felonies. Some states have enhancement statutes so if a suspect has been previously convicted of a burglary, then even a burglary of a coin-operated machine may be a felony.

Burglary of vehicles in the United States is quite extensive. According to the city of Austin, Texas (2014), police work over 10,000 burglaries of vehicles each year. This number does not reflect the dark figure of crime (those crimes not reported to the police). Police agencies across the United States have combated vehicle burglaries with smart campaigns such as the Lock it, Remove it, or Lose it campaign.

Scope of Burglary in the United States

According to the Uniform Crime Report (2012), there were 2,103,787 burglaries reported in 2012 in the United States. Of these burglaries, 74.5% were residential in nature. A majority of the residential burglaries occurred during the day when the victims were away. This is particularly true in modern times as most of the household members work to support a modern lifestyle. This was not always the case as many women prior to the 1970s did not work outside the household. Consequently, in today's time there are many empty residences during the day while the occupants work. Conversely, the majority of burglary of buildings occurred during the night. This also makes sense because businesses close for the day and leave an empty building during the nighttime hours (Figure 6.2).

In 2012, there were an estimated 2,103,787 burglaries, a decrease of 3.7% when compared with 2011 data:

- The number of burglaries decreased 5.6% when compared with 2008 and was down 2.4% when compared with the 2003 estimate.
- The estimated number of burglaries accounted for 23.4% of the estimated number of property crimes.
- By subcategory, 59.7% of burglaries involved forcible entry, 33.9% were unlawful entries, and 6.3% were attempted forcible entry.
- Victims of burglary offenses suffered an estimated $4.7 billion in property losses in 2012; overall, the average dollar loss per burglary offense was $2230.
- Burglaries of residential properties accounted for 74.5% of all burglary offenses.

Figure 6.2 The FBI's overview of burglary in the United States. *Note*: The FBI's Uniform Crime Report for 2012.

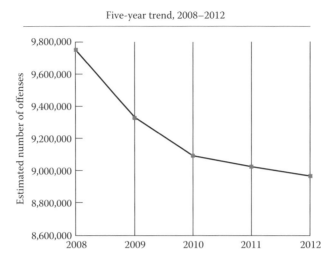

Figure 6.3 Property crime offense figure. *Note:* The FBI's Uniform Crime Report for 2012.

Burglary is considered a property crime. According to the Uniform Crime Report data, the trend in property crime has taken a significant dip in recent years and this includes burglary (Figure 6.3).

According to the UCR, of all property crimes in 2012, larceny–theft accounted for 68.5% and burglary accounted for 23.4%. As one would expect, there are seasonal differences in the crime rates for burglary. According to Lauritsen and White (2014), household burglary exhibited seasonal patterns, with rates of victimization typically highest in summer and lowest in winter or spring.

According to the National Crime Victimization Survey, there tends to be a high rate of underreporting of burglary among other property crimes. In 2012, victims reported to police about 52 property crimes per 1000 households. The rate of property crime not reported to police increased from 86.1 per 1000 households in 2011 to 101.9 in 2012 (Trueman et al., 2013).

Proactive Preventative Measures

Situational crime prevention comprises opportunity-reducing measures that are directed at highly specific forms of crime, involvement of the management, design or manipulation of the environment in as systematic and permanent way possible, and making crime more difficult or risky as judged by a wide range of offenders (Clarke, 1997).

In response to property crime, the general public, the business community, and the police have developed strategies to prevent burglaries. The public at large many times approaches burglary prevention from a reactive view and as a response to victimization. It is after a burglary that the victim feels unsafe in their home and thus will take action to limit the possibility of a repeat occurrence. This could be in the form of installing a monitored security system to installing closed-circuit television (CCTV) surveillance. Many neighborhood associations hire policing agencies or private security to perform additional patrol in their neighborhoods.

The most popular method of burglary prevention is a home or business security system. Modern alarms systems have made rapid advancement over the last 15 years. Electronic sensors can detect glass breaking, a change in frequency of sound waves, and changes in the temperature of a room. When an alarm is activated, a call is made from a central unit in the home to the alarm company. The alarm company contacts the home owner or the local police department. If the alarm company cannot make contact with the home owner, then the police department is notified. The police then respond to the alarm. Many alarm systems now allow wireless remote control of the system. With an advanced alarm system like this, when an alarm is activated, the home owner is also notified through cell phone technology or through an app on a smart phone. With some alarm systems, the owner can see real time through CCTV into their home through their phone application. Home owners can also remotely activate the alarm system, reset it, and turn off and on lights in the home.

We know that burglars choose easy targets. Therefore, residents should make sure that their home is secure at all times. When residents go out of town, they need to make certain that newspapers and/or advertisements do not accumulate in and about their home. In addition, there are timed light switches that can be purchased to control the home lighting while the residents are away. For the burglar who does surveillance on a home prior to a break-in, this may thwart that effort and the burglar would search for an easier target.

Most law enforcement agencies also conduct free close property patrol checks. This is where a law enforcement agency will send a police patrol by a residence to check on it while the occupants are away. In Vernon, Texas, the police officers get out of their vehicles and conduct a walk around inspection on the home. These checks are conducted by officers on all three shifts depending on the workload. Each of the officers completes a form detailing the times and days that the officer checked on the property and if any unusual condition existed, which is then sent to the home owner when they return.

Many law enforcement agencies have campaigns to inform the public of the power of burglary prevention. One prevention strategy is Operation ID. This strategy involves marking or engraving a person's property with an identifying number (generally a driver's license number, which is easily recognized and traced by law enforcement) and displaying a window decal to discourage burglary and/or theft. Citizens may call the police department crime prevention unit to make a "house call" with the engraving tools. Some law enforcement agencies allow citizens to bring items to the police department for engraving, but with bulky items, it is most oftentimes easier for the officer to make a house call. It is also important for home owners to write down serial numbers of electronic devices. Some police agencies have formatted forms that can be given to the home owner for this specific purpose.

Many police agencies conduct home and business security surveys. Usually, officers assigned to a community policing or crime prevention unit will conduct a hands-on security survey. This entails assessing the strengths and weaknesses of a home or business as it relates to the security of the home or building. The police agency generally will give the business or home owner a copy of a printed report with suggestions that the owner can take to harden their target so to speak.

Many urban communities have built entire subdivisions inside walled and secured sections. These gated communities generally have a guard shack that is staffed with a security member who then checks the residents as they enter the community. Some neighborhoods have an electronic gate that a resident either uses a special code number or has a magnetic card that is read to open the gate. In addition to subdivisions using the gated community concept, many apartment complexes have also incorporated this type of perimeter protection. In addition, many apartment complexes hire security officers to patrol the premises. Some apartment facilities employ off-duty police officers to work security of the facility. Using a community policing approach, the apartment complex allows the officer to live in the community for a reduced rate or at no cost at all in exchange for part of the salary that they receive. These types of arrangements are organized through the police department, which has administrators who approve them. The idea behind these types of security arrangements is that the police officer and their families live in the complex and get to know the residents. The officers know who belongs at the complex and who doesn't. In addition, as fully certified police officers, they tend to get more respect from the residents than a hired security officer.

Police agencies across the country have instituted burglary of vehicle campaigns to include catchy slogans such as Lock it or Lose it or Lock it, Remove it, or Lose it. These campaigns are designed to induce the public to remove their valuables from their vehicles thus eliminating the target. These are widespread campaigns that have had some success.

Investigative Techniques

Residential Burglaries

Burglaries of residential properties accounted for 74.5% of all burglary offenses, and investigation into these types of burglaries generally begins with a victim returning home and noticing that there was a break-in. The police are then called to respond. Some residents have burglar alarms that are triggered, and thus, an immediate police response is warranted. When responding to an alarm call, the responding officer should not run code 3 to the scene rather the scene should be approached quietly. Always approach a burglary alarm as if it is an active crime scene with the perpetrator inside the home. Most departments send two units to respond to a burglary in progress. Many departments treat alarm calls differently than an active burglary in progress that should be treated as noted earlier as an active scene.

As the arriving officers approach the scene, they should be observant of people and/or vehicles that are in close proximity to the location of the call. Many burglars will park their vehicle away from the actual target residence, depending on what the intended theft will entail. Some burglars who work in teams may have a vehicle circling the block and/or in close proximity to drive up quickly to load the stolen property. Many times the vehicles that are used are stolen or the driver is an unauthorized user of the vehicle. Consequently, careful observation is critical upon approaching the scene. Once on the scene, with backup, the responding officers should make sure that the residents either have evacuated the home or that they do so prior to officers entering the home.

Investigating the Point of Entry

Officers clearing a residential home burglary may do so with a K9 unit if possible. If not, then a team of two officers should clear the residence. Depending on the department resources and policy, a detective may be called for the collection and preservation of any evidence left at the scene by the burglars. If the department allows for patrol officers to investigate the burglary, then a careful walk-through should be conducted. During this initial walk-through, the officer will identify the point of entry (forced or not) as well as the point of exit. More than 70% of all residential burglaries have forced entry. With this information, examining doors and windows is critical to locate the point of entry.

Careful inspection of a forced entry may reveal evidence in the form of shoe marks on a kicked door or toolmarks if a burglar used a tool to force open a door or window. Police can process toolmark evidence found in the area where the forced entry was made. Burglar tools may reveal unique characteristics that distinguish this tool from any other tool. This is from wear and tear of the tool as well as the manufacturing process of the tool. The characteristics of each tool can be transferred onto a surface when the tool is used to force open a door or window and "scratched" marks into the surface of the receiving object. Many police departments have a collection of toolmarks that are used as a standard for comparison of tools recovered in burglar arrests. In the absence of a questioned tool, examinations of the mark that was made may be observed to determine what type of tool produced the mark and whether the mark is of any evidentiary value. The investigating officer may use either photographic evidence of the toolmark or silicone casting. Generally, all evidence is photographed before being collected and this includes toolmark impressions. Photographs have much less evidentiary value than that of a casting (FBI, 2014).

When the point of entry is a window, the burglars generally break out the glass and remove the jagged pieces so that they can either lift the window or crawl through the window. If the burglar did not wear protective gloves, then fingerprints may be located on these pieces of glass which the officer may find below the window. Consequently, detailed inspection of the glass is essential to evidence collection. In addition, if the burglar did crawl through a window, the officer may find blood on glass left in the window frame. Locating trace evidence at the point of entry is crucial. Knowing that the offender had to enter through this point of the residence may offer the officer evidence in the form of hairs, bodily fluids, clothing fibers, footprints, etc.

Evidence Collection at the Scene

The actual recovery of trace evidence is consistent with the collection methods with other crime scenes. The officer should use the standard methods of evidence collection and follow the policy of the department related to collection and preservation of evidence. Once inside the residence, the evidence collection should follow the likely path that the burglars took inside. The victims should assist the investigator at this point with the identification of items that are missing or that have been disturbed. Fingerprint evidence may be located on drawers that the burglar opened or attempted to open. Unless on glass, fingerprints are oftentimes difficult to locate as well as to collect successfully. Due to the CSI effect, victims do like to see investigators locating fingerprints and they expect that a mountain of evidence will be collected. It is important to walk the victim through the realities of evidence collection so that they are satisfied with the investigation and/or at least understand why fingerprints are not found or collected.

At the point of exit (which may also be the point of entry), evidence may be present in the form of shoe prints, or anything that the burglar dropped. Also, there may be drag tracks through the grass, dirt, or ground surface. Depending on the conditions,

In Vernon, Texas, a burglary was reported and investigated. The burglary took place while the residents were out of town. When they returned, they discovered that they had been victims of a burglary. Although there was minimal evidence located and/or collected at this burglary scene, a neighborhood canvas was conducted. During the interviews with the neighbors, one particular neighbor recalled that they saw a U-Haul trailer parked outside of this residence sometime after midnight. Vernon, Texas, only has one U-Haul rental location. A records check of the individuals that rented a trailer revealed a suspect who was later brought in for questioning. The suspect eventually confessed to the crime. The stolen items were recovered and returned to the victim. Consequently, a neighborhood canvass cannot be overstated as a great investigative tool in working burglaries.

Figure 6.4 Neighborhood canvas produces lead.

evidence such as show impressions may be collected. Again, the standard collection methods should be used.

A neighborhood canvas should be conducted to identify if any of the neighbors saw or heard anything related to the burglary or anything out of the ordinary. In addition, the officer should look for any items that may have been dropped from the burglar in the surrounding areas (Figure 6.4).

It is a reality of the world that some burglaries are reported fraudulently. A home owner or business owner may attempt to cover other losses through insurance recovery of stolen property that has actually not been stolen. The interview of the reporting person and/or owner of the property is important to determine that the reported burglary was an actual burglary and not staged by the owner for insurance purposes.

Investigators should analyze crime patterns and methods of operation (modus operandi) of previous burglaries in the vicinity. Comparisons should be made of the burglaries to determine if the possibility exists of any patterns that may point to the same perpetrator(s) who may be responsible for more than one burglary. The way that entry was made into the residence as well as the nature of items taken and how the burglary as conducted may all be compared. Consequently, data analysis is important.

Commercial Burglaries

Commercial burglaries or burglaries of a business are distinguished from residential burglaries as the penalty for these types of burglaries is generally lower than that of a residential burglary. In most state criminal codes, a burglary of a business is still considered a felony crime, although a lesser felony than that of a residential burglary. Commercial burglaries can be either rudimentary or rather sophisticated.

Rudimentary commercial burglary may consist of a burglar throwing a rock through a plate glass window giving easy entry into the business. The burglar then enters and takes items that are within easy grasp. Another popular way to gain entry into a business is by crashing a vehicle through the front door/window. Typically, the vehicles used in this type of entry are stolen. These types of rudimentary burglaries are called "smash and grabs." Many times shoe stores and/or clothing stores face this type of quick burglary threat. If a vehicle was used to smash the front of the business, it may contain evidence. Consequently, if a vehicle is left at the scene, the investigator would process it for evidence as if it was involved in any other crime. Department policy dictates the process of securing the vehicle as evidence. In addition, if the vehicle was stolen, the particulars of the theft may also reveal clues in the case.

More sophisticated commercial burglaries may involve a team of people. This could include a lookout (wheelman) and front men (who actually perpetrate the actual break-in). These types of burglaries are typically well planned out. The burglars know what they are looking for and may have advanced break-in tools. Characteristically, these tools include bolt cutters, pry bars, blow torches used for cutting, drills, sledge hammers, wire cutters, and police scanners. Commercial burglars may know of a safe inside a business. If the burglar(s) is attempting to defeat a safe, they may use one of several techniques: *Punching*, which involves removing the safe's dial and then using a sledge hammer and punch (screwdriver or chisel) to disable the safe's locking device. *Pulling*, a device is attached to the safe's dial and it is removed exposing the safe's locking mechanism, which is then disabled. *Peeling*, consists of peeling apart a corner of the safe exposing the locking device that can then be defeated. *Ripping*, is where the burglar uses a tool (cutting torch) or device to cut into the safe's exterior thus exposing the contents of the safe. *Drilling*, is when the safe's dial is drilled into exposing the locking device to defeat. *Blasting*, is where explosives are used to defeat the locking mechanism.

Coin-operated machines as well as ATMs are also targeted for burglary. These machines produce immediate results for burglars as they contain cash. Coin-operated machines are attacked similarly to a safe with the goal to defeat the locking mechanism, which gives the burglar access to the money. You find coin-operated machines outside grocery stores, in hotels, at highway roadside parks, and at many business locations. In addition, most self-service car washes have a change machine that is desirable for burglars. ATMs present a challenge for burglars as they are generally very heavy and secured well to the locations where they are. Many times a burglar will gain access to an ATM in a similar fashion to a smash and grab. If the burglar can use a stolen truck to back into a business that has an ATM and can dislodge it, they may be able to carry away the entire ATM. Otherwise, it may take too long to defeat the ATM.

Burglary of Vehicles

Theft of money, vehicle equipment such as stereos, or any property that is left inside a vehicle is considered burglary of a vehicle. These types of burglaries are generally a lower classification of crime. In Texas, burglary of a vehicle is a Class A misdemeanor, which is punishable up to a year in jail. There are endless ways to gain access to a vehicle. The easiest is when the driver leaves the vehicle unattended and unlocked. Many burglaries of vehicles occur this way, as an unlocked vehicle presents an easy opportunity. If a vehicle is locked, the burglar may gain access by smashing a window, using a slim jim and/or prying the window away from the doorframe, and using a rod to unlock the car door. Once inside, the burglar takes what they believe to be valuable. This type of burglary can happen very quickly and at any location that a vehicle is left at to include outside of a residence. Increasingly, burglar of vehicles included recreational vehicles (RVs) as they contain televisions and expensive audio equipment. The investigating officer should look for fingerprints on the car windows. Oftentimes the burglar will look inside a vehicle and place their hands on the glass. This is beneficial as glass is a favorable surface to recover fingerprints. The investigator should determine if any CCTV exists in the area where the burglary of a vehicle was located. Furthermore, obtaining as detailed a report of the items stolen is essential to recovery should the items be sold at pawnshops.

Summary

Burglary is a crime that has multiple facets. The criminal definition includes a theft or attempted theft or other felony crime while entering into a residence, building, business, vehicle, or coin-operated machine. Investigation into burglary starts with locating the point of entry into the victim's property whether that is a residence, business, or vehicle. Evidence collection and analysis at the point of entry is vital for developing modus operandi of the burglar as well as collection of identifying evidence to tie the perpetrator to the crime. Standard evidence collection and preservation protocol is used at a burglar scene. Investigation into burglary is usually conducted by a detective or criminal investigator but may also be conducted by a patrol officer depending on the size and availability of resources of the responding law enforcement agency.

The general public has turned to law enforcement for recommendations of crime prevention measures, which they can take to diminish the opportunity of a burglary. From Operation ID to Lock it or Lose it, law enforcement attempts to be proactive in their fight against burglary. However, for the general public, burglary still tends to be a reactionary crime, whereas it is after a person is victimized that they take protective measures to help decrease their risk for future burglaries.

Questions for Discussion

6.1 Discuss the different definitions of burglary.
6.2 What are the elements of the crime of burglary?
6.3 How is a burglary different from a robbery?
6.4 Why do burglary trends show a seasonal pattern?
6.5 Discuss the proactive measures that residents have taken to prevent burglaries.
6.6 Characterize the advances made in home protection alarm systems.
6.7 Discuss how the first responding officer(s) should approach the scene of a reported burglary.
6.8 Why is it important for officers to assume that a burglar is still in the residence when responding to the initial call?
6.9 What items may be collected as evidence of a burglary?
6.10 Discuss the different methods used to defeat a safe.

References

Austin, Texas Police Department (2014). Austin Police Department auto theft/burglary of vehicle report. Retrieved from: http://www.austintexas.gov/department/auto-theft. Accessed on January 11, 2014.
Clarke, R. (1997). *Situational Crime Prevention: Successful Case Studies*, 2nd edn. Guilderland, NY: Harrow & Heston.

Federal Bureau of Investigation (2012). Uniform crime report. Retrieved from: http://www.fbi.gov/about-us/cjis/ucr/crime-in-the-u.s/2012/crime-in-the-u.s.-2012/tables/7tabledatadecpdf. Accessed on January 11, 2014.

Federal Bureau of Investigation (2014). Tool mark examinations. *Handbook of Forensic Services.* J. Coleman (Ed.). Quantico, VA: An FBI Laboratory Publication. Retrieved from: http://www.fbi.gov/hq/lab/handbook/examtool.htm. Accessed on January 11, 2014.

Lauritsen, J. L. and White, N. (2014). Seasonal patterns in criminal victimization trends, Office of Justice Programs. NCJ 245959.

Trueman, J., Langston, L., and Planty, M. (2013). Criminal victimization, 2012, Office of Justice Programs. NCJ 243389.

Investigation of Health-Care Fraud

7

STEPHEN A. MORREALE

Contents

Chapter Objectives	100
Chapter Outline	100
Investigation of Health-Care Fraud	100
Scope and Breadth of the Issue	101
Birth of Medicare	103
Surveillance and Detection	103
Centers for Medicare and Medicaid Services	104
Fraud Prevention System	104
Pay-and-Chase Conundrum	104
Federal Law Enforcement Efforts	105
Nursing Homes and Assisted Living Facilities	105
Patient or Elder Harm	106
Who Might Call?	106
Types of Schemes	107
Using Analytics to Detect Schemes	108
Pharmaceutical Fraud	108
Drug-Related Crimes Can Constitute Fraud	108
Quality of Care	109
Transportation Fraud	109
How Are Violations Uncovered?	109
Hotline	109
Organized Criminal Groups	109
Provider Fraud	111
Exclusion/Sanction Action	111
Cybercrime Unit	111
SIUs for Insurance Carriers and Fraud Investigative Units	111
Medicaid Fraud Control Units	112
Genesis of a Case	112
Qui Tam	112
Employee Complaints	113
Using Labor Records as an Investigative Tool	113
Access to Information	113
Research Fraud	113
HIPPA Privacy Violations and Medical Identity Theft	114

    Enforcement Actions   114
    Useful Certifications for Investigators   114
Conclusion   115
Questions for Consideration   115
References   116

Chapter Objectives

After reading this chapter, you should be able to

1. Determine the breadth and depth of health-care fraud in America
2. Understand the types of schemes relating to health-care fraud
3. Understand the benefit of involving federal and state agencies in cases involving patient harm of potential fraud linked to state and federal health-care benefits
4. Understand the difference between fraud, waste, and abuse
5. Better understand the agencies involved with investigating health-care fraud

Chapter Outline

Birth of Medicare
Scope and Breadth of the Health-Care Fraud Issue
Schemes Found in Health-Care Fraud
The Pay and Chase Conundrum
Federal Law Enforcement Efforts
Nursing Homes and Assisted Living Facilities
Patient Care Issues
Useful Certifications for Investigators

Investigation of Health-Care Fraud

In your day-to-day investigative work, you may come upon issues related to health care (HC), quality of care, various forms of patient abuse, and patient harm or issues related to people bilking senior citizens to buy insurance and pay for medical advice or duping elderly citizens to pay for products or services that are never delivered or unnecessary.

It can be beneficial, as you are presented with facts and circumstances that lead you to believe that there is a potential for an HC-related nexus to the case. There are often enhanced penalties that can apply if there is a connection to state or federal health insurance or entitlement programs. Engaging the assistance of state and federal investigative agencies can assist you in seeking justice for victims with many acts against the interest of our senior citizens or those who are most vulnerable.

HC expenditures in the United States are rising from an estimated $2 trillion in 2006 to an estimated $5 trillion in 2020. It is estimated by the Federal Bureau of Investigation (FBI) and the NCAA that fraud occurs in approximately 3%–10% of the billing events.

According to Centers for Medicare and Medicaid Services (CMS) data, in 2012, hospital expenditures were $892 billion, physician and clinical services worth $566 billion, and prescription drug expenses estimated $261 billion. In the same year, Medicare expenses were $580 billion, with Medicaid expenses set at $416 billion. By the sheer numbers, there is much opportunity for fraud, waste, and abuse.

It is important to note that most HC providers are honest, well-intentioned professionals making an effort to provide quality HC. With the sheer volume of providers seeking the ability to provide services to Medicare patients, applications for provider numbers are generally approved before confirming the existence of a clinic or a facility. Since there is often a lag in time between issuance of a provider number and a check to confirm whether a provider of facility is actually in existence, unscrupulous providers often test the system by sending small billings and seeking payment. By law, most claims submitted must be paid within 30 days.

When they see that payment has been made without question, significant bills are submitted, generally paid, and after receipt of proceeds, the facility, clinic, or provider will close up shop and run with the money. Quite often, the fraudsters seek a nominee or straw owner, and set up shop nearby, to seek more billing opportunities.

Scope and Breadth of the Issue

HC fraud is a growing issue in the United States and exists at the state level, federal level, and private insurance carrier level. Each fraudulent offense requires a certain level of sophistication to successfully commit the fraud and to prevent or investigate the crime. HC is a highly regulated industry with regulators from the state and federal levels. Many entities involved in HC provision are subject to cyclical audits or surveys. These include site visits, review of procedures, health and safety checks, and review of documentation and equipment.

Only a commitment to understanding and recognizing evolving schemes will allow investigative units to ferret out such fraud arrangements and keep the schemers in check. In order to identify potential fraud, data analysis units have been established to develop methods to dig into the massive amounts of data looking for patterns, changes in practices and spikes, and fluctuations in billing. The focus needs to be widespread and covers all lines of the HC insurance business. Much like the efforts in drug suppression, where pressure needs to be focused on a variety of drugs, HC fraud focus should be spread over durable medical equipment (DME) agencies, drug benefits, home HC agencies, hospice, hospitals, outpatient clinical procedures, and skilled nursing facilities (SNF), among others. This can create a sentinel effect to hold down fraud attempts.

Credit card companies rely on their in-place systems and algorithms to pay attention to variations in customer habits. These same approaches are being modified to conduct data surveillance on billing at the Medicare and Medicaid programs and with HC insurance companies. CMS has been criticized for not having systems in place to identify vast swings in billings until it is too late and money has been paid to a provider or supplier.

The cost of HC is staggering in the United States. The FBI estimates that HC fraud costs American taxpayers $80 billion a year (FBI, 2014). Of this amount, $2.5 billion was recovered through False Claims Act cases in fiscal year (FY) 2010. Most of these cases were filed under qui tam provisions (NHCAA, 2014). According to the

National Health Care Anti-Fraud Association (NHCAA), the most common types of fraud committed by dishonest providers include the following:*

- "Billing for services that were never rendered, either by using genuine patient information—sometimes obtained through identity theft—to fabricate entire claims, or by padding claims with charges for procedures or services that did not take place."
- "Billing for more expensive services or procedures than were actually provided or performed, commonly known as 'upcoding'—i.e., falsely billing for a higher-priced treatment than was actually provided (which often requires an accompanying 'inflation' of the patient's diagnosis code to a more serious condition consistent with the false procedure code)."
- "Performing medically unnecessary services solely for the purpose of generating insurance payments—seen very often in nerve-conduction and other diagnostic-testing schemes."
- "Misrepresenting non-covered treatments as medically necessary covered treatments for purposes of obtaining insurance payments-widely seen in cosmetic-surgery schemes, in which non-covered cosmetic procedures such as 'nose jobs' are billed to patients' insurers as deviated-septum repairs."
- "Falsifying a patient's diagnosis to justify tests, surgeries, or other procedures that aren't medically necessary."
- "Unbundling–billing each step of a procedure as if it were a separate procedure."
- "Billing a patient more than the co-pay amount for services that were prepaid or paid in full by the benefit plan under the terms of a managed care contract."
- "Accepting kickbacks for patient referrals."
- "Waiving patient co-pays or deductibles for medical or dental care and overbilling the insurance carrier or benefit plan (insurers often set the policy with regard to the waiver of co-pays through its provider contracting process; while, under Medicare, routinely waiving co-pays is prohibited and may only be waived due to 'financial hardship')."
- Gang visits—There are services that are provided in a group setting within an organized living community. This may be at a social service center or group home, assisted living facility (ALF) or SNF. Previous schemes include several group therapies, such as physical or occupational therapy, speech therapy, behavioral therapy, or podiatry treatments (clipping vs. debridement). While these services are acceptable, some unscrupulous providers bill these services as if they were provided individually, in a private setting, rather than billing a lower per patient fee for group treatment.
- Theft of funds from senior citizens can be construed as HC fraud by certain states. When money is taken from a Medicaid or Medicare beneficiary, the government insurance programs need to take on a greater share of the costs. It is the position of many state from which the funding is being provided, that this constitutes Medicaid fraud.

The aforementioned bullets represent the potential that may be an indication of potential HC fraud.

* NHCAA, 2014, www.nhcaa.org/resources.

Birth of Medicare

The advent of social insurance in the United States occurred well before the Affordable Care Act, also known as "Obamacare." Attempts to introduce social medicine or coverage or medical insurance for senior citizens were met with serious opposition. Lobbying efforts by representatives for both the American Medical Association (AMA) and the American Hospital Association (AHA) (Marmor, 2000) held off the implementation until 1965. President Lyndon Johnson established the program as a part of his view toward the "Great Society."

There was a great deal of concern and distrust with suggestions that the federal government would control medical care. The AHA and AMA insisted that the claims processing should continue to be with the "Blues" or their spin-offs across the United States since they had experience with handling claims for HC services.

At the outset, the Social Security Administration, a component of the then— Department of Health, Education, and Welfare, had oversight of Medicare and Medicaid. In 1977, the Health Care Finance Administration (HCFA) was established for oversight of the programs, and later renamed Centers for Medicare and Medicaid Services.

In the early days, there were Program Integrity Units established within the Blues (Blue Cross and Blue Shield). These units began as "surveillance units" focused on review of billings and review of data to look for spikes in billing and identify outliers and patterns of billing that merit further review for potential identification of fraud, waste, or abuse (CMS, 2008).

Later, as potential contract fraud occurred, there were concerns that units working inside the payer, Blue Cross organizations might be coopted and asked not to report or cover up issues when information was sought by investigative agencies. In fact, in several cases, this was found, and contract fraud was difficult to prove. In these cases, former employees were identified and sought out for leads and statements.

Surveillance and Detection

Over time, the fraud and surveillance units were moved outside the parent units, those claims-processing organizations. The names of the units changed from Program Integrity Units to Program Safeguard Contractors (PSC) and Benefit Integrity Support Centers to Zone Program Integrity Contractors (ZPIC). Most recently, CMS announced that they will be awarding contracts for unified program integrity contractors. These units are intended to have oversight for fraud detection work along all lines of business, which includes home health agencies, hospitals, doctors, diagnostic testing centers, SNFs, DME suppliers, and the Medicare drug program.

As the contracts were awarded, the units were moved further and further away from the affiliated contracts or Medicare Administrative Contractors (MACs). This was done because of the experience of CMS and, previously, HCFA with contractor fraud.

As of 2014, there were seven zones for oversight of several states or territories, with several contracts awarded to organizations that have established investigative units. These units are made up of fraud investigators, data analysts, and statisticians. The current group of contractors includes Health Integrity, Cahaba, Advanced Med, and SafeGuard Services. Each of these contractors has access to claims data and maintains liaison with the MACs and with the Office of Inspector General (OIG) for Health and Human Services (HHS), the Medicaid Fraud Control Units (MFCU), the FBI, state Departments of Health, and the U.S. Attorney's Office.

Centers for Medicare and Medicaid Services

Most work for CMS of this nature is completed by contractors, ranging from claims processing to medical review to fraud identification and detection. These units are independent; each focused on a specific role and rarely appears to be in sync with one another.

There are contractors to review the quality of care and provide surveys of facilities; contractors to process claims and conduct site verifications of new providers; contractors to ferret out fraud, handle incoming complaints, and handle education of providers and beneficiaries; and contractors to deal with appeals of any recover and repayment attempts (CMS, 2015).

Fraud Prevention System

In 2010, CMS awarded a contract to establish a Fraud Prevention System to provide leads to the ZPIC with potential leads for potential fraudulent activity. This contractor is charged with running data analysis to identify anomalies in billing and payments. These leads are provided on a rolling basis to the PSC and focus on spike billing, medically unbelievable charges, and beneficiary sharing. Medically unbelievable charges focus on providing and billing for services that exceed 24 h in a day or billing for services of 350–360 days per year at a high volume.

Once the PSC receive the leads, they process them, cross-check them in their investigative database, and determine whether the provider is a known subject or there is an existing pending investigation. Otherwise, the leads can be sent to data analysts or investigators for a work-up to determine if the lead, the high billing pattern, can be substantiated and a case initiated.

Pay-and-Chase Conundrum

By law, most individual provider billing claims must be paid within 30 days. As a result of negotiations, it was agreed that the Blues would pay facilities prospectively. That means that hospitals could draw funds from a pool, based on the previous year's billings and earnings. If issues are found, inquiries are made for supporting documentation. If necessary, the claims can be denied, and thus, the payments can be suspended or reversed. Any money owed can be taken from future payments. The notion that money is paid before a claim is substantiated creates the "pay-and-chase" model. If the money to be recovered is from an existing facility or provider, it is relatively easy to recover the funds. Education is provided to help the facility bill and document properly.

In some places, clinics are established, which are no more than storefronts, allowing for quick billing. This makes it hard for investigators to recoup the funds that were attained under questionable or illegal manner, when the money has already been paid and moved:

- Data analysis and big data.
- Reliance on beneficiary and family vigilance.
- HC insurance fraud—Virtually all insurance carriers have established special investigative units (SIUs) to address attempts to defraud.

Federal Law Enforcement Efforts

During the Reagan Presidency, the Inspector General (IG) Act established IG offices in most of the federal agencies. In 1978, The U.S. Department of Health and Human Services (DHHS) established the IG's Office. At the time, HHS was the largest civilian federal agency and focused on providing services and entitlements including Medicare and Medicaid.

The Office of Investigations (OI) serves as the police and investigative agency for DHHS. A primary focus is HC fraud. The investigative arm is relatively small compared to other federal investigative agencies. There are less than 500 special agents, who operate in field offices throughout the United States and Puerto Rico. Some states have as few as two agents assigned, while some of the other more populated states have a greater number of agents assigned. Several of the more populous states such as New York, Florida, and California have several dozen special agents dedicated to HC fraud investigation.

In 1996, as a result of the Health Insurance Privacy and Portability Act (HIPPA), the FBI was granted concurrent jurisdiction to investigate HC fraud. Over the years, OI has gained and lost positions. According to OI HQ, there are approximately 500 special agents, and the FBI has assigned upward of 1000 agents dedicated to HC fraud.

More recently, HC fraud task forces and strike forces have been established in high-fraud areas, including Miami, New York, Los Angeles, Detroit, and others, called Health Care Fraud Prevention and Enforcement Action Team (HEAT). The Joint Department of Justice–Health and Human Services (DOJ–HHS) Medicare Fraud Strike Force is a multiagency team of federal, state, and local investigators designed to fight Medicare fraud. The Force uses Medicare data analysis techniques and an increased focus on community policing to combat fraud.

The U.S. Attorney's Offices have been directed to focus on HC fraud as a priority. As a result, most U.S. Attorney's Offices have created special units to prosecute both civil and criminal cases.

The Medicare Fraud Strike Force (HEAT) now includes nine U.S. cities: Baton Rouge, Louisiana; Brooklyn, New York; Chicago, Illinois; Dallas, Texas: Detroit, Michigan; Houston, Texas; Los Angeles, California; Miami, Florida; and Tampa Bay, Florida (HHS, 2014a,b).

According to the OIG, in 2012, federal antifraud efforts led to the recovery of $4.13 billion to the Medicare trust fund. This was accomplished through investigative efforts, prosecution, civil and criminal fine, and recoveries and recoupment.

Nursing Homes and Assisted Living Facilities

Many nursing home beds are paid for, at least in part, by Medicare or Medicaid. In limited circumstances, nursing homes will have beds that are only "private-pay" beds. In circumstances where the quality of care is questioned, patient harm or death occurs; consideration should be given to potential HC fraud.

With nursing home suspicious deaths, abuse, and thefts, these events take on an extralayer for investigations since it is one of the most heavily regulated HC sectors by both the state and federal governments.

These crimes are often seen as economic crimes or white-collar crimes. More recently, units have been created in prosecutor's offices focusing on HC fraud or corruption units. Many of the clinical operators in HC fraud schemes are licensed at the state and federal levels. These licensing agencies can be contacted and notified of the suspected activity on the licensed individual or entity.

Patient or Elder Harm

In our society, those who are senior citizens are seen as a vulnerable population. Whether they are living on their own or in a SNF, ALF, or senior housing, there are those who will prey on this population or take advantage of their trust.

Patient harm can include injuries caused from poorly performed or unnecessary surgical procedures, assaults on nursing home patients, or unnecessary services and tests, bruising, and falls resulting from poor care or oversight.

Many law enforcement agencies have established senior citizen liaison officers. These officers provide training and services for this special population. Many of them need home health assistance. Some of the staff for home health agencies earn the trust of their patients. There are situations where thefts of money, jewelry, and prescription drugs have occurred. Again, if any funds to pay for services come from state or federal sources, there is the potential to involve state or federal investigative, regulatory, and oversight agencies to assist in the investigation. This can open up opportunities for sanctions beyond criminal charges.

Who Might Call?

As in many crimes, it is often the local police that are alerted to potential fraud at the outset. HC fraud can extend from patient care, theft of property from patients, to observed discrepancies behind the scenes. As a local or state officer, you may find difficulty in obtaining certain records without a subpoena or warrant. Many records are protected by HIPAA laws and regulations, with even greater protection afforded to psychiatric records.

State and federal investigators are granted with the primary authority to investigate HC fraud. These agencies have authority to seek records, sometimes by letter and other times using a federal administrative warrant, which can be signed by the special agent in charge of the IG's Office. This may serve as an opportunity to collaborate and gain access to records that may be needed in your investigation.

Prior to serving in federal law enforcement, as a young officer, I was called to a complaint of an unusual number of controlled prescription drugs being received by an animal research office. It is often the local police that will be the initial responders. In this case, the call had come from a suspicious employee, concerned with the number of boxes of controlled substances being received by a medical researcher. A good number of boxes were found to have a high number of pills that were popular on the drug scene.

The researcher had a DEA prescribing number. As the investigation ensued, interviews with staff and the researcher uncovered that the drugs were not used for the boars that were being used for experiments. Instead, it was found that the doctor had been using the drugs for personal use and to entice woman for his pleasure.

After developing the facts, and recognizing that the actions of the researcher violated both state and federal statutes, it was decided that the case would better fall in the federal arena, since the prescribing was done using a DEA number. DEA was notified and handled the case through the U.S. Attorney's Office, with charges filed in U.S. District Court. In this matter, no local testimony was required, since the researcher plead guilty.

There are specific federal and state laws that may apply specifically to and elder fraud and abuse. These can be very helpful to know when considering potential criminal of civil actions in a case.

Calls for service may start with medical calls. In a Connecticut case, a nursing home patient was rushed to an emergency room suffering from dehydration and open, untended wounds. The triage nurse felt that the man seemed like he had "been in a dumpster" not a HC facility. Because of perceived mistreatment and poor patient care, the hospital staff called the local police, who in turn called for assistance from both the OIG and state MFCU since it was found that at least some portion of the patient expenses were borne by taxpayer funds. Again, it is often local police that will be the initial responders.

Types of Schemes

A number of agencies have focus on HC fraud and drug diversion crimes. For the U.S. Government, the primary responsibility for fraud against the Medicare and Medicaid programs rests with the OI for the OIG, U.S. DHHS. This group of approximately 500 special agents spread across the United States and Puerto Rico serve as the policing arm for HHS, Medicare program.

In the 1990s, the FBI was granted concurrent jurisdiction for HC fraud. The FBI created investigative units focusing on HC fraud, generally supervised under the public corruption and white-collar investigative squads.

Federal legislation was passed to provide funds to investigate and prosecute HC fraud cases at both the civil and criminal levels.

Due to the recent payment for drugs, DEA has joined several of the task forces. Much of the fraud detected has been aimed at federal Medicare programs and the federal/state funded Medicaid program. These two programs derive funding from HHS and CMS. State pay a portion of the cost for Medicaid, as a result, scheme detected and charged for Medicaid fraud can be prosecuted at either the federal or state levels.

There are issues of patient harm and the quality of care when poorly performed or unnecessary surgical procedures.

In Vermont, an elderly patient was being seen to handle cataracts. The patient was being seen for a procedure by an ophthalmologist. On one day, the patient underwent a surgical procedure on one eye. The patient was scheduled for an additional procedure for the other eye.

On the day of the scheduled surgery, the doctor was sick and his office canceled the appointment. A family member decided to take their mother to another ophthalmologist for a second opinion. During an examination, it was determined that the patient did not have cataracts and did not have any recent surgery on her eye.

This led to a complaint with the local police who contacted the OIG to conduct a joint investigation. It was found that the doctor routinely was taken advantage of elderly patients, by diagnosing cataracts and recommending a surgical procedure for relief. It was found that dozens of Medicare beneficiaries had been duped, and Medicare was charged and paid for unnecessary services.

Using Analytics to Detect Schemes

Big data drives the billing and payment for many services provided through Medicare, Medicaid, and other federal insurance programs. Algorithms can help PCSs.

In most states, there is interest from the MFCU, assigned to the Attorney General's Office. If there is any portion of payment from either Medicare or Medicaid, it can be useful to contact the offices to seek their advice or participation in an investigation.

There are specific federal and state laws that may apply specific to the state and federal and elder fraud and abuse.

Remember, in HC facilities, many of the employees are licensed. As a result, they are held to a higher standard and their behavior can lead to licensure review. The certified nursing assistant (CNA), nursing staff (RN), and physicians (MD) are generally licensed by the state. Each state has a licensing board. These boards accept complaints and will work with police agencies in situations where conduct or behavior is questionable or illegal. In addition to legal actions through the courts, there is the possibility for the suspension or revocation of the practitioner's license.

Pharmaceutical Fraud

Over the years, Medicare and Medicaid have modified policies to allow for payment of certain drugs. In certain circumstances, there are schemers that will work in hospice or have a relative in a hospice with access to painkilling drugs including OxyContin. There are others who are able to acquire a Medicare number and create false scripts. Some present themselves at a pain clinic, pay in cash for a prescription and then with a false identity, submit the scripts for themselves for OxyContin and then go to a pharmacy to pick up the filled prescription, using a Medicare number. Some obtain prescriptions for a 30-day vial of 900 OxyContin pills. Ironically, the copay for drugs is $0.50 or a dollar for those who are Medicaid patients.

It's not unusual for police to receive a phone call from a suspicious pharmacist. This is often where the police will be the first to learn of this particular attempt or scheme. The federal government gets involved in this because they are paying a great portion of the cost of these drugs; therefore, when one fraud is involved, it can become a federal violation. This of course is a state law violation and therefore can be prosecuted in either jurisdiction.

Drug-Related Crimes Can Constitute Fraud

Several years ago, federal government decided to provide prescription drug benefits. At the state level, Medicaid provides terrace assistance for prescription drugs. In some cases, detectives may run into are schemes where drug seekers look to coopt identification of beneficiaries or court a beneficiary themselves. In most states, the copay can sometimes be as cheap as $0.50 per prescription. The main schemes to obtain large quantity prescriptions for OxyContin drew the attention of state investigators as well as federal investigators. The OIG and DEA began to focus on false scripts and scripts that were written for people who were seeking upward of 900 OxyContin per month based on serious pain.

Quality of Care

CMS (Medicare and Medicaid) have concerns over the quality of care for patients paid for by state and federal insurance. There has been a push to identify situations where Medicare recipients are not properly treated, are subjected to abuse, poor quality of care, unnecessary diagnostic tests, where patient harm occurs. When this is found, you might consider contacting the state MFCU or the OIG.

Transportation Fraud

In many situations, patients need to receive ambulance services. However, there have been many unscrupulous ambulance services that have billed Medicare illegally. In a recent case, American Medical Response was charged and entered into a settlement agreement for $20 million with the Department U.S. Attorney's Office in Boston.

In other instances, ambulance companies have "upcoded" in order to bill more money for services. In a case in northern Maine, during an ice storm, ambulance companies were asked to transport ambulatory (walking) senior patients from one place to a safe, heated facility. Basic life support and advanced life support (ALS) vehicles were used. If the company had billed for chair car service, there would be no issue. Instead, they billed Medicare and Medicaid for ALS services, easily a more than $350 per person overcharge or "upcode."

How Are Violations Uncovered?

Hotline

A hotline was created to accept calls for potential waste, fraud, or abuse of departmental funds. The main function of the HHS-IG is to protect the Medicare trust fund. This hotline is well advertised on every explanation of benefits, which is mailed out after any service that has been billed for.

When a service does not look familiar, beneficiaries are encouraged to call the Medicare hotline. Medicaid has a similar arrangement. This is one way that potential fraud, waste, or abuse is brought to the attention of the insurance provider.

Organized Criminal Groups

As with many crimes, where there is substantial opportunity for the fraudulent attainment of money, certain groups organize to benefit from any potential moneymaking enterprise. It is not unusual in urban areas for organized criminal groups to set up and take advantage of people and opportunity.

In cities as widespread as New York, Miami, Los Angeles, San Juan, and Detroit, certain groups exploited weaknesses in the system. For example, in Miami, a group of

South American and Cuban citizens worked with the social center in an urban area. These groups identified social service providers who had access to newly arrived immigrants. They offered "finder's fees."

In the Brighton Beach section of New York City, Russian-organized crime has found that HC fraud can be lucrative. Schemes included setting up medical clinics, with "kickback rooms" to pay patients for the privilege of submitting multiple claims for service in their names.

In Miami, storefront clinics were created to give the appearance of an infusion therapy clinic. Many of these were set up in neighborhoods with a high immigrant population. Unscrupulous nonmedical clinic operators sought the assistance of employees at senior citizen centers and drop-in neighborhood social clubs to help identify potential individuals that were willing to sign for Medicare or Medicaid insurance. Once this was done, individuals were contacted and agreements were made for these new "patients" to be picked up by then, provided breakfast and taken to storefront clinics. Once at these storefront clinics, patients waited several hours. This gave the appearance of an active clinic providing medical services. At times, they would be brought into a room and provided with infusions of vitamins, rather than medications. Documentation for these infusions would be created to show that the "patients" had serious disease up to and including HIV. The illusion was that these patients required expensive infusions picking up to 3–4 h per session, with the ability of charging government health insurance providers up to $8,000–$10,000 per session.

These same patients would be transported in the afternoon for lunch and brought to another storefront clinic. For another 4 h, they would wait in the waiting or treatment rooms, and then be brought home being paid between $200 and $250 per session in cash. These patients were told not to talk to any authorities or they would lose their opportunity to earn money and get medical treatment. Because so many of these were non-English-speaking recent immigrants, many with distrust for police officials from their native country, it was rare that investigators could get anyone to talk.

This scheme in Florida was isolated to Dade and Broward County. It is estimated that nearly $1 billion was bilked by the storefront clinic operators.

In another South Florida case, a DME supplier billed Medicare for $150 million for prosthesis over a 6-month period. Again, in South Florida counties of Broward and Dade, this DME supplier billed and was paid $150 million for prosthetic legs. When investigators received complaints from patients about billings for artificial legs, they found that there were thousands of artificial legs billed for buying unscrupulous DME supplier. This would have meant that tens of thousands of patients in only two counties had lost their legs in accidents or by surgical means.

When the case came forward, the judge not only commented that he was displeased with the supplier but also voiced displeasure with the government for not having recognized this potential fraud patterns much earlier than when the billings had approached $150 million.

It is a shame that some of the techniques used to anticipate and detect fraud with credit card companies are not adopted by Medicare and Medicaid. When I traveled to Russia on a detail for DEA, I used my American Express to make a few purchases for a watch and jewelry. Immediately after the purchases, my wife was called at my home by a fraud staffer from American Express. They inquired as to whether there was any reason for a charge to be added to my AmEx in Russia. My wife was able to verify that I was traveling and the alert was canceled.

Unfortunately, those same alerts do no help to stem the tide of HC fraud. While "big data" is reviewed by fraud contractors for Medicare, it takes time to determine spikes in billing. The criticism is that these spikes are not found in the early stages, and often, significant sums have been paid to the unscrupulous operators.

In cases throughout the United States, the HC industry has produced many organized crime factions to abuse the system for illegal profit. In recent cases, Russian-organized crime syndicates were found to control elements of billing companies, clinics and social service agencies.

Provider Fraud

While the great majority of medical providers are responsible, caring practitioners, there are some that take advantage and violate the faith and trust of their profession. Many cases have been investigated that have caused doctors, dentists, podiatrists, nurse practitioners, and physical therapists to be convicted and excluded from future medical practice.

Exclusion/Sanction Action

When someone is found in violation of the law surrounding their involvement in HC, the department (U.S. DHHS) has the authority to bar the entity or individuals from participating in HC or related provision of services, for a period of time, up to life. As with all government actions, an individual or entity has the right to appeal the decision. This is a powerful tool to keep thieves from committing more crime.

Cybercrime Unit

With the proliferation of the Internet, e-mail, and hacking/virus schemes, OI launched a cybercrime unit in 2000. Agents and computer recovery specialists were trained to assist at search warrant sites and create mirror images of hard drives and other electronic storage devises, so the information could be seized and analyzed for potential evidence. Of course, since then, there has been a proliferation of mobile devices with send and storage capabilities that must be considered when collecting evidence. With the introduction of "cloud computing," many vendors (service providers) are needed to help gain access to all records for consideration in an investigation.

Warrants must include language seeking any/all devices used in the conduct of business to create, store, and access medial or billing records. The imaging of storage devices allows the law enforcement agency to obtain information, without disrupting the practices ability to continue to provide medical care to patients in clinics, physician's offices or hospitals and SNF.

SIUs for Insurance Carriers and Fraud Investigative Units

Many HC insurance organizations have established SIUs to ferret out fraud and abuse schemes against the carriers. This might focus on providers, suppliers, beneficiaries or employees. Many of the investigators working in SIUs have a background in accounting, auditing, while some are retired detectives, federal investigators. Many obtain the certified fraud examiner (CFE) designation by preparing and taking the test. See the succeeding text for more details.

Medicaid Fraud Control Units

MFCU are state law enforcement agencies located in 49 states. MFCUs are mandated by federal law to investigate and prosecute Medicaid fraud and patient abuse. Most are overseen by the State Attorney General's Office, some fall under the State Police and/or the State Department of Public Safety.

Only North Dakota is without an MFCU. This is allowed based on a waiver granted after the state's chief law enforcement officer certifies that there is not a significant volume of fraud in that state. These units are provided with a grant from U.S. DHHS for 75% of the cost, with each state responsible to pay the remaining 25%. The MFCUs investigate complaints of patient harm, theft against patients paid, at least in part by Medicaid.

Genesis of a Case

There are several ways that investigations are initiated. CMS has set up a hotline to allow for beneficiaries or other concerned individuals to lodge complaints about quality of care, over billing, services not rendered or other Medicare-related issues. These calls are logged and researched and sent forward to contractors or to local OIG/investigations offices for review and consideration.

Qui Tam

Qui Tams are a growing source of investigative referrals. Anyone can file a qui tam through a court, but generally, a relator or "whistle-blower seeks the assistance of a lawyer to represent their interests." Black's Law Dictionary defines a qui tam action as "an action brought by an informer, under a statute, which establishes a penalty for the commission or omission of a certain act," and provides that if any money is recovered in a civil action, part of the penalty may go to any person who will bring such action and the remainder to the state or some other institution.

Qui tam is a provision of the Federal Civil False Claims Act that allows private citizens to file a lawsuit in the name of the U.S. government charging fraud by government contractors and others who receive or use government funds and share in any money recovered.

Some of the improvements included the trebling of damages, expanding the role of the qui tam relator, guaranteeing the relator a set percentage of the money that the government recovers, and the whistle-blower protection clause (Morreale, 2005a).

By trebling (tripling) the damages of the amount of fraud discovered, the role of the qui tam relator was expanded by the 1986 amendment because, before, the relator did not have the right to play a role once the government intervened in the case. Although the government has the primary role if they intervene in the case, the relator "shall have the right to continue as a party to the action." This clause gives you and your attorney the right to watch the justice department's handling of the case before settlement and allows you to go to the judge if you believe that the case is not being handled well or not in your best interests.

Before the 1986 amendment, the court could arbitrarily set the percentage of award for the qui tam relator. The 1986 amendment guaranteed a minimum of 15% of the recovery and a maximum of 30%.

The whistle-blower protection clause is one of the strongest protection clauses in federal law. It protects not only the relator but also anyone who investigates, initiates, testifies in furtherance of, or assists in a case. In Section 3730(h), whistle-blowers that have proven harassment are entitled to "all necessary relief necessary to make the employee whole" including "reinstatement with the same seniority status… two times the amount of back pay, interest on any back pay, and compensation for any special damages." This clause not only helps the relator keep their job if they are still employed while the case is proceeding but also makes a company think twice about harassing any employees who cooperate with exposing the fraud. Unfortunately, this clause does not help subcontractors and independent contractors who want to cooperate with the investigation (Morreale, 2005a, p. 6).

Employee Complaints

Another source of referrals is from disgruntled, dissatisfied, or uncomfortable employees. Generally, these complaints will come directly to the HHS-IG's OI. At times, the employee will contact the PSC. In these instances, the contractor must immediately notify a manager of the regional office for HHS/investigations. Generally, the employee will be contacted to better understand the complaint in depth.

Using Labor Records as an Investigative Tool

One way that investigators can attempt to locate potential witnesses is to look to state labor records. It is not uncommon for OIG and other HC fraud investigators to seek year-to-year listings of employees and compare to identify employees who are no longer at a facility. Locating former employees can offer opportunities to approach and interview them. In many cases, there are employees you may encounter that have left on bad terms and harbor some animosity and offer valuable information about the former employer. As in finding a jilted lover to try to gain information on a former boyfriend or girlfriend, identifying former employees may provide significant detail and provide some inside information on the practices in the organization.

Access to Information

Information is freely available by accessing the Internet. There are a number of different reports available for download by visiting www.oig.hhs.gov. There is substantial information relating to investigative and administrative action taken in the semiannual report to Congress as well as federal regulation notices, hearings testimony, reports, and publications.

Research Fraud

According to the Health Care Fraud and Abuse Control (HCFAC) Program Annual Report issued by U.S. DHHS (2013), monetary results during FY 2012, the federal government won or negotiated over $3.0 billion in HC fraud judgments and settlements, and it attained additional administrative impositions in HC fraud cases and proceedings. As a result of these efforts, as well as those of preceding years, in FY 2012, approximately $4.2 billion was deposited with the Department of the Treasury and the CMS, transferred to other Federal agencies administering HC programs, or paid to private persons during the FY. Of this $4.2 billion, the Medicare trust funds received transfers of approximately $2.4 billion during this period, and over $835.7 million in Federal Medicaid money was similarly transferred separately to the treasury as a result of these efforts. The HCFAC account has returned over $23.0 billion to the Medicare trust funds since the inception of the program in 1997.

HIPPA Privacy Violations and Medical Identity Theft

The HIPAA was passed by Congress in 1996 to address the concerns for privacy and security of individually identifiable health information and HC records. In recent years, many records have been preserved in electronic form, including doctor notes, test results, and diagnostic testing images.

As so many law enforcement agencies have found, there are countless complaints of breach of privacy, computer records, fraudulent charges and theft of identity, these same schemes have reached HC matters. There are a series of regulations detailing steps that providers must take to insure network protection and privacy of all electronic records. Breaches must be reported to authorities immediately.

There are issues surrounding attempts for "bad guys" to obtain access to medical identify numbers. Obtaining such information gives others the potential to bill, obtain drugs, medical equipment, and services illegally.

In a Connecticut hospital, a clerk in the billing office began to download documents, which had patient data, including DOB, insurance identification numbers, and other HC data. The clerk gather as much of the information in both printed and electronic form, then resigned. They sold the information to unscrupulous providers who attempted to use the information to generate billing lines for submission to insurers.

Enforcement Actions

In FY 2012, the DOJ opened 1131 new criminal HC fraud investigations involving 2148 potential defendants. Federal prosecutors had 2032 HC fraud criminal investigations pending, involving 3410 potential defendants, and filed criminal charges in 452 cases involving 892 defendants. A total of 826 defendants were convicted of HC fraud–related crimes during the year. Also in FY 2012, DOJ opened 885 new civil HC fraud investigations and had 1023 civil HC fraud matters pending at the end of the FY. In FY 2012, FBI HC fraud investigations resulted in the operational disruption of 329 criminal fraud organizations and the dismantlement of the criminal hierarchy of more than 83 criminal enterprises engaged in HC fraud.

The amount reported as won or negotiated only reflects federal recoveries and therefore does not reflect state Medicaid monies recovered as part of any global, federal–state settlements.

In FY 2012, HHS' OIG excluded 3131 individuals and entities. Among these were exclusions based on criminal convictions for crimes related to Medicare and Medicaid (912) or to other HC programs (287), for patient abuse or neglect (212), and as a result of licensure revocations (1463). In addition, HHS' OIG imposed civil monetary penalties against, among others, providers and suppliers who knowingly submitted false claims to the federal government. HHS' OIG also issued numerous audits and evaluations with recommendations that, when implemented, would correct program vulnerabilities and save program funds (Health Care Fraud and Abuse Control Program Annual Report, 2013).

Useful Certifications for Investigators

There are two organizations for those interested in gaining more information and education on HC fraud schemes and investigative approaches. The Association of Certified Fraud Examiners (ACFE) and NHCAA offer information and certifications.

The ACFE offers the CFE. This certification takes a broad approach to fraud at many levels, not just HC fraud. This credential draws many HC fraud investigators. The CFE is a well-respected, well-received credential. Many people who achieve this designation find work in the insurance industry, banking, private investigation, and special investigation units.

The NHCAA offers the accredited health-care fraud investigator certification. Many HC fraud investigators seek this credential. There are continuing education requirements to maintain the credentials.

These credentials can be of great help to retiring detectives looking for investigative opportunities in the private sector. Many contract companies and insurance companies have special investigative units, staffed with HC investigators and fraud investigators. These units focus on fraud, waste, and abuse against the company.

Conclusion

This chapter was intended to provide an overview of the status of HC fraud in the United States. In countless police encounters, there may be a nexus to HC fraud. Many complaints come from family members, seniors that feel they have been taken advantage of, or staff members of facilities where patient harm or theft has occurred. These are cases that almost always are reported to local police. The work of most detectives is multifaceted. It is rare that there are specializations in units focused on HC. These cases often come to the attention of police agencies during other investigations.

It is valuable to understand the existence of potential HC fraud charges, as a support for investigating certain crimes. Detectives can leverage several federal or state enforcement agencies to help investigate and seek additional charges in matters with a nexus to potential patient harm or HC fraud. Complaints that are investigated might be an assault, stolen items, death, missing drugs, and medical identity theft. Some of these cases may have the added layer of HC fraud. If so, you should consider reaching out to an MFCU, the HHS' OIG/OI, the FBI Health Care Squad, or the State Boards of Health Care Registration or Licensing.

With the growing graying of America, police investigators should be cognizant of the rise in fraud schemes aimed at an aging population and those who are trusting and yet vulnerable to being duped by unscrupulous service, medical equipment, and HC providers.

Questions for Consideration

7.1 Do existing state laws for fraud and theft sufficiently address the issue of HC fraud?

7.2 With the rise in identity theft, should you consider medical identity theft in some circumstances?

7.3 Why would a detective seek assistance from a federal or state agency focused on HC fraud?

7.4 What is meant by the pay-and-chase conundrum?

7.5 What federal agency might a detective consider reaching out to for guidance and assistance in a suspected HC fraud case?

References

Association of Certified Fraud Investigators (ACFE). (2015). Accessed at http://www.acfe.org.

CMS. (September 2008). Best Practices for Medicaid Program Integrity Units Interactions with Medicaid Fraud Control Units, Centers for Medicare and Medicaid Services, Medicaid Integrity Group.

Centers for Medicare and Medicaid. History of Medicare. http://www.cms.gov/About-CMS/Agency-Information/History/index.html. Accessed February 2, 2015.

Federal Bureau of Investigations (FBI), Healthcare Fraud. (2014). http://www.fbi.gov/about-us/investigate/white_collar/health-care-fraud. Accessed February 2, 2015.

HHS (2014a). Work plan. http://oig.hhs.gov/reports-and-publications/archives/workplan/2014/Work-Plan-2014.pdf.

HHS (2014b). Semi-annual report. https://oig.hhs.gov/reports-and-publications/archives/semiannual/2014/SAR-S14-Web-Final.pdf.

Marmor, T. R. (2000). *The Politics of Medicare: Second Edition (Social Institutions and Social Change)*, Aldine Transaction.

Morreale, S. A. (September/October 2005a). Fraud in the American health care system takes on many forms: An insider's view of how violations are uncovered and what happens as a result. *Journal of Health Care Compliance*, 7 (5), 13–22. Aspen Publications.

Morreale, S. A. (September/October 2005b). While most health care professionals offer caring, ethical service, some are much less scrupulous. *Journal of Health Care Compliance*, 7 (5), Aspen Publications.

National health Care Anti-Fraud Association (NHCAA). http://www.nhcaa.org. Accessed September 15, 2014.

U.S. Department of Health and Human Services. (2013). Health Care Fraud and Abuse Control (HCFAC) program annual report.

White-Collar and Financial Fraud Investigations

FRANK DIMARINO

Contents

Chapter Objectives 117
Chapter Outline 118
Definition of White-Collar Crime 118
Examples of White-Collar Crime 119
    Embezzlement 119
    Fraud 120
    Other Types of White-Collar Cases 122
Initiatives in Investigating White-Collar Crime 124
    FBI Financial Intelligence Center 124
    U.S. Department of the Treasury Financial Crime Enforcement Network 124
        Commercial Databases 127
        Law Enforcement and Regulatory Databases 127
    General Investigative Strategies 127
    Collection of Information through Local Sources That Aid Investigations 128
Trends in White-Collar Crime and Future Investigative Techniques 129
Questions in Review 131
References 131

Chapter Objectives

After reading this chapter, you should be able to do the following:

1. Provide a definition of white-collar crime.
2. Explain how white-collar crime differs from other types of crime.
3. Explain what a "Ponzi" scheme is and how to investigate such a case.
4. Explain the crime of embezzlement and how to investigate embezzlements.
5. Explain how banks are used to commit fraudulent schemes and the investigative tools that can be used to analyze financial transactions.
6. Discuss the five types of white-collar crimes by providing definitions and methods of investigation.
7. Summarize the role of financial centers and enforcement networks that provide support to law enforcement.
8. List items of evidence that should be considered in white-collar cases and how such items can be collected.
9. Identify future trends in white-collar crime and how investigators can anticipate where future crimes may be committed.

Chapter Outline

Definition of White-Collar Crime
Examples of White-Collar Crime
Embezzlement
Fraud
Other Types of White-Collar Cases
Initiatives in Investigating White-Collar Crime
FBI Financial Intelligence Center
U.S. Department of Treasury Financial Crime Enforcement Network
General Investigative Strategies
Collection of Information through Local Sources That Aid Investigations
Trends in White-Collar Crime and Future Investigative Techniques

Definition of White-Collar Crime

White-collar crime is, at its core, lying, cheating, and stealing. In 1939, sociologist Edwin H. Sutherland first introduced the term "white-collar crime" in an address to the American Sociological Society as an attempt to create a classification of offenders. He defined "white-collar crime" as "a crime committed by a person of respectability and high social status in the course of his occupation."[1] Sutherland's focus was on assessing the qualities of the offender, rather than the characteristics of particular crimes.

Sutherland, while exploring new territory in characterizing criminals, claimed that there is a "significant category of crimes that are committed by persons of wealth, respectability," and "social status."[2] Sutherland would be surprised as to how correct this criminal classification is true in recent decades when we consider the felony convictions of Martha Stewart, Kenneth Lay, Jeffrey Skilling, Andrew Fastow, Bernard Ebbers, Richard Scrushy, and Bernard Madoff—all corporate executives who were already millionaires before they committed their crimes. Clearly, financial crimes committed by such high-status offenders who serve as corporate leaders in a position of trust are more troubling than those committed by low-status persons.[3]

Bernard Madoff, a financial advisor to hundreds of victims, for example, pleaded guilty to 11 federal crimes after bilking investors out of billions of dollars from his elaborate Ponzi scheme. As we will learn in more detail,

> a Ponzi scheme is a fraudulent business enterprise that attracts investors with the promise of high returns. Unbeknownst to investors, there is no underlying wealth-generating mechanism or business plan. Instead, money brought into the scheme by new investors gets redistributed as "dividends" to early investors.

The Federal Bureau of Investigation (FBI) has interstate jurisdiction to investigate white-collar crimes and often will work in partnership with state and local investigators. Internet crime reports can originate with private citizens. The FBI defines white-collar crime as

> those illegal acts which are characterized by deceit, concealment, or violation of trust and which are not dependent upon the application or threat of physical force or violence. Individuals and organizations commit these acts to obtain money, property, or services; to avoid the payment or loss of money or services; or to secure personal or business advantage.[4]

The U.S. Department of Justice, Bureau of Justice Statistics, defines white-collar crime more broadly as

> nonviolent crime for financial gain committed by means of deception by persons whose occupational status is entrepreneurial, professional or semi-professional and utilizing their special occupational skills and opportunities; also, nonviolent crimes for financial gain utilizing deception and committed by anyone having special technical and professional knowledge of business and government, irrespective of the person's occupation.[5]

A cornerstone to any definition of white-collar crime is deception and a lack of physical force. As advances in technology occurs and the criminal mind becomes more devious, white-collar crime has an ever-broadening scope. White-collar crime can be committed by a broad range of offenders from managerial corporate executives engaged in insider trading to tech savvy common individuals running a phishing scheme on the Internet.[6]

White-collar crime, therefore, can be considered as illegal or unethical acts that violate fiduciary obligations or public trust for the purpose of advancing personal or organizational gain. We will next turn our attention to a list of white-collar crimes with examples of each.

Examples of White-Collar Crime

The broad definition of white-collar crime allows or recognizes both traditional forms of economic crime (e.g., embezzlement, bank fraud, money laundering, and insurance fraud) and high-tech crimes (Internet fraud, intellectual property theft, and "drive-by" ransomware scams).

The following is a partial list of white-collar crimes, an explanation of the crime, and a list of investigative techniques to launch an investigation.

Embezzlement

Embezzlement is the taking, withholding, using, secreting, or conversion of money or property for the defendant's own purposes or gain that had been entrusted to the defendant's care by virtue of the defendant's employment or occupation.[7] This definition presupposes that the embezzled property must have been in the lawful possession of the defendant at the time of its appropriation, and the defendant has the knowledge that the appropriation is contrary to the wishes of the true owner of the property.[8]

White-collar defendants, convicted of embezzlement of funds with the amounts in parentheses, have held such positions as city comptroller ($53 million),[9] transit agency finance director ($370,000),[10] administrative assistant for nonprofit corporation ($5.1 million),[11] head bank teller ($264,000),[12] corporate accounts payable clerk and assistant controller ($900,000),[13] corporate electronic invoicing specialist ($940,000),[14] university vice president and chief information officer ($650,000),[15] golf club bookkeeper ($60,000),[16] and chief executive officer of commodity futures business ($215,000,000).

In many cases, the defendant had a special relationship of trust or a fiduciary relationship to care for the funds over which he or she had control. Also, when the defendant has held a position in government or similar organization, the defendant's sentence is enhanced for his or her violation of public trust.

Intent must be proven for a conviction. In embezzlement investigations, evidence needs to be gathered to demonstrate that the defendant had the intent to deprive another of his or her property.[17] The defendant must have the knowledge that he or she was "interfering with the property of another" to satisfy the intent requirement.[18] Most often, proof of criminal intent must be shown through circumstantial evidence that shows how the defendant came into possession of the funds, what falsehoods the defendant employed to conceal the conversion of funds, and how the defendant spent or disposed of the funds.[19]

Warning signs that embezzlement is occurring include (1) an employee who suddenly has an improved standard of living with no extra income to explain it, (2) sudden or protracted decrease in company's profits or holdings, (3) disorganization of financial records, (4) unexplained changes in revenue or expenses or increased write-offs, and (5) extremely loyal employees who never take vacations so that only they manage the books with sufficient auditing practices in place.

Detectives and investigators need to be aware of potential defenses that may be asserted by a defendant in an embezzlement case. The defendant may try to show the legal nature of his or her possession or action. For instance, the defendant may try to show that he or she intended to return the property or made total repayment of the amount taken. If the defendant makes timely restitution, such action may negate a criminal intent depending upon the timing of the restitution and the surrounding circumstances. On the other hand, evidence that the defendant did not personally benefit from conversion of the property will not generally excuse unlawful possession.

Some defendants may assert that as a result of corporate customs and practices, the organization acquiesced in the defendant's practices or agreed to the defendant's usage of the funds. Such a defense rarely prevails provided that fraudulent intent can be shown through concealment, deception, and personal gain. If a defendant's actions precluded the organization from knowing the true, complete material facts, then no organization could validly acquiesce into the defendant's conversion of funds.

Other defenses that may be raised by defendants include entrapment, raising the question of the defendant's predisposition to commit the crime; diminished mental capacity, raising the question of the defendant's mental capacity to form criminal intent; or the statute of limitations, raising the question of statutory inapplicability as to when the crime was committed.

Fraud

Banks and other financial institutions are often the victims of crimes. Those who harbor criminal intent are readily tempted to unlawfully gain access to accounts with high-dollar amounts in bank accounts. They may also seek to take advantage of the banking process that must follow regulations concerning transfers of money. Crimes that impact bank accounts and similar assets are known as financial institution fraud crimes.

Financial institution fraud crimes are not typically "whodunit" crimes where identity of the perpetrator is the major focus of the investigation. In bank robberies, for example, the focus on the investigation is primarily the identity of the perpetrator. The act of how the robbery occurred is comparatively straightforward. Similar criminal offenses involving violence, such as murder and assault, and arson involve the investigation of who exactly was the perpetrator.

For the most part, the investigation of financial institution crimes focuses more on how the crime was committed and the circumstances that demonstrate criminal intent. Often, the identity of the perpetrator is known.

The crux of the financial investigation typically involves determining the nature of the crime, the means used to commit the crime, the methods used to obtain illegal access to funds, and the type of concealment used to cover up the crime. Proof of facts that demonstrate the criminal intent to defraud is also necessary.

Financial investigations involve the collection and analysis of documents, account statements, and monetary transactions. Importantly, these investigations also involve "following the money" by tracing where the money went once it was unlawfully received. Many times, fraudsters will use financial institutions, such as banks, to deposit their ill-gotten gains into accounts. They may also engage in other banking transactions where they will wire funds, transfer funds, or shelter funds.

Bank fraud involves a scheme to defraud a financial institution or to get money or property owned or controlled by a financial institution by using false pretenses, representations, or promises. Depending upon the jurisdiction, a defendant can be found guilty of bank fraud if the government can prove beyond a reasonable doubt:

1. The defendant carried out a scheme to defraud or to get money, assets, or other property from a financial institution by using false or fraudulent pretenses, representations, or promises about a material fact
2. The false or fraudulent pretenses, representations, or promises were material
3. The defendant intended to defraud the financial institution

A "scheme to defraud" includes any course of action intended to deceive or cheat someone out of money or property.

A statement is "false" or "fraudulent" if it is "about a material fact that the speaker knows is untrue or makes with reckless indifference as to the truth" and makes with intent to defraud. A "half-truth" about a material fact made with the intent to defraud is encompassed in this definition.

"Intent to defraud" means that the defendant acted with the specific intent to deceive or cheat someone, usually for personal gain or to cause financial loss to someone else.[20]

Similar evidentiary proof requirements exist for health-care fraud,[21] wire fraud,[22] and mail fraud.[23] The standard for proving a scheme to defraud with the specific intent to deceive or cheat someone apply to each of these crimes.

Detectives need to be aware of potential defenses that defendants may assert in fraud cases. Typically, such defenses focus upon the lack of intent to defraud. The defendant may assert, for example, that he or she was merely engaging in conduct that others had also engaged in and was not considered to be wrongdoing.

The astute detective, however, during the course of the investigation, looks for "badges of fraud." Badges of fraud are circumstantial pieces of evidence that point to conscious, willful, and knowing fraudulent intent.

For instance, if the defendant engaged in elaborate methods of concealment, such activity indicates fraud. Concealment indicates a violation of an ethical standard or knowing violation of the law. Concealment, which implies affirmative steps to disguise wrongdoing, is more significant than the simple omission to disclose a fact.

Other badges of fraud may involve the timing of the criminal activities, the variance from established business practices, and the involvement of persons who stood to benefit from the transactions.

In short, each fraud case provides its own unique set of badges of fraud and building circumstantial evidence typically requires "leaving no stone unturned" during the investigation. Each piece of evidence needs to be evaluated to determine how it provides insight into the defendant's intent to commit the crime.

Other Types of White-Collar Cases

Although embezzlement and fraud are the two primary white-collar offenses, as technology advances occur and governmental programs become prolific, white-collar crime spreads wherever there is an opportunity to obtain money or funds through illegal means. The following chart contains categories of white-collar crime, a description of the crime, and the beginning steps that a detective should take to initiate an investigation.

Crime Category	Description	Initial Investigation
Advance fee scheme	Victim pays money to fraudster in anticipation of receiving something of greater value—such as a loan, contract, investment, or gift—and then receives little or nothing of value. Such schemes may involve "work-at-home" or "cancer research" fee schemes.	Obtain any documents indicating payments. Interview victim to determine representations made to victim before paying advance fee.
Computer fraud	Violations enforced under Title 18, U.S.C., Section 1030 include unauthorized access to protected computers, theft of data such as personal identification used to commit identity theft, and denial of service attacks used for extortion or disruption of e-commerce and malware (malicious software) distribution to include viruses intended for financial gain.	Trace evidence of the crime must be located, captured, and documented in a forensic manner to be preserved for production at trial. Electronic access logs must be collected with a strict chain of custody process. The local U.S. Secret Service Electronic Crimes Task Force provides technical expertise, research, and aggressive investigation in cases that have significant community impact.
Corporate fraud	Corporate wrongdoing including accounting schemes involving false entries designed to deceive investors or shareholders, self-dealing by corporate executives, kickbacks, misuse of corporate property for personal gain, or obstruction of justice.	If the information comes from a corporate whistle blower, a comprehensive interview should occur to gather information and documents while maintaining the identity confidential. If probable cause can be established, consider a search warrant.
Identity theft	Occurs when fraudster assumes victim's identity to perform a fraud or other criminal act.	Determine how fraudster obtained victim's identity: theft of wallet, rifling through trash, and accessing credit or bank information. Also determine what is

(Continued)

Crime Category	Description	Initial Investigation
		specifically used to commit the fraud: name, social security numbers, dates of birth, Medicare numbers, addresses, birth certificates, death certificates, passport numbers, financial account numbers, passwords, or biometric data (fingerprints, or iris scans).
Insurance fraud	Insurance contracts between the insured and insurer are meant to manage legitimate risks and to spread the risk of loss among the pool of insureds. Any scheme to exploit the insurance contract by deceiving one of the parties in order to receive money to which they are not entitled is insurance fraud. Insurance contracts include casualty, property, disability, and life insurance. Insurance fraud includes the following schemes: (1) misrepresentation to the insurer, (2) embezzlement of premiums or insurance benefits, (3) staged auto accidents, (4) bodily injury fraud, (5) workers compensation fraud, (6) disaster relief fraud, and others.	Insurance fraud perpetrators include dishonest policyholders, insurance industry insiders (such as agents, brokers, and claims adjusters[24]), medical professionals (such as chiropractors and others specializing in treatment of soft tissue injuries), and attorneys (who circumvent the antifraud measures imposed by insurers). Investigators need to follow the money trail by interviewing victims who suffered loss and reviewing documents related to claim sand payments. In appropriate cases, cooperating witnesses and informants may provide crucial information. Investigators should contact the state insurance investigation bureau and the Coalition Against Insurance Fraud for investigative support.
Internet fraud	Any cybercrime that uses the Word Wide Web and whose perpetrators use the Internet to obtain money from unsuspecting victims. Criminal schemes include criminal spam, phishing, spoofed or hijacked accounts, international reshipping schemes, cyberextortion, auction fraud, credit card fraud, intellectual property rights, computer intrusions (hacking), economic espionage (theft of trade secrets), and other traditional crimes that migrate to the online environment.	There are a growing number of joint cybercrime task forces with resources from federal, state, and local agencies. A detective should coordinate with the Internet Crime Complaint Center (IC3). IC3 receives Internet-related complaints, conducts research and analysis, and, through automated matching systems, identifies links and commonalities and groups complaints with similar information. IC3 prepares reports in support of investigations.
Medicare fraud	Senior citizens are frequent targets of Medicare schemes, especially by corrupt medical equipment manufacturers who offer seniors free or lower-priced medical products in exchange for their Medicare numbers. Because a physician has to sign a form certifying that equipment or testing is needed before Medicare pays for it, con artists fake signatures or bribe corrupt doctors to sign the forms. Once a signature is in place, the manufacturers bill Medicare for merchandise or service that was not needed or was not ordered.	Investigators should coordinate with special agents of the Office of Inspector General, U.S. Department of Health and Humans Service, for technical assistance and analysis related to criminal activities.

(Continued)

Crime Category	Description	Initial Investigation
Ponzi schemes	"Ponzi" schemes promise lucrative financial returns far in excess of traditional investments. Instead of investing the funds of victims, however, the fraudster provides "dividends" to initial investors using the funds of subsequent investors. The scheme collapses when the fraudster flees with all of the proceeds or when a sufficient number of new investors cannot be found to allow the continued payment of "dividends." "Ponzi" scheme is named after its creator— Charles Ponzi of Boston from the 1900s. This type of crime continues to present day as evidenced by the prosecution of Bernie Madoff.	Investigators need to conduct thorough interviews of victims, carefully detailing the specific representations made by the con artists participating in the scheme. Many times, a pattern establishes repeat representations that can be proven false and made with intent to defraud. Any and all printed or electronic matter provided from initial contact with the victim through to the last payment needs to be collected and preserved.

Initiatives in Investigating White-Collar Crime

FBI Financial Intelligence Center

Conducting a financial fraud investigation is like assembling a jigsaw puzzle. All the pieces of information need to be evaluated and assessed and then assembled together to get a complete picture. Analysts need to review evidence and link together individual pieces of evidence to provide a sketch of criminal activity. The Financial Intelligence Center was formed in 2009 to identify potential investigative targets committing mortgage fraud. Since 2009, its mission has broadened to include securities and commodities fraud, health-care fraud, money laundering, procurement fraud, and public corruption.

The Financial Intelligence Center reviews "big data" that come from the FBI, other law enforcement agencies, and consumer complaint websites. According to the FBI's description of the work conducted by the center, computer programs are used to establish common themes that emerge from similar scams and similar names. These data are analyzed to target potential subjects or suspicious activities. Data analysis, reports, and spreadsheets are provided to field agents who may be assigned to task forces with local and state law enforcement authorities.

The Financial Intelligence Center has its counterparts in several states. For instance, the New York City Financial Intelligence Center seeks to integrate already existing data streams concerning persons, places, or businesses so that analyses can be provided to law enforcement to support investigative activity or to provide actionable information concerning "criminal trends and threats impacting the fiscal health of the city's economic structure."[25]

U.S. Department of the Treasury Financial Crime Enforcement Network

Numerous law enforcement agencies, including the FBI, maintain a proactive approach when investigating white-collar fraud that may involve money laundering. As defined by the U.S. Department of Justice, money laundering is

The process by which criminals conceal or disguise the proceeds of their crimes or convert those proceeds into goods and services. It allows criminals to infuse their illegal money into the stream of commerce, thus corrupting financial institutions and the money supply, thereby giving criminals unwarranted economic power.[26]

On average, the FBI alone investigates over 300 cases involving money laundering each year. As a result of their investigative activities, $18.4 million have been returned as restitutions with similar high-dollar amounts for fines and other recoveries.

Typically, in an investigation where money laundering may be a crime, a parallel financial investigation is conducted to find and locate the monetary proceeds of criminal activities and to prove their connection to underlying crimes.

Suspicious activity reports (SARs) are one of the government's main weapons in the battle against money laundering and other financial crimes since these reports generate leads that law enforcement agencies use to initiate investigations into fraudulent activities and related money laundering offenses. The Bank Secrecy Act requires financial institutions and money service businesses, securities and futures firms, insurance companies, casinos and card clubs, and other types of financial institutions to file a SAR whenever they suspect money laundering, financial fraud and abuse, discovery of illicit funds, or other similar activities.

According to the FBI, many individuals launder money to conceal illegal activity, such as bank fraud, securities and futures fraud, public corruption, health insurance fraud, tax evasion, commercial real estate loan fraud, and even drug trafficking and terrorism. Money laundering provides a conduit for criminal conduct by permitting criminals to maintain control over their proceeds and ultimately to provide a legitimate cover for their illegal sources of income. Law enforcement officials estimate that each year, 1–2 trillion dollars worldwide are laundered through different types of financial institutions and businesses.

Some examples of suspicious activities that may trigger the filing of a SAR include as follows:

- A bank customer, a retired CPA, frequently sends and receives money transfers of more than $2000 to and from many different people.
- A customer conducting an $11,000 cash transaction attempts to bribe a bank employee not to file a currency transaction report.
- The bank customer refuses to explain what he or she is doing and implies that the teller has no business for being curious.
- The bank customer deposits precisely $10,000 in cash and advises the teller that he or she need not prepare a currency transaction report because the deposit is below the reporting level.

SARs must be filed by a financial institution in the following circumstances. First, a report must be made whenever bank insider abuse is suspected. If a financial institution detects any criminal violation against the bank or a transaction conducted through the bank, where the bank may have been the actual or potential victim, and the bank can identify one of its directors, officers, employees, agents, or other affiliated person as having committed or aided a criminal act, regardless of the amount involved, a report must be filed within 30 days.

Second, any violation aggregating $5000 or more where a suspect can be identified must be reported if the bank was an actual or potential victim. If the suspect has used an alias, then information regarding the true identity of the suspect or group of suspects, as well as alias identifiers, such as drivers' licenses or social security numbers, addresses, and telephone numbers, must be reported.

Third, any violations aggregating $25,000 or more regardless of a potential suspect must be reported. Whenever the bank suspects a criminal violation involving or aggregating $25,000 or more in funds or other assets, where the bank believes that it was an actual or potential victim, it must be reported although no suspect can be identified.

Last, any transactions that are suspected to be connected with money laundering or structuring must also be reported. Structuring is conducting financial transactions at financial institutions to evade the reporting requirements of federal regulations. Notably, if the bank believes that a transaction has no business or apparent lawful purpose or is not the sort in which the particular customer would normally be expected to engage, and the bank knows of no reasonable explanation for the transaction, then the bank must report the details of the transaction.

On a periodic basis, prosecutors from each of the 94 U.S. Attorneys' offices gather in their districts to meet with special agents from the FBI, the Internal Revenue Service (IRS), the U.S. Secret Service, the U.S. Postal Service, Immigrations and Customs Enforcement, and local investigators to review and evaluate SARs to determine next steps in criminal investigations related to banking crimes.

The author, Frank DiMarino, as an assistant U.S. attorney and the financial institution fraud coordinator in the Southern District of Georgia, participated in such consultative meetings to evaluate the information disclosed on SARs on a monthly basis. According to his experience, SARs are one of the most valuable tools to proactive law enforcement. Frequently, targets and criminal schemes were identified that warranted investigation, indictment, and prosecution.

Each agency during a SAR Task Force meeting would bring unique information to the consideration of the potential criminal matter identified by the SAR. For instance, Customs has access to information about imports, exports, and about travel out of the country. Detectives and local law enforcement investigators bring insight about local business practices and business leaders. The IRS, under certain circumstances, can access tax return information, which helps determine whether the money in question has a lawful or unlawful source. The Postal Service can provide mail covers, identify the holder of a post office box, track money orders, or even ask the mail carrier what he or she has observed when delivering mail to target locations. Names and identifying information would be searched in Narcotics and Dangerous Drugs Information System (NADDIS) and other databases.

Financial institutions are required to retain for 5 years from the date of filing the SAR: (1) a copy of the SAR and (2) the business records of any supporting documentation. Financial institutions must make such documentation available to the Financial Crimes Enforcement Network (FinCEN).

FinCEN collects the following information from commercial and law enforcement databases that may be helpful to task force detectives conducting white-collar crime investigations.

Commercial Databases

- International corporate/financial records
- Public records
- Corporate financial information
- Social security numbers
- Real estate information
- Business information
- Stock market insider transactions
- Court cases, tax liens/judgments
- Names, addresses, and phone numbers

Law Enforcement and Regulatory Databases

- Automated Commercial System
- Nonimmigrant Student Database
- Currency and Banking Retrieval System
- INTERPOL Case-Tracking Systems
- Postal Inspection Service
- Department of Homeland Security, U.S. Citizenship and Immigration Services Central Index System
- Treasury Direct Securities System
- National Association of Securities Dealers
- NADDIS
- Treasury Enforcement Communications System (TECS)

Financial institutions expect that SARs will be treated as law enforcement–sensitive material. Inappropriate disclosure of SARs could frustrate that expectation and have a chilling effect on both the quantity and the quality of future SAR filings. Moreover, SARs may contain information concerning how a bank discovered suspicious activity, possibly allowing other potential wrongdoers to take preventive action to avoid being detected. Therefore, it is essential that law enforcement agencies and prosecutors take measures to ensure that the existence of a SAR or its contents are not disclosed unless absolutely necessary or required by law. Bank employees are also prohibited by law from notifying any person involved in the suspicious activity that has been reported to the government.

SARs have triggered closer scrutiny of banking transactions that have victimized financial institutions and ordinary citizens. This investigative activity continues with the recent Interagency Financial Fraud Enforcement Task Force established in 2009.

General Investigative Strategies

White-collar criminal investigators accept the fact that such cases involve voluminous documents. These cases are document intensive and a clear method of organizing and archiving records so that documents may be presented at trial and used for further investigations that are crucial. White-collar prosecutions often involve defendants with substantial monetary resources who are able to afford zealous and expensive attorneys, sometimes former prosecutors. White-collar prosecutions also often involve not only individuals but also an organization, such as a corporation or a government body.

The detective must be ready to handle investigations that involve not only individual defendants but also multiple and joint defendant. Defendants who join together in a joint defense agreement assert a united front, share information among each other, and seek to defeat the prosecution's strategy of having one defendant testify against one of more codefendants.

Federal grand jury subpoenas are powerful tools to obtain documentary evidence about wrongdoing. The "subpoena duces tecum" allows the grand jury and investigative team covered by grand jury confidentiality restrictions to obtain bank records, computer databases, accounting records, corporate records, and other similar documents that would aid a criminal investigation. The Fifth Amendment privilege against self-incrimination does not apply to an individual's records or to corporate records so long as the government did not compel the individual to create the record. The Fifth Amendment privilege does apply, however, to the production of personal, as opposed to corporate, records when a target of the grand jury investigation has been subpoenaed to produce such records.

Use immunity, a promise by the government not to use the testimony of a testifying witness or the fruits of such testimony, may be granted to an individual to compel his or her testimony about the records. Granting a witness use testimony involves the calculation of not being able to use derivative evidence obtained from the testimony and likely litigation about what constitutes derivative use of the testimony.[27] Nonetheless, in appropriate circumstances, use testimony is a valuable tool to obtain information about records. In addition, use immunity may be used to further the investigation into unknown suspects or the criminal leaders of the enterprise.[28]

Another method to obtain information from a witness, depending upon the circumstances and the needs of justice, is to offer a witness a nonprosecution agreement in return for cooperation or testimony leading to the conviction of others. Such agreements are negotiated arrangements and may include whatever reasonable terms the defense and prosecution agree on. The agreements are enforceable against the government and if the other party withdraws from the agreement, they may be prosecuted.

Collection of Information through Local Sources That Aid Investigations

The white-collar investigator can obtain much information about the subjects and targets of an investigation through gathering data, facts, and knowledge from the following sources:

- Bankruptcy records from the Federal Bankruptcy Courts
- County and state records of civil actions and criminal convictions
- County records of divorce
- County and state records of licenses
- County records of probate and death
- Secretary of State records of corporations, limited liability corporations, and other business entities

- State Vital Statistics Bureau
- County records of real estate transactions and land transfers
- County record of Uniform Commercial Code index of liens, financing statements, and debtor transactions
- National Crime Information Center including 21 files related to stolen items and vehicles, identity theft, and wanted persons
- National Law Enforcement Telecommunications System including motor vehicle and drivers' data to state criminal history records
- TECS II regarding border observations and interactions
- Tax files (local, state, and federal)
- Bank accounts
- Credit card accounts
- Loan records
- Currency transaction reports
- SARs
- Wire receipts
- Canceled checks
- Certified or other mail receipts
- Corporate records
- Telephone records
- News reports and articles
- Arrest records

Information from computers including website history, databases, electronic files, and other digital evidence can be forensically investigated by the FBI Computer Analysis Response Team (CART) who provides services to local, state, and federal investigators. CART examiners are experts at extracting records from digital media even after the computer components have been intentionally damaged.

Trends in White-Collar Crime and Future Investigative Techniques

According to a 2010 survey by the Bureau of Justice Statistics of American households, nearly one in four households was victimized by white-collar crime during the previous year.[3] According to the Federal Trade Commission (FTC), a federal agency responsible for detecting and preventing fraud, deception, and unfair business practices in the marketplace, in 2010, among all fraud complaints made to the FTC, at least 56% of company scammers made initial contact with the victim over the Internet (45% by e-mail and 11% through a website). The FTC reports that only 19% of first contacts were made by phone.[29] It is clear that the Internet provides criminals with very little setup cost, little time investment, and relative anonymity to carry out fraudulent schemes.

A majority of American households generally believe that white-collar crime has contributed to the current economic crisis that began in 2009.[3] Nearly half believe that law enforcement is not devoting enough resources to combat with collar crimes.[3]

The first decades of the twenty-first century have seen computer literacy grow exponentially, technological advances expand, and mobile devices proliferate to send e-mails and text messages, complete banking and purchasing transactions, as well as become tools for consumer payments.* The white-collar investigator will need to continuously learn of technological improvements and methods of detecting criminal activity using more advanced digital forensics.

As economic conditions evolve, the white-collar investigator will need to be vigilant to detect new fraudulent scams. For example, as mortgages became worthless and the real estate bubble collapsed, mortgage fraud materialized in a new form by seeing foreclosure rescue companies preying on distressed homeowners and criminals who target senior citizens with the lure of reverse mortgages.

As Bitcoin or other virtual currencies take hold, criminals are likely to transfer money by using such digital transfers, especially in countries with little or no regulation. Criminals may use anonymous prepaid credit cards. For state and local white-collar investigators, they should be observant for criminals who may prey on smaller banking institutions to launder ill-gotten gains and inject money into the banking system to avoid reporting controls of larger financial entities.

As the baby boomer population continues to ages and as the demand increases for health care and benefits, there is a corresponding rise in losses from health-care fraud. We're talking billions of dollars every year. Examples of health-care fraud are abundant. Such fraud may involve one-person schemes involving perhaps an unethical physician to criminal enterprises and corporate-level campaigns. Such investigations are necessarily document intense, and the astute investigator will secure the assistance of the federal agencies that have the resources to conduct interstate investigations.

Investment fraud and accounting fraud continue to flourish despite significant prosecutions that have closed accounting firms. The state and local investigator should be aware of businesses who report that their expenses have taken a significant jump or whose revenue has fallen drastically for no apparent market reason. Embezzlement wherever there is an opportunity to hide the unlawful conversion of funds remains a temptation among office workers, professionals, and government employees. Investigators will need to know how to craft federal grand jury subpoenas to obtain documents for review. Also, the traditional methods of investigation that involve cooperating witnesses, confidential informants, and undercover operations have proven productive in many white-collar investigations. Also, conducting surveillance and interviews, running court-ordered wiretaps, and executing search warrants are usually part of a comprehensive investigation where the criminal scheme is complex and the subjects employ sophisticated means to conceal wrongdoing.

To stay ahead of criminal schemes, law enforcement will need the technology to collect, analyze, and share high volumes of electronic evidence, rapidly and efficiently. High-level forensic accounting and analysis is mandatory. Also, rapid response teams such as the FBI CART unit are needed to collect electronic evidence before destruction.

In all fraud cases, the criminal investigator must examine the contents of the subject's mind. Simply, an investigator must marshal sufficient evidence that not only establishes how a fraudulent scheme was perpetrated but also proves that when the perpetrators did the transactions, they knew that they were engaged in conduct that was criminal in nature. Investigators must collect evidence that show what the perpetrators were thinking.

---

* In September, 2014, Apple announced a new application that allows iPhone 6 users to pay with "contactless payment technology and unique security features." https://www.apple.com/iphone-6/apple-pay/ (accessed September 14, 2014).

Criminal defendants who raise such defenses as having acted in good faith, lacked any criminal intent, made a mistake of fact, relied on a lawyer's or other professional's advice, or acted negligently but not willfully often put the government to the test of proving beyond a reasonable doubt that the defendant knew they were acting criminally with the requisite fraudulent intent. Neither stupidity nor risky behavior is a crime even though many victims may suffer a loss.

For a successful prosecution, investigators need to access and analyze e-mails and text messages that perpetrators have shared with each other and their victims. Establishing a timeline is crucial that provides a history of financial transactions and the underlying electronic messages that occur around the time of the transactions. These electronic jottings often provide a significant window into the white-collar criminal's mind and provide persuasive evidence of criminal intent.

Questions in Review

8.1 Explain the crime of embezzlement and how to investigate embezzlements.
8.2 Explain how banks are used to commit fraudulent schemes and the investigative tools that can be used to analyze financial transactions.
8.3 Discuss five types of white-collar crimes by providing definitions and methods of investigation.
8.4 Explain the roles of the following investigative units:
    a. FBI Financial Intelligence Center
    b. U.S. Department of Treasury Financial Crime Enforcement Network
8.5 List items of evidence that should be considered in white-collar cases and how such items can be collected.
8.6 Identify future trends in white-collar crime and how investigators can develop investigative leads.

References

1. Sutherland, E. (1983). *White-Collar Crime: The Uncut Version.* New Haven, CT: Yale University Press, p. 7.
2. Green, S. P. (2004). The concept of white collar crime in law and legal theory. *Buff. Crim. Law Rev.* 8(1), 1–34.
3. Huff, R., Desilets, C., and Kane, J. (2010). *The 2010 National Public Survey on White Collar Crime.* Fairmont, VA: National White-Collar Crime Center, p. 9. http://www.nw3c.org/docs/research/2010-national-public-survey-on-white-collar-crime.pdf?sfvrsn=8 (accessed August 24, 2014).
4. U.S. Department of Justice, Federal Bureau of Investigation. (1989). *White Collar Crime: A Report to the Public.* Washington, DC: Government Printing Press.
5. Bureau of Justice Statistics, U.S. Department of Justice. (1981). *Dictionary of Criminal Justice Data Terminology,* 2nd edn. Rockville, MD: National Criminal Justice Reference Service.
6. Huff, R., Desilets, C., and Kane, J. (2010). *The 2010 National Public Survey on White Collar Crime.* Fairmont, VA: National White-Collar Crime Center, p. 11. http://www.nw3c.org/docs/research/2010-national-public-survey-on-white-collar-crime.pdf?sfvrsn=8 (accessed August 24, 2014).
7. *Black's Law Dictionary,* 9th edn. (2009). Embezzlement. Available at Westlaw.

8. United States v. Stockton, 788 F.2d 210, 216–217 (4th Cir.), cert. denied, 479 U.S. 840, 107 S.Ct. 147, 93 L.Ed.2d 89 (1986).

9. http://www.fbi.gov/chicago/press-releases/2013/former-dixon-comptroller-rita-crundwell-sentenced-to-nearly-20-years-in-federal-prison-for-53.7-million-theft-from-city (accessed September 7, 2014).

10. Levesque, W. R. (2003, June 18). Hospice employs ex-embezzler. *St. Petersburg Times* 2003 WLNR 15695031.

11. http://www.fbi.gov/washingtondc/press-releases/2013/former-employee-pleads-guilty-to-embezzling-more-than-5.1-million-from-non-profit (accessed September 7, 2014).

12. http://www.fbi.gov/memphis/press-releases/2014/former-head-teller-pleads-guilty-to-bank-embezzlement (accessed September 7, 2014).

13. http://www.fbi.gov/sacramento/press-releases/2014/tracy-woman-pleads-guilty-to-embezzling-from-health-plan-of-san-joaquin-and-agilent-technologies (accessed September 7, 2014).

14. http://www.fbi.gov/atlanta/press-releases/2013/former-cox-employees-charged-with-embezzlement (accessed September 7, 2014).

15. http://www.fbi.gov/pittsburgh/press-releases/2014/former-fairmont-state-vice-president-convicted-on-embezzlement-tax-charges (accessed September 7, 2014).

16. http://www.fbi.gov/albany/press-releases/2014/diane-schmaler-pleads-guilty-to-dorset-field-club-embezzlement (accessed September 7, 2014).

17. United States v. Ford, 631 F.2d 1354, 1361 (9th Cir. 1980).

18. United States v. Scott, 789 F.2d 795, 798 (9th Cir. 1986) (intentional sale of another's property with knowledge of facts making crime satisfies intent under Title 18, U.S.C., § 641).

19. United States v. Brown, 742 F.2d 359, 361 n.1 (7th Cir. 1984).

20. Neder v. United States, 527 U.S. 1, 25 (1999).

21. Title 18, United States Code, Section 1347.

22. Title 18, United States Code, Section 1343.

23. Title 18, United States Code, Section 1344.

24. http://www.fbi.gov/jacksonville/press-releases/2013/boat-insurance-fraud-conspirators-indicted (accessed September 13, 2014).

25. New York City Criminal Justice. Fighting financial fraud. http://www.nyc.gov/html/cjc/html/fraud/fic.shtml (accessed August 24, 2014.)

26. Federal Bureau of Investigation. Financial crimes report to the public, fiscal years 2010–2011. http://www.fbi.gov/stats-services/publications/financial-crimes-report-2010–2011/financial-crimes-report-2010-2011#Asset (accessed September 6, 2014).

27. 18 U.S.C. §§ 6602-6004 (2003).

28. United States Attorneys Manual § 9-27.600, *Entering into Non-Prosecution Agreements in Return for Cooperation—Generally* (August 12, 2002).

29. National Criminal Justice Reference Service. (2012), *Statistical Overviews*, Section 6, Identity theft, p. 13. https://www.ncjrs.gov/ovc_archives/ncvrw/2012/pdf/StatisticalOverviews.pdf (accessed September 14, 2014).

Investigations Involving Computers and Analysis

Collection and Preservation of Digital Evidence

MARK MCCOY AND RACHAEL ELLIOTT

Contents

Chapter Objectives	135
Chapter Outline	136
What Is Digital Evidence?	136
Legal Issues	138
Handling Digital Evidence at the Crime Scene	139
General Investigative Questions	140
Questions Specific for Identity Theft/Financial Crimes	140
Questions for the Victim	140
Questions for the Suspect/Target	140
Investigative Questions for Internet Crimes against Children	140
Questions for the Victim	140
Questions for the Suspect/Target	141
Investigative Questions for Intrusion/Hacking (Network)	141
Home Network Questions	141
Business Network Questions	141
Investigative Questions for Crimes Involving E-Mails	141
Questions for the Victim	141
Questions for the Suspect/Target	142
Investigative Questions for Instant Messaging/Internet Relay Chat Crimes	142
Questions for the Victim	142
Questions for the Suspect/Target	142
Seizure of a Computer	142
Seizure of a Cell Phone or Other Mobile Devices	144
Documenting a Digital Crime Scene	144
Packaging and Transporting Digital Evidence	144
Antistatic Bags	145
Questions for Discussion	145
References	145

Chapter Objectives

After reading this chapter, you should be able to do the following:

1. Ensure the digital evidence is seized with the proper legal authority.
2. Recognize, identify, seize, and secure all digital evidence at the scene.
3. Document the entire scene and the specific location of the digital evidence found.

4. Collect, label, and preserve the digital evidence.
5. Package and transport digital evidence in a secure manner.

Chapter Outline

What Is Digital Evidence?
Legal Issues in the Search and Seizure of Digital Evidence
Handling Digital Evidence at the Crime Scene
Documenting a Digital Crime Scene
Packaging and Transporting Digital Evidence

What Is Digital Evidence?

As technology rapidly advances, the way we view evidence at all types of crime scenes changes. Digital evidence can now be found in every type of crime and in most crime scenes. In the following diagram, the U.S. Department of Homeland Security has developed a list of potential digital evidence associated with a wide variety of crimes (U.S. Department of Homeland Security, 2007).

Computer fraud investigations:

- Account data from online auctions
- Accounting software and files
- Address books
- Calendar
- Chat logs
- Customer information
- Credit card data
- Databases
- Digital camera software
- E-mail, notes, and letters
- Financial and asset records

Child abuse and fornography investigations:

- Chat logs
- Digital camera software
- E-mails, notes, and letters
- Games
- Graphic editing and viewing software
- Images
- Internet activity logs
- Movie files
- User created directory and file names that classify images

Network intrusion investigations:

- Address books
- Configuration files
- E-mails, notes, and letters
- Executable programs
- Internet activity logs
- Internet protocol address and usernames
- Internet relay chat logs
- Source code
- Text files and documents with usernames and passwords

Homicide investigations:

- Address books
- E-mails, notes, and letters
- Financial asset records
- Internet activity logs
- Legal documents and wills
- Medical records
- Telephone records
- Diaries
- Maps
- Photos of victim/suspect
- Trophy photos

Domestic violence investigations:

- Address books
- Diaries
- E-mails, notes, and letters
- Financial asset records
- Telephone records

Financial fraud and counterfeiting investigations:

- Address books
- Calendar
- Currency images
- Check and money order images
- Customer information
- Databases
- E-mails, noters, and letters
- False identification

- Financial asset records
- Images of signatures
- Internet activity logs
- Online banking software
- Counterfeit currency images
- Bank logs
- Credit card numbers

E-mail threats, harassment, and stalking investigations:

- Address books
- Diaries
- E-mails, notes, and letters
- Financial asset records
- Images

- Internet activity logs
- Legal documents
- Telephone records
- Victim background research
- Maps to victim locations

Narcotics investigations:

- Address books
- Calendar
- Databases
- Drug recipes
- E-mails, notes, and letters

- False ID
- Financial asset records
- Internet activity logs
- Prescription from images

Software piracy investigations:

- Chat logs
- E-mails, notes, and letters
- Image files or software certificates
- Internet activity logs

- Software serial numbers
- Software cracking utilities
- User-created directories and file names that classify copyrighted software

Telecommunication fraud investigations:

- Cloning software
- Customer database records
- Electronic serial numbers
- Mobile identification numbers

- E-mails, notes, and letters
- Financial asset records
- Internet activity logs

Identify theft investigations:

- hardware and software tools
  - Backdrops
  - Credit card reader/writer
  - Digital camera software
  - Scanner software

- Identification templates
  - Birth certificates
  - Check cashing cards
  - Digital photo images
  - Driver's licenses
  - Electronic signatures
  - Counterfeit vehicle registrations
  - Counterfeit insurance documents
  - Social security cards

- Internet activity related to ID theft:
  - E-mails and newsgroup postings
  - Deleted documents
  - Online orders
  - Online trading information
  - Internet activity logs

- Negotiable instruments
  - Business checks
  - Cashier's checks
  - Credit card numbers
  - Counterfeit court documents
  - Counterfeit gift certificates
  - Counterfeit loan documents
  - Counterfeit sales receipts
  - Money orders
  - Personal checks

Digital evidence can be defined as any information that has been stored or transmitted digitally (USLegal, 2001–2014). Digital evidence can be considered latent, or hidden, like DNA and fingerprints. It can quickly cross jurisdiction lines and be easily damaged and altered (National Forensic Science Technology Center, 2014). Examples of digital evidence can include, but are not limited to, e-mails, documents, spreadsheets, text messages, pictures, and videos. These digital evidence items can be stored on any type of digital media. Some examples of different types of digital media are computer hard drives, some printers, thumb drives, gaming systems, cellular phones, MP3 players, tablets, and some of the newer appliances that have built-in televisions.

Digital devices play an important role in the lives of nearly everyone across the globe. While we usually think of computers, mobile phones, and tablets as sources of digital evidence, digital storage devices vary in many ways. Some of these devices can be easily identified in a crime scene, while others can be deceiving. They can range in size and appearance, which make them easy to hide. Some examples of different devices can be seen below.

Digital evidence can also be stored electronically at Internet service providers or other off-site locations. Some examples of this information can be found with cell phone service providers, "cloud" services, and Internet providers. Gathering this information can sometimes prove challenging and in most cases requires some form of legal service.

Legal Issues

A computer or other digital media can be used differently in different crimes. There are three main ways digital media can be utilized to commit a crime. The first is when the computer was used as an instrument to commit the crime, for example, when a computer is used to gather information and stalk someone. The digital device is used to facilitate the criminal activity. The second is when the computer itself is the target of the crime (Hailey, 2003). When a computer system is hacked in order to gather useful information is an instance of a computer being the target of the crime. These types of attacks on computers and computer networks are what we traditionally identified as computer crimes. The third is when the computer is used as a repository of evidence and this will typically be the most common type of digital evidence. An example of this kind of investigation is when child pornography is stored on the computer. Digital evidence can include evidence leading up to, and including, the crime, and it can include evidence after the crime has been committed. Just as any other criminal investigation, there must be probable cause to justify the seizure of digital evidence. The plain view exception to a warrant gives legal authority to seize the electronic device, but it does "not" give the proper authority for a search of the device's contents. This is a very common mistake made by law enforcement officers; it is important to remember that typically we are seeking to look at and review the files and digital data stored on the digital devices. Consent can be given for a search of a digital device. Just like any other search, consent can only be given by a person with the proper authority. When obtaining consent, it is important to make sure the documentation states the person is giving permission to seize the device and for a future examination to be conducted by a forensic examiner. If your agency already has a document used for consent of electronic evidence, it should be used. If a form needs to be created, it is suggested to consult your local district or state attorney. It is also important to remember that consent can be retracted at any time. For this reason, it is safest and most preferred to obtain a search warrant. Search warrants are typically written for the search and seizure of electronic storage devices, like computers and cell phones, or to obtain service records, billing, and subscriber information from service providers. The role of the computer in the crime, as well as why you believe it would contain evidence, should be stated in the search warrant affidavit. In addition, the specific description of the evidence you are looking for must be included. It should also be explained why you believe electronic evidence will be found at the location of the search.

Handling Digital Evidence at the Crime Scene

It is a common misconception that investigators can look at digital evidence at the crime scene or at any time a digital device is discovered. However, the mere starting of a computer or looking at a file on a computer will alter the original evidence. Digital evidence should be approached just as any other evidence. Agency procedures should be put in place to ensure the integrity of the evidence is maintained. The first step in this procedure should be to make sure no one has access to any digital media. This can help prevent the damage of any digital evidence. It is important to keep in mind the existence of wiping programs used to erase evidence, and it is important to realize there are remote capabilities with some devices that can allow remote wipes to be performed. Something that can be helpful to the investigators, as well as the digital forensic examiner, would be to ask some specific questions regarding the evidence. Some general questions and electronic crime–specific questions suggested by the U.S. Department of Homeland Security (2007) can be found in the following.

General Investigative Questions

- When and where was the computer obtained? Was it purchased used or new?
- Who has access to the computer?
- How many people use the computer, and what are their names/usernames?
- What is the level of computer experience for each user?
- What times of day do the individual users access the computer?
- Where are other electronic media, such as CDs and thumb drives, stored?
- Does the computer require a username and password? What are they?
- Is there any software that requires a username or password? If so, what is it?
- How is the computer connected to the Internet (i.e., dial up, cable, DSL, LAN)?
- What is the e-mail provider/username for the suspect or victim?
- Is there remote access to the computer?
- Is there encryption software being utilized?

Questions Specific for Identity Theft/Financial Crimes

Questions for the Victim

- Has there been any unusual activity on any of your accounts?
- What, if any, accounts have been compromised?
- Have you recently applied for any credit cards or loans?
- Have you provided any personal information to any one person or organization?
- Is any of your personal information maintained on your computer?
- Have you had any bills or financial statements that do not arrive regularly in the mail?

Questions for the Suspect/Target

- Does the computer contain any software used for making checks or other financial documents?
- Is there software on the computer that can be used for manipulating photographs?
- Are there scanned or manipulated forms of identification?
- Was the computer used for any online purchasing?

Investigative Questions for Internet Crimes against Children

Questions for the Victim

- Has the victim been online in any chat rooms?
- What type of chat/e-mail client does the victim use?
- What is the victim's e-mail address or online chat room name?
- Who is on the victim's "buddy" list in chat rooms?
- Has the victim provided any information about their true name, age, and location to anyone online?

- Does the victim use the Internet, e-mail, or chat from any other computers? If so, where?
- What were specific sexual acts observed in images or electronic communications?
- Has the victim received any pictures or gifts from the suspect?

Questions for the Suspect/Target

- Where are all the computers the suspect uses?
- Does the suspect store information remotely, such as an external hard drive or online storage?
- What is the suspect's online identity or chat room name?
- Has the suspect communicated electronically with anyone?
- How does the suspect communicate with these people (i.e., e-mail, chat)?
- Did the suspect knowingly view any child pornography using the computer? If so, how did the suspect obtain these images?
- Did the suspect share these images with anyone else?

Investigative Questions for Intrusion/Hacking (Network)

Home Network Questions

- Can all the network cables be actually traced back to their respective computers?
- Is there an individual person associated with each computer?
- Is the network connected to the Internet? If so, how is it connecting?
- Where is the DSL/cable modem located? Is it currently connected?
- Who is the Internet service provider?
- Is there more than one computer that can connect to the Internet?
- Is there a wireless network?

Business Network Questions

- Who observed the illegal activity first? Are there any other witnesses to this activity?
- What type of illegal activity was observed?
- Who is the network administrator? What is their contact information? (Note: The network administrator should not be contacted by the first responder.)
- Are there any current/former employees that are a suspect?
- Is there a diagram of the network available?
- Are there computer logs that are maintained? If so, can those logs be secured for further investigation?
- Are there any other law enforcement agencies that have been contacted?

Investigative Questions for Crimes Involving E-Mails

Questions for the Victim

- What is the victim's e-mail address and Internet service provider?
- What are all usernames and e-mail accounts used by the victim?

- Obtain printed copies of any e-mails received by the victim. (*Note*: Do not turn on the victim's computer to print these e-mails.)

Questions for the Suspect/Target
- What is the suspect's e-mail address and Internet service provider?
- What are the usernames and e-mail accounts for all e-mail accounts used by the suspect?
- What software/usernames are used by the suspect and associated passwords?

Investigative Questions for Instant Messaging/Internet Relay Chat Crimes

Questions for the Victim
- Has the victim had the logging/archiving feature activated during chat sessions?
- What is the victim's online screen name(s) and e-mail address(es)?
- Does the victim have any copies of the material already printed?
- What type of software/chat client does the victim use?

Questions for the Suspect/Target
- What is the suspect's online screen name(s) and e-mail address(es)?
- What software/usernames are used by the suspect and their associated passwords?

While these types of questions are not all inclusive, they provide an excellent starting point for detectives at the crime scene and will provide valuable information for digital forensic examiners processing the evidence in the laboratory.

Seizure of a Computer

After all persons have been removed, it is important to determine if the computer is on, off, or simply in a state that appears to be off. If the computer is on, we must determine if it is a stand-alone computer or if it is connected to a server. If it is connected to a server, contact someone knowledgeable for assistance. If it is a stand-alone machine, check to make sure there are no destructive processes running. Next, determine if the computer is on a network. If a network is present, determine if there is any data transfer on that network. If data transference is present, document that information and call for assistance. If no transfer is happening, isolate that machine and check for any encryption programs actively running. If encryption software is found, interview the suspect for any information. Keep in mind this interview may not produce good information.

   After all these steps have been taken, pull the plug from the back of the computer. If it is a laptop, remove the battery and power cord. If the computer appears to be off, perform a sleep test to ensure it is truly off by simply moving the mouse or something. If it is found to be on, follow the steps described earlier. If the computer is off, it should remain off and simply pull the plug from the back of the machine as described previously. Then documentation and preparation for packaging and transport should be done. A step flowchart of the aforementioned steps of a computer can be seen below.

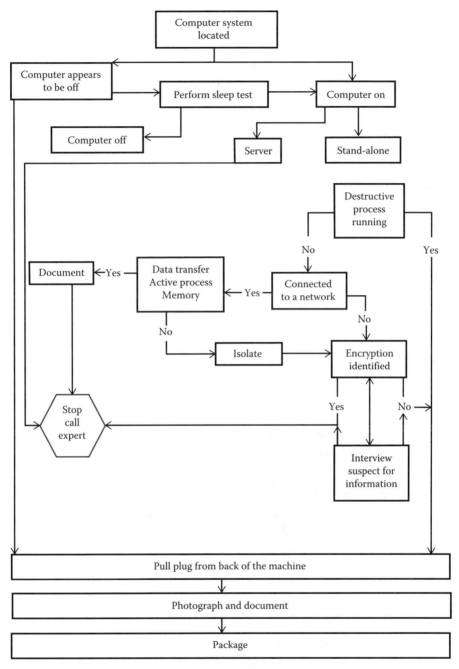

Adapted from the International Association of Computer Investigative Specialists,
Basic Computer Forensic Examiner Course, Maitland, FL, May 2014.

Seizure of a Cell Phone or Other Mobile Devices

As with a computer, if it is already off, leave it off. It is also important to remember when seizing a portable device to also seize any power cords that go with it. In some of the older cellular phones, if the battery dies, data can be lost. It may be necessary to plug it in to a power source to avoid this issue. It is also essential to make sure it is not connecting to the network. Remember, some devices have a built-in remote wipe capability that a user can initiate as long as the device is connected to the network. There are some current recommendations for removing a cell phone from the network. The phone can be turned off, placed in a faraday bag, placed in an all-metal paint can, wrapped in tin foil, or simply turned off. In addition, if the device has a passcode, ask the suspect for the code. They may not give it to you, but it never hurts to ask. If you don't have it, "do not" make guesses. The phone will eventually lock up, and then even someone with the correct passcode will not be able to gain access.

Documenting a Digital Crime Scene

The first thing done to document the digital crime scene, as with any other scene, is to photograph the scene. In addition to the overview photographs and close-ups, pictures of how any cables or cords are attached may be necessary. After photographs are taken, it may also be necessary to record and mark the location of cables for future reference. Remember some things in the scene that are not digital in nature may still be important, such as manuals, books, and notes found around the computer.

Documenting digital evidence.

Packaging and Transporting Digital Evidence

The packaging and transportation of digital evidence is important just as with any other type of evidence. Methods for packaging digital evidence should include steps to protect the media from physical damage and damage from electromagnetic sources. Physical damage can come from a multitude of things, some of which can be obvious. It can be caused by heat/cold, moisture, or living creatures. Electromagnetic sources of damage can be cell phones, radios, and the magnets found in speakers. When packaging or storing digital evidence, "never" use plastic bags. There are storage containers made specifically for the packaging of digital devices, such as antistatic bags. Packaging that is also acceptable for digital media could be paper bags or cardboard boxes.

Antistatic bags.

Antistatic Bags

When using any of the proper packaging material, precautions should be taken to ensure the devices are also being protected from physical damage that could be done during transport. Be aware of where the items are being placed in the vehicle for transport. Do not place them near the radios, speakers, in a place where moisture could accumulate, or somewhere the temperatures are too extreme. In addition, just like any other evidence that is seized, proper chain of custody must be maintained.

Questions for Discussion

9.1 What can be considered digital evidence?
9.2 What are some crimes that could involve the use of digital evidence?
9.3 What are important legal issues to consider when obtaining digital evidence?
9.4 What should be considered when packaging and transporting digital evidence?

References

Hailey, S. (2003, September 19). What is computer forensics. Retrieved from Cyber Security Institute website, http://www.cybersecurityinstitute.biz/forensics.htm (accessed on April 11, 2011).

International Association of Computer Investigative Specialists (IACIS). (May 2014). Basic Computer Forensic Examiner Course, Maitland, FL.

National Forensic Science Technology Center. (2014). *A Simplified Guide to Digital Evidence.* Largo, FL: National Forensic Science Technology Center. Retrieved from http://www.crime-scene-investigator.net (accessed on July 24, 2014).

U.S. Department of Homeland Security. (2007). Best practices for seizing electronic evidence v. 3.1. A pocket guide for first responders. Washington, DC: United States Secret Service.

USLegal. (2001–2014). *Definitions.* Retrieved from USLegal website, http://definitions.uslegal.com/d/digital-evidence (accessed on July 24, 2014).

Cybercrime Investigation: An International Perspective

10

SZDE YU

Contents

Chapter Objectives	147
Chapter Outline	147
Define Cybercrime	148
International Cybercrime Operations	150
Political Motives	150
Financial Motives	151
Other Motives	153
International Cybercrime Investigations	154
Tracing the Perpetrator	154
Tracing the Money	157
Other Clues	158
Challenges	159
Summary	160
Question for Discussion	161
References	161

Chapter Objectives

After reading this chapter, you should be able to do the following:

1. Understand the nature of cybercrimes.
2. Understand cybercrime's transnational operation.
3. Understand the challenges faced in investigating international cybercrimes.
4. Understand what evidence is relevant in cybercrime investigation.

Chapter Outline

Define Cybercrime
International Cybercrime Operations
Political Motives
Financial Motives
Other Motives
International Cybercrime Investigations
Tracing the Perpetrator
Tracing the Money

Other Clues
Challenges
Summary

Define Cybercrime

According to the International Criminal Police Organization (INTERPOL), cybercrime is one of the fastest growing crimes, and it is estimated that cybercrime has cost the world billions of dollars every year (INTERPOL, 2014). Although we should always be cautious about the accuracy of these estimates, it is fair to say that cybercrime has moved beyond just a few computer geeks trying to show off their computer skills as many traditional criminals are now exploring how to facilitate their criminal activities through the relative freedom and elusiveness provided in the digital world. Moreover, cyberspace can readily extend reach to a wider selection of victims, often across geographic boundaries. If criminals do not respect the law, we cannot expect them to be stopped by a human-defined borderline. For criminals, physically passing a borderline entails certain difficulty, while in cyberspace, the difficulty of going international is minimal. In fact, the number one reason that discourages criminals from operating on an international level in cyberspace is the language barrier. However, this barrier is becoming more and more conquerable owing to modern technologies that offer instant translation on the Internet or on a handheld electronic device.

Since cyberspace offers more opportunities and seemingly more anonymity, it did not take long before a variety of cybercrime started burgeoning on the Internet. Although INTERPOL was right about cybercrime's fast growth, it was wrong in implying cybercrime is a single category of crime. Cybercrime consists of a wide range of criminal activities, and it is improper to discuss them as one phenomenon as if they can be understood all at the same time. The only thing they share so as to be categorized as cybercrime is the involvement of a computer or a computer network. Besides this commonality, they can be quite distinctive with regard to their motives, nature, impact, and skills required. It is also unwise to assume cybercrime as fundamentally different from traditional crime because the prevalence of modern technologies has substantially blurred the line. Before we classify cybercrime, it is important to note that a computer in the context of cybercrime refers to any electronic devices that can be programmed to carry out computational operations and possess the capacity to access the Internet. Hence, a tablet, a cell phone (especially smartphones), as well as a laptop or desktop should all be seen as a computer.

Cybercrime has been defined as "computer-mediated activities that are illegal" (Yar, 2006, p. 10). Some scholars prefer to include deviant acts (e.g., sexually explicit content) in the discussion of cybercrime, but we will focus on illegal acts with the understanding that the details of law could vary. Apparently, this broad and inevitably vague definition does not suffice when it comes to criminal investigation. In the following, we will classify cybercrime according to the different nature of the crime.

The first type of cybercrime is "stealth" (e.g., data theft and hacking), which does not require interaction with the victim. Preferably, the victim never notices the crime. In this type of cybercrime, the goal is to acquire or alter whatever digital data they are targeting (sometimes unintended data might be included). For example, in 2013, the third largest retail corporation in the United States, Target Corp., reported a data breach on debit and credit cards used by customers in Target stores (RT, 2014). The incident was categorized by the U.S. government as a cyberattack, but essentially, it is criminals stealing sensitive data from the victims. This type of cybercrime is in general financially motivated as the stolen data can be resold for profit. However, it could also entail a political agenda, such as hatred toward American companies or big corporations. Espionage is another salient possibility. It is important to remember that a criminal motive can be multidimensional, meaning the crime could be serving more than one purpose (Yu, 2013).

The second type of cybercrime is "deception," which normally requires the victim's response in order for the victimization to be accomplished. The goal is to deceive the victim so that he or she will voluntarily offer sensitive information that the criminal is seeking. The rampant phishing e-mails roaming on the Internet nowadays would be a good example. If the recipient does not respond, the attempt would end in failure. Deception can be further classified into two subcategories: general target and specific target. For the most part, deception in cybercrime aims at the general Internet users without targeting a particular person but occasionally a victim could be specifically chosen based on certain characteristics. The motive is mostly financial but it could be more complex than one single motive, depending on the parties involved.

The third type of cybercrime is "destruction" (e.g., cybervandalism and malware). The goal is to result in a destructive impact on a computer, a website, or a network. This type of cybercrime is generally associated with a political motive, but it could also be simply someone showing off computer skills. In some cases, the criminals might demand a ransom to capitalize on fear of destruction (e.g., ransomware). The victim usually is chosen because of its symbolic meaning (e.g., White House website represents American government), but it could be random as well. In fact, most computer viruses were distributed over the Internet without a specific target. The extreme form of this type of cybercrime can be regarded as cyberterrorism or cyberwar.

The fourth type of cybercrime is "transaction." Like businessmen, criminals in these crimes aim to sell products, such as drugs, sex, data, or even regular household items. They might be selling legal items in a criminal way, such as selling clothes via e-mail spam, or they could be outright selling illegal items. Sometimes, they do not really sell for money, but rather they exchange their criminal possessions with like-minded people electronically, such as child pornography. In any events, they need to advertise what they have in some way to attract potential clients. Conceivably, the production or acquisition of the advertised goods could very well be another crime in itself. Therefore, although there may not be always a clear victim in these transactions, victimization may still exist either pre- or posttransaction. From an investigative point of view, the chain of events should be looked into altogether, instead of focusing on only the transaction itself.

The last type of cybercrime is much more personal and therefore usually targets a specific victim. This type is called "affliction," such as cyberbullying and cyberstalking. Acquaintance between the perpetrator and the victim can be expected. The goal is usually other than monetary gains or political statements. Rather, mostly the perpetrator seeks gratification from knowing the victim is being tormented by such affliction or from invading the victim's privacy. Without sufficient gratification or with too much fun, the crime is likely to escalate either way. When escalated, the affliction could be carried over from the digital world into the physical world. Once again, it is naïve to think cybercrime and street crime are always separated. Some incidents of hacking may fall into this category as well, if the real target is the person instead of the organization or data. Likewise, a computer virus could be planted on a specific person's computer to exert affliction. Hence, it is important to note that the typology introduced here does not mean to assert that one crime can only fall into one category. The imperative is to identify the nature of the crime, rather than be bound by the label of the crime.

After the nature is identified, investigators then look into motive, means, and opportunity. The same motive could result in different natures of crime. For example, when the motive is money, some criminals choose to sell black market drugs (i.e., transaction) while others could choose to engage in online scams (i.e., deception). The same nature does not guarantee the same means. For example, cyberbullying and hacking into the victim's computer to spy on him or her can both be affliction in nature, but the means (i.e., computer skills) required to accomplish these offenses can be vastly different. Moreover, the means should not solely define the nature. For instance, vandalizing someone's blog might seem to be destruction, but if such vandalism is merely a way of afflicting suffering on this particular person, it should be seen as more of affliction than destruction. As for opportunity, it can be argued that as long as you have an online presence, there is opportunity for you to be victimized in cybercrime, and likewise, you can always find opportunity to commit a cybercrime. Despite the prevalence of opportunity, investigators ought to pay special attention to who is privy to such online presence, especially when the access to it is supposed to be private. To illustrate, you may have an e-mail account or a website (i.e., online presence), but it does not mean everybody would know about it or have access.

This chapter discusses cybercrime investigation with an emphasis on the international perspective. The assumption is the readers already possess a decent understanding on cybercrime in general. It is crucial to understand what cybercrime is and how it might manifest in different forms as mentioned earlier.

International Cybercrime Operations

Political Motives

The transnational nature of cybercrime lends itself well to international operations. Some of these international operations are driven by political motives. Political motives are traditionally seen in the destruction type of cybercrime. Chinese hackers have been known for launching attacks on the U.S. government's web infrastructure. According to the Center for Public Integrity, Chinese hackers crashed the Federal Election Commission's computer system during the federal government shutdown in 2013 (CNN, 2013). These foreign hackers also have launched numerous cyberattacks on U.S. companies in the past few years (Vijayan, 2013). It has been suspected that the Chinese government could be behind these organized hacking activities. Although these acts are usually referred to as cyberattacks, in many of these incidents, hackers are actually attempting to steal data, which makes such attacks more in line with stealth rather than destruction. Several hacker groups are for hire to engage in espionage, such as Hidden Lynx or Icefog. Their goal is to steal industrial secrets and sell them to the highest bidder or whoever hires them. These groups rarely use the stolen data themselves, so after theft, they usually need to engage in the transaction type of cybercrime subsequently. Although seemingly these hackers are working for money, their political motivation should never be discounted. Many of these hacker groups are possibly backed by a government and only attack targets in a foreign nation. In 2013, a confidential report prepared for the Pentagon alleged Chinese hackers have stolen various weapon designs from the U.S. military (CBS News, 2013). Of course, China is not the only country that utilizes cyberattacks for political reasons. According to Edward Snowden, the U.S. National Security Agency runs an Office of Tailored Access Operations (TAO) as a vast hacking unit on behalf of the U.S. government (Stevens, 2014). TAO's operations allegedly range from counterterrorism to cyberattacks to traditional espionage (Stevens, 2014). The U.S. government also has been suspected to be involved in the creation of a computer virus, Stuxnet, which was used to target Iranian nuclear facilities in 2009 and 2010 with some success (Zetter, 2013).

Besides these government-related (allegedly) operations, some international cybercrimes could be orchestrated by politically extremists, such as terrorists. Terrorists could resort to cyberterrorism when traditional attacks are being foiled at an increasing rate. Sometimes, they simply make a threat to a foreign country via the Internet. In 2011, Taipei police received an e-mail sent from the United States by self-proclaimed "Aryan Nation" threatening to attack four skyscrapers in Taiwan (Culpan and Ong, 2011). Despite the absence of actual attacks, a threatening e-mail like this can already be seen as an international cybercrime. To date, there have not been major cyberterrorist events recorded. Some incidents that might have been described as cyberterrorism in the media are merely cybervandalism or at best cyberattacks mentioned earlier. Nonetheless, cyberterrorism is more than just a movie plot. It is perfectly possible when terrorists come across a weakness exploitable in a computer system that can result in devastating effects, such as air traffic systems, nuclear power plant systems, or emergency dispatch systems. In 2014, a Malaysia Airlines Flight 370 went missing for several days, and some people suspected this incident might result from a terrorist plot that had a cyberterrorism component in it (The Week, 2014).

When politics is involved, people tend to develop double standards due to conflicting political stances. However, it is important to note that form a legal point of view, a crime is a crime. It is hypocritical to condemn the act when other people do it to us, while trying to justify it when we are doing the same thing to others. In 2013, a Taiwanese fisherman was brutally murdered by the Philippine Coast Guard. While the two governments were negotiating for a solution, the people in Taiwan were losing patience. Consequently, some hackers in the name of "Anonymous" launched cyberattacks on several Philippine network infrastructures. Figure 10.1 shows the message left on Philippine domain registry website. Although this was seen as righteous payback by most Taiwanese people, at the same time, they were worried about counterattacks from Philippine hackers, which did occur, but were much less successful.

Financial Motives

Money has always been a strong motivation for people and criminals alike. Theoretically, the bigger the market is, the more money can be made. Although cyberspace is ideal for doing international business, some restraints are still in place. For instance, when shopping on Amazon.com, you would notice many items are only available on American soil because the sellers will not or cannot ship them overseas. This "foreignness" restraint applies to criminal activities as well but such restraints could sometimes be seen as a safeguard by criminal-minded people. In 2010, a public university in upstate New York received complaints about credit card charges issued by the university's various financial services. The credit card

Figure 10.1 Hackers attack on Philippine DNS website.

owners never visited that university but their credit card bills indicated expenses on campus. A further investigation revealed that the university had been unwillingly used by some cybercriminals to validate stolen credit card numbers. Allegedly, this was operated overseas in East Europe, and therefore, the foreignness that hinders international shopping on Amazon.com is now protecting these cybercriminals from being identified.

Financial motives can be found in almost all types of international cybercrime. For example, almost everyone who uses e-mail has received at least one or two messages from some Nigerian princes or some British lottery agencies claiming you are entitled to an unexpected fortune. The author of this chapter has done some extensive investigation in these online scams and found that despite the deceptive nature of scam, most of them are surprisingly honest about their nationality. Scammers probably do not want the victim to send money to the wrong country, and they are not afraid to disclose which country they reside in because they count on the foreignness as protection. Figure 10.2 shows an example of international scam e-mails.

Besides scam and stealing from a foreign country, some financially motivated criminals use other methods in their international operations. Human trafficking is one example, even though it is not normally considered a cybercrime. Trafficking a person cannot be accomplished via the Internet, but enticing victims to come to you is perfectly feasible on the Internet. Every year, many teenagers run away from home to meet some "friends" they met online and end up being sold as sex slaves. Moreover, global marketing for sexual services is also suitable online. Not all sex services require physical contact. Many porno websites offer pay-per-view video streams, and this type of service can be operated anywhere around the world. As stressed, cybercrime is not necessarily a unique category distant from traditional crimes. Many old crimes now have incorporated a digital component. Drugs, guns, and any other contraband can all be purchased on the "Deep Web." The Deep Web sites are the websites (e.g., Silk Road) that exist on the Internet but they cannot be indexed by the major search engines (e.g., Google). In other words, they are only accessible through special software, such as Tor (https://www.torproject.org/).

Dear Sir/Madam

I am Mr. Minto Mansoor, there is a Foreign customer of our financial institution with some good financial asset, although now late. We tried to find a possible successor to no avail. I want you to stand as the successor to this fund. I want you to know that this deal is risk free for you as we keep the transaction confidential.

It involves the transfer of sum US$ 9.8 million Dollars. I shall perfect all legal documents in your name to make you the legal beneficiary to the funds, Once the funds are transferred to your nominated account then we will share the proceeds in a ratio of 45% for me, 45% for you and 10% for the less privileged. Please it is a secret deal.

Kindly respond with the following information below for further details if you are interested in this business.

1: Full names
2: Private Phone:
3: Fax number.
3: Your residential address.

Hope to hear from you shortly as your response will be confidential and will be given immediate attention. Call or Fax me on the below details.

Kind Regards,

Mr. Minto Mansoor.
Tele/Fax: +27-865-111-808
South Africa.

Figure 10.2 A scam e-mail.

In contrast, there are crimes that are strictly cybercrime for they can only exist in the digital world, such as digital piracy. People in Asia can download a song from America with ease, whereas Americans can find a Japanese animation on the Internet in a few seconds. As mentioned, the only real hurdle is the language barrier. With peer-to-peer software, the whole world can be sharing pirated digital files, and for the most part, the participants (or perpetrators) do not even know or care where the sources of downloading are. In the world of digital piracy, nationality is simply irrelevant. Transferring a digital file across borderlines is too easy and virtually free. Therefore, digital piracy is indeed the most prevalent international cybercrime, and annually, it has cost copyright holders nearly 4.4 billion in music piracy (RIAA, 2014) and 63.4 billion in software piracy (BSA, 2011).

Other Motives

Although most cybercrimes seem to stem from a financial or a political motive, there could be other motives. Many people who illegally make digital intellectual property available (called crackers rather than hackers) do not engage in digital piracy for money. They simply share pirated files without charging a fee. Some of them do this for fame, as they want to be recognized in the underground cyberspace even though their true identity probably is still hidden. Some crackers do not care for either money or fame. They do it because they can.

It is one way of self-assurance in which they do not need to be recognized personally as long as they know other people would appreciate their contribution. It is the psychological gratification they seek, or they could be simply altruistic. Some may be doing it to harm a particular copyright holder. For instance, it is a well-known fact in the IT world that Microsoft is not the most popular software company, and therefore, many people would love to see the company's profit dwindle on account of digital piracy. This type of motive arguably could be political but the political statement is usually less obvious.

Some pedophiles exchange illegal materials to make like-minded friends, regardless of money or politics. Some students hack the school's Banner system to change grades without a financial or political motive. There are people launching a cyberattack for personal vendetta rather than political agenda. The affliction type of cybercrime mostly does not involve a financial or political motive, either. The bottom line is that no motive is exclusive to only one type of cybercrime. The same motive can result in different criminal acts and the same criminal act could be motivated by different reasons. However, when it comes to international cybercrime (except altruistic digital piracy), politics and money are predominantly the motive. When other motives are involved, the cybercrime is more likely to be a local operation.

International Cybercrime Investigations

As cybercrime starts to grasp more attention in law enforcement, most agencies are confounded with jurisdictional issues. When a murder occurs in New York City, more often than not, the NYPD has the jurisdiction over the crime. However, when a hacker living in Russia attacks servers around the world, the jurisdictional issue becomes much more complex because international collaboration is vital in investigation and yet it is often unattainable. To resolve this, the Council of Europe adopted an international treaty, called Convention on Cybercrime, in 2001 in an effort to harmonize laws in different nations with regard to cybercrime and promote cooperation among participating nations (Convention on Cybercrime, n.d.). As of March 2014, 42 nations including nonmembers of the Council of Europe have ratified this treaty. In 2006, the United States also ratified this treaty, and it took effect on January 1, 2007 (Council of Europe, 2014). Despite this treaty's intention to unite governmental forces to fight international cybercrime, it is not without criticisms. Obviously, many nations do not participate (notably, China and Russia), but the most salient concern is regarding privacy, because under this treaty, governments should be granted power to monitor citizens' online activities and share citizens' information with foreign governments in the name of combating cybercrime. The treaty also requires signatory nations to criminalize certain behavior so as to harmonize a common legal framework that eliminates jurisdictional hurdles, whereas the said behavior could be protected by some nations' constitutions (e.g., racism and freedom of speech). These concerns are beyond the scope of this chapter, but they are important to note. Investigators ought to be aware of the power at their disposal and the potential abuse of such power.

Tracing the Perpetrator

Tracking down a criminal in the physical world is already challenging at times, but it is even more difficult in cyberspace. The biggest challenge is the lack of the offender's physical presence at the crime scene or the lack of a well-defined crime scene to begin with, which changes the definition of "opportunity" in criminal investigation. In theory, everyone with access to cyberspace has opportunity. Victims in cybercrime typically only detect victimization after the fact. By the time the crime is reported, much evidence could have been inadvertently deleted or contaminated, considering the volatility of digital evidence. For example, in Figure 10.2, the contact information provided by the scammer was initially legitimate, because they needed the victim to be able to contact them. However, it expired very quickly and became untraceable thereafter. Hence, in cybercrime investigation, the major determinants for success are the ability to promptly identify suspects and the ability to trace the suspect's whereabouts. As discussed, the foreignness of international cybercrime normally offers a safeguard for criminals because even if you know who they are and where they are based in, you may not be able to take any action. This is why international collaboration, such as the Convention on Cybercrime, is believed to be warranted. Nonetheless, before any international assistance can be acquired, investigators still need to identify suspects and have an idea at least which nation the perpetrators operate in.

In most cases, an IP address is the most crucial clue. IP stands for Internet Protocol. In order for computers to communicate with one another and form a network, they must use the same communications protocol. The Internet is essentially formed by connecting numerous computers that use the Transmission Control Protocol/Internet Protocol (TCP/IP). Each computer is then assigned an address (i.e., IP address). The most common version of IP address is IPv4, a 32-bit number. In a Windows operating system, the user can find the IP address allocated to the local machine by checking the "Details" of "Local Area Connection Status" (Windows, n.d.). Figure 10.3 shows an example of the IPv4 address. On a Mac, the IP address can be found by checking the "System Preferences."

Because IPv4 addresses are running out due to the increasing number of machines connected to the Internet, IPv6, a 128-bit number, has been deployed in 2000s. An IPv4 address can be represented as IPv6. In principle, if investigators can identify the IP address, they would be able to know where the machine is located. All IP addresses are supposedly registered by the Internet service provider (ISP), so a simple "whois" search may reveal who registered the IP address in question. Figure 10.4 shows the registration information on the IP address given in Figure 10.3. If a cyberattack was launched from the aforementioned IP address, then it seems the attack originates from the United States, and the additional information should help shed more light. The same principle can apply to tracing the origin of an e-mail by examining the header information.

However, tracing the IP address is limited in its capacity to identify a suspect. First, an IP address at best indicates a machine or a device. Investigators still need to establish reasonable proof that the suspect was the person using this device to commit a crime. Second, one IP address can be shared among several machines (especially on WiFi), just like one computer could be shared among several users. Third, many IP addresses are dynamic, which means the ISP does not always allocate the same IP address to the same device, such as most smartphones do not have a permanent IP address. Conversely, the same IP address could be used by a different computer at a different time. These limitations are the reason why the time factor is extremely important. Without specifying what time the crime occurred, it would be difficult to link an IP address to a particular computer, let alone a particular person. Moreover, IP addresses can be hidden. A proxy, VPN, and Tor are a few popular methods used by cybercriminals to disguise their IP address. As a result, a criminal operating in the United States could appear to come from Finland,

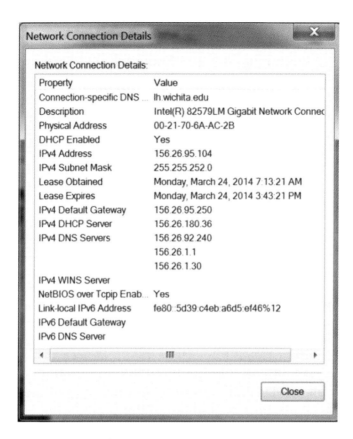

Figure 10.3 IPv4 address on Windows 7.

156.26.95.104 - Geo Information

IP Address	156.26.95.104
Host	156.26.95.104
Location	US, United States
City	Wichita, KS 67260
Organization	Wichita State University
ISP	Wichita State University
AS Number	AS22245 Wichita State University
Latitude	37°69'36" North
Longitude	97°48'04" West

Figure 10.4 Whois information on IP address.

for example. There are also cyberattacks launched through botnets. A botnet is usually created through infecting numerous computers around the world to gain control over these computers without the rightful owner's knowledge. Criminals then use these unwilling participants in the botnet to perform a task, such as a distributed denial of service attack or sending spam e-mail. In these cases, tracing the perpetrator by the IP address could be futile, although it is not entirely impossible.

Notwithstanding, not all cybercriminals are computer savvy or careful enough to eliminate traces. An IP address is still a reliable clue when you try to track down a pedophile that has been downloading child pornography onto his or her personal computer, or a student who is downloading pirated motives in the dorm room. Certainly, it is more complicated in international operations, but the fundamentals are similar. You cannot expect foreign agencies to be of much help when you have no idea where the crime originates.

Lastly, it is important to note that even though cybercriminals can be elusive and hard to catch, they still live in the physical world. Sometimes, their crimes require a physical presence to be fully accomplished. For instance, a pedophile can hide on the Internet to lure victims but eventually he or she has to show up if he or she desires to have any physical contact with the victim. Sometimes, despite their computer skills, cybercriminals may not be as good at other aspects of their life. For example, in 2000, two Russian hackers, Alexey Ivanov and Vasiliy Gorshkov, flew to Seattle to apply for a job in a computer security company. When Ivanov and Gorshkov thought their life was about to get better owing to their computer skills and bragged about their hacking accomplishments during the job interview, they did not know the company was a shell created by the FBI. The lure was so successful that the FBI tried the same gambit again in 2004, although the outcome this time was less successful (Poulsen, 2008; Jahnke, 2005). The point is even if investigators cannot win in the digital world, there might be other ways of tracing the perpetrator, such as social engineering. Social engineering is the attempt to influence people without force so that they would accomplish a goal that may or may not be in their best interests. For instance, a person might befriend you to earn your trust and convince you to reveal your personal information when he or she plans on using such information to benefit himself or herself or to hurt you. Social engineering has long been a crucial part of crime, including many cybercrimes, especially the deception type. Investigators should be mindful of this component in cybercrime investigation rather than solely fixate on the computer component. Social skills and computer skills can be equally important in cybercrimes.

Tracing the Money

When the perpetrator is elusive, another important clue in crime is money. As discussed, money is a strong motive in many cybercrimes. While criminals hide their identities and digital footprints, the money they are seeking is often hard to hide and hard to give up. Unlike street drug dealing, in cybercrime, the money is unlikely to be in cash. Without cash, financial payment is mostly traceable. A stolen credit card, when used, will result in a transaction record that indicates when and where even if the transaction takes place online. More often than not, receiving a payment would also expose the perpetrator's identifiable information, such as bank account information. Even a PO box rented under a fake name still helps in placing the perpetrator's physical presence. Although digital currency, such as Bitcoin, does offer more secrecy in black market transactions in cyberspace, the transactions are not untraceable. They are just encrypted, which means it requires more effort to acquire evidence, whereas the criminal is also less able to alter it. Moreover, when money is stored somewhere, either online or in a bank, the connotation is the authority may seize it upon good reasons or at least freeze the account pending investigation. Unless the criminal forsakes the account completely, any access or attempt to access could give away some traces, such as the IP address used to log on the website.

Hence, by following the money, investigators could be led to viable suspects or persons of interest to say the least. Many thieves can successfully steal credit card numbers without being detected, but they become vulnerable when they use a physical address to deliver the goods purchased with the stolen card. By monitoring the money flow, the criminals' entire operation could be outlined. This is especially useful in international cybercrime investigations. Some criminals believe they are safe as long as they set up an oversea account to receive payments, but it may not be true. In 2010, a Chinese technology company was blackmailed by unknown hackers. The hackers demonstrated their ability to disrupt the company's business and asked for $250,000. The money was wired to an account in a foreign country. Although the Chinese law enforcement had no authority to touch that account, they never ceased monitoring it. Three months later, when someone transferred some of the money to an account in Hong Kong, the investigators were able to follow the money and identify the suspects living in Hong Kong, who then led the police to the mastermind hiding in Western Europe. Although the Chinese police were not able to apprehend this mastermind, they at least dismantled this ring's operation in China and more importantly learned a great deal about how cybercriminals operate internationally. It is noteworthy that more and more cybercrimes are committed by a group of criminals as organized crime (INTERPOL, 2014), and therefore, the ability to move the money quickly after the crime becomes even more critical because all participants want to get paid and disgruntled criminals might start talking.

Criminals will always keep evolving and adopt new schemes. The central principle to keep in mind is that when investigators determine money is the motive, they should immediately try to examine the money transfer mechanism used in the crime. Following the money can be beneficial as discussed. By cutting the money flow, at times, criminals would be forced to make a desperate move and thus increase chance to make mistakes. Furthermore, if the criminals do not seem to care about money, investigators ought to be alert enough to consider alternative motives. Sometimes, money is secondary to the true cause or it could be merely a ruse serving to distract investigation (e.g., terrorism).

Other Clues

Not all cybercrimes are about money, so tracing the money might not apply. When tracing the perpetrator directly does not seem easy either, many investigators would choose to give up because they believe they have hit a dead end. Actually, there are other clues that are often overlooked. Many cybercriminals aim at no specific targets in their operations, including international operations. They choose whatever is convenient. For instance, when some Nigerian scammers sent you an e-mail trying to defraud you of your money, they did not choose you, the person; rather, they sent the e-mail to you only because they have your e-mail address, along with others. The address was likely collected by automated software programs from the website. In other words, you were targeted because your contact information was conveniently attainable. Some hackers choose their targets by port scanning, which identifies vulnerable servers they can break into. In this manner, they are also choosing conveniently accessible targets. When criminals operate in this impersonal fashion, they tend to engage in trial and error and result in many failed attempts. Unfortunately, because it failed, the attempt does not usually draw sufficient attention from law enforcement. When was the last time someone reported receiving computer viruses blocked by antivirus programs? When cybercrime fails, it tends to be seen as annoyance rather than criminal activity. Sometimes, they are still not seen as crime even when they are successful.

This is a shame because much intelligence could be derived from those failed attempts. For example, if law enforcement actively investigates the content in spam e-mails, a noticeable amount of criminal activities can be easily identified, ranging from counterfeit goods, illegal drug sales, sex trades, digital piracy, to international fraud rings (Yu, 2011). With proper analysis and proactive approaches, valuable intelligence is practically delivered by criminals themselves. Nonetheless, most people, including law enforcement agencies, still think e-mail spam requires nothing more than a delete button. Failed attempts in other types of cybercrime can also be valuable. Computer viruses must come from a source, such as a website or a program, so even if infection is averted, investigation can still be carried out to trace the source. Failed hacking attempts often leave behind some trails that indicate the origin of the attack. By collecting information on these failed attempts over time, the knowledge gained from the analysis could become helpful in future investigations.

Some other clues may be derived from the victim by studying victimology. Victimology is the study of the victim's role in crime. Although many cybercrimes are indiscriminate of victims, studying known victims can still learn about the criminals' habit. For example, in 2012, the author created a new e-mail address to register on a reputable website and did not use this e-mail address for any other purposes. Three weeks later, this address started to receive spam e-mails. Considering that e-mail address was only associated with this website, it would suggest a strong possibility that this website had a data breach that allowed cybercriminals to attain members' e-mail addresses from the website's database. Another possibility is this website was selling user information to spammers. Either way, a crime has occurred. Without studying victimology in this case, it would be hard for investigators to narrow down the source to this particular website. When the victim is specifically chosen, victimology will be even more helpful in narrowing down suspects with motive and opportunity.

International collaboration is critical when victimology indicates victims with international backgrounds. In addition to language issues, the victim's different culture and social background should also be taken into consideration. In 2009, a Chinese international student was accused of possession of child pornography in the United States, but a further investigation revealed that the female in the questionable pornographic photos was actually a 25-year-old Japanese woman wearing high school uniforms. The misunderstanding stemmed from the American investigators' unfamiliarity with Asian culture.

Challenges

Culture is a salient challenge investigators are faced with in international cybercrime investigation. Due to different cultures, different nations at times have trouble enacting compatible laws to criminalize certain computer-related activities. For example, not all nations have the same view on child pornography, especially when it comes to computer-generated pornography and the definition of "child." Another example is that cyberattack on a foreign government or corporation is not always deemed illegal, considering many governments are actually sponsoring these clandestine activities. When the popular sentiment is that if I am the victim, it is crime, but if I am the attacker, it is for good cause, there is practically no hope to expect any nations to actively deal with their patriotic hackers. When the national laws fail to reconcile internationally, it makes investigative collaboration much more difficult. Even if the law is enacted in response to international pressure, such as the Convention on Cybercrime, the implementation and enforcement of the law might not be always as advertised. This is because each nation has different priorities. Given limited resources, sometimes, it is simply not in their best interests to devote too much to solving a crime overseas. Moreover, training adequate personnel to be capable of handling cybercrime investigation takes time and funds. As technology is advancing rapidly, it is not easy to equip enough investigators with sufficient expertise to catch up.

Even if we are confident in our own expertise, we normally cannot vouch for our international partners. Sloppy work done by a foreign agent could be detrimental to a case, while the domestic investigators may have little control over that. The deficiency on the foreign partner's end could include the inability to find all evidence, to collect all evidence without integrity issues, to efficiently process evidence, and to adequately preserve evidence for international sharing. In some sensitive cases, the concern also involves the willingness to honestly share accurate information and evidence.

It should be noted, by "evidence," we are not merely referring to digital evidence. It is a common misconception that in cybercrime investigation, investigators should focus on finding digital evidence. Although digital evidence is truly crucial, traditional evidence could prove to be critical in a cybercrime as well. For example, investigators can trace an IP address to a machine, but how do they prove who was actually using that machine? In this case, conventional evidence, such as fingerprints and eyewitnesses, could play an important role in expelling reasonable doubt. As mentioned, social engineering can be a component in many cybercrimes, and therefore, searching for evidence should be extended in that direction as well. In contrast, some people falsely believe digital evidence is only relevant to cybercrime. Today's technologies have long changed that. Even in street crimes, relevant evidence could be found in a mobile phone, a tablet, a GPS device, a surveillance camera, and so on. In 2014, Jules Bahler allegedly robbed a Michigan bank with a submachine gun. What led the FBI to his arrest was a selfie he shared on Facebook in which he was holding that submachine gun (Moye, 2014). Although bank robbery is not a cybercrime, one important, albeit circumstantial, piece of evidence in this case was a digital photo.

Summary

Cybercrime can be domestic as any other crimes, but its electronic nature lends well to transnational operations. Accordingly, investigation of these operations requires international collaboration to overcome jurisdictional issues. While efforts are being made to establish a harmonized partnership internationally, hardship is still prevalent. First, not all nations are willing participants in these efforts. Second, even among participants political agenda sometimes prevail over crime solving. Nevertheless, international cybercrime has become a trend on account of the rampant growth in amount and drastic expansion in scope of cybercrime. Tracing the perpetrator in international cybercrime can be challenging because skilled criminals would know how to conceal their true identity and origin, and even if they are not so skilled, much information can only be acquired with help from a foreign agency while cooperation is not a guarantee. Despite this, investigators by no means should simply assume cybercriminals are untraceable. There are things worth trying, such as IP address lookup. Furthermore, it is important to be mindful that criminals do not live in cyberspace, so the social aspect of cybercrime should not be ignored. When identifying the perpetrator directly is impracticable, tracing money sometimes offers another avenue to the perpetrator's identity.

Challenges always exist in any type of criminal investigation, including international investigations. Incompetence, inefficiency, hidden agenda, language barrier, and the lack of funding are among the most common hurdles. The key to successful international cybercrime investigation is effective communication among international agencies. Sharing information is the essence, but it is a delicate issue regarding what information to share and how to share it. Even agencies working for the same government often withhold information from one another for various reasons. Nonetheless, these are agency-level issues, and individual investigators normally have little control over them. On an individual level, to offer adequate assistance, investigators ought to at least possess sufficient knowledge and skills in handling evidence. Both digital evidence and traditional evidence (e.g., physical evidence and testimonial evidence) should be looked for in cybercrime investigations. Some clues (e.g., spam e-mails or online classified ads) are available in plain sight but are often overlooked because of their seeming trivialness. A systematic collection and analysis might prove to be helpful in mapping out cybercriminals' activity.

Question for Discussion

10.1 What is international cybercrime? What elements make a cybercrime international?
10.2 Explain how different types of cybercrime might share the same motive.
10.3 If you are cyberbullied on Facebook, how do you trace the perpetrator for his or her real-life identity? How do you prove that?
10.4 What is a botnet? What may the use of botnet impede investigation?
10.5 What role does "social engineering" play in cybercrime and investigation?
10.6 What are the challenges in international investigations?
10.7 If an American bank's online banking system is attacked and the bank claims the attacks originated from a foreign nation, what do you do as the principal investigator? Outline your investigation procedure.

References

BSA. (2011). 2011 piracy study. Retrieved April 10, 2014 from http://globalstudy.bsa.org/2011/.
CBS News. (2013). How Chinese hackers steal US secrets. Retrieved March 12, 2014 from http://www.cbsnews.com/news/how-chinese-hackers-steal-us-secrets/.
CNN. (2013). Report: Chinese hackers attacked crucial government election website. Retrieved March 12, 2014 from http://politicalticker.blogs.cnn.com/2013/12/17/report-chinese-hackers-attacked-crucial-government-election-website/.
Convention on Cybercrime. (n.d.). Retrieved March 22, 2014 from http://conventions.coe.int/Treaty/EN/Treaties/Html/185.htm.

Council of Europe. (2014). Convention on cybercrime. Retrieved March 22, 2014 from http://
conventions.coe.int/Treaty/Commun/ChercheSig.asp?NT=185&CM=&DF=&CL=ENG.

Culpan, T. and Ong, J. (2011). Taiwan security stepped up after 'Aryan Nations' terror threat. Retrieved
March 12, 2014 from http://www.bloomberg.com/news/2011-09-15/taiwan-security-stepped-
up-after-aryan-nations-terror-threat.html.

INTERPOL. (2014). Cybercrime. Retrieved March 3, 2014 from http://www.interpol.int/Crime-areas
/Cybercrime/Cybercrime.

Jahnke, A. (2005). Alexey Ivanov and Vasiliy Gorshkov: Russian Hacker Roulette. Retrieved March
24, 2014 from http://www.csoonline.com/article/219964/alexey-ivanov-and-vasiliy-gorshkov-
russian-hacker-roulette.

Moye, D. (2014). Bank robbery suspect posts submachine gun selfie on Facebook before alleged
crime. Retrieved March 28, 2014 http://www.huffingtonpost.com/2014/03/10/jules-bahler_
n_4936115.html.

Poulsen, K. (2008). Valve tried to trick Half Life 2 hacker into fake job interview. Retrieved March 24,
2014 from http://www.wired.com/threatlevel/2008/11/valve-tricked-h/.

RIAA. (2014). Scope of problem. Retrieved April 10, 2014 from https://www.riaa.com/physicalpiracy.
php?content_selector=piracy-online-scope-of-the-problem.

RT. (2014). Target part of a broader cyber-attack, Russian hackers allegedly involved. Retrieved
March 6, 2014 from http://rt.com/usa/retailers-hacker-attack-russian-750/.

Stevens, R. (2014). Snowden reveals massive National Security Agency hacking unit. Retrieved March
12, 2014 from http://www.globalresearch.ca/snowden-reveals-massive-national-security-agency-
hacking-uunit/5363265.

The Week. (2014). Flight MH370: Investigators probe hijack or cyber attack. Retrieved March 20,
2014 from http://www.theweek.co.uk/world-news/flight-mh370/.

Vijayan, J. (2013). China-based hacking group behind hundreds of attacks on US companies.
Retrieved March 12, 2014 from http://www.computerworld.com/s/article/9242476/China_
based_hacking_group_behind_hundreds_of_attacks_on_U.S._companies.

Windows. (n.d.). Find your computer's IP address. Retrieved March 24, 2014 from http://windows.
microsoft.com/en-us/windows/find-computers-ip-address#1TC=windows-7.

Yar, M. (2006). *Cybercrime and Society*. Thousand Oaks, CA: Sage Publication.

Yu, S. (2011). Email spam and the CAN-SPAM act. *International Journal of Cyber Criminology*,
5(1), 715–735.

Yu, S. (2013). Behavioral evidence analysis on Facebook: A test of cyber-profiling. *Defendology*,
16(33), 17–30.

Zetter, K. (2013). Legal experts: Stuxnet attack on Iran was illegal act of force. Retrieved March 12, 2014
from http://www.wired.com/threatlevel/2013/03/stuxnet-act-of-force/.

Use of Crime Analysis in Criminal Investigations

11

DENIESE KENNEDY-KOLLAR

Contents

Chapter Objectives	163
Chapter Outline	163
Word about Crime Mapping	165
Administrative and Operational Analysis	165
Strategic Crime Analysis	166
Intelligence Analysis	167
Criminal Investigative Analysis	168
Geographic Profiling	168
Tactical Crime Analysis	169
Data Used in Tactical Crime Analysis	170
Linking Cases and Identifying Patterns	171
Types of Patterns	171
Induction and Deduction	173
Principle, Key, and Related Cases	173
Generating Leads	174
Clearing Cold Cases	174
Questions for Discussion	175
References	175

Chapter Objectives

After reading this chapter, you should be able to

1. Define crime analysis
2. Explain the primary purpose of crime analysis
3. Describe criminal investigative analysis
4. Explain various types of patterns
5. Compare and contrast inductive and deductive reasoning

Chapter Outline

Administrative and Operational Analysis
Strategic Crime Analysis
Intelligence Analysis
Criminal Investigative Analysis
Tactical Crime Analysis

Types of Patterns
Induction and Deduction
Principle, Key, and Related Cases

Crime analysts and officers trained in crime analysis techniques can offer valuable assistance to criminal investigators. Most crime analysis techniques can be applied in an investigation to aid in the understanding of information; an analyst can help make sense of information already known to the investigator and can help the investigator in the search for new information. Crime analysis is another tool in the investigator's arsenal.

In October 2002, John Allen Muhammad and Lee Boyd Malvo murdered 10 people and wounded 3 others in a series of sniper attacks in the Washington, DC, area. The attacks occurred across several areas in Maryland, Virginia, and Washington, DC. The multijuris-dictional nature of the investigation involved officers and agents from numerous local, state, and federal agencies. As part of their investigation, the police used spatial crime analysis techniques to link the attacks and to recognize which shootings were likely parts of the pattern (Shillingford and Grossman, 2014) (Figure 11.1).

Detectives have long recognized the value of having a visual representation of crime locations. Being able to "eyeball" the criminal landscape often helps detectives to identify patterns and link cases. Throughout most of the twentieth century, most police precincts contained a map of their city on which detectives could plot out crime locations using different colored push pins. In the twenty-first century, detectives work with crime analysts who perform sophisticated spatial analysis with state-of-the-art geographic information system software and who utilize queryable national and local databases to recognize patterns, link cases, and generate leads.

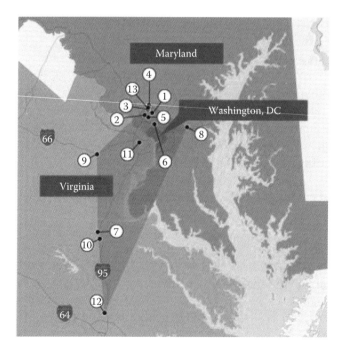

Figure 11.1 A spatial analysis of the October 2002 Washington, DC, area sniper shootings.

"Crime analysis" is still an emerging discipline. As such, it lacks a standardization of practice and training that professions eventually develop and resists a single, accepted definition. Different authors have defined crime analysis in numerous ways (see, e.g., Peterson, 1998; Bruce, 2004; Paulsen et al., 2010; Paynich and Hill, 2010; Santos, 2013). However, they all share a common thread identifying crime analysis as a methodological analysis of crime data in order to provide decision-making and investigative support to police. It is "the systematic study of crime and disorder problems as well as other police-related issues…to assist the police in criminal apprehension, crime and disorder reduction, crime prevention, and evaluation" (Santos, 2013, p. 2). As this definition demonstrates, crime analysis techniques can be used in many different support functions for police and administrators. This chapter will focus primarily on those methods used in police investigation. However, it is worthwhile to briefly discuss other forms of analysis as well.

Word about Crime Mapping

"Crime mapping" is the creation of a visual representation of the places in which crimes occur by plotting out their locations on a map. The process involves plotting crime location data on a digital map in order to make comparisons with other factors in the environment (Shillingford and Grossman, 2014). For example, one can examine crime locations in relation to other environmental features like roads, parks, or schools to understand the nature of the places in which crime occurs (e.g., whether drug crimes are more likely to occur near schools or whether a series of robberies are occurring near bus stops). One can use mapping to examine temporal variables like time of day or day of the week (e.g., the time of day car thefts are most likely or the day of week people are most likely to drive drunk). Mapping can also be used to examine crime in relation to demographic features like income level, age, or education of victims, suspects, or even neighborhoods (e.g., age of rape victims, average income of a neighborhood). All of this can be used by the analyst to aid police in identifying patterns, linking cases, developing investigative leads, or predicting trends.

This practice is based upon the simple concept that the place in which crime happens matters. A crime does not happen just anywhere; it happens in a particular place for a reason and a key aspect in understanding crime is understanding "where" it happens (and why it happens there). An offender made a journey to that place and chose to commit his or her crime there, rather than in any of the other places he or she had traveled to that day. His or her victim also made a journey to that place, yet remained unvictimized in all of the other places he or she had been that day. The nature of the crime space is an essential element of the criminal event. The spatial analysis of crime is "an integral part of the process…(of) crime analysis" (Harries, 1999, p. 1) but it is not the only technique utilized by analysts. This chapter will not focus on any single methods, but will provide an overview of techniques.

Administrative and Operational Analysis

The primary purpose of this type of analysis is to inform police administrators and policy makers about issues of police operations or other legal and/or political concerns. Administrative analysis may involve a presentation of crime statistics in areas surrounding area high schools to the local school board or a presentation of the frequency of officers' use of stop-and-frisk tactics to police administrators and command staff. Operational analyses, however, examine a department's policies and procedures in order to determine their effectiveness. For example, an analyst may be asked to study whether the department's use of sobriety checkpoints on holiday weekends had an appreciable effect on the number of motorists driving while intoxicated in order to determine if such checkpoints should be continued, discontinued, or discarded in favor of some other action. These types of analyses are intended to assist policy makers in deciding optimal allocation of police resources.

Strategic Crime Analysis

Strategic crime analysis is the examination of "crime problems and other police-related issues to determine...patterns of activity (and to) evaluate police responses...and procedures" (Santos, 2013, p. 61). This type of analysis involves employing statistical methods to study the data contained in electronic databases. Analysts can use any police database that contains relevant information about crime and disorder. Most commonly, this process uses the data collected by and contained within the department's computer-aided dispatch (CAD) system or its record management system (RMS).

The CAD system is designed to monitor police dispatch and response. It is not the same thing as the 911 system, but it is linked to it. Dispatchers take information about calls for service from the 911 system and enter it into the CAD in order to dispatch officers, monitor officer activity in the field, and record communications between officers and dispatch (Santos, 2013). The CAD links the information from the 911 call or other call for service to other police databases (i.e., the arrest, incidents, known offenders, sex offender databases) to gather additional information about the location or suspect. The system sends this compiled information to responding officers in the field via patrol car terminal. More modern systems may also be equipped to send this information to officers using tablets or smartphones. So a police officer responding to a call to a location can have information about previous calls to the same address or a police officer who makes a traffic stop can access information about the driver and vehicle (Figure 11.2).

A strategic crime analysis using CAD data may involve something along the lines of studying the day, time, and place that the most noise complaints are made in a neighborhood or correlating reports of suspicious persons or vehicles with reports of burglary or trespass. The purpose is to understand what type of crime or disorder problems exist in an area. Understanding the long-term problems in a community by studying when calls are made, where they are made, and the nature of the complaints allows police to formulate a plan of response and to decide where and how to allocate limited resources most effectively.

The department's RMS is another important source of data for the strategic crime analyst as it contains information on crime incidents, arrests, and police personnel, among other things. The Law Enforcement Information Technology Standards Council (LEITSC) of the International Association of Chiefs of Police describes an RMS as "an agency-wide system that provides for the storage, retrieval, retention, manipulation, archiving, and viewing of information, records, documents, or files pertaining to law enforcement operations" (2008, p. 10). It contains all of the information known to police about a case from

Figure 11.2 A CAD workstation.

beginning to end and any and all records pertaining to law enforcement operations including, but not limited to, calls for service, arrests, crime incidents, accidents, warrants, citations, witnesses, contacts, personnel records, and investigative case management (LEITSC, 2008). Additional databases may be maintained within the RMS pertaining to persons (e.g., victims, known associates), property (e.g., recovered or seized property), or vehicles.

Strategic crime analysts may use data from the RMS in order to understand crime problems within the community with the aim of assisting police in problem-solving efforts. Appropriate topics might be something like an analysis of ultimate disposition of stolen vehicles (i.e., are they recovered, destroyed, or never found) or the percentage of sexual assault cases that are cleared by arrest.

Intelligence Analysis

Intelligence analysis is used to identify the activity of criminal networks and organizations. This type of analysis may be useful in the investigation of many different criminal syndicates such as organized crime groups, gangs, drug traffickers, cyberfraud and identity thieves, human-trafficking rings, and terrorist cells. It may be used for both single agency investigations and interjurisdictional cooperative efforts. Police in neighboring southwestern states may cooperate with each other as well as federal agencies to track the activity of immigrant smugglers and human traffickers across national and state borders, or local police may use it to determine the extent of gang communications in the local jail.

The data typically used for this sort of analysis are usually generated by police investigative efforts. It includes an examination of things such as witness statements, evidence gathered in an undercover operation, informant information, surveillance reports, telephone and electronic communication, and travel information. The intelligence analyst will compile as much information as possible from all of these various sources in order to link persons of interest to each other and to various locations and to determine their relationships and roles within the organization.

Criminal Investigative Analysis

Criminal investigative analysis is the preferred modern term for the practice popularly known as "criminal profiling." Due in part to the misrepresentation of profiling in popular television shows, books, and movies (Santos, 2013) and differences in the types of profiling employed by modern analysts, many practitioners have come to prefer describing what they do as "criminal investigative analysis." Regardless of what it is called though, the purpose is to create a profile of an unknown offender that enables investigators to "identify and prioritize suspects" (Santos, 2013, p. 60).

Criminal investigative analysts develop an offender profile through an inductive process that involves examining characteristics of the crime and crime scene in order to infer personal characteristics of the offender. This, in turn, allows case investigators to narrow their focus or suspect pool. The process, as originally developed by agents at the Federal Bureau of Investigation, proceeds in a series of stages (Petherick, 2014):

- *Stage 1—Profile inputs.* The analyst collects as much information about the crime as he or she can. In addition to things like physical evidence, autopsy reports, crime scene photos, and police reports, he or she also finds out as much as he or she is able about the victim and his or her life.
- *Stage 2—Decision process models.* The information gathered in Stage 1 is integrated in Stage 2 to look for patterns regarding crime type, offender's intent, victim and offender's risk, and time and location factors.
- *Stage 3—Crime assessment.* The second and third stages often coincide because as the analyst is looking for patterns, he or she is also using that information to reconstruct the crime. Assessment is made regarding the timeline of events and the likely behaviors and motivations of both the offender and the victim.
- *Stage 4—Criminal profile.* The analyst uses the information gathered and generated in the previous stages to compose a profile of the characteristics that the unknown offender would be likely to display. This may include things such as personal and criminal background, personality traits, pre- and post-offense behavior, habits, family situation, employment, and relationship status, among other things. The profile is based upon what is known about offenders who have committed similar crimes in similar ways in the past with the assumption that the current offender will be comparable in terms of personality traits, behavior, and lifestyle.
- *Stage 5—Delivery to investigative team.* The analyst offers the profile to the investigating officers so that they may generate new suspects or narrow down existing ones based upon how well they "fit" the profile.

Geographic Profiling

One specific type of profiling that is of particular interest to analysts who utilize crime mapping is a practice called geographic profiling. Like other types of profiling, the purpose here is to aid police in identifying a suspect or narrowing down a pool of potential suspects. Only, instead of using crime scene information to infer characteristics about the offender, geographic profilers use crime locations in order to determine a likely area of residence for an unknown offender in a series of crimes.

An example to the uses of a geographic profile can be demonstrated by the case of serial rapist Randy Comeaux. In 1999, police in Lafayette, LA, used geographic profiling to assist in the investigation of a series of rapes that had gone cold. (A single rapist was suspected of being responsible for as many as nine rapes.) The task force that had been assembled to investigate the rapes had been disbanded in 1998, but the lead investigator had learned of the practice of geographic profiling from a colleague and decided to give it a try in the hopes of narrowing down the suspect field (Chernicky, 2000). The profile identified the boundaries of an area in which the suspect was likely to reside. This information, in conjunction with an anonymous tip made to police, led to the DNA identification and eventual confession of Randy Comeaux, a former Lafayette police deputy (Weiss and Davis, 2004). As it turned out, Comeaux did indeed live in the identified zone at the time of the rapes.

Geographic profiling was developed in the early 1990s by a former Vancouver police officer named Kim Rossmo, as part of his doctoral dissertation research. It is based upon the idea that the criminal will behave spatially in certain predictable ways (Paulsen et al., 2010; Petherick, 2014). Career criminals will occupy limited, specific space as they go about their daily activities. Like everyone else, the geographic areas they frequent will be specific and consistent. They will live in one place, work in another, shop in yet another, and travel consistent routes between these places. Rossmo (1993) posited that serial offenders will be most likely to commit their crimes within these familiar activity spaces, yet also outside of a "buffer zone" area around their residence where they would be most likely to be recognized. In addition, Rossmo (2000) proposes a "least effort principle" that suggests that people will generally opt for a course of action that requires the least amount of effort when given a choice of actions. So, criminals are likely to commit crimes in places that are not only near but also easy to get to. For example, a serial rapist may avoid a nearby housing development that is gated and secure and opt for a development that is easier to access that is a little farther away.

These theoretical concepts formed the basis of criminal geographic targeting, the computer model utilized by two of the most popular geographic profiling computer programs (Paulsen, 2005). The analyst enters information about a series of crimes (or crimes believed by investigators to have been committed by the same offender) into the program, and, using Rossmo's algorithm, it generates a map in which areas of the offender's likely residence are indicated in colors coded for different degrees of probability. Investigators may then use that map to compare to suspect lists or to focus their investigative efforts within (Figure 11.3).

The accuracy of profiling (geographic or otherwise) remains unclear (Paulsen, 2005), so it is important to note that any type of profile is only ever meant to be a tool for investigators to use to gain some additional insight. It is never sufficient enough, in and of itself, to be solely relied upon. Profiles should always be considered only in addition to other pieces of evidence.

Tactical Crime Analysis

Tactical crime analysis (TCA) is the type of analysis most frequently used in criminal investigation. Paulsen et al. (2010) define TCA as "the comprehensive identification, evaluation, analysis, and resolution of specific criminal activity problems" (p. 4). The goals of

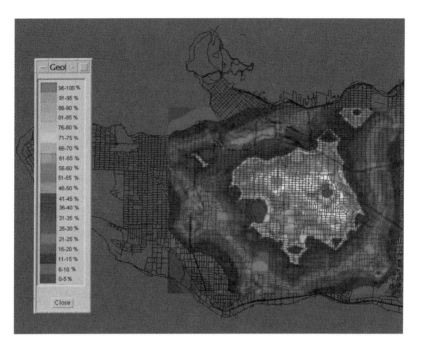

Figure 11.3 An example of a geographic profiling map.

this type of analysis include identifying patterns, generating investigative leads, identifying suspects, and clearing open cases. A tactical crime analyst uses information from police reports of recent crimes to understand the nature of the events in order to aid in their investigation. TCA can be applied to many different types of crime but is generally most useful in investigating crimes where the offender is not known to the victim and that are most likely to repeat (i.e., burglary, motor vehicle theft, robbery, and sexual assault). To this end, TCA serves three main functions: identifying patterns through linking open cases, identifying potential suspects, and linking closed cases to open ones in order to clear them (Santos, 2013).

Data Used in Tactical Crime Analysis

TCA requires that the analyst first be able to recognize and identify "repeat incidents." "Incidents" are events that incur a police response. They may result from calls for service, or an officer may come upon them while on patrol. They are not limited to crimes. In fact, frequently they are not. Incidents include disturbances (e.g., noise complaints, barking dogs, loud parties), alarm calls, traffic accidents and stops, field stops, and reports of suspicious activity, people, or vehicles. Incidents become repeat incidents when two or more similar incidents occur in the same place or are committed by the same person (Santos, 2013).

Repeat incidents may not always be readily apparent as such, and it is the job of the analyst to be able to recognize them in the available data. Typically, this involves an examination of data from the CAD system as well as the reports filed by the responding officers to look for incidents repeating at a single location or incidents of similar type of activity. For example, repeat drug dealing activity may be evident in the data not just by drug arrests but also by analogous or related activity as well. There may have been fights or disturbances in the area, reports of suspicious persons or vehicles, and citations for loitering that demonstrate the repeating nature of the activity through numerous incidents even if only one arrest for drug dealing was made. Incidents that may be part of a repeating burglary pattern would not necessarily be limited to burglary calls or arrests. It's likely that reports of alarm calls, suspicious vehicles, or trespass would have also been made. Analysts need to be familiar with the nature of crimes and the ways in which they are likely to occur so they know which types of incidents to examine as part of a potential series or pattern. Education and experience with crime is therefore essential for a crime analyst. A crime analyst cannot simply be a statistician. He or she must have an understanding of crime and criminal behavior.

The data used for tactical analysis are a mix of qualitative and quantitative. It most frequently comes from CAD logs of calls for service and from reports made by responding officers,* and it may also include information garnered from other sources such as witness statements, briefings, and field interviews. Any source that can provide information on how, when, and where an incident occurred (time of day, day of week, date, location, location type, crime type, suspect behavior, victim behavior, suspect characteristics, victim/property characteristics, vehicle descriptions, etc.) is useful to the analyst.

Linking Cases and Identifying Patterns

TCA relies upon the ability of the analyst to identify crime patterns by linking cases based upon similar characteristics (i.e., crime type, suspect behavior, victim choice). Criminologists have long recognized the phenomenon that a large amount of crime is committed by a relatively small cohort of repeat offenders (Wolfgang et al., 1972), so linking crimes and looking for patterns make sense. However, it is not uncommon for a crime pattern to go undetected by investigating officers. Investigators may miss evidence of case linkage for many reasons, but often, it's simply a matter of not looking for a pattern (Paulsen et al., 2010). For this reason, an analyst trained in examining large sets of data for patterns can be a valuable asset to an investigation.

Types of Patterns

The International Association of Crime Analysts (IACA) defines a crime pattern as two or more crimes that are treated as a single unit of investigative analysis and meet the following criteria: (1) they share at least one point of similarity in terms of crime type, offender or victim behavior, type of victim or target, type of property targeted, or location that makes them distinct from other crimes that have occurred within the same time frame; (2) the victim and offender are strangers to each other; and (3) the crimes occur within a limited length of time (IACA, 2011a,b; Santos, 2013). A pattern is neither a trend nor a chronic problem. That is, it is a short-term problem, not a persistent or long-term one.

---

* Depending upon the needs of the analysis, the analyst may need to supplement report information with information from interviews with the officers and witnesses.

The IACA (2011) recognizes seven primary types of crime patterns.

1. **Series**: A group of similar crimes thought to be committed by the same individual or group of individuals acting in concert.
   Examples: Four commercial arsons citywide in which a black male, between the ages of 45–50 years, wearing yellow sweatpants and a black hooded sweatshirt and a yellow "Yankees" cap, was observed leaving the commercial structures immediately after the fire alarm was triggered; five home invasion-style robberies involving two to three white males in their 20s wearing stockings over their faces, displaying a silver, double-barreled shotgun, and driving a red 1980s Pontiac Trans Am.

2. **Spree**: A specific type of series characterized by high frequency of criminal activity within a remarkably short time frame to the extent that the activity appears almost continuous.
   Examples: A rash of thefts from auto at a parking garage over the course of 1 h; multiple apartments in a high-rise building burglarized during daytime hours on a single day.

3. **Hot Prey**: A group of crimes committed by one or more individuals, involving victims who share similar physical characteristics and/or engage in similar behavior.
   Examples: Five home invasion robberies of Asian immigrant families occurring throughout the city over 6 weeks; seven fraudulent check scams targeting elderly victims over 1 week; 10 robberies committed by different offenders of intoxicated persons walking home alone from the bars on the weekend over 2 months.

4. **Hot Product**: A group of crimes committed by one or more individuals in which a unique type of property is targeted for theft.
   Examples: Sixteen thefts of GPS units from vehicles at residential and commercial places in 3 weeks; 25 burglaries of vacant homes and construction sites for the purpose of taking copper wiring and piping over 3 months; 20 thefts of laptops and smartphones occurring throughout a college campus the first month of school.

5. **Hot Spot**: A group of similar crimes committed by one or more individuals at locations within close proximity to one another.
   Examples: Eight daytime burglaries over the past 4 weeks at a suburban residential subdivision, with no notable similarities in method of entry or known suspects; 10 commercial burglaries over the course of 3 weeks at businesses located within a half-mile radius during overnight hours.

6. **Hot Place**: A group of similar crimes committed by one or more individuals at the same location.
   Examples: A local movie theater that has experienced 15 thefts from auto, several incidents of graffiti on the building and 2 strong-arm robberies in the parking lot over the course of 1 month, an apartment community that has experienced two stranger-on-stranger sexual assaults, several drug-related shootings, and seven residential burglaries within 6 weeks.

7. **Hot Setting**: A group of similar crimes committed by one or more individuals that are primarily related by the type of place where crimes occurred.
   Examples: Eleven late night robberies of 24 h convenience stores throughout the city by different offenders over 2 weeks; five burglaries of duplex homes adjacent to abandoned railway beds over one weekend; 14 theft from commercial vans/trucks parked at night in residential neighborhoods over 3 weeks (pp. 3–4).

Identifying the type of pattern that exists is important because appropriate police responses will vary depending on the nature of the pattern. For example, tactical responses to hot spot or hot place patterns would focus less on suspect identification and more on deterrence efforts such as directed patrol, whereas a series or spree would benefit from suspect identification methods such as geographic profiling. Understanding the type of pattern allows analysts to work with investigators and administrators in determining the best use of police resources in response.

Induction and Deduction

Pattern identification may proceed as either an inductive or deductive process of reasoning. "Deductive reasoning" is a "top-down" approach that works from the general to the specific. In looking for a pattern with this type of reasoning, the analyst starts with considering all crimes of a certain type and then looks for commonalities between them, thereby narrowing down cases based upon characteristics that they have in common (Santos, 2013). For example, suppose an analyst is looking for a pattern of serial homicides. He or she starts with data for all homicides. From there, he or she reduces focus to murders of women. He or she then further reduces the field to murders of women aged 18–30 years, then murders of women aged 18–30 years with long dark hair, then murders of women aged 18–30 years with long dark hair who were lured from a public place, and so on until he or she arrives at a number of cases that are linked by as many shared characteristics as possible.

"Inductive reasoning" is the opposite, in that it is a movement from the specific to the general. What this means for pattern identification is that the analyst will start with a single case and then seeks to link it to others based upon similarities. Using the previous example of the serial homicide pattern, the analyst would start with a single case of a 24-year-old woman with long dark hair who was lured from a public place and murdered by strangulation. He or she would then link it to two more cases of women, aged 19 and 28 years, respectively, with long dark hair that were also lured from a public place and strangled. He or she then examines other homicide cases that may share some, if not all, of those same characteristics. For example, other cases where a woman was lured from a public place and strangled, but who had blonde hair, and a woman with long dark hair who was strangled, but not lured, and so on.

Neither of these methods is necessarily "better" than the other, and the process the analyst uses will largely depend upon the needs of the investigation.

Principle, Key, and Related Cases

When a potential pattern is identified, the analyst fine-tunes it by identifying key characteristics and determining which cases best fit the pattern. First, he or she examines all of the possible pattern cases and selects the "principle case." This is the case for which he or she has the most detailed information and which best exemplifies the pattern (Santos, 2013). This case will serve as a point of comparison for other cases and their inclusion into the pattern will be based upon the degree of similarity to the principle case. Of particular note in the principle case are those characteristics of the crime or the offender that are most distinctive. These things will prove to be most indicative of subsequent cases likely being part of the pattern. Suppose the principle case in a series of bank robberies has the following characteristics: the robber enters the bank wearing a Halloween mask of former President Richard Nixon. He approaches a female teller and hands her a note that reads "Give me all your mony (sic) or I'll blow the place up" and threatens her with a handgun. It is his mask and the misspelled note that are particularly distinctive and would be most helpful in telling related cases from other unrelated robberies.

Next, the analyst will identify "key cases." These are cases that share the most points in common with the principle case, though not all of them. In our bank robbery series, a key case might involve the robber wearing the Nixon mask and spelling money incorrectly in his note, but perhaps approaching a male teller and threatening him with a knife instead of a gun. It could still be considered part of the pattern because it shares many of the more distinctive aspects.

Finally, the analyst looks for "related cases." This involves expanding his or her search to find additional cases that share characteristics of his or her pattern but appear to have a less tenuous connection. The analyst in our example may find a case in other robbery reports of a man who robbed a convenience store wearing a Nixon mask. While a lot of the traits are different, the presence of something as distinctive as the mask makes it plausible to consider it as part of the pattern.

Generating Leads

In addition to pattern analysis, investigators often approach tactical crime analysts for assistance in generating leads for possible suspects. Through examining the information from various cases linked in a pattern, the analyst can compile descriptions of potential suspects or vehicles. For instance, suppose a witness in one case described a white man with brown hair, and a witness in another linked case described a tall man with a mustache, and two other witnesses in other linked cases stated that he fled the scene in a blue Nissan Sentra. All of this can be compiled into a single description (a tall, white man with brown hair and a mustache driving a blue Nissan Sentra) that investigators can focus on in identifying their suspect. The analyst may also be able to use the composite description to search databases of known offenders or vehicles to pinpoint a name or address for a potential suspect.

Clearing Cold Cases

TCA is also used to clear cold or unsolved cases by linking them to other cases for which investigators have identified or arrested a suspect. This may even enhance the chances of making an arrest or gaining a prosecution by providing new, additional evidence against a suspect. Identifying these cases is akin to linking current, open cases to a pattern. Here, the analyst examines closed or cold cases to determine if they share enough characteristics with cases in which a suspect is identified as to suggest that they were committed by the same person. Clearly, in this sort of situation, detectives need to conduct further investigation in order to prove that his or her cases were indeed committed by the same party. What the analyst provides is the lead to suggest that the cases may be related.

Crime analysis is an emerging discipline. It is both "a profession and a set of techniques" (IACA, 2011), and its aim is to help police to be more effective and better informed.

In the twenty-first century, crime analysts will become an essential part of every police organization. Even officers who do not do analysis themselves will need to understand what analysts can do and how they can assist officers in their primary duties of crime prevention and criminal apprehension.

Questions for Discussion

11.1 Discuss a number of ways in which police might be able to use crime mapping to understand and respond to motor vehicle theft in their jurisdiction.

11.2 Think of an example for each of the different types of crime analysis discussed in this chapter.

11.3 Describe how you would identify a pattern of convenience store robberies in your jurisdiction. Is your method inductive or deductive?

11.4 Think of an example for each type of pattern described in this chapter.

11.5 If you needed to convince policy makers in your jurisdiction to devote more resources to crime analysis training for police officers, what arguments would you make?

References

Bruce, C. W. (2004). Fundamentals of crime analysis. In C.W. Bruce, S.R. Hick, and J.B. Cooper (Eds.), *Exploring Crime Analysis: Readings on Essential Skills*, pp. 11–36. North Charleston, SC: Booksurge LLC.

Chernicky, D. (2000, April 27). Profile leads to conviction in La. Serial rape cases. Retrieved from http://articles.dailypress.com/2000-04-27/news/0004270008_1_serial-rapist-serial-rapes-crime-sites (June 27, 2014).

Harries, K. (1999). *Mapping Crime: Principle and Practice*. Washington, DC: United States Department of Justice, Office of Justice Programs, National Institute of Justice.

International Association of Crime Analysts. (2011a). Crime pattern definitions for tactical analysis (White Paper 2011-01). Overland Park, KS: Author.

International Association of Crime Analysts. (2011b). What is crime analysis? Retrieved from http://www.iaca.net/dc_about_ca.asp. Accessed on June 2014.

Law Enforcement Information Technology Standards Council International Association of Chiefs of Police. (2008). Standard functional specifications for law enforcement records management systems. Retrieved from Office of Justice Programs website: https://it.ojp.gov/documents/leitsc_law_enforcement_rms_systems.pdf. Accessed on June 2014.

Paulsen, D. J. (2005). Connecting the dots: Assessing the accuracy of geographic profiling software. *Policing: An International Journal of Police Strategies and Management* 29(2), 306–334.

Paulsen, D. J. and Bair, S. (2010). *Tactical Crime Analysis: Research and Investigation*. Boca Raton, FL: Taylor & Francis Group.

Paynich, R. and Hill, B. (2010). *Fundamentals of Crime Mapping*. Sudbury, MA: Jones and Bartlett Publishers.

Peterson, M. B. (1998). *Applications in Criminal Analysis: A Sourcebook*. Westport, CT: Praeger.

Petherick, W. (2014). *Profiling and Serial Crime: Theoretical and Practical Issues*, 3rd edn. Waltham, MA: Anderson Publishing.

Rossmo, D. K. (1993). A methodological model. *American Journal of Criminal Justice* 27(2), 1–15.

Rossmo, D. K. (2000). *Geographic Profiling*. Boca Raton, FL: CRC Press.

Santos, R. B. (2013). *Crime Analysis with Crime Mapping*, 3rd edn. Thousand Oaks, CA: Sage Publications, Inc.

Shillingford, D. and Groussman, J. (2014, January 1). Using GIS to fight crime. Retrieved from http://www.iso.com/Research-and-Analyses/ISO-Review/Using-GIS-to-Fight-Crime.html#fig1 (June 5, 2014).

Weiss, J. and Davis, M. (2004). Geographic profiling finds serial criminals. *Law and Order* 52(12), 32–38.

Wolfgang, M., Figlio, R., and Sellin, J. (1972). *Delinquency in a Birth Cohort*, 2nd edn. Chicago, IL: University of Chicago Press.

Specialized Investigations

IV

Gang Investigations

12

JOHN P. MCLAUGHIN

Contents

Chapter Objectives	179
Chapter Outline	179
Introduction	180
Defining a Gang	181
How and Why Gangs Came to Be	181
Growing Gang Populations	182
Gangs in the Military	182
Gang Members in Law Enforcement	183
Impact on Society	183
Relationship between Gang Art and Violence	184
Clothing	185
Numerology	185
Investigative Information and Procedure	187
Informants	187
Relationship between Gangs and Drugs	188
Cross-Agency Sharing	188
Court Testimony	189
Broken Promise	190
Policing in the Digital Age	190
Electronic Surveillance	190
Social Media	191
Conclusions	191
Questions for Review	192
References	192

Chapter Objectives

After studying this chapter, you should understand the following concepts:

1. What constitutes a gang?
2. How gangs impact our society?
3. How to conduct a gang investigation?
4. Gang operations in the digital age.

Chapter Outline

Introduction
Defining a Gang

Impact on Society
Investigative Information and Procedure
Policing In the Digital Age
Conclusions
Questions in Review

Introduction

Street gangs have become an increasingly major concern for law enforcement agencies. A gang's impact can have social, political, and economic repercussions. This chapter will present a broad overview of gangs in communities mostly focusing on the metro New York region with additional information for other areas in the United States. This subject matter evolves on a daily basis: their role in society has dramatically changed especially with the advancing technology of the Internet. By using *burner* cell and smart phones, gangs are able to communicate in ways we never thought possible a decade ago. This chapter will also discuss various ways law enforcement can combat gangs to protect people (children, women, and senior citizens) from victimization.

Gangs are as diverse as our American communities. The core identity of each gang is based upon race, gender, economic standing, or other subset characteristics that bond a member of people in need of definition and to stand out from the general population. The main difference between gangs and the rest of criminal society is an overwhelming dedication to committing violent acts for proving one's deviant reputation in addition to posing a significant threat to rivals and law enforcement. Gangs use severe violence to show their strength against *the system*, and to test, initiate members' stamina for admission into their group. Or rather said, senior members physically assault their new recruits for a predetermined amount of time. Females who want to join a predominantly male gang will be *sexed* in: they have sex with a predetermined number of the male *original gangsters* (also known as OGs).

Gangs are no longer on the outer fringe of society. They have become part of the everyday existence in every kind of community across the United States. Former Speaker of the House Newt Gingrich stated in a U.S. News World News report that

> Gangs are as old as America itself and a part of our historical and popular culture. However, fueled by the global nature of the drug trade, gangs are increasingly international operations, with many of the largest and most vicious gangs operating in America hailing from South America. With the infrastructure in place to move and distribute drugs from across the border, the danger exists that they will use their network to, for the right price, traffic terrorist and weapons into the country. For the first time, gangs are presenting a growing threat not only to our personal safety, but to our national security. Since combating gangs will ultimately require a strong local effort, it is essential that Americans learn about the threat and demand strong actions from all levels of their government (Gingrich, 2005).

To form a gang, a group of people band together for a common ideal and/or against a common enemy. In the following chapter, the gangs will be described in the context of immigration from South America. Please remember that not all immigrants are members of or are affiliated with the gangs described in the following text, but that these South American immigrant and second-generation members serve as an example.

We also will be discussing gangs of African Americans in the context of minority culture in urban America. While there are also notable branches of Asian-American gangs, they are not nearly as exhibitive or prevalent in American popular culture.

Law enforcement now has to rise to the challenge of identifying gangs, conduct undercover operations, and help disband gangs using the number of tools available in coordination with the legal system of both state and federal regulations. This chapter attempts to assist that law enforcement understand the histories and differences between gangs, in addition to how officers and detectives must approach and maintain relationships with gang member informants through trial testimonies. A table of important information to review has been included at the center of the chapter that you may bookmark for a reference guide. At the end of this chapter are various scenarios that law enforcement may be confronted with and how to handle situations legally and safely.

Defining a Gang

There is no standard definition of a gang. However, what most law enforcement agencies do agree upon is that a gang of three or more members must have a permanent power in their originating community and brand themselves with a symbol, a color, and/or a number; they identify with (discussed in more detail in the succeeding text) and commit criminal acts to build their fearsome reputation and alarm the general public. Gang members go by different monikers such as sets, posse, and crews. There is as much diversity among gangs as there are nongang communities. They exist in urban, suburban, and rural America, even in seemingly peaceful regions such as the Hawaiian Islands. Crip symbols of pitchforks and the Star of David (McLaughlin, 2007) have been painted across various places in Maui and Kwai. Identifying a gang and profiling gang members as well as quelling a community's gang presence still requires adherence to the rights guaranteed in the first amendment (free speech and assembly) and following criminal process of law.

How and Why Gangs Came to Be

Since the beginning of time, people have gathered into groups for protection, warmth, and a desire to belong to something greater than themselves. Gangs satisfy the basic human needs for love, to feel wanted, and to be respected if their immediate family fails them. The individual who claims to provide these needs holds the greatest power over the group.

According to the U.S. Department of Justice (DOJ), there are currently over 30,000 individual domestic gangs with over 1.4 million members. There are multiple lists of criteria different agencies use to identify a person as a gang member, some of which may be contradictory with each other. The range of age groups, the kinds of criminal acts they commit, and a gang member's duration within and out of a group. For this latter point, it is most difficult to define a former gang member if they participated as a minor but not as an adult. Should someone be held accountable for the mistakes of their youth?

The DOJ identifies gang members with seven markers. Most law enforcement agencies identify a gang as groups with three or more official members involved in criminal activity as defined by law. The Nassau County Police Department in New York uses

14 identifiers to label a person a gang member. Then, if the person in question has no continuous contact with the Nassau County Police Department for 3 years, he or she is erased from the list.

A foremost reason that gangs form in a particular neighborhood is due to a significant population of *broken* homes. A predominantly matriarchal-run household with little time spent on setting reasonable rules and enforcing reasonable discipline, minimum wage working (or on public assistance) single mothers raising children at or below the poverty line creates an overwhelming environment. Children are often left to their own devices with almost no constant adult supervision: the *latch-key* effect. As a result, they seek love and structure from whoever can. Gangs in their neighborhood seem to provide such emotional support and identity. They think they have found a better family that offers them a better present and future.

Historically, gangs also served as a rebellion against an oppressive majority population. The notorious Five Points on the lower east side of Manhattan was for the Irish to band together as newly arrived immigrants among the established WASP ethnicities (German, English, Dutch, etc.). This tradition has carried through the centuries to today's recognized El Salvadorian gang MS-13. However, unlike them, contemporary gangs victimize their own communities by using knowledge of the language, customs, and fears. This is compounded by knowing illegal immigrants from their *turf* will not go to the police. Under this umbrella of the so-called security, the gang's activities may include dealing drugs, prostitution, or a form of extortion called *taxing*. A gang will charge the neighborhood elders to keep an eye out for and prevent trouble, charge local drug dealers to rent their corners, and other such examples of *protection*. The gangs seek ultimate control over their land and people.

Growing Gang Populations

The pictures in the following text show the difference in gang populations from the early 1990s to 2010. In 20 years, membership has not only increased but that almost no region of the United States is isolated or resistant to (potential or occurring) gang membership and activity. The areas of Southern California, southeast Florida, and Chicago are consistently higher.

Gangs in the Military

A Federal Bureau of Investigation (FBI) report titled *Gang Related Activity in the U.S. Armed Forces Increasing* dated January 12, 2007, outlined the threat of gang members in the military. Of the over 2.5 million citizens that serve domestically and internationally, less that 1% of the military are gang members, equaling to an estimation of 10,000 soldiers and sailors (gangland video basic training). This population is similar to the size of a large military base. This number is so large because of the pressure to recruit new military personnel and informal renunciation of gang membership is not strictly enforced.

Thus, criminal acts committed by gang members in the military (as charged to by their gang superiors or on their own) on foreign soil are perceived not as gang acts but as performed by the U.S. Military. From such doings of gang symbol graffiti to homicide and rape, these are exploited as outright disrespect for the hosting foreign country. Stationed in enemy and ally territories alike (including Afghanistan, Iraq, Germany, Japan, and even

Greenland), according to Sgt. Jeffrey Stoleson of the U.S. National Guard in 2006, these become political crises.

When gang members of the military return home and reenter civilian life (whether on leave, in reserve, or are discharged), they are equipped with the training tactics that domestic law enforcement are not usually taught or are experienced with. Weapons, explosive, ambush, and other techniques are then applied to their gangs' methods of offensive or retaliatory violence. Thus, combat from abroad is assimilated into urban and suburban street life. Not only are gang members enticed to join the military to better their credentials when back with their gang, but the extreme measures used in the armed forces pose a threat to domestic everyday confrontations. Unless an individual recruit is sincerely interested in leaving the gang for a different life, gang member recruits are only troubled with the military's threat of dishonorable discharge before completing basic training.

Gang Members in Law Enforcement

As with recruiting soldiers for the U.S. military, state and local law enforcement agencies must recruit enough people to keep their communities safe. However, police departments are thus pressured to hire from communities with significant high rates of gang membership and gang activities. While there are very strong standards and background checks are conducted, some gang members can slip through the cracks. For example, in the late 1990s, the LAPD formed Community Resources Against Street Hoodlums, an anti-gang unit abbreviated as CRASH. However, because of Officer Rafael Perez's illegal action of stealing 2.7 kg of cocaine from evidence and selling it back on the street, in addition to other offenses, 4 other officers were arrested and 70 were investigated. These corrupt officers tainted the LAPD's reputation, CRASH, and as a result, almost 100 narcotics cases were overturned with more reexamined. A federal judge ruled that under the RICO statutes, the LAPD could be the equivalent to a criminal enterprise. The $300 million that the city of Los Angeles received from a tobacco settlement was used to pay off gang members for wrongful incarceration reparations, instead of putting the money toward improving beneficial community programs and infrastructure (Reavill, 2000). One sign of how this event's impact is still felt is that currently, California law enforcement agencies with significant gang membership to combat are reaching to other states for police recruitment.

Impact on Society

The impact of gangs can be visually evident in a poverty-stricken local economy with closed storefronts and the various graffiti tags seen across town. The former example is a cyclical effect. The gangs use tactics such as shaking down pedestrians or stealing from bodegas to increase the likelihood that people will not want to shop in that area. Those businesses loose customers and eventually close. The gangs will then move into those abandoned spaces to conduct their business. Paradoxically, to prevent such *shakedowns* in the first place requires a stronger police presence, which requires increasing taxes to hire more patrol units. As the current economic state of wage ranges in relation to quality of life, to pay these higher taxes necessitates that both parents work to support their children with the basics of shelter, heat, food, clothing, and supplies to attend school. If both parents' working hours do not correlate with the children's after-school schedules, then they have a much higher probability of becoming prey for the gangs' initiation incentives. As their surrogate family, the gang will claim to provide what their own parents cannot: love, attention, respect, and money. Thus, gangs will always try to take advantage of the community's weaknesses.

Relationship between Gang Art and Violence

There are two kinds of graffiti: *urban art* that takes inspiration from and gives back to the community with a positive message simply using the building's surfaces as a medium. And then there is gang graffiti, which is blight in communities used for a variety of reasons:

1. *Territory*: To let other gangs, the police, and the public know which gang controls the specific neighborhood. Turf is a major commodity to all gangs. As mentioned earlier, it is their place of recruitment and of business. The street corner or the strip mall is a marketplace for exchanging illegal goods like drugs. Members use an area of turf as their epicenter to which they spread out from and return to. Businesses in this vicinity suffer the most from direct and threatened violence. Marking the blocks with a gang's symbol or code acts like checkpoints and borders between public and gang property.
2. *Memorialization*: Perpetuating the myth of a gang member's immortality and sometimes sacrifice, their image and/or name is artistically rendered. It is a message that members are not forgotten by the gang, other gangs, the community, and any other public audiences who come across it.
3. *Homicidal threat*: 187 refers to the California penal code for homicide. Pairing this tag with the name of a gang member or law enforcement agent is equivalent to a public notification that a person's life is in danger. Because most of the public is not familiar with this signal, despite its rather unnoticed use in popular culture, this threat may not be reported.

To know how to decipher street graffiti is an important tool. Law enforcement's response should be swift, but steps should first be followed before the graffiti is removed:

1. *Read It*: Do you recognize the graffiti? Has it been seen and used before? What was its meaning in that previous circumstance? Do you think this holds the same meaning or is it different? Does this tag pose a threat to someone, represent a new gang's name, and mark their turf?
2. *Record It*: Take a picture of it with your cell phone camera or other device. Write down or text a few describing details: Where is this graffiti located? Can it be easily seen by the public or in a more conspicuous area? Is there anything special or new that should be taken into consideration? Also, take note of any other details about the people or place this graffiti is.
3. *Report It*: Notify the proper gang or intel unit that handles this area, along with the photo you took.
4. *Remove It*: After local enforcement or other proper authorities have been notified and taken steps to record and seek more information, the graffiti should be removed completely in a timely fashion (Figure 12.1).

Figure 12.1 Gang graffitti threatening law enforcement. (Photo by John McLaughlin, 2014.)

Clothing

Style of dress can in some cases identify membership in a gang. Most members wear oversized clothing such as baggie pants and 3XL shirts. The purpose of this is twofold. One, it can make the individual appear larger than he is. It is easy to conceal weapons and drugs. And two, clothing can also conceal the outlines of a person's body, making it a more difficult target to hit. Although other subcultures wear larger size clothing, like skateboarders and hip-hop aficionados, primary color cotton T-shirts are just one of many indicators to look out for.

Although sneakers are not a strong indicator of gang membership, members of MS-13 particularly wear the Nike brand, while the rival Salvadorians With Pride prefer Adidas. These two footwear identifiers have been observed and confirmed for the last 15 years from law enforcement interviews. But more than just the style or comfort, high price indicates wealth. New Air Jordans can be expensive. Additionally, in correction facilities, sneakers can be the only means of individual or gang expression.

Not only what they wear but how the items are worn can clue law enforcement into, as well as rival gang members, to which they belong to by simply seeing which side their pant leg or arm sleeve is rolled up. Dedicating a side of the body to the left or right visually shows commitment to a specific gang. While there is no definitive rule as to which side reflects which gang, Bloods usually prefer the left and the Crips prefer the right.

Numerology

As previously discussed but not fully explored, gangs use various numbers to convey messages. If the graffiti-drawn name of a gang member or law enforcement is accompanied by a 187, this is a threat to the person's life. The following information is an overview but is subject to change:

People Nation/Bloods: Associated with the number 5. They were made up of 5 street gangs in the Compton area of Los Angeles, California, named Block Swan, Piru Brims, Bounty Hunter, and Bishop. The term *031* means, "I have love for my Bloods." A fashion trend in the 1990s was a clothing line developed in Hollis, Queens, New York, called, *For Us By Us*, or F.U.B.U. Many of those items displayed a large 05, thus becoming very popular with the Bloods' community. In relation, the five-pointed star represents their values of life, love, loyalty, understanding, and knowledge.

Folk Nation/Crips: Associated with the number 6 because one of the founding members, David Barksdale, of the Gangster Disciples in Chicago referred to himself as King David. Barksdale wore a large Star of David necklace. The six-pointed star is used by this gang, representing the six values of life, love, loyalty, understanding, knowledge, and wisdom.

The Almighty Latin King and Queen Nation: Associated with the number 360, representing a complete circle. All are supposedly equal in this closed/exclusive society. The number 1-4-18 is also widely used. The term *mor del Rey* (Kings Love) is used only by the Latin Kings. Each letter represents a number: A = 1, B = 2, C = 3, etc. We also see this with outlaw motorcycle gangs such as Hell's Angels, whose number is 81 to show their affiliation, especially in the phrase, "support your local 81."

MS-13 or Mara Salvatruca: Associated with the number 13. There has been some debate over this but is generally considered that M is the 13th letter in the alphabet and because 213 is the area code for Southern California, where the majority of MS-13 members are from. This gang also uses Roman numerals to show gang affiliation, like XIII (Table 12.1).

Table 12.1   Basic Gang Information

Gang	Color	Number	Affiliation	Ethnic Background	Graffiti Symbol
Crips	Blue	6	Folk Nation	African American	
Bloods	Red	5	People Nation	African American	
MS-13	Blue and white	13	None	South American	
Latin Kings	Black and gold	360	People Nation	Hispanic	
NETAS	Red, white, and black	150	People Nation	Hispanic	
Trinitarios	Black and green	3	None	Hispanic	Picture Unavailable
18th Street	Black and red	18	None	All nationalities	

Investigative Information and Procedure

Policing has radically changed these past several years. Not only does the 24/7 news cycle rely upon immediate updates, but also with the relatively new and increasing use of smart phone video and picture recordings, along with their uploading to social media platforms, any story that shows alleged police impropriety or shocking violence is not carefully considered as possible out of context.

Informants

As information is the key to success in war, politics, and business, the same can be said for law enforcement. The first step to undercover investigate a gang is recruiting an informant. Gangs must generate revenue to operate; thus, they rely on black market or illegal enterprises such as narcotics, prostitution, and protection. They need to interact and build relationships with nongang members, or rather *the public*, in order to sell their illegal goods and services. This is a weakness in each gang system.

An informant is a trusted member of the gang, yet who also understands there is greater opportunity cooperating with investigating detectives for a lesser, or almost no, prison sentence. The informant will vouch for the undercover detective's credibility and make the introduction to gang leaders.

There are three main categories why a gang member would become an/your informant, but no matter their reason, always verify the information with other sources:

1. *Money*: As an incentive to cooperate, information can be paid for their assistance that ranges from a couple dollars to potentially tens of thousands of dollars. However, some may become greedy and rely on their handlers for a better lifestyle. These types may just give you a lot of information that might not end up meeting the case's intel standards.
2. *Revenge*: A gang member may want to see a rival punished for something that has caused them physical or emotional injury, especially if their ego has been bruised. They see the investigating detectives as doing the dirty work; usually, law enforcement does not mind getting involved in these problems as long as it gets the drugs and guns off the streets. Their information, however, may especially be more frequently about their specific target and not your case's overall objectives.
3. *Less Prison Time*: This is by far the most valuable and trusted informant because they are usually more long-term thinking about the benefit from a reduced or eliminated sentencing. An informant will understand giving misinformation could lead to law enforcement suffering a severe setback and thus their deal may be revoked.

How valuable are informants? Consider this metaphor: A group of people that socialize with each other on a daily basis form close bonds. Whether they are a sports team, families in a neighborhood, or coworkers, their unique characteristics become very familiar. When a new person enters this group to play, to live next door, or take over someone else's job, they need to be vouched for as someone who will fit into the group and who can be trusted or otherwise they are greeted with suspicion. This new person needs an informant to make introductions and create that immediate trust.

However, protection of informants can prove difficult. In one case, 15-year-old Olivia Mendoza was killed by MS-13 for they believed she was an informant attempting to leave the gang. Her body was found in Old Westbury along a dark road. Olivia was murdered by the same people she thought were supposed to be her family.

Relationship between Gangs and Drugs

Currently, marijuana is a gang's preferred illegal business operation. Despite Colorado and Washington among others having decriminalized it (as of this writing the federal government still considers marijuana a Schedule 1 drug), there is relatively little risk of prison time. The all-cash business dealing marijuana provides great advantages such as no taxes, no overhead, no permits, and just straight profit. Thus, protecting their turf with violence and intimidation keeps their *storefront* open.

Gangs cannot go to the police for protection and go to small claims court over a bad deal, and they can't fill out paperwork for taxes. The more violent the gang is, the more threatening their reputation, and the more secure their turf is. If no one messes with them, they can continue about their business and then make more profit.

Gangs also recruit people who know how to convert cocaine to crack, called *chefing*. Though the ingredients are cocaine and baking soda and water, the art of cooking a batch of crack requires with someone with skill to stretch the cocaine enough and come out with a quality product. These street chemists are in high demand. Heroin has also made a big comeback to the Long Island region. It is easy for gang members from the suburbs to ride the train into Brooklyn or many of the New York City boroughs and buy a sleeve of heroin (100 Gags) for sometimes as little as $60 to sell it back on Long Island for over $100.

Cross-Agency Sharing

All areas of law enforcement need to be utilized when confronting gangs and keeping them under control. Intelligence and investigative techniques need to be shared among all agencies:

Patrol force: Usually, the first contact gangs have with law enforcement. Police officers will conduct field interviews documenting the location, size, and makeup of gang members. Police will also be the first to spot and identify gang graffiti. Some departments have resource officers inside of schools and have insight into new gangs forming or fights that may occur. Enforcement of public nuisance laws such as open alcoholic containers, making loud noises, or other quality of life issues will demonstrate to the public that gang activities will not be tolerated.

Narcotics investigations: Gangs are fueled by money earned through drug dealing, in most cases, marijuana. And the beginning of decriminalization of marijuana has made it more viable to deal. Less risk of a prison sentence equals more untaxed money to be made. Currently, marijuana is legal in two states: Colorado and Washington. Most states have decriminalized possession of marijuana for personal use. However, to the federal government, marijuana is still a Schedule I drug and is illegal to sell or possess without proper documentation. This has created a vacuum not seen since the prohibition era of alcohol. Gangs that are dealing drugs need to protect the location or *turf* where they sell as well as their product and the gang members that sell marijuana. This is done through means of violence. It also exposes gang members to arrest and criminal prosecution.

Corrections department: Offers a wealth of information into the life of a gang member. Prison records of visitors to gang members, information from correspondence, and material taken from cells can deliver valuable information on gang activity.

Probation and parole officers: Helps keep gang members who have been convicted of a crime accountable for their actions. A program such as Operation Night Watch in Nassau County, New York, is an example of how probation officers can curb the gang problem. Most conditions for release for a defendant include monitored supervision. This includes the right for probation officers to spot check a probationer's residence or workplace. Operation Night Watch includes a partnership with local law enforcement, which will check on gang members and any involvement with gang material, drugs, or other violations.

District Attorney's Office: The start of every criminal investigation begins with gathering as much intelligence as possible. Informants, as previously stated, are among the most reliable. This is mainly due to the fact that they are exchanging information to lessen a prison sentence or for other reasons. Proffering help establishes the structure and hierarchy of the gang and what crimes they have committed and weapons the gang may have. With the restructuring of drug laws on both the state and federal levels, less defendants agree to cooperate with law enforcement and opt for drug provision programs. This in turn has created a shortage of human sources and intelligence.

Federal law enforcement agencies: Offering a wide variety of assistance, agencies such as the FBI; the Bureau of Alcohol, Tobacco, Firearms and Explosives; the U.S. Immigration and Customs Enforcement; and the U.S. Marshals Service have provided equipment and manpower in stopping that gang menace. Federal RICO laws provide for longer prison sentences and establish gangs such as MS-13, Bloods, Crips, and the Latin Kings as a criminal enterprise.

Court Testimony

No one knows your case like you do. Think about how much time and effort is spent bringing a case to court and its successful prosecution. Prosecutors, defense attorneys, and legal aid counsel handle thousands of different cases in a short time. Even though an active detective is responsible for hundreds of cases each year, all under stress from supervisors and complainants, it is your ultimate responsibility to know each of their details. Because you have been involved from the start, you know the strengths and weaknesses, the statements taken, and the evidence invoiced. Testifying at preliminary hearings and grand juries requires complete preparation! You cannot and should not enter the courtroom hoping those memories or pieces of information will "just come to you." Go over your testimony beforehand, and communicate with the prosecutor to go over any left out details or weaknesses in the case or their planned examination of you on the stand. Also, attempt to consider the defense attorney's questions under cross-examination. You do not want to give the jury an opportunity to find fault of your understanding of the case's investigation.

Broken Promise

Gangs are a socioeconomic product. When jobs are scarce and poverty is prevalent, it creates anger and resentment. Our youths need to feel a sense of pride about them. They need to feel wanted and to be a positive member of society. Unfortunately, this is becoming harder for them to find at home. Apprenticeships with labor organization in which individuals would learn a trade may be helpful. Volunteer work for those in need may also help empower some of these kids that are susceptible to joining a gang.

Gang leaders promise their recruits to fill the void for at-risk youth: those who have been mistreated and abused or who are just looking for excitement. The gangs use terms such as *family*, *brother*, and *sister*. When asked about their gang, members will profoundly proclaim, "these are my people." The gang members will state that they share everything, similar to the promotional language of a utopian commune from the 1960s.

The reality is when a member is of no more use to the gang's objectives, they will have no use for the member. When incarcerated, no one from the gang will put up the money to pay the mounting bills, put in the member's commissary, or visit him or her; mostly due to that, all correctional facilities keep records of who received visitors and their names. The member is abandoned from the outside while incarcerated.

Inside the prison walls is a different story. Members of one gang who are incarcerated together or prisoners who form a gang inside the facility do so to provide protection from the other gangs. For the former group, the gang's outside doctrine is reinforced inside. While for the newly formed gang, members are hardened and can withstand the violence that occurs. In a perverse way, incarceration promotes gang membership.

Policing in the Digital Age

Electronic Surveillance

Electronic surveillance is law enforcement and investigators' greatest tool to acquire information and/or solve a case. In the form of security camera footage to data stored on personal cell phones, such devices are used as evidence for, by, and against suspects. It is necessary to get a court order whenever and as soon as possible to protect the evidence's inclusion for trial. The contact names for drugs and weapons, photos, videos, text transmissions, and other information garnered from these devices are invaluable. Without a court order or other affirmed statement of proper reception (even if voluntarily given from the suspect or informant), such evidence can be suppressed.

Additionally, inconspicuous recording devices that record an officer's wrongdoing or lie can discredit the officer's evidence or testimony. Prior to conducting an investigation with a suspect, do a thorough pat-down for any electronics. Even a highly respected officer can get caught for a transgression. For example, seasoned Bronx NYPD Detective Christopher Perino was sentenced for lying under oath: found perjured for testifying that he did not interrogate the 17-year-old suspect Eric Crespo. Detective Perino's attempt to recover the handgun used in the crime was recorded on the suspect's MP3 player. It shows "Detective Perino grilling him for more than an hour – and prosecutors had to cut a deal to salvage the case" (Block, 2009).

Social Media

Current gang trends show that gang members are using social media more frequently and without the knowledge that authorities are monitoring these websites. Gang members can be seen in web videos committing all types of criminal acts in addition to throwing up gang hand signs and displaying allegiance to their gangs. No crime can be solved sitting in a squad room watching YouTube videos. But this type of evidence can greatly enhance a gang investigation and prosecution by showing the individual is a willing participant and member. Evidence of a gang member throwing up hand signs or rapping about his street *cred* is a powerful tool in demonstrating culpability to the court. Investigators need to familiarize themselves with these applications that are online. Investigators also need to learn the steps needed to memorialize these pictures, videos, and text to present in court. Some of this content is taken down within a few hours of their original posting. Investigators need to learn to especially familiarize themselves with navigating and utilizing the sources listed in the following. For identifying gang members, research for undercover operations, and learning more information as gangs develop, these are excellent sources because they are personalized and self-created with little administration:

1. *Twitter*: Similar to text messages but limited to 140 type characters; members can post anything from a status update to assault threats, drug deal information, bragging about crimes committed, etc. While profiles and *tweets* can be public, users have the opportunity to make them private, block followers, and also send direct messages (DMs), which are never public.
2. *Facebook*: Users can create specific individualized pages about themselves that they can make public or keep private. Members can connect with *friends*, *like* someone's status update, post pictures and captions for social events or illegal activities, post their current locations, and other *apps* for sharing information. In addition, they can create event with invites for any occasion whether a legal party or disguised as an illegal meeting.
3. *Instagram*: Users can post pictures with short text captions of almost anything (the site has few censorship regulations) and follow each other.
4. *YouTube*: Users post videos of anything they capture on their smart phones or that are professionally produced. Subscribers as well as the entire public that can access the site can view these videos. Subscribers can post their comments to the videos for simulated conversations. These videos can be used for recruitment, bragging, and claiming responsibility for certain crimes; in addition, they are used with permission by traditional media for television and can be reposted on other websites.

Conclusions

Gang membership and violence is no longer confined to the neighborhoods; they sprang from but have crossed state and international borders. Members are able to travel physically and send their messages across the Internet to influence and affect all those who come across it. Incidents will occur that present threats to both police and suspects. But to combat gangs, in the future, current law enforcement agents need to be trained to handle situations as if always in the public eye with the potential for internal scrutiny. Training is a sensitive issue because it is time consuming and expensive, but there is greater expense when a police force is not properly trained.

Combating street gangs is a difficult task. They adapt to police enforcement while continuing to operate in the criminal world. One example of this is *flying* the flag of their gang in public. For most gangs, this means simply wearing a bandana in their gang's color. But, in the case of MS-13 (which display blue bandanas), they adapted by painting the inside of their pants pockets blue. When out in public they would turn the pocket inside out; but should police be in view, they would push the pockets back inside. Or, as seen in the table earlier, a Latin King member uses a tattoo of playing cards in order to hide the ALQK moniker.

Additionally, the public should also be informed about the nature of policing. The job is difficult, and in some cases, violence is needed to counteract a violent act in effecting arrests or stopping a violent situation from becoming uncontrollable.

Questions for Review

12.1   What constitutes a gang?
12.2   Explain the growth of gangs in the United States.
12.3   Why do gangs use tattoos?
12.4   What crimes do gangs generally engage in?

References

Bilchik, S. (October 1998). Gang members on the move. *Juvenile Justice Bulletin*. Retrieved from the Office of Juvenile Justice and Delinquency Prevention website: http://www.ojjdp.gov/jjbulletin/9810_1/gang8.html. Accessed March 4, 2014.

Block, D. (September 22, 2009). NYPD Detective Christopher Perino, Convicted of Perjury, is sentenced to 4 months in jail. *New York Daily News*. Retrieved from website: http://www.nydailynews.com/news/crime/nypdperjury-sentenced-4-months-jail-article1.404669. Accessed March 4, 2014.

Crowley, K. (September 23, 2004). Gang Vengeance. *New York Post*. Accessed March 4, 2014.

Gingrich, N. (June 29, 2005). *Gangs: A Threat to National Security*. Retrieved from the Fox News website: www.foxnews.com/story/2005/06/29gangs-threat-to national-security. Accessed March 4, 2014.

McLaughlin, J. (April, 2007). Gangland: The complete season one. Marketed and distributed the U.S. by New Video, A&E television networks History Channel, New York.

McLaughlin, J. (February, 2014). Graffiti used to Threaten Police. Uniondale, NY.

Miami New Times. http://blogs.miaminewtimes.com/riptide/gangmap.jpg.

Reavill, G. (November, 2000). *The Dirtiest Cop Alive Maxim Article*. Retrieved from the Dirty Writers Blog: http://dirtywriters.blogspot.com/2006/02/dirtiest-cop-alive-maxim-article.html. Accessed March 4, 2014.

Handling Informers

13

DAVID LOWE

Contents

Chapter Objectives   193
Overview of Dealing with Informants   194
Law/Policy in Handling Informants   194
   United Kingdom's RIPA   195
   Policies on the Use of Informants in Other States   195
      Australia   195
      United States   197
Ethical Issues in Handling Informants   199
   Motives and Incentives to Inform   199
   Informants: The Necessary Evil   200
   Ethical Handling of Informants   200
   1968–1997 Irish Troubles: A Case
   Study in Unethical Police Handling of Informants   201
Recruiting Informants   203
Evidence of Informants   204
   Immunity from Prosecution/Reduction in Sentence   204
      United Kingdom's Serious Organised Crime and Police Act 2005   204
      U.S. New Jersey Brimage Guidelines   205
   Informant Witness Anonymity in Criminal Trials   205
      United Kingdom's Coroners and Justice Act 2009   205
      Canada's Confidential Informant Privilege   206
Questions for Discussion   207
References   208

Chapter Objectives

This chapter examines the law and policy in handling informants looking at a number of countries from the U.K., U.S. and Australia. This leads onto an analysis of the ethical issues related to recruiting and handling informants. The chapter concludes by examining legal issues related to the use of evidence from informants in criminal trials, in particular the legal position in the U.K., the U.S. and Canada.

After reading this chapter, you should be able to do the following:

1. Appreciate the requirement for statutory/policy provisions in handling informants.
2. What motivates a person to become an informant and assess the quality of the information they provide.
3. Appreciate the ethical implications in handling informants.

4. Identify methods of recruiting informants.
5. Understand issues behind informant immunity from prosecution, potential reduction in sentencing, and anonymity in criminal trials.

Overview of Dealing with Informants

Snitches, snouts, touts, and grasses are just some of the colloquial terms used to refer to those who pass on information to the police. As the majority of the academic work, policy documents, reports and judicial case reports in this area refer to people who pass on information as informants, for consistency this chapter will use the term informant. An informant is a person who actively seeks damning knowledge information on target groups/individuals, rather than the one who simply passes information onto the police (Lieberman 2007, Jones-Brown and Shane 2011, p. 5, Miller 2011, p. 206).

In policing, the use of informants in criminal investigations is seen as a cost-effective means of detection, especially in dealing with serious and organized crime (Williamson and Bagshaw 2001, p. 50), with police officers encouraged to exploit the full potential of informants and to cultivate such contacts (Audit Commission 1993, p. 32). While the importance of informants has been globally accepted as important to detective work by both practitioners and researchers (Miller 2011, p. 203), informant use has also been seen to create conflict within agencies within the criminal justice system as well as creating major tensions and conflicts within the police organization itself (Dunningham and Norris 2000, p. 68). This conflict tends to emanate from the very nature of who the informants are and how they are handled by the police, an issue examined in this chapter when we examine the ethical issues in handling informants. Another potential source of this conflict is in the fact that in some national states, there are no statutory provisions governing the use of informants in criminal investigations, and in some jurisdictions, there is not even a policy guiding officers in their use that attempts to ensure a degree of uniformity in informant handling. Regarding the relationship between the police and other criminal justice agencies, another source of conflict is in the admissibility of evidence that informants give in criminal trials and maintaining their anonymity. These issues are addressed in the following text.

Law/Policy in Handling Informants

When examining the process of how police officers handle informants, there is no consistency in protocols and procedures between nation-states. Some like the United Kingdom have mandatory statutory guidelines that must be followed, while other nation-states vary between mandatory and recommended policy guidelines, with some having no guidance at all. In some nation-states, the format of guidelines can change as seen in the United Kingdom where prior to the police use of informants being governed by the Regulation of Investigatory Powers Act 2000 (RIPA) and its accompanying codes of practice, like most other states, the use of informants was governed by a policy document under the former Home Office guidelines. This section will examine the impact of legislation and policy in the police handling of informants.

United Kingdom's RIPA

In essence, RIPA tightened up the procedures governing the recruitment and use of informants that RIPA refer to as covert human intelligence sources.* RIPA was introduced to replace the Home Office policy. This came about as a result of decisions by the European Court of Human Rights (ECtHR) in cases like *Khan v. United Kingdom.*† *Khan* was concerned with the use of covert surveillance by the police, and the ECtHR held a Home Office policy document that is not an act prescribed by law (a statute) that is required under the limitations given in Article 8 of the European Convention on Human Rights (right to privacy) for the state to interfere with this right. As a result, RIPA significantly changed the law governing the police use of surveillance in the United Kingdom. RIPA defines an informant as one who covertly establishes or maintains a personal or other relationship with a target (person or organization) to obtain information or gain access to another person to gain information to be passed on to the state agencies.‡ Another key change on informant handling is the accompanying codes of practice that provides guidance to the police in applying RIPA when handling informants. While a breach of the codes of practice will not always amount to unlawful action by a police officer, such a breach is likely to result in any information obtained by an informant during an investigation that could be used as evidence in a criminal trial being rendered inadmissible. One significant change in RIPA and its codes of practice is that informants are managed by a handler§ and a controller.¶ The controller has to be a rank above that of the handler and their role is to maintain a general oversight in the use of the informant by the handler.** Under RIPA, a risk assessment is carried out prior to, during, and at the end of the use of the informant regarding the tasking they are asked to do and the likely consequences should it become known that the person was an informant.††

Under the previous Home Office guidelines, risk assessments were carried out, but recording how they were managed was not as rigorous as RIPA. Under RIPA, the handler must continually report to the controller.‡‡ These reports include informing the controller when and where any meetings or contact will be made with the informant, the conduct of the informant, and the safety and welfare of the informant.§§ Under RIPA, it is not acceptable for the handler to meet the informant on their own without the knowledge of their supervisor/line manager acting as a controller, and RIPA encourages the handler to be accompanied by a colleague during any meetings with the informant. This is to provide corroboration that the handler was acting ethically with the informant.

Policies on the Use of Informants in Other States

Australia

Concerned with corruption undermining the use of informants, in criminal investigations Australian state governments have considered introducing policies regarding the use of

---

*   Section 26(1)(c) RIPA
†   (2000) 8 EHRC 310
‡   Section 26(8) RIPA
§   Section 29(5)(a) RIPA and paragraph 6.7 Codes of Practice: Covert Human Intelligence Sources
¶   Section 29(5)(b) RIPA and paragraph 6.9 Codes of Practice: Covert Human Intelligence Sources
** Paragraph 6.8 Codes of Practice: Covert Human Intelligence Sources
†† Paragraph 6.14 Codes of Practice: Covert Human Intelligence Sources
‡‡ Section 29(5)(b) RIPA
§§ Paragraph 6.15 Codes of Practice: Covert Human Intelligence Sources

informants. In 1993, the New South Wales' Independent Commission Against Corruption put forward recommendations regarding the recruitment and handling of informants that included the following:

1. When recruiting informants, an assessment is made of the potential informants through an evaluation of the information likely to be supplied and the characteristics of the individual.
2. A preregistration assessment stage of the informant be introduced that includes consideration of the informant's motives/suspected motives, informants' personality/psychological makeup, drug use, police's previous experiences with the informant, anticipated dangers or potential problems in the handling of this informant, and the nature/quality of the information the informant is likely to pass on.
3. Police officers be trained in the handling of informants, police officers instructed regarding the consequences in developing informant relationships and introducing procedures in managing police officer/informant relationships.
4. Introduce mechanisms of accountability that involves notifying supervisors of meetings with informants, completing an informant contract/informant information report, involving police supervisors in the handling of informants, and employing informant case officers (1993, pp. 81–83).

Many of these recommendations echo concerns in the recruitment and handling of informants around the world, and some of these concerns were behind the introduction of the statutory provisions in the United Kingdom's RIPA legislation. While acknowledging the distinct benefits derived from the police use of informants in criminal investigations, Western Australia Parliament's Corruption and Crime Commission 2011 reports into corruption risks of controlled operations, and informants identified the risks informant use poses to law enforcement. As a result, the commission recommended developing and implementing "...robust internal policies and procedures for mitigating risks inherent to its own investigations" (Western Australia Parliament Joint Standing Committee on the Corruption and Crime Commission 2011, p.28). From both the 1993 New South Wales report and the Western Australian Parliament's report, no policy on police procedure in dealing with informants has been formalized and introduced as mandatory for officers to follow.

Although no specific policy has been introduced regarding informant use by the police, the New South Wales' Parliament has introduced the Law Enforcement (Controlled Operations) Act 1997 where a controlled operation is one conducted for the purpose of obtaining evidence and frustrating or arresting persons involved in criminal activity or corrupt activity.[*] A police officer can apply for the controlled operation in which the application outlines the nature of the activity that is being investigated[†] to be authorized by a chief executive officer[‡] (which includes the commissioner of the New South Wales Police).[§] The act is clear in what activities are not permitted in the authorization and they include the following:

---

[*] Section 3(1) Law Enforcement (Controlled Operations) Act 1997
[†] Section 5 Law Enforcement (Controlled Operations) Act 1997
[‡] Section 6 Law Enforcement (Controlled Operations) Act 1997
[§] Section 3(1) Law Enforcement (Controlled Operations) Act 1997

1. Inducing or encouraging another to engage in criminal activity or corrupt conduct
2. Engaging in conduct that is likely to endanger the health or safety of another participant or the result in serious loss or damage to property
3. Engaging in conduct that involves the commission of sexual offenses*

Under the act, a civilian participant, which would include an informant, cannot be authorized to participate in a controlled operation unless the chief executive officer is satisfied that it is impracticable for an officer to participate in that aspect of the operation and it is also impracticable for that civilian participant to participate without having to engage in that activity.† While there would appear to be a degree of statutory control, unlike the United Kingdom's RIPA, the act itself lacks specifics in how informants should be handled as it is not solely focused on handling informants and is more concerned with preventing any form of corrupt activities by police officers during criminal investigations.

United States

The 2006 attorney general's guidelines regarding the use of confidential informants are mandatory but only apply to U.S. federal agencies such as the FBI or the Drug Enforcement Agency and do not apply to U.S. police departments at state, county, or municipal level. As with other nation-states, we see a similarity of conditions and protocols that officers must follow regarding the use of informants in criminal investigations. Among the factors officers have to take into account in determining if a person is suitable to become an informant includes the person's age, the person's motivation in providing information, the risk that person might adversely affect a criminal investigation, that person's reliability and truthfulness, and his or her prior criminal record (2006, pp. 8–9). The guidelines state that approval of using a person as a high-level informant is required. High-level informants are those who are part of an enterprise that has national or international sphere of activities. The activities have to be of a high significance to the federal agencies' objectives or where the informant would be involved in serious criminal activity, corruption, or violence (2006, p. 3). The approval must be granted by the Confidential Informants Review Committee (2006, p. 13).

In handling the informant, the officer must not impede or interfere with any investigation or arrest of the informant, and the officer cannot reveal to the informant information relating to other investigations being conducted against the informant. Also, the agent cannot exchange gifts or receive anything of more than a nominal value from the informant, nor can the officer socialize with the informant except where it is necessary for operational reason (2006, p. 17), and the officer cannot authorize the informant to engage in any activity that constitutes a misdemeanor or a felony otherwise than the activity authorized (2006, p. 19). Due mainly to concerns over corruption and informants committing crime while being handled during investigations, we see similarities in the policy and procedure recommended in using informants where a constant theme running through a number of national states' policies is strict control, recoding of informant usage, and accountability.

---

* Section 7(1) Law Enforcement (Controlled Operations) Act 1997
† Section 7(3) Law Enforcement (Controlled Operations) Act 1997

In 2005, the FBI examined the agency's application of the 2002 guidelines and reported that out of 120 confidential informant files, they found guideline deficiencies in 104 (87%) of the files they examined. The deficiencies they found included failure of officer's evaluation on suitability of a person to be an informant, failure of officers to give the informant the required instructions, failure to obtain a proper authority to permit an informant to engage in illegal activities, and failure to report unauthorized illegal activity by informants (2005, paragraph VI). Concerns how guidelines were not being adhered to by the FBI have not abated. In August 2013, Congressman Lynch wrote to the attorney general of the U.S. Department of Justice requesting that the guidelines be revised in order to enhance the accountability and transparency in the FBI's use of informants and to protect the public against authorized and unauthorized informant crime. Congressman Lynch's concern was that in 2011 the FBI approved of 5658 instances of illegal activity by informants.* The focus of his concern was the U.S. parliamentary scrutiny of and the accountability of federal agencies, in particular the FBI's authorizing of person's becoming informants. As a result, he forwarded a bill, the "Confidential Informant Accountability Act 2013" in the House of Representatives. If enacted, the bill would require a report from the federal agencies governed by the attorney general's informant guidelines revealing the total number of crimes authorized and the category of crime, the amount of drugs involved if it is a drug crime, the amount of money if the crime was a theft or robbery, and if the crime was authorized or unauthorized along with informing the state each crime took place in.

In another study on the use of informants in the state of New Jersey, Jones-Brown and Shane found that written policies regarding the use of informants existing at state, county, and municipal level were problematic as at state level they found the use of informant policies was disjointed and spread through various documents. The county policies differ from each other, and in some cases that difference was substantial as written policies did not exist in all of the municipal police departments. This is contrary to the Commission on Accreditation of Law Enforcement Agencies' recommendations. They also found that among those police departments that had policies governing the use of informants, police officers were not uniformly aware of the existence of the policies and neither were they trained in them leaving what they said as "… room for intentional and unintentional violations" (2011, p. 4).

What is important, especially in police jurisdictions where there is little or no mandatory guidance in the police use of informants, is that officers follow good practice that has been adopted where the procedures in using informants are more tightly controlled. This includes the following:

1. Having an officer of a higher rank of the officer handling the informant to act as a controller in order that the controller can oversee proceedings and guide and support the handling officer.
2. A risk assessment is carried out, which assesses the risk to the informant of the activity they will be expected to carry out, the potential risk of unacceptable criminal activity the informant may carry out, and, based on the informant's behavior and connections, the potential traps that could lead to corrupt activity between the informants and officers handling them. This risk assessment should be ongoing and carried out by the controlling officer while the informant is deployed.

---

* The document can be retrieved from http://www.documentcloud.org/documents/742049-fbi-oia-report.html (date accessed May 27, 2014).

3. That all contact with the informant and what information they pass on to the handling officer are recorded and retained.
4. The handling officer is accompanied by a second officer to corroborate what is said during contact with the informant.

All of these points are related to protecting not only the informant while active in the field but also the officer handling that informant, as the next section will explain why such concern exists in using informants in criminal investigations.

Ethical Issues in Handling Informants

Motives and Incentives to Inform

Previous studies on informants show that incentives and motivation to inform range from receiving money for information passed on, revenge, and taking out criminal competition to looking for a favor from the police officer handling them (Billingsley 2001, p. 86). Rosenfeld et al. state the incentives and motivation to inform, which include fear (of the police), greed, revenge, altruism, a reduced jail term, and even the need for self-esteem (2003, p. 292). Miller's research found that the financial motivation of being paid to inform was the second most common motivation of his sample to inform, with the first most common being the reduction in sentence or reduced charges (2011, pp. 211–221).

Millar identified four classifications of motivation for a person to become an informant:

1. Those who are "hammered" into compliance—These are individuals who have been "turned" or "flipped" following their arrest and have only agreed to inform due to legal duress, that duress being how the pending criminal charge will be dealt with should the person agree to comply with the officer's request to inform.
2. The bounty hunter—Motivated by money, this category of informant works on a contingency fee basis that can be problematic as the fee may only be payable upon the successful prosecution of the individual they are informing on. The potential danger with this category of motivation as in their desire for money the informant could potentially fabricate situations, give false testimony, or even plant evidence to ensure a successful prosecution.
3. Vengeful informants—This is a motivation driven by revenge and could be other criminals desirous of removing competition, a "friend" responding to rumors, or scorned partners in intimate relationships with the individual they are informing on.
4. Police buff—They tend to be eccentric citizens and police fans who may have on occasion useful information, but who generally have poor-quality information as they are not usually submerged in criminal subcultures (Miller 2011, pp. 214–215).

From the studies carried out, the motivation factor that appears to cause most concern is the informant looking for a favor from the police officer. The criminal informant could be looking for the handler to turn a blind eye to their criminality while passing on information regarding the "bigger criminal" (Colvin 1998, p. 41). This relationship between the handler and the informant has been regarded as a form of police corruption with the potential to lead to payments being made by immune criminals to police officers (Sanders et al. 2010, p. 328). For Clark, this is the reversal of the informant and handler role where criminals actively recruit potentially corrupt officers, protect the officer from exposure, and reward the officer with money commensurate with the value of intelligence provided (2001, p. 41). As Lieberman states, it is an imperative that officers understand the motivation of informants who come forward with information (2007, p. 2).

Informants: The Necessary Evil

It is recognized by both practitioners and academics that the use of informants is central and an important source of information in criminal investigations (Bean and Billingsley 2001, p. 25, Lieberman 2007, p. 1, Miller 2011, p. 203). The most effective informant is the person who has contact/involvement with criminals and Greer's categorization of informants is still a useful model to use. Greer states the categories of informant hinge on two variables, one being the relationship between informants and the people upon whom they inform with and the other being the relationship with the police to whom the informant supplies their information (1995, p. 510). He categorizes informants as follows:

1. "Casual observer"—who is an "outsider" as they have no connection or relationship with the person, they pass information onto the police as they have observed an incident and bring it to the attention of the police.
2. "One-off accomplice witness"—who is an "insider" as they have some connection or relationship with the person on whom they are passing information onto the police. They are passing information onto the police out of contrition or because of the possibility of lesser charges.
3. "Supergrass"—who not only has a connection or relationship with the person on whom they are passing information onto the police, but they also have inside information on the crimes being planned or committed by that person, and the supergrass informs the police of multiple incidents of crime (Greer 1995, pp. 11–12).

While witnesses who have no connection with criminals that pass on information are of course important sources in criminal investigations, it is the supergrass category of informants who are necessary to cultivate if police officers want to gain that valuable inside information. As Lieberman points out, the use of confidential informants can lead investigators to their key targets as they are insiders who have the ability to go places and speak with people who are inaccessible to the police (2007, p. 1). To gather such information entails police officers not only having to handle informants who are criminals because they are more effective in gathering the required information (Miller 2011, p. 206), but the officers also have to handle criminal's morals and values that potentially lead to police corruption and unethical behavior (Crous 2009, p. 117).

Ethical Handling of Informants

In handling informants there is a degree of deception by the officer where the deception includes placing a person who is an informant into a criminal circle to gain the criminal target's trust. As this deception is concerned with being effective in proactive policing where the aim is to prevent serious crime being committed, this deception can be justified on the grounds of the role of the informant being essential to be effective in carrying out this task during the criminal investigation (Williamson and Bagshaw 2001, pp. 55–57). Williamson and Bagshaw term this justification as "ends-based thinking" where the need to tackle high crime rates as well as serious crime justifies the deception in police dealings that includes the deception of criminals indulging in crime to have forfeited their right to fair treatment (2001, p. 57). Such thinking in this type of crime control also involves a moral justification where to warrant the use of immoral methods, it is only through the use of an informant can information be obtained to confirm police suspicion that another is committing crime and that crime is of sufficient seriousness (examples include drug dealing, human trafficking, pedophilia-based sexual crimes) (Harfield 2012, pp. 79–80). In such circumstances regarding a suspect's moral rights, Harfield says:

> The moral rights of victims/potential victims to be protected from serious crimes or to have such a crime investigated and prosecuted as fully as possible must, in the circumstances, outweigh the suspect's moral rights to privacy. (2012, p. 80)

Even where an officer warns the informant only to play a minor role, that officer cannot take into account the possibility of the informant feeling it necessary to play a more active role, and as a result, the handling officer does not know the true extent of the informant's involvement in planning a crime and the degree to which they were the primary instigator (Dunnighan and Norris 1998, p. 22). This raises an important issue that in the desire to obtain information, to what degree does the officer allow their informant to engage in criminality in order to obtain that information? For Harfield this is an important question. He makes the point that the more involved the informant becomes in criminality, there is the correlative increase in the moral wrongs committed by the informant that compounds the cumulative moral harm (2012, p. 81). As he says:

> Assuming that the given law is not itself immoral, committing crime is itself a moral harm. This in turn gives rise to a further moral harm: committing crime in order to prosecute crime undermines the very purpose of the criminal justice system and the integrity of its actors and agencies. (2012, p. 82)

1968–1997 Irish Troubles: A Case Study in Unethical Police Handling of Informants

A good example of how this can escalate was seen during the 1968–1997 Irish Troubles in Northern Ireland where republican terrorist groups such as the Provisional Irish Republican Army (PIRA) (mainly Roman Catholic) wanted independence from British rule and loyalist terror groups such as the Ulster Defence Association and the Ulster Volunteer Force (mainly Protestant) carried out a campaign to remain under British rule. This was a vicious terrorist campaign that was fought on two fronts. The PIRA deployed their England Department's Active Service Units (ASUs) on the British mainland where their activities were policed by the United Kingdom's secret service Military Intelligence Section 5 (MI5) and the United Kingdom's police department Special Branch's Counter-Terrorism Unit (CTU). In Northern Ireland, British Army Intelligence, MI5, and the police, the former Royal Ulster Constabulary (RUC), policed the activities of PIRA and the loyalist groups. Crucial to preventing acts of terrorism was the use of informants who were active within these terrorist groups. Rather than recruiting and then placing informants into certain positions within terrorist organizations (McGartland 1997, Bamford 2005, p. 591, Hewitt 2010, p. 64) on the British mainland, one method of informant recruitment by the English Special Branch CTUs was through recruiting those already active in or who had a connections with PIRA terrorist cells (O'Callaghan 1998, Bamford 2005, p. 591). The main reason why English Special Branch CTUs had to adopt this approach is they found it difficult to place agents in the PIRA's England Department's ASUs as the ASUs based in England contained no more than four members and consequently were difficult to penetrate. As Sarma points out, PIRA's "…England Department was an example of the effectiveness of the ASU format and the internal security it provided" (2005, p. 171). As a result, English Special Branch CTUs had to rely on informants who had a peripheral connection with operatives in PIRA's England Department and who were willing to come forward as volunteers or had been turned by CTU officers following their arrest and detention in police custody.

This was not the case for the RUC in Northern Ireland. It is important to differentiate the practices between the RUC Special Branch and English Special Branch during the Troubles, which was such a violent conflict that it has been described as the United Kingdom's Vietnam (Ryder 1989, p. 6). The RUC recruited and placed individuals as informants into Loyalist groups where some RUC Special Branch officers were accused in the complicity of those informants' actions in killing not only members of PIRA but also lawyers whose main clients were republicans and Irish Catholics that were suspected of connections with PIRA's republican cause (Punch 2012, pp. 121–135). At that time, the United Kingdom's Home Office guidelines on the use of informants was the only policy English and Northern Irish Special Branch CTUs had to follow. The guidelines stated the police should never use an informant to encourage another to commit a crime; police officers should not counsel, incite, or procure the commission of a crime and protecting informants does not grant the informant immunity from arrest or prosecution for the crime they fully participate in (Police Ombudsman for Northern Ireland 2007, paragraph 31.5). While there is no empirical evidence that English Special Branch CTUs followed the informant handling guidelines during the Troubles (which can be due to lack of access granted by the respective agencies to empirical research), there is evidence from the 2007 Ballast Report that they did follow the guidelines (Police Ombudsman for Northern Ireland 2007, paragraph 31.3). In contrast, a number of reports carried out following the Troubles from the 2003 Stevens Report (Punch 2012, pp. 123–124) and the 2004 Corey Report (Moran 2010, p. 20, Punch 2012, pp. 136–138) to the Ballast Report (Police Ombudsman for Northern Ireland 2007, paragraph 31.2), along with empirical work reveal that the RUC Special Branch did not abide by the Home Office guidelines (Bamford 2005, pp. 600–603, Sarma 2005, p. 168, Moran 2010, pp. 19–20, Punch 2012, p. 120) and the officers were associated with the unauthorized killings.

Placing a degree of context into this example, Clark points out that corruption in and around the use of informants is not rampant and neither is it out of control (2011, p. 49), but the behavior of some of the RUC officers at that time is a classic example of those rare occasions where standards fall, supervision fails, and officers become vulnerable to temptation where "…under such circumstances the dangers of [informants] and police officers becoming corrupt are high" (Clark 2001, p. 38). In addition to this, ethically, such behavior undermines the trust upon which social interaction is based (Harfield 2012, p. 92). Even with the pressure officers face in their desire of getting a result in the ends-based thinking during an investigation, this reason cannot be used to condone unethical handling of informants.

Recruiting Informants

The traditional way of recruiting informants is with persons who are in police detention following their arrest or with every offender police officers meet. This method of informant recruitment has changed little over the years (Gill 2000, p. 187, South 2001, p. 69). From her research, Turcotte also makes the point that the police must ensure that relationships built up with informants are power imbalanced in their favor (2008, p. 296). In 1976, the United Kingdom's Special Branch recruited the "paid-in-kind" informant who had been arrested and recruited during their suspect interview by the officers as officers had some form of hold over the informant including the threat of bringing charges for some minor offenses (Bunyan 1977, pp. 137–138). This method of informant recruitment has been criticized as being held in police custody is characterized by enforced dependency, frustration, isolation, and fear; hence, it is not surprising that those detained in police custody are more likely to succumb to propositions to provide information (Dunninghan and Norris 1998, p. 21). This has been a global method of informant recruitment. In Australia's New South Wales state's Independent Commission Against Corruption's 1993 discussion paper on police informants, while it mentions how police officers were encouraged to cultivate informants, it says there has been little guidance in applying the most appropriate ways of recruiting them (1993, p. 20). Citing New South Wales detective training material, it says that every person arrested is a potential informant and they should be cultivated accordingly adding

> Never miss an opportunity to stop and speak to criminals ... Always treat their womenfolk and families with the utmost respect and courtesy, particularly when searching their homes. ...conduct your interrogation in a proper manner. Then if you feel he is a potential informant be friendly towards him, try and oblige him with any small favour he may request ...If he requests a packet of cigarettes, do so at your own expense. He may supply you with the correct identity of some person responsible for committing a crime and your small outlay will be repaid tenfold. (1993, p. 21)

While the language in this guidance indicates the social values of the day that may not be appropriate today, the message regarding recruitment still has not changed in today's policing environment.

The police practice of "turning" (Turcotte 2008, p. 294) or "flipping" (Miller 2012, p. 212) suspects into informants following arrest is an area that has courted academic and media controversy. Using police policy documentation, Innes found that a range of tactics were used by officers to recruit informants, "...according to the officer's assessments of the individual concerned and what they believed would be the most effective approach" (Innes 2000, pp. 367–382). Examining Canadian police documents, Turcotte found that the methods recommended to encourage offenders to inform were not through physical coercion but through the use of mind games (2008, p. 296). All the empirical work on informants found that a variation of mind games were used by the police to recruit informants ranging from

1. Exaggerating the offenses a suspect may be charged with
2. Threatening the potential of long prison sentences the suspect may receive should they be charged and tried for the offenses they were arrested for

3. Where there is more than one suspect, officers would imply to one that the other suspect is talking and about to make a deal
4. The financial implications of informing that can range from the officers saying how much an informant can earn or, if the suspect does not inform, what they could lose if convicted (Innes 2000, p. 368, Norris and Dunningham 2000, p. 387, Rosenfeld et al. 2003, p. 392, Lieberman 2007, p. 3, Turcotte 2008, p. 296, Jones-Brown and Shane 2011, p. 53, Miller 2011, p. 212)

Although Turcotte says none of the officers in her research sample used physical coercion, there appears to be little argument that the aforementioned tactics are coercive as they are aimed at intimidating a suspect in police custody. Where a person under arrest in police detention is made an offer by the police of bail as an alternative to being remanded in custody, this choice is one of very restricted autonomy with an adverse consequence in the event of noncooperation. For Harfield, such an approach by the police is inherently "coercive in character" (2012, p. 91). In such circumstances, how such offers are made is important as guidance from the independent prosecuting agencies such as the Crown Prosecution service in the United Kingdom and the district attorney in the United States should be sought. Inducements that cannot be realized should not be made to encourage persons to become informants, especially to those being recruited when detained in police custody.

Evidence of Informants

There are occasions where the information passed on by informants becomes evidence in criminal trials. This in itself has courted controversy on two counts regarding arrangements for reducing the potential sentence an informant may face for their involvement in the criminal activity they informed on and, for those who are a witness in a criminal trial, their anonymity. Here, we will look at some examples of how some nation-states' jurisdictions have dealt with this issue.

Immunity from Prosecution/Reduction in Sentence

United Kingdom's Serious Organised Crime and Police Act 2005

Sections 71 and 72 of the Serious Organised Crime and Police Act 2005 (SOCPA) introduced statutory guidance for the prosecution to introduce evidence from an informant in a criminal trial. One reason being the use of informants is the most economical investigative method of piercing the shield of criminal activity (Colvin 1998, p. 38, Williamson and Bagshaw 2001, p. 55, Sanders et al. 2010, p. 326). This can range from a reduction in the length of a possible custodial sentence to the informant being immune from prosecution.[*] However, conditions are placed on this immunity as it must be appropriate to do so[†] and is only granted by a specified prosecutor like the Director of Public Prosecutions[‡] who will give the offender a written notice to this effect laying out the conditions of the

---

[*] Section 71 Serious Organised Crime and Police Act 2005
[†] Section 71(1) Serious Organised Crime and Police Act 2005
[‡] Section 71(4) Serious Organised Crime and Police Act 2005

immunity.* While this immunity is an incentive to tackle organized crime, this power is wide and can be applied to lesser offenses (Owen et al. 2005, p. 48). The aim of this statutory provision was to clarify and strengthen the common law provisions concerned with encouraging criminals assisting law enforcement agencies by passing on information and evidence against other criminals (Corker et al. 2009, p. 261). Since the commencement of Sections 71 and 72 of SOCPA, Corker et al. found that due to the complexities of using the statutory provisions, prosecutors were disinclined toward using these provisions, staying with the common law provisions instead where it is the court that makes decisions regarding immunity (2009, p. 262).

U.S. New Jersey Brimage Guidelines

In *State v. Brimage*,[†] the Supreme Court of New Jersey was asked to consider through a negotiated plea agreement to waive a mandatory minimum sentence under Section 12 of the Comprehensive Drug Reform Act 1987. In order to ensure a degree of uniformity, the court ordered the New Jersey attorney general to review new plea offer guidelines that all 25 New Jersey counties had to follow where these guidelines include minimum and standard sentences and eliminate the provisions that encourage inter-county disparity. The guidelines had to specify permissible range of offers for particular crimes and be explicit regarding bases for upward and downward departures. The court added that the New Jersey attorney general could also provide for differences in treatment among various offenders based on specific factors of flexibility among the counties, adding that in all plea offers, the individual characteristics of the crime and the defendant such as whether the defendant is a first or second time offender must be considered. Also, the prosecutors must state on the record their reasons for choosing to waive or not to waive the mandatory period of parole ineligibility, and if the prosecutor departs from the guidelines, they must give reasons why they are departing and state them clearly on record.[‡]

Informant Witness Anonymity in Criminal Trials

United Kingdom's Coroners and Justice Act 2009

Sections 86–97 of the Coroners and Justice Act 2009 make provisions regarding the anonymity of witnesses in criminal trials. The U.K. Parliament introduced these provisions following a House of Lords decision in *R v. Davis*[§] where seven witnesses to a murder feared for their lives, including three who identified Davis as the gunman. At Davis' trial the judge ordered that the witnesses gave evidence under a pseudonym, their addresses and personal details that might identify them were withheld from the court, the witnesses gave evidence behind a screen so they could only be seen by the judge and the jury, and the witness' natural voices were subject to mechanical distortion to Davis and his counsel to prevent recognition.[¶] Davis' appeal was that he was denied the right to face his accuser,

---

* Section 71(1)–71(3) Serious Organised Crime and Police Act 2005
† (1998) 706 A.2d 1096
‡ (1998) 706 A.2d 1096 at III paragraph C
§ [2008] UKHL 36
¶ [2008] UKHL 36 at paragraph 3

a long-established principle of the English common law. The House agreed with Davis and allowed his appeal. In the decision, Lord Mance said that

> ...any further relaxation of the basic common law principle requiring witnesses on issue of dispute to be identified and cross-examined with knowledge of their identity and permitting the defence to know and put to witnesses ...relevant questions about their identity is one for Parliament to endorse and delimit, not for the court to create.

This is what the U.K. Parliament did where in order to protect the safety of a witness or another person or to prevent serious damage to property or in order to prevent real harm to the public interest,[*] the prosecution can apply for a "witness anonymity order" where

1. The witness' name and other identifying details can be withheld or removed from materials disclosed to any party in the criminal proceedings
2. The witness may use a pseudonym
3. The witness is not asked questions of any specified description that might lead to the identification of the witness
4. The witness is screened (except to the judge and jury)
5. The witness' voice is subjected to modulation[†]

On an application the prosecutor must inform the court of the identity of the witness but is not required to identify the witness' identity or information that might lead to the witness being identified to any other party in the proceedings of their legal representatives.[‡] The act also allows defendants to make such an application in relation to any witnesses they wish to call where again they must inform the court of the identity of the witness, and this includes the prosecutor but not any other defendant or their legal representative.[§] As would be expected, there are conditions attached to the application of a "witness anonymity order" that includes where the credibility of the witness is relevant and needs to be assessed, where the witness might be the sole or decisive evidence implicating the defendant, and whether the witness' evidence can only be properly tested if their identity is disclosed.[¶] While the 2009 Act's provisions are written to cover a number of categories of witnesses, it is clear that this will include informants' evidence that could be submitted in U.K. criminal trials.

Canada's Confidential Informant Privilege

While having no statutory provisions through its common law, Canada has developed legal procedures for dealing with informant privilege and revealing the identity of an informant at criminal trials. In summary, there is a duty not just on the police but also on the Crown prosecutors and the courts not to release any information that risks revealing the identity of a police informant.[**] This principle has been recognized for some time in Canada and

---

[*] Section 88(3) Coroners and Justice Act 2009
[†] Section 86(2) Coroners and Justice Act 2009
[‡] Section 87(2) Coroners and Justice Act 2009
[§] Section 87(3) Coroners and Justice Act 2009
[¶] Section 89(2) Coroners and Justice Act 2009
[**] *Named Person v Vancouver Sun* (2007) 224 C.C.C. 1 (3d) (S.C.C.) at paragraph 17

is seen as being of fundamental importance to the workings of the criminal justice system.[*] The rationale behind this is to protect informants from the risk of retribution, which was recognized in *R v. Barros* to encourage cooperation from future informants where the court said:

> ...the privilege encourages other potential [informants] to come forward with some assurance of protection form reprisal. ... The obligation to protect confidential sources clearly goes beyond a rule of evidence and is not limited to the courtroom.[†]

One important principle in this privilege is that the Crown prosecutors cannot rely on material that is withheld under informant privilege to help prove the guilt of a defendant as Mister Justice Fish held in *R v. Basi*, the prosecution cannot introduce withheld information as evidence at a trial without first providing that evidence to the defense.[‡] The only occasion the defense can challenge informant privilege is when the defendant can show their innocence is at stake.[§]

Not every nation-state has similar provisions related to informant immunity and offers of reduction in sentencing regarding informants during criminal trials. Especially for informants who are classed as confidential informants (those active within criminal circles involved in serious and organized criminal activity), revealing their details in an open court imperils the personal safety of the informant and potentially their family members. Regarding the use of informants in criminal investigations, one constant theme is the importance of the information they pass on. Unless there are sufficient safeguards in place, one can see why officers are reluctant to pass on informants' personal details, especially when that information becomes evidence to be used in a criminal trial against the investigation's main criminal target.

Questions for Discussion

13.1 Why are strict controls in the use of informants in criminal investigations important?

13.2 Why are risk assessments important to the police when deciding to deploy informants during a criminal investigation?

13.3 Why are informant-motivating factors important to consider when deciding to recruit and deploy a person as an informant?

13.4 What ethical considerations should be considered in using informants in criminal investigations?

13.5 How should officers approach the recruitment of a person who has been arrested and who is in police custody as an informant?

13.6 Should informants who are involved in criminal activity be granted immunity or at the least a reduction in sentence?

13.7 Why is informant anonymity important when they are potential witnesses in criminal trials?

---

[*] *R v. Leipert* (1997) 112 C.C.C. (3d) 385 (S.C.C.) at paragraph 10
[†] *R v. Barros* (2011) 273 C.C.C. (3d) 129 (S.C.C.) at paragraph 30
[‡] *R v. Basi* (2009) 248 C.C.C. 257 (S.C.C.) at paragraph 51
[§] Ibid at paragraph 40

References

Audit Commission (1993) *Tackling Crime Effectively Management Handbook Volume 2*. London, U.K.: Audit Commission.

Bamford, B.W.C. (2005) The role and effectiveness of intelligence in Northern Ireland. *Intelligence and National Security*, 20(4), 581–607.

Bean, P. and Billingsley, R. (2001) Drugs, crime and informers. In Billingsley, R., Menitz, T., and Bean, P. (Eds.), *Informers: Policing, Policy, Practice*. Cullompton, U.K.: Willan Publishing.

Bunyan, T. (1977) *The History and Practice of the Political Police in Britain*. London, U.K.: Quartet Book.

Clark, R. (2001) Informer and corruption. In Billingsley, R., Menitz, T., and Bean, P. (Eds.) *Informers: Policing, Policy, Practice*. Cullompton: Willan Publishing, 38–49.

Colvin, M. (1998) *Under Surveillance: Covert Policing and Human Rights Standards*. London, U.K.: Justice.

Corker, D., Tombs, G., and Chisholm, T. (2009) Sections 71 and 72 of the serious organised crime and police act 2005: Wither the Common Law? *Criminal Law Review*, 261–271.

Crous, C. (2009) Human intelligence sources: Challenges in policy development. *Security Challenges*, 5(3), 117–127.

Dunninghan, C. and Norris, C. (1998) Some ethical dilemmas in the handling of police informers. *Public Money & Management*, 18(1), 21–25.

Dunningham, C. and Norris, C. (2000) The detective, the snout, and the audit commission: The real costs in using informants. *Howard Journal*, (98), 67–86.

FBI. (2012) Federal Bureau of Investigation Annual Otherwise Illegal Activity report. Retrieved from http://www.documentcloud.org/documents/742049-fbi-oia-report.html (accessed May 27, 2014).

Gill, P. (2000) *Rounding Up the Usual Suspects: Developments in Contemporary Law Enforcement Intelligence*. Aldershot, U.K.: Ashgate.

Greer, S. (1995) Towards a sociological model of police informants. *British Journal of Sociology*, 46(3), 509–527.

Harfield, C. (2012) Police informers and professional ethics. *Criminal Justice Ethics*, 31(2), 73–95.

Hewitt, S. (2010) *Snitch: A History of the Modern Intelligence Informer*. London, U.K.: Continuum Books.

Independent Commission Against Corruption (1993) *Policy Informants: A Discussion Paper*. Sydney, New South Wales, Australia: Independent Commission Against Corruption.

Innes, M. (2000) "Professionalising" the role of police informant. *Policing and Society*, 9(4), 357–384.

Jones-Brown, D. and Shane, J. (2011) *An Exploratory Study of the Use of Confidential Informants in New Jersey*. Newark, NJ: American Civil Liberties Union of New Jersey.

Lieberman, B. (2007) Ethical issues in the use of confidential informants for narcotic operations. *The Police Chief*, 74(6), 1–5.

Lynch, S. (August 23, 2013) Congressman Lynch Urges Attorney General Holder to Strengthen Guidelines on FBI Confidential Informants. Retrieved from http://lynch.house.gov/press-release/congressman-lynch-urges-attorney-general-holder-strengthen-guidelines-fbi-confidential (accessed May 27, 2014).

McGartland, M. (1997) *Fifty Dead Men Walking*. London, U.K.: Blake Publishing.

Miller, J.M. (2011) Becoming an informant. *Justice Quarterly*, 26(2), 203–220.

Moran, J. (2010) Evaluating special branch and the use of informant intelligence in Northern Ireland. *Intelligence and National Security*, 25(1), 1–23.

O'Callaghan, S. (1998) *The Informer*. London, U.K.: Bantam Press.

Owen, T. et al. (2005) *Blackstone's Guide to the Serious Organised Crime and Police Act 2005*. Oxford, U.K.: Oxford University Press.

Police Ombudsman for Northern Ireland (2007) Investigate report (Ballast report). Belfast, U.K.: Information Directorate.

Punch, M. (2012) *State Violence, Collusion and the Troubles: Counter Insurgency, Government Deviance and Northern Ireland.* London, U.K.: Pluto Press.

Ryder, C. (1989) *The RUC: A Force under Fire.* London, U.K.: Methuen.

Sanders, A., Young, R., and Burton, M. (2010) *Criminal Justice,* 4th edn. Oxford, U.K.: Oxford University Press.

Sarma, K. (2005) Informers and the battle against republican terrorism: A review of 30 years of conflict. *Police Practice & Research,* 6(2), 165–180.

South, N. (2000) Informers, agents and accountability: Some matters arising from the use of human information sources by the Police and the Security Service. In Billingsley, R. Menitz, T., and Bean, P. (Eds.), *Informers: Policing, Policy, Practice.* Cullompton, U.K.: Willan Publishing, pp. 67–80.

Turcotte, M. (2008) Shifts in police-informant negotiations. *Global Crime,* 9(4), 291–305.

US Attorney General's Guidelines Regarding the Use of Confidential Informants (2006) Office of the Attorney General, Washington, DC. Retrieved from https://www.fas.org/irp/agency/doj/fbi/dojguidelines.pdf (accessed May 27, 2014).

Western Australia Parliament Joint Standing Committee on the Corruption and Crime Commission (2011) Corruptions risks of controlled operations and informants. Report No. 15 in the 38th Parliament. Perth, Western Australia, Australia: Legislative Assembly, Parliament of Western Australia.

Williamson, T. and Bagshaw, P. (2001) The ethics of informer handling. In Billingsley, R., Menitz, T., and Bean, P. (Eds.), *Informers: Policing, Policy, Practice.* Cullompton, U.K.: Willan Publishing.

Investigations by Police of Police

14

ROCCO DEBENEDETTO

Contents

Chapter Objectives   211
Chapter Outline   211
Overview of Law Enforcement Corruption and Misconduct   212
Police Culture and Lessons Learned from the NYPD   214
   Lessons Learned   215
How to Conduct an Internal Affairs Investigation   216
   Intake Process   219
   Investigation   220
   Evidence Assessment   223
   Report Preparation and Findings Determination   223
   Evaluating the Effectiveness of an Internal Affairs Investigation   224
References   225

Chapter Objectives

After reading this chapter, you should be able to do the following:

1. Identify common corruption and misconduct issues that impact police departments across the United States.
2. Recognize the root causes of police corruption and misconduct, including common types of incidents.
3. Understand the components of an efficient and effective internal affairs investigation.
4. Distinguish between different types of evidence and sources of information and understand the strengths and weaknesses of each.
5. Evaluate the effectiveness of law enforcement corruption and misconduct investigations.

Chapter Outline

Overview of Law Enforcement Corruption and Misconduct
Police Culture and Lessons Learned from the NYPD
How to Conduct an Internal Affairs Investigation
Evaluating the Effectiveness of an Internal Affairs Investigation

Overview of Law Enforcement Corruption and Misconduct

In an ideal world, the need for internal affairs investigators would not exist. In a Utopian government, the police would simply be a stable presence, adhering itself to the countless clichés, which adorn police cruisers globally: "to protect and serve"; "in partnership with the community"; "honor, respect loyalty"; and "courtesy, professionalism and respect." There are few certainties here on earth—death and taxes aside—one cultural phenomenon we can be assured of is that for as long as state and municipal governments empower law enforcement, there will be dishonest and corrupt police officers among the rank and file who will use their enormous powers and authority granted by their badge to violate the very laws they swore an oath to protect and enforce.

Simply stated, police misconduct and corruption are abuses of police authority ranging from excessive use of force to bribery. Both misconduct and corruption can be either procedural (of or pertaining to the violation of departmental rules, codes, procedures, or guidelines), criminal (referring to violations of state and federal laws), or unconstitutional (officers who violate the civil rights of others). While misconduct involves the violation or selective enforcement of certain laws, guidelines, or procedures, corruption is the exploitation of police authority to attain profit or another material benefit for themselves or others (Police Corruption and Misconduct, 2014). Rampant police misconduct is often, but not always, a symptom of larger law enforcement corruption within the department; thus, it can be perceived to be the manifestation of a macro problem on the micro level. Usually, misconduct hints toward corruption when it is widespread and repeated either with the approval of or acquiescence of superiors; thus, it is safe to say that "misconduct gets police officers fired; corruption gets chiefs fired" (Courtemanche, 2011).

The issue of police corruption in the United States came to the attention of those who dared to look shortly after the first police departments were created and staffed. In the mid- to late 1800s, political parties ran the municipal government and all related agencies and, therefore, could handpick their police force as long as the directives of these political parties, which often required officers to "look the other way," were blessed by the politically connected. The culture and environment of this era accepted corruption, which further led to individual officers acting independently, seeking additional measures to benefit themselves financially or otherwise. Officers accepted bribes to ignore criminal activity and demanded money from business owners guaranteeing "protection." Reform efforts did not begin in earnest until the start of the twentieth century (Police Corruption and Misconduct, 2014). Though widespread corruption declined somewhat, it was still a serious problem.

In the 1920s, prohibition greatly increased corruption throughout police departments nationwide. Massive amounts of money were being made by bootleggers who in turn paid off police officers to allow their illegal activities to continue. Police corruption came to the forefront in 1929, prompting President Hoover to direct the creation of the Wickersham Commission, which recognized that prohibition was not only unenforceable, but carried a great potential for police corruption (Police Corruption and Misconduct, 2014).

Police corruption and misconduct again reached a precipice during the Civil Rights Movements of the 1960s and 1970s. While there was less monetary gain from the actions of some police officers during this period, widespread violations of constitutional rights coupled with the police brutality enacted mainly against people of color—much of it broadcasted on national television—were an eye opener for much of the country.

The Knapp Commission in 1972 highlighted many corrupt practices of the New York City Police Department (NYPD) including bribery and large-scale participation in gambling and prostitution rackets. Introduced was systemic payoffs, rewarding those officers "on the pad" who allowed illegal activities to proceed without police intervention. Further, during the subsequent investigation, Frank Serpico's testimony revealed a crucial issue that was known to all police officers of the time, namely, the "code of silence," "blue curtain," or "blue wall," among numerous other names referring to the sense of alienation and betrayal police officers felt in testifying against or even reporting other officers for misconduct. It was learned that officers would rather stand in silence than "rat out" those within the ranks committing criminal acts. The commission's recommendations, which notably included prosecution for police misconduct, were implemented, but largely ineffective (Hall, 2002).

During the 1980s and early 1990s, as the drug trade became more lucrative and concurrently more violent, specific misconduct in these dangerous areas became pervasive with police officers throughout the nation being implicated and formally charged with the stealing and selling of narcotics, as well as organized murders of rival drug lords. One notorious case took place in 1994 in New York City's 30th Precinct, located in Harlem, dubiously nicknamed "The Dirty Thirty." Two sergeants and twenty-seven police officers were arrested and charged with faking police radio and 911 emergency calls to cover up illegal raids on drug dealers' apartments, during which they seized drugs and stole large amounts of cash; officers were charged with conspiracy to distribute cocaine, among other drug-related charges (Corruption in the Dirty Thirty, 1994). A subsequent report by the federal General Accounting Office in 1998 discovered definitive evidence of growing police involvement in "drug sales, theft of drugs and money from drug dealers, and perjured testimony about illegal searches." This report also highlighted a disturbing development in police corruption as individuals no longer acted independently with regard to narcotics, but seemed to be "working in small groups to protect and assist each other" (Rabkin, 1998). This marked another turning point as the revelation of widespread law enforcement involvement in narcotics spurred ambitious efforts by police departments across the United States to root out these issues through rigorous training for officers, the establishment of community-policing programs and the evaluation and subsequent revision of organizational rules, as well as the development and institution of prevention and control mechanisms. The most novel development during this period centered on the establishment of joint police and civilian complaint review boards, with the most drastic system-wide reforms being instituted by the NYPD, including the establishment of a Commission to Investigate Allegations of Police Corruption and the Anti-Corruption Procedures of the Police Department (the "Mollen Commission") in 1992, a revamped and empowered Civilian Complaint Review Board in 1993, and the full-time Commission to Combat Police Corruption in 1995. Findings from these commissions cited "police culture" as a defining component reinforcing negative behavior either directly or through indifference, that is, the "blue wall," and making departmental reform extremely difficult as a result (NYPD Preventing Crime and Corruption, 1997).

Police Culture and Lessons Learned from the NYPD

Although "police culture," as discussed in the media, seems to have a negative connotation, the term is more complex referring to the "merging of two major components: (1) the image of impartial and professional crime fighters that the police have of themselves, and (2) a system of beliefs and behavior not described in published manuals or agency value statements" (Hall, 2002). Police culture is formed by shared attitudes, beliefs, values, assumptions, and experiences, many of these commonalities unique to law enforcement, further strengthening the cohesiveness of the group (Martin, 2011). While some elements of police culture are universal such as camaraderie, others vary according to department as a result of nuances in organizational structure, leadership, etc.

As briefly alluded earlier, police culture was cited in Milton Mollen's 1994 report into police corruption in New York City as a principle factor contributing to widespread corruption within the NYPD. Mollen stated that corruption flourished within the NYPD "because of a police culture that exalts loyalty over integrity; and because of the silence of honest officers who fear the consequences of ratting on another cop no matter how grave the crime…" Thus, in an environment that is perceived as hostile, the police culture offers its members reassurance that they will be protected in the line of duty and supported against external threats and that they will maintain secrecy when confronted with external investigations. In sum and substance, police officers believed that they must protect their own and therefore loyalty was valued above integrity, that is, the "blue wall" (Hall, 2002). Although police officers are most often associated with the term, the "blue wall," a code of silence in one form or another exists in most professions, as the desire for self-protection and group inclusion, further reinforced by the fear of being ostracized, is a facet of human nature. A national survey (1998) of police officers by the Police Foundation found that 52.4% agreed that "It is not unusual for a police officer to turn a blind eye to improper conduct by other officers." In addition, another survey conducted between 1999 and 2000 indicated that 79% of police recruits acknowledged the existence of a code of silence, thus indicating that officers are indoctrinated into the code of silence before they are even out on the street (Hall, 2002).

Indoctrination into the negative facets of police culture is a major roadblock to conducting internal affairs investigations as officers are usually uncooperative, not forthcoming, and sometimes blatantly untruthful and devious. Tactics range from legal means, whereby officers simply refuse to cooperate and seek legal representation, to officers reporting sick en masse ("the blue flu") to create operational issues or even attending a courtroom under the guise of solidarity, but in actuality intending to intimidate a witness from testifying. Over time, the cultural and organizational reinforcement of this "us versus them" mentality causes a conflict between an officer's ethics and integrity pitted against his brother officers and the overall culture into which he had been indoctrinated (Noble and Alpert, 2009). The following recent incidents highlight the pervasiveness and complexity of police officer corruption; incidents range from extremely complex money rackets to more simple abuse of authority with police culture playing a contributing role in each:

- In Sunrise, Florida, it was discovered that police intentionally lured cocaine and other drug dealers to their suburban town—even arranging for purchases to occur in local family restaurants—in an effort to bust the buyers and seize the assets. Police even paid one informant more than $800,000 over the past 5 years for her success in drawing drug dealers into the city. "Under long-standing state and federal forfeiture laws, police can seize and keep ill-gotten gains related to criminal activities, such as the money a buyer brings to purchase cocaine and the car driven to the deal" (O'Matz and Maines, 2013).

- Ten Atlanta law officers were arrested for taking payoffs to protect cocaine deals taking place in crowded shopping centers and school parking lots. Officers were accused of using their guns, badges, and authority to facilitate drug deals under orders of a street gang (Visser, 2013).
- Eight current and former New York police officers were arrested and charged in federal court with accepting thousands of dollars in cash to transport M-16 rifles and handguns, as well as what they believed to be stolen merchandise across state lines (Rashbaum, 2011).
- Five San Francisco police officers and one former cop were indicted by federal grand juries in connection with a corruption investigation launched after videos surfaced that showed plainclothes officers allegedly entering rooms at a residential hotel without legitimate reasons. An indictment says the officers beat or threatened residents at the hotel and falsified records. In another case, the indictment says these officers stole money, drugs, and personal items from hotel residents that they either kept or sold (Almasy, 2014).

Lessons Learned

Since 1894, the NYPD has experienced corruption scandals and commissions of inquiry, followed by reform and decline into subsequent commissions on a roughly 20-year cycle (NYPD Preventing Crime and Corruption, 1997). The most recent commission, the Mollen Commission, cited police culture within the NYPD as one of the major causes of corruption, as well as a serious impediment to investigating misconduct and corruption incidents. This commission also concluded that the current investigative structure, the Internal Affairs Division, was largely ineffective at combatting the problem and therefore was reorganized and reconstituted to more adequately respond to and investigate police misconduct and corruption incidents (after a reorganization it became the Internal Affairs Bureau [IAB]). The major conclusion of the Mollen Commission was that present "corruption is characterized by brutality, theft, abuse of authority and active police criminality." Two noteworthy developments came out of research associated with the Mollen Commission of Inquiry, namely,

1. A proactive approach is necessary if police corruption was to be effectively addressed
2. An independent internal investigative police unit is the most effective and efficient structure for tackling police corruption (NYPD Preventing Crime and Corruption, 1997)

It was discovered that police agencies typically do not have a mechanism in place to proactively address misconduct and corruption issues before they become pervasive and trigger either a complaint or an inquiry. It was recognized that once corruption starts and is allowed to persist—either through acquiescence or indifference—commanders lose control of their officers, and eventually the police force loses the confidence and respect of the community. The most effective internal affairs body is one that is internal to the police department it serves and is staffed by officers who understand police culture, thereby allowing them to more efficiently collect evidence and investigate corrupt police officers. Most departments throughout the country do not have the resources or volume to justify its own internal affairs unit. The effectiveness of these two principles was clearly articulated by NYPD IAB Chief Charles Campisi, when he stated that "over the past 10 years the NYPD has grown by 42% to a size of 55,000 officers. Due to the approach adopted by the NYPD in this time period to deal with corruption and misconduct, in spite of the increase in size of the agency, there has been a 50% drop in complaints of serious misconduct and corruption and a 60% decrease in the number of shooting incidents" (Newham, 2003). The objective of the reengineered IAB was to establish a unit that was both reactive, investigating all serious complaints thoroughly, and proactive, in that information from complaints is categorized, catalogued, and analyzed to identify problem officers or units where it is evident that problematic behavior is commonplace rather than an isolated event.

One facet of the NYPD's proactive approach to combatting corruption involves "integrity testing," whereby an officer is presented with a real-life situation that provides the opportunity to commit misconduct. Integrity testing is either targeted, where it is focused toward either a targeted or random officer, which increases the notion of an omnipresent IAB as officers do not know where, when, or how they are being tested until they fail and are eventually presented with evidence supporting that fact. A simple example of an integrity test is a staged motor vehicle accident, where an officer is left in charge of inventorying the contents of the vehicle, while the occupants are transported to the hospital. The vehicle will usually contain electronics, cash, and other things of value to entice the officer, whose actions will be captured via an installed video camera (Newham, 2003).

Present-day anti-corruption strategies build off of the Mollen Commission findings and are based on three broad concepts:

1. Establishing an effective internal affairs function to serve as a deterrent to corruption and serious misconduct
2. Revamping organizational systems, more specifically supervision, training, and discipline
3. Creating systems of external accountability to promote a relationship between the community and law enforcement

In totality, the broad system-wide efforts enacted by the NYPD in the 1990s demonstrate that effective reform of a large police service is possible (NYPD Preventing Crime and Corruption, 1997). Many lessons learned, both from the Mollen Commission itself and empirically through instituting system-wide reforms of the NYPD, can be generalized and applied throughout other police departments across the United States.

How to Conduct an Internal Affairs Investigation

To accurately conduct an internal affairs investigation, it is necessary to first understand the root causes of police misconduct and corruption. Despite the numerous commissions of inquiry, research studies conducted by criminologists, and the multiplicity of phrases and terms created to describe police corruption, the issue simply boils down to the negative aspects of human nature. Robert A. Verry takes this concept further in his book, *Mechanics of a Police Internal Affairs Investigation*, where he distills the causes of all police corruption and misconduct down to seven categories: (1) apathy, (2) gluttony, (3) greed, (4) lust, (5) pride, (6) resentment, and (7) wrath (collectively, the "seven deadly sins").

Apathy leads to an officer viewing his job as nothing more than a paycheck and results in a reactive, indifferent officer who attempts to avoid any additional work and merely tries to stay under the radar. Apathetic officers are easy to discover by an investigator as they tend to disobey departmental rules, write less summonses, make fewer arrests, and submit sloppy and error-filled and incomplete paper work. Not to mention, an officer's apathetic behavior often results in additional work for those around them, as well as a defiant attitude toward superiors causing other officers to openly talk about the apathetic officer's behavior long before an investigator receives a formal complaint (Verry, 2011).

Gluttony gradually emerges slowly as an officer may accept a free cup of coffee from a local vendor believing it to be a nice gesture from the store owner. This gesture can slowly manifest itself in the officer's mind as a deserved benefit of being a public servant, thereby leading to excessive exploitation of his/her badge to obtain free items, upgrades, or special accommodation—and perhaps more importantly—a feeling of insult when his/her badge does not garner the same respect from others. This type of misconduct is often difficult to discover until an issue arises whereby someone refuses to convey a benefit on the officer, thus triggering a complaint (Verry, 2011).

Greed is one of the most heinous causes of police misconduct, often resulting in an officer using his or her badge to conduct crimes for profit. While apathy and gluttony are more passive causes of corruption, greed is much more conscious and premeditated as an officer knows that they are breaking the law and continues to do so anyway to obtain profit. Common examples of this "sin" that are easily discernable to the trained investigator include complaints of theft. For example, a vehicle was pulled over and was searched as it was believed to contain narcotics; this was determined to be unfounded; however, a complaint is later filed indicating that cash and other valuables are now missing from the glove compartment and trunk of the vehicle. Another red flag that something is amiss regarding an officer's behavior is often indicated by an officer living beyond their means, driving an expensive car and the acting frivolous display of lavish items. These signs may warrant an investigator's attention (Verry, 2011).

Lust manifests itself by an officer exploiting the inherent power and authority of the position to obtain sexual favors in exchange for pardons from wrongdoing. A common example is a complaint received by a female motorist who was stopped and molested or during a house arrest where an individual is strip searched for no apparent reason. Red flags for investigators may include an officer constantly getting others to cover for his or her infidelities and an officer who pays an inordinate amount of time and attention to enforcing offenses committed by women (Verry, 2011).

Pride is unique in that it is a precursor to, and influencer of, all the other "sins." Pride, while useful to an extent during the workday, as an officer needs to occupy a position of superiority with greater authority than the general public, can spill over into one's personal life with disastrous consequences (Verry, 2011). Red flags for an investigator include domestic violence complaints; personal issues with family, friends, and neighbors; and allegations of child abuse.

The last two "sins," resentment and wrath, are much more difficult to identify than the others. Resentment causes officers to act immorally in order to attain something at any cost that they believe they deserve, while wrath is the internalization of anger and hatred that presents itself in either self-destructive behavior or overly aggressive behavior toward others. While these internal issues should surface during preemployment psychological testing, oftentimes these issues go undetected for years until a police officer's internalization of wrath and resentment causes him or her to begin to act irrationally. For example, an officer was disciplined by a blonde female superior earlier in the day and later that day arrests a blonde female for jaywalking (Verry, 2011).

The root causes of police misconduct and corruption can inform and assist investigators to take a proactive and not only a reactive approach to rooting out departmental misconduct and corruption. Now, it is necessary to discuss the most common kinds of police misconduct that investigators will most often encounter. The following nine common types of police misconduct all stem from the seven root causes identified earlier and include (1) absenteeism, (2) alliances, (3) bribery, (4) dishonesty, (5) embezzlement, (6) influencing, (7) kickbacks, (8) nepotism, and (9) cronyism (Verry, 2011).

Investigators have several tools at their disposal as they investigate allegations of police misconduct. The following sampling of methodologies presents general guidelines on how to conduct an investigation into common misconduct issues. In investigating absenteeism, the investigator must maintain not only accurate records of attendance but also all documentations pertaining to days missed, tardiness, etc. Regarding alliances, investigators should focus on relationships that could lead to the officer's position being compromised such as an officer hanging around a known establishment where organized crime operates or being in a close personal relationship with known criminals. Bribery is often extremely difficult to prove as it involves two guilty parties. An investigator must look for any patterns of summonses or citations issued as well as any other paper trail that may hint toward this criminal act. Dishonesty usually occurs when an officer has already been engaged in other forms of misconduct and attempts to cover up their misdeeds or the misdeeds of others. Sadly, many officers who would not have been fired if they owned up to their initial misdeed do get fired for being dishonest when the truth eventually surfaces. Embezzlement is another common kind of police misconduct, whereby an officer misappropriates funds, which have been entrusted to him or her. Embezzlement also usually involves the manipulation of records and data that often leaves a paper trail for the discerning investigator. Influencing occurs when an officer uses his authority to influence or secure a favor for someone in return for material gain. Kickbacks involve a police officer who ensures that another party obtains something from a police officer (or department) in exchange for some type of material gain. For example, a vendor may have a personal relationship with an officer who works in purchasing and therefore obtains information regarding a particular bid ahead of schedule, thus gaining an unfair advantage. Another example is a retired police officer—many of whom work in the security and private investigations field—contacting a friend, who is an active officer, and asking him or her to utilize the criminal justice system to run a background check for personal or professional reasons. Similar to many of the types of misconduct listed earlier, kickbacks often leave paper trails and digital fingerprints leading to the target officer for the trained investigator to uncover. The last two common types of misconduct, namely, nepotism and cronyism, concern the bestowing of a special privilege on an individual either due to their familial relationship with the person with regard to the former or due to friendship in the case of the latter. Common examples include a nephew of the chief being fast tracked through the hiring process even though other applicants are more qualified. Now that the root causes and most common types of police misconduct and corruption have been discussed, it is time to identify the investigation process from complaint to adjudication, if applicable (Verry, 2011).

Intake Process

While many ongoing investigations are proactive in nature searching for paper trail inconsistencies and odd officer behavior, many investigations are reactive, beginning when internal affairs receive a complaint and determine that the allegations are worthy to warrant an official investigation. "Intake" refers to the process and procedures associated with receiving, analyzing, and cataloguing complaints from multiple sources (Noble and Alpert, 2009). Complaints can take many forms, to include written or oral, in person or anonymous, electronic or paper, and internal or generated from outside the department. A public complaint form should be available upon request at all police stations and other municipal offices (Noble and Alpert, 2009). Some municipalities have electronic complaint forms that can be accessed from the Internet and completed anywhere an individual has access to a computer. Regardless of the form in which the complaint is received, it is a recommended practice that the IAB or similar type unit accept all complaints to best gain insight into the public's perception of the police force. All complaints need to be documented and either determined to be credible and serious enough to warrant an investigation or deemed unfounded. Complaints can range from irrational verbal reports of police misbehavior to formal complaints indicating widespread corruption in a police department. Nonsupervisory personnel who receive a complaint should always be required to immediately summon a supervisor to verify the complaint and ensure it is properly directed. Nonsupervisory personnel are often not trained to adequately investigate a complaint and may run into a conflict of interest if they are tasked with accepting and lodging a complaint made against a peer officer (Noble and Alpert, 2009). If a supervisor receives a complaint about another supervisor, a superior officer should be summoned to receive the complaint, and so on and so forth. The IAB or similar agency should make all efforts to make the process as simple as possible, even offering tutorials on how to complete a complaint and assistance for foreign language complainants. All of the earlier defined processes and procedures ensure that police departments are accurately receiving and responding to public complaints.

Following the receipt of a complaint, it is the role of the IAB or similar agency to analyze and catalogue a complaint; if the complaint is determined to be serious and credible, the IAB or similar agency will assign a trained investigator who should begin to collect data, gather evidence, and conduct interviews. Proper classification of a complaint is a crucial step that must occur immediately following initial intake. Classification or cataloguing ensures that the received complaint is investigated in an appropriate fashion; it determines where, when, and how a complaint is investigated and resolved. Most internal affairs units catalogue complaints into major categories such as "administrative" complaints and "criminal" complaints. Administrative complaints are addressed in a vastly different manner than criminal complaints, as criminal complaints may result in an officer being prosecuted or placed in jail rather than only leading to internal disciplinary action, such as being formally written up, docked time, and possibly suspended.

Subcategories within both categories are also utilized to further classify complaints and determine that the appropriate investigator is assigned to the complaint (Noble and Alpert, 2009).

Investigation

After a complaint has been received, analyzed, categorized, and assigned, assuming the complaint was deemed to be serious, the investigation commences. Investigations should be as impartial as possible, removing any actual or perceived bias, prejudice, or self-interest, and simply be based upon the gathering and assessment of facts and evidence.

Depending upon the type and categorization of the complaint, investigations are either administrative or criminal in nature. Administrative investigations primarily focus on investigating the employee misconduct through gathering evidence and identifying supporting material regarding the alleged offense. A secondary purpose of administrative investigations is to uncover material that may be grounds for broadening the investigation, such as repeated absenteeism, insubordination, or disregard of department directives. Additional information may also lead the investigator to uncover the involvement of other officers related or unrelated to the original allegation. Findings from administrative investigations are more useful than just supporting the investigation at hand. Findings can be used to identify various officer behaviors that may help explain other acts of misconduct, as well as to identify inefficient or ineffective policies and procedures and to better design officer training to help mitigate the specific misconduct incident initially under investigation.

The first step in conducting an investigation is to form a detailed investigative plan listing an inventory of evidence collected to date: testimony, interviews to be conducted, those who require follow-up interviews, information to be collected from said interviews, and time frames for evidentiary collection. Further, investigators should produce a list of investigative documents that need to be obtained such as medical records, financial records, police reports, prior complaints, and any other relevant document that may have been prepared. A seasoned investigator will also structure the timing of interviews to achieve a tactical advantage, obviously, much more easily accomplished during an administrative investigation than a criminal investigation. The investigator may also wish to seek feedback from his or her peers or supervisor to ensure that all investigatory steps are accounted for and that he or she did not overlook any details. Following the formalization and approval of the investigative plan, an investigation can finally commence.

Securing, collecting, and analyzing evidence is the crux of both the administrative and criminal investigations. Evidence can stem from both internal and external sources, with the internal sources of information to include information discovered on mobile data terminals (MDTs), police radio audiotapes, dispatch logs, payroll records, police video cameras, and reports prepared and other internally produced memoranda. External sources of information may include a crime scene, review of area CCTV or other surveillance video, witnesses, information gleaned from conducting an area canvass, and medical and financial records, among other evidentiary sources external to the police department. Internal sources, specifically information derived from MDTs, offer insight into the state of mind of the officer through capturing internally sent messages, identifying other officers on duty at the time of the incident, and gathering other useful information. For example, during the Rodney King case, officers utilized the MDT to brag about their use of a Taser as well as to send numerous comments littered with racial slurs. Police radio audiotapes also offer a window into the state of mind of the target officer as conversations usually occur between the police dispatcher and the assigned officer prior to the officer responding to the scene of the incident (Noble and Alpert, 2009). Video, if captured, can help objectively demonstrate the sequence of events at the scene of the incident that can augment the investigator's interpretation of interviews from witnesses. Incidents involving law enforcement, by their very nature, create significant amounts of paper work and supplemental documentation that should be compiled and examined by an investigator during any investigation.

While other internal sources of information discussed earlier are objective and not easily manipulated, documentation may be manipulated and even edited by the target officer or accomplices to cover up misconduct. Therefore, all documentation associated with a particular incident needs to be analyzed to determine its credibility. The most common information an investigator will want to know regarding a particular document is its authorship, the time of its creation, that the document was drafted in accordance with a defined process, and that it followed an approved and consistent chain of custody (Noble and Alpert, 2009). The document in question should also be compared against other similar documents by the same author to determine if it is standard or if the structure, tone, etc., seems to be uncharacteristic. Documentation should be examined according to the earlier defined methods regardless of whether it was internally or externally provided.

Complaints of misconduct sometimes arise immediately following an incident, thereby forcing the investigator to immediately secure a crime scene to ensure that no evidence is added, removed, or altered. An investigator will want to clearly demarcate the scene by establishing physical boundaries; control access and maintain a log of all visitors; preserve the original scene as much as possible through video, drawings, or photography; conduct walkthroughs of the scene with witnesses to better understand the sequence of events and how they may have impacted on the current state of the scene; and finally systematically and methodically collect, evaluate, and catalogue evidence from the scene. Very often a crime scene is initially established and investigated by first responding patrol officers, detective investigators, and others (assistant district attorney, assistant medical examiner) with a required and authorized jurisdictional presence. Understanding that the investigation may be bifurcated for an extended period (at times for its duration), internal investigators must ensure that the integrity of the crime scene is not compromised and remains intact.

Other external sources of information include financial and medical records and witnesses associated with the scene of the misconduct or privy to misconduct conducted by the target officer. Medical records are quite useful when conducting an investigation regarding the use of excessive force by a target officer. Complainants are usually more than willing to allow an investigator access to their medical records, usually believing that they corroborate their accusation of excessive force (Noble and Alpert, 2009). Financial records are primarily used to examine misconduct incidents, whereby it is believed that an officer is profiting from his or her crimes. Due to the criminal nature of this type of misconduct, a search warrant or prior authorization from the target officer is usually required before these records can be obtained. Witnesses are a crucial source of information that can yield much for a skilled interrogator but must be carefully handled so as to not result in "cross-contamination" of witness testimonies. Most witnesses are attempting to convey their story of the incident in as much as detail as possible and may leave out certain pieces of information that another witness may remember; thus, it is useful to hear the unadulterated versions of all witnesses' stories rather than a rehearsed and less correct consensus version. This can be done by securing and segregating witnesses so that one witness' version of events cannot correctly or incorrectly inform another's story. Further, interviews should be conducted with as little time lapse as possible from the actual time of the incident to avoid memory gaps that naturally occur with the passage of time (Noble and Alpert, 2009).

Interviews are almost always conducted during an internal affairs investigation for both the administrative and criminal varieties and, while briefly discussed earlier, are essential sources of information for the investigator. An investigator will need to navigate the line between art and science to be successful at conducting structured, tactful, and efficient interviews. Witnesses will often be uncooperative, deceitful, and misleading (often as a result of the code of silence discussed earlier), and it is the job of the investigator to sift through all of the information presented and uncover useful information to mark as evidence. Experienced and effective investigators develop valuable skills that when used correctly induces the interviewee to reveal crucial information that he or she did not intend to divulge. Once evidence is collected, catalogued, and analyzed, the investigator should begin to interview witnesses, according to his or her investigative plan, to include those associated with, involved in, or aware of the particular misconduct in question. Often, the original interview list will expand as the investigation continues. Initial interviews are typically structured to obtain the basic answers to who, what, where, when, how, and why regarding the incident, with more detailed questions occurring as the investigation progresses, and follow-up interviews are conducted. Planning the order of the interviews is also very important as it allows the investigator to control the process and avoid contamination of witnesses. The investigator will want to interview the person with the broadest perspective of the incident, followed by individuals who may know more about particular facets of the incident to gain a complete understanding of exactly what happened (Noble and Alpert, 2009). Seasoned investigators will cite numerous other tricks of the trade, such as building rapport with the interviewee before difficult questions are asked, carefully structuring the order of questions to control a witness from having selective memories and altering their story, and lastly, realizing that more than 90% of all communication is nonverbal, and assess body language and other subtle cues that may tell more than actual statements, among numerous other strategies.

While the terms "interview" and "interrogation" are often used interchangeably, interrogations are much more methodical in their approach, thus requiring additional degrees of planning. Interrogations are designed to obtain information that would not otherwise be divulged by the interviewee. The first step in preparing for an interrogation is to conduct a case analysis of witness statements and other evidence collected to date to help formulate a theory regarding the incident in question. Interrogations are the last interviews to take place and are usually only conducted when an investigator is reasonably sure that a subject has important information regarding the case. Sequences of interrogations should be structured so that the officer who is most likely to divulge the most is interviewed first, followed by those with a lesser degree of culpability and so on and so forth. The setting is just as important as the planning portion of an interrogation. The environment should be free of distracting influences, and the number of people present should be limited to as few as possible (Noble and Alpert, 2009).

Evidence Assessment

During the course of an investigation, all evidences will be collected, studied, and assessed for credibility. Statements given during interviews can be categorized as conflicting, admissions, or confessions. Conflicting statements may occur because of perceptual differences between witnesses—which is common and acceptable—or may point out a lie or inconsistency in a target officer's story if several other witnesses perceived the incident differently. Admissions are when a target officer admits that he or she was in fact at the scene of the incident, but did not commit any misconduct. Admissions, when assessed in light of additional sources of evidence, may support a circumstantial determination of proof on the part of the investigator. Confessions are similar to admissions with one distinct difference; the officer in question admits that he or she was involved in misconduct. Confessions must be received in a voluntary manner without the withholding of food, bathroom privileges, or water and without the threat or implied threat of force or an investigator risks having all evidence obtained from a confession thrown out in court (Noble and Alpert, 2009). Further, all witnesses must be analyzed to determine their credibility. This is usually done by assessing their demeanor and understanding of the event in question, prior statements, character, reputation for honesty, etc.

Evidence collected can be categorized as direct, circumstantial, physical, or exculpatory. Direct evidence is evidence that directly proves fact beyond a reasonable doubt. Direct evidence can be testimony or documentation that can either prove or disprove that misconduct occurred. Circumstantial evidence is evidence that indirectly links the officer in question to the misconduct. For example, an admission, as discussed earlier, demonstrates that the target officer was present during the misconduct incident, but that he or she was not involved. Taken together with other direct evidence, circumstantial evidence is admissible. Physical evidence refers to the tangible evidence collected during an investigation, such as a weapon, vehicle, or records requested. Exculpatory evidence is evidence that directly points to the target officer's innocence (Noble and Alpert, 2009). All types of evidence to include records, photographs, videos, and statements must be clearly and methodically documented in the investigative report.

Report Preparation and Findings Determination

A written report must clearly indicate the specific misconduct incident investigated, the complainant, the target officer, all persons interviewed, the investigative methodology, and most importantly, the findings. The content and quality of the report is critical, as it will inform judgments regarding the quality of the overall investigation. The narrative needs to clearly articulate the who, what, where, when, why, and how of the case and explain the methodology utilized to determine answers and to support findings. Evidence needs to be clearly presented and organized to allow a reader to follow the investigator's train of thought regarding the incident. Typically, a good report will go through numerous drafts and revisions, even being reviewed by superiors before it is finalized and distributed to the departmental hierarchy.

Depending on the nature of the misconduct incident and the organizational structure of the department where the misconduct occurred, the adjudication can be carried out by the precinct or unit commander, an internal panel of police managers, an outside oversight agency, or even the Chief of Police (Noble and Alpert, 2009). These methods all have their strengths and weaknesses, but it is up to the department to choose how to best ensure a complete, nonbiased investigation. Findings should be clearly stated and marked as unfounded, exonerated, unsubstantiated, founded, or other misconduct noted. After the determination of findings, disciplinary action and/or criminal prosecution usually follows.

Evaluating the Effectiveness of an Internal Affairs Investigation

Despite efforts to combat misconduct and corruption within the law enforcement community, recent polls demonstrate that only "56% of people rated the police as having a high or very high ethical standard." For comparison, 84% rated nurses as having a high or very high ethical standard, clearly demonstrating the divergence between the publics' perception of individuals from these two careers that both intend to serve the public good (Martin, 2011). While some researchers cite high-publicized cases of police corruption as contributing to this perception (partly accurate), the issue is not that simple as statistics also largely support the public's perception and indicate that although much has been done to combat misconduct and corruption, there is still a great deal of work to be accomplished. For example, during the period from 1992 to 2008, approximately 2000 NYPD officers were arrested that is an average of 119 per year. Further, while the number of complaints logged by internal affairs has tripled since 1992, the number of investigations pursued over the same period has halved. For example, IAB receives and logged more than 14,700 tips in 1994, yet only investigated 2,258, which accounts for approximately 15%. In 2006, the department received nearly 45,000 tips and investigated only 1,057, approximately 2%, thus indicating a disturbing trend (Baker and McGinty, 2010). Therefore, it is necessary to continuously assess and evaluate the effectiveness of internal investigations and the organization or bureau tasked with leading investigations not only to identify issues and risks but to improve efficiency and other metrics of performance.

The starting point for evaluations is usually the investigators themselves. Investigators are examined from both quality and efficiency perspectives. For example, how many investigations were carried out by the particular officer in question and were these cases primarily simple or complex in nature? Assessments based upon volume and complexity allow comparisons to be made both internally to other investigators and externally outside the organization. Efficiency is measured by checking the timeliness and quality of reports. The number of drafts and revisions often indicates quality issues and has a direct negative impact on efficiency. Other ways of assessing quality are much more in depth, requiring the evaluator to reexamine the evidence to understand how the investigator structured his or her report (Noble and Alpert, 2009). While this method is much more time intensive, supervisors should periodically assess investigator quality in this manner.

Detailed metrics should be developed, and evaluations and internal audits should also be conducted to ensure the policies, procedures, and processes of the internal affairs unit are successful in identifying, addressing, and reducing acts of misconduct and corruption. Organizations can fall short in several respects: unqualified or uncommitted investigators, improper or ineffective supervision and management, and less than full support from senior management and/or local government to name a few. Internal evaluations and audits not only help to strengthen an internal affairs unit by identifying weaknesses and correcting small issues before they become larger ones but also help to enhance the public perception of their police department in holding those few "bad apples" accountable for their misconduct while ensuring that the overwhelming majority of good and honest officers within the department hold and value integrity above loyalty.

> If citizens cannot trust that laws will be enforced in an evenhanded and honest fashion, they cannot be said to live under the rule of law. Instead, they live under the rule of men corrupted by the law.

Dale Carpenter*

References

Almasy, S. (February 27, 2014). San Francisco corruption probe ensnares five cops and one retired officer. CNN. Retrieved May 27, 2014.

Baker, A. and McGinty, J. (March 26, 2010). N.Y.P.D. confidential. *New York Times*. Retrieved May 21, 2014.

Bayley, D. and Perito, R. (2011). Police corruption: What past scandals teach about current challenges. United States Institute of Peace—Special Report.

Corruption in the 'Dirty 30' (September 30, 1994). *New York Times*. Retrieved June 8, 2014.

Courtemanche, Jr. R. (November 1, 2011). Internal affairs: An evolution in organizational culture? *Police Chief*.

Hall, R. (September 19, 2002). A brief discussion of police culture and how it affects police responses to internal affairs investigations and civilian oversight. Retrieved May 27, 2014.

Martin, R. (May 1, 2011). Police corruption: An analytical look into police ethics. Retrieved May 27, 2014.

Newham, G. (2003). Preventing police corruption: Lessons from the New York City Police Department. Centre for the Study of Violence and Reconstruction, Johannesburg, South Africa.

New York Police Department: Preventing Crime and Corruption. (1997). Independent Commission against Corruption.

Noble, J. and Alpert, G. (2009). *Managing Accountability Systems for Police Conduct: Internal Affairs and External Oversight*. Long Grove, IL: Waveland Press.

O'Matz, M. and Maines, J. (October, 2013). Cops, cash, cocaine—How sunrise police make millions selling drugs. *Sun Sentinel*. Retrieved June 17, 2014.

Police Corruption and Misconduct (2014). History, Contemporary Problems, Further Readings. http://law.jrank.org/pages/9248/Police-Corruption-Misconduct.html. Retrieved June 2, 2014.

Rabkin, N. (June 29, 1998). Law enforcement: Information on drug-related police corruption. Retrieved June 1, 2014.

Rashbaum, W.K. (October 25, 2011). 8 Officers charged with gun trafficking in U.S. corruption case. *New York Times*. Retrieved May 27, 2014.

Verry, R. (2011). *Mechanics of a Police Internal Affairs Investigation*. Flushing, NY: Looseleaf Law Publications.

Visser, S. (February 13, 2013). 10 Metro police officers face corruption charges. *The Atlanta Journal-Constitution*. Retrieved May 27, 2014.

---

* Mr. Carpenter is an American legal commentator and Earl R. Larson Professor of Civil Rights and Civil Liberties Law at the University of Minnesota Law School.

Investigation of Occult Groups

15

GORDON A. CREWS

Contents

Chapter Objectives	228
Chapter Outline	228
Introduction	229
Terminology, Titles, and Labels Used	230
First Amendment Protections	230
"Cult Cops" and "Ghostbusters"	231
Genesis of Labels	231
Impact on Police Training and Education	232
Satanic Panic and the CSI Effect	233
Satanic Panic	233
CSI Effect	234
Defining and Identifying Occult-, Satanic-, and Alternative-Belief-Related Crime	235
Crimes Most Often Linked to Occult Involvement	235
Inherent in Some Activities	236
Questionable Crimes	236
"Types" of Individuals Involved	237
Levels of Involvement	238
Satanic Tourism and Legend Tripping	239
Factors Involved in the Identification and Investigation of a Possible Cult, Occult, Alternative Belief Crime Scene	240
Investigating Occult-Related Crime	240
Recognizing Occult Symbols and Rituals at the Crime Scene	241
Occult Crime Scene Clues	241
Other Potential Questions That Should Be Considered	242
Traditional Materials Used by Criminal Investigators	242
Occult Crime Scene Identifiers	242
Occult Holidays	243
Potential Indicators of Dangerous Occult-Related Behavior	244
Symbols of the Occult and Alternate Religions	245
Developing Probable Cause for a Search Warrant	246
Clothing and Jewelry	246
Games, Books, Wall Hangings	246
Weapons	247
Ritual Items	247
Barriers to Effective Law Enforcement Involvement in Occult, Satanic, and Alternative Belief System Crime	247
Barriers	247
Overcoming Barriers	248

Conclusion   249
Questions for Discussion   249
References   250

Chapter Objectives

After reading this chapter, you should be able to do the following:

1. Discuss the impact of the First Amendment of the U.S. Constitution upon the investigation of possible occult-related crime.
2. Define the terms "cult cops" and "ghostbusters" and their evolutionary impact upon the investigation of possible occult-related crime.
3. Explain the impact that "Satanic panic" and the "CSI effect" upon these types of investigations.
4. Describe the characteristics of individuals involved in negative or dangerous types of occult behaviors.
5. Discuss the factors involved in the identification and investigation of a possible cult, occult, and alternative belief crime scene.
6. Discuss the possible barriers to effective law enforcement involvement in occult, Satanic, and alternative belief system crime.

Chapter Outline

Introduction
Terminology, Titles, and Labels Used
First Amendment Protections
"Cult Cops" and "Ghost Busters"
"Satanic Panic" and the "CSI Effect"
Defining and Identifying Occult-, Satanic-, and Alternative-Belief-Related Crime
Crimes Most Often Linked to the Occult
Types of Individuals Involved
Levels of Involvement
Satanic Tourism and Legend Tripping
Factors Involved in the Identification and Investigation of a Possible Cult, Occult, Alternative Belief Crime Scene
Investigating Occult-Related Crime
Recognizing Occult Symbols and Rituals at the Crime Scene
Traditional Materials Used by Criminal Investigators
Developing Probably Cause for a Search Warrant
Barriers to Effective Law Enforcement Involvement in Occult, Satanic, and Alternative Belief System Crime
Conclusion
References

Introduction

Over the past 40 years, considerable attention has been given by the public, news, and media to the perceived exponential increase in the amount of "occult- and Satanic-" related crime in the United States. While historically there has been very little evidence of this actually occurring, rumors, legends, misrepresentations, and unsupported reports of it have substantially impacted America and the rest of the world. A growing number of countries are experiencing a new phenomenon of their youth becoming interested and involved in various occult, Satanic, and alternative belief systems and practices. Unfortunately, some of this behavior involves criminal, antisocial, and very unsafe/risky behaviors. Depending upon the political and social culture, it can actually place these young people's lives at risk by their government and family. It appears that Western influence and attempts to democratize various parts of the world have brought about negative influences as well as positive ones.

Many international youth and young adults (Crews and Montgomery, 2001) are mimicking activities, practices, and belief systems they are reading about on the Internet and seeing through media outlets. The problem is that many of the incidents and activities they are learning about either *never occurred* or where *grossly misrepresented* on the web. Moreover, many social media sites universally accessible allow individuals to create, exaggerate, manipulate, and even fake events and actions that may or may not have even happened.

A major contributing factor (Crews and Montgomery, 1996) to these issues is that there is very little serious examination of the problem of actual occult-, ritualistic-, or Satanic-related violence and crime. Most social scientists consider the topic unworthy of any serious academic consideration. Therefore, sound, evidence-based, unbiased information for those in the criminal justice system to use in addressing what crime does occur is scarce. Unfortunately (Religious Tolerance, n.d.), others, like fundamental Christians, overly zealous television and media producers, and others with personal agendas, have given enormous time and energy to spreading misinformation, panic, and hysteria. Ironically, this information seems to be that which finds its way into the hands of those responsible in dealing with it such as parents, teachers, and law enforcement. Even those with good intentions (Crews and Montgomery, 2001) and motivation can become harmful and actual contributors to problems they are trying to prevent when they have incorrect or biased information at their disposal.

As with the investigation of any type of criminal behavior (Osterburg and Ward, 2013), law enforcement must use the soundest practices and sound evidence possible in order to be effective. Panic and misinformation can no longer be the foundation for law enforcement efforts to deal with suspected occult or Satanic criminal behavior or crime scenes. Given the importance of the police function in any society, there is far too much potential for harmful impacts on the lives of witnesses, victims, and suspects with anything less.

A major problem (Finkelhor et al., 1991) immediately apparent in an historical examination of the investigation of any occult-related crime is simply the lack of education and understanding. Most law enforcement personnel, albeit the general public too, are unfamiliar with the world of the "occult" in general much less the ways in which it can be used and/or abused by criminal offenders. This lack of knowledge in the general public has led to panic, hysteria, stereotyping of others, and unnecessary problems between parents/teachers and young people. This lack of knowledge in law enforcement has led to wrongful prosecutions, accusations against innocent individuals, and lack of identification of actual culpable individuals. At a minimum, it can cause communities' undue fear, parents to overreact, educators to miss proper warning signs, and the separation of people based on imaginary lines where none need to exist.

The purpose of this chapter is to offer, at a minimum, information for the criminal investigator to consider when he or she is faced with a potentially occult-related crime or behavior. Very often simple "food for thought" can help one realize their own lack of knowledge, personal biases, prejudice, and limitations. The vast majority of law enforcement officers desire to be as effective as possible in carrying out their sworn duty to "serve and protect." This sometimes requires an officer to step out of their "comfort zone" and face the reality of that in which they may become involved. This is no truer than found in the duties of the criminal investigator.

Terminology, Titles, and Labels Used

Throughout this chapter, labels such as "occult," "Satanic," or "alternative belief system" are used interchangeably for the sake of discussion. This is in no way meant to imply they are the same thing or universally defined in the same manner. The definitions of these terms are, as with many things in culture, in the "eyes of the beholder." The one involved in a particular belief system or behavior will ultimately be the sole individual to truly know what they are doing and why. They will be the one who has defined and qualified all systems, terms, practices, and terms they use. As will be discussed extensively, the police investigator must keep this fact at the forefront of their mind in examining these types of suspected crimes or criminal involvement.

The information discussed in this chapter is not offered to contribute to the misconception that all "occult" activities or interests are "evil" or "Satanic." Nor does it wish to contribute to the false belief that all of the belief systems or practices discussed have a natural inclination toward criminal behavior. Investigators are encouraged to review the vast information available on these interests and belief systems. Caution should be advised though to determine the source and potential personal agenda that may exist for the writer or group producing the material.

Some who practice these activities do sometimes break the law, some do use them as an excuse to commit their crimes, and others use them to "cover up" the true motivation of their crime. Each individual event, incident, crime, and/or individual must be evaluated upon their own merits with no assumptions or stereotypes in mind. This is a very basic idea in criminal investigation, but one that must not be forgotten.

First Amendment Protections

As with all areas of the police function (Osterburg and Ward, 2013; Brandl, 2014), law enforcement officials must be vigilant in their efforts to serve and protect their respective publics. This vigilance is no more important than when it comes to ensuring the due process protections enjoyed by Americans and those on its soil. It has to be remembered that most (Legal Information Institute, n.d.), if not all, occult and paganistic belief systems and practices are protected by the First Amendment of the United States Constitution.

While many may view these practices as "different or strange," they are still protected by the freedom of religion aspect of this amendment.

The first pronouncement of the First Amendment (Legal Information Institute, n.d.), stating that "Congress shall make no law respecting an establishment of religion," is generally interpreted as meaning that the federal and state government cannot establish a national church/religion or excessively becoming involved in religion in the United States, particularly to the benefit of one religion over another. While the "Free Exercise Clause" states that "Congress shall make no law respecting an establishment of religion, or prohibiting the free exercise thereof...," the Supreme Court of the United States has consistently held, however, that the right to free exercise of religion is not absolute.

Historically (Anti-Defamation League, 2012), the court has held that convictions for criminal acts committed in the name of religion do not violate the First Amendment. The court has generally reasoned that to do otherwise would potentially set precedents for a wide range of religious beliefs including those as potentially extreme as human sacrifice. The court has stated (*Reynolds V. United States*, 1878), "Laws are made for the government of actions, and while they cannot interfere with mere religious belief and opinions, they may with practices." Therefore, when it comes to occult, pagan, and Satanic practices, the First Amendment protects one's alternative belief, but not all aspects of the practice.

"Cult Cops" and "Ghostbusters"

Since the early days of policing (Crews et al., 1996), many officers have become, either by choice or need, experts in specialized fields such as gang violence, organized crime, terrorism, or arson. The last 40 years have forced many police officers to become acquainted with the occult, cults, and various forms of ritualistic violence. Some experience one unusual event that may have peaked their interest where others may have been assigned to become "overnight experts" in order to deal with a rash of crimes or activities in their jurisdiction.

Genesis of Labels

This labeling occurred in the late 1970s and early 1980s when police officers were becoming overwhelmed with so-called "cult and ritualistic violence" calls and complaints. These situations involved everything from older women suddenly realizing (or after seeing a paraprofessional counselor) that they were either ritualistically sexually abused by their "Satanic parents" to having been sold by their parents to some new "devil-worshipping cult" to become a "breeder" for the group. They ranged from accusations that the teenager next door "Satanically sacrificed" one's pet black cat to unsubstantiated rumors of the local day care center being a cult headquarters where children were ritualistic sexually abused each day.

Police officers (Crews and Montgomery, 1996) who were interested in investigating (or assigned to) these types of crimes were considered by some to be "odd" or "strange." Jokes started in many departments that these officers were "cult cops" or "ghostbusters." Over the following decades, these nicknames would change from humorous tags and labels to actual titles that were revealed by many officers trying to make a name for themselves in lectures, interviews, and training programs. Currently, these titles are used as negative labels placed upon anyone who is overzealous, misinformed, or benefiting from spreading fear and panic. While the term used to be just used for actual police officers, it has become one used for anyone who is "uncovering the hidden through of the Satanic conspiracy in the United States," obviously supporting the idea that one *does* exist.

Impact on Police Training and Education

Unfortunately (Victor, 1991b), "cult cops" and "ghostbusters" had a major impact on establishing and supporting the earliest rumors of a vast "Satanic conspiracy." They helped "validate" to the public that this *conspiracy* was responsible for up to 50,000 human sacrifices a year in the United States, involved people in the highest levels of government and civilian life, and recruited new members through heavy metal music and role-playing games such as *Dungeons & Dragons*.

Numerous police "Satanic cult seminars" and police academy classes arose across the country (California Office of Criminal Justice Planning, 1993). Traditional police jargon was used to describe people who were evil, dangerous, and very eager to recruit young adults into their groups. This jargon was combined with a plethora of terms such as "cult and ritual" by these so-called "cult crime experts," but they were never truly or fully defined nor clarified. By not doing this, speakers implanted in their audiences superstitious connotations of evil, the demonic, and the supernaturally criminal as plausible causes.

Still in the twenty-first century (Toth et al., 2008), law enforcement officials flock to training seminars about Satanic cults and crime, albeit new groups like "goth," "juggalos," and the "trench coat mafia" are the new culprits. Many of these seminars offer a world view that interprets any unusual occurrence, interest, or behavior as a sign of increasing participation by Americans in antisocial belief systems. The seminars further claim that Satanism has spawned gruesome crimes and aberrant behavior that might presage massive increases in violent crime.

An examination of most of the "training materials" and "sources" (Hicks, 1990) used in police training in this subject area is very often no more than newspaper stories and anecdotal information. Much of this current training teaches officers to quickly infer false *cause–effect relationships*. Conclusions (Lanning, 1989) are to be drawn from very weak and circumstantial evidence. This has caused a great deal of the law enforcement model of cult crime to be ill-considered, based on nondocumented secondary sources or other unsubstantiated information, and is rife with errors of logic. Such errors include false analogies, faulty cause–effect relationships, and broad, unsupported generalizations. The new "cult crime model" (Richardson, 1991) betrays an ignorance of a larger academic context of anthropology, sociology, psychology, and history, which is vital to a proper perspective on these types of behaviors and interests.

This rapidly developed (Crews, 1996) as the basis of many law enforcement publications and reports. People were warned that almost any unusual event or crime scene could be an occult-related crime. People should be warned to vigilantly watch for any items that could be in any remote way connected to any "occult" practice or belief. If any are found then, in fact, an occult-related crime had occurred or was about to occur. This implied to many parents, social workers, and teachers that there was some inherent connection between reading books on the occult and crimes like murder or suicide. This steered them away often from looking at other causes that may have led to the violence (i.e., being jilted by a girlfriend, a history of psychiatric treatment for depression, etc.).

This was compiled by the fact (Coleman, 1986) that most newspaper accounts never mentioned other attributes of a crime scene since only those touched by a nameless, faceless evil will suit the reader's interest for an explanation of why seemingly "normal" children commit such horrific acts. And the same newspaper article would ultimately be reproduced and circulated at "cult seminars" to substantiate the so-called "Satanic connection."

The negative and counterproductive results of this are obvious. As noted earlier (California Office of Criminal Justice Planning, 1993), "cult cops" do not readily define their terms. The words "cult," "occult," "Satanic," and "ritual" find casual usage; the words imply with demonic and evil associations. "Evil" is, indeed, the operative word. Law enforcers who have mixed *cult crime theories* with their professional world views have transformed their legal duties into a confrontation between good and evil. While police officers are viewed as "crime fighters," they are to do this by being civil servants and honoring the motto painted on the sides of many police patrol units, "to serve and protect." Obviously, this must mean to do so for all.

Satanic Panic and the CSI Effect

Two of the criminal investigator's worst enemies are concepts that entered the American culture and nomenclature in the 1970s and 2000s, respectively: *Satanic panic* and *the CSI effect*. Both are responsible for a great deal of misunderstanding and misinformation that has led to enormous confusion, panic, fear, and hysteria in communities across the United States. Obviously, all of which make the criminal investigator's job much more difficult. The best defense for the police officer is to be as familiar with these phenomena as possible and aware of the impact they may have upon any criminal investigation. They can also further help the citizens they serve by taking every opportunity to educate the public and fellow criminal justice colleagues of the existence and impact these concepts can have on the proper response to criminal behavior and public safety.

Satanic Panic

The phenomenon of *Satanic panic* (Victor, 1993) originated during the 1970s and gained widespread acceptance during the 1980s and 1990s. This period in American history was rampant with outlandish claims that a vast underground network of Satanists were in control of secular society. These reports were fueled by many fundamentalist Christians in the United States. The 1970s and 1980s witnessed the proliferation of so-called "authoritative" works being published and disseminated to the American public. Works such as *The Satan Seller* by Mike Warnke (1972) and *Michelle Remembers* by Smith and Pazder (1980) became actual training materials for educators, parents, and law enforcement. Self-proclaimed "Satanic experts" such as these joined a large number of individuals spreading panic and fear into local communities across the United States.

Satanic panic (Victor, 1993) spread to society at large when law enforcement agencies began accepting the incredible claims of evangelical Christians at face value. Police agencies used these false allegations as the basis for investigations of any and all perceived occult activity often committed by harmless neo-paganism groups or bored teenagers. The assumption became that these activities were part of the broader *Satanic conspiracy*

(Frankfurter, 2008), which they were lead to believe existed. As more crimes were being "linked" to Satanic rituals by American law enforcement, the popular media began to "validate" this false information to the public in news reports. They naively believed that if law enforcement reported it, it must be true and factual.

By the early 1990s (Sills, 1990), *all* of these "authoritative pieces and speakers/trainers" were proven to be fraudulent and their "information" self-created. A pivotal work during this time was the book *Satanic Panic: The Creation of a Contemporary Legend* by Dr. Jeffrey S. Victor in 1993. He examined the phenomenon of *Satanic panic* and offered that there is no evidence for the actual existence of organized Satanic cults.

Unfortunately, these revelations have had little effect on those who wanted to believe such an extremely organized evil underground did exist to promote "Satan on earth." More importantly, many of the materials developed, published, and printed during this period are still being used by police academies across America in the twenty-first century. Over time, past use by law enforcement officials of these materials has somehow validated their use for current police officers. This obviously is very disturbing in that false and inaccurate information is being given as fact to an entirely new generation of police officers almost daily.

The impact that this was having, and continues to, was that some criminal investigators (Victor, 1989) fell into the same traps that made so many ineffective in the 1970s and 1980s (i.e., identification of *backward masking* on albums, the *Dungeons & Dragons* board game, and *heavy metal music* in general as the cause of all social ills). As America attempted to deal with juveniles who were "dabbling with various types of dangerous occult and Satanic practices," those in pivotal roles to have positive impacts did not. In turn, many young people were damaged and families destroyed for no reason.

CSI Effect

Most police officers (Roane, 2005) are well aware of the issue *the CSI effect* or, as known by some, the *CSI syndrome*. The *CSI effect* is named after a television program that first aired in 2000. *CSI: Crime Scene Investigation* involved a fictional team of crime scene investigators who solved murders in Las Vegas, Nevada. The show greatly exaggerated criminal investigation techniques and procedures and the capabilities of police crime labs. These exaggerations (Heinrick, 2006) have greatly impacted public perception and the U.S. criminal justice system over the last decade. Such shows are responsible for raising crime victims' and jury members', even criminals', real-world expectations of forensic science. This is especially true in crime scene investigation and DNA testing.

It has become very apparent (Roane, 2005) that many juries have come to demand more forensic evidence in criminal trials. This has greatly raised the stakes for standard of proof required for criminal prosecutions. Such increased public awareness of forensic science has also increased the demand for forensic evidence in police investigations. These demands have greatly increased the workloads for crime laboratories across the country. Another result of the *CSI effect* is the drastic increase in forensic science programs at the university level, though many new programs have been criticized for inadequately preparing (in understanding of role and skill set) their students for real forensic work. Finally (Heinrick, 2006), many argue that shows such as this actually teach criminals how to conceal evidence of their crimes, thereby making it more difficult for investigators to solve cases.

The potential impact that either of these phenomena can have on the criminal investigator is obvious. For those who are investigating potentially occult or Satanic crime, they will probably experience both of them at the same time. An effective investigator will be able to recognize when faced with these and know how to manage them. Their own personal biases/beliefs, fears, and lack of knowledge first, then those of others second.

Defining and Identifying Occult-, Satanic-, and Alternative-Belief-Related Crime

One of the most difficult areas of this type of investigation is defining and identifying occult-, Satanic-, and alternative-belief-related crimes. Some law enforcers (Mueller, 1992) have recommended the creation of a new criminal category specifically called "occult crime," arguing that such a category is necessary to measure the actual extent of crime related to the occult. Other law enforcers have adamantly argued against this creation, claiming that such a category would not only be superfluous but that no crime category should exist for a specific belief system. Other law enforcers simply offer that anyone of any belief who commits a crime, whether or not to further their beliefs, has committed a crime, not just an occult crime, Satanic crime, or for that matter, a "Christian" crime.

Still, many (Clark, 1988; Lyons, 1988; Larson, 1989; Johnston, 1989; California Office of Criminal Justice Planning, 1993; Crews, 1996) have attempted to develop the proper definition of these types of crimes. The following is a list of many proposed definitions for "occult-related crime":

- It involves a crime that is occult motivated, involved with secret knowledge of an occult group, and uses certain rituals to change physical science.
- It is in some way motivated by a person's belief either in religion or in theory.
- It is motivated by nontraditional or occult beliefs and committed to further an occult belief system.
- It is any illegal activity in which the "trappings" of the occult are present.
- It is committed by two or more individuals who rationally plan the crime and whose primary motivation is to fulfill a prescribed occult ritual calling.
- It encompasses ceremonial actions and/or ritualistic acts, involves occult-related behavior patterns, and is motivated by a belief in some occult ideology.

No matter what definition is used, law enforcers must be careful not to interchangeably and synonymously use the terms occult crime, Satanic crime, and/or ritualistic violence.

Crimes Most Often Linked to Occult Involvement

In general, law enforcers assume (Richardson, 1991; Mueller, 1992; Perlmutter, 2003) that several specific crimes can have occult linkages: trespassing, vandalism, theft, graffiti, arson, and animal sacrifice. There is a second category of crimes whose assumed links to crime are either supported or denied by law enforcers: suicide, kidnapping, murder/human sacrifice, and ritualistic abuse.

Inherent in Some Activities

Many law enforcement investigators (Richardson et al., 1991a) share a common belief that physical evidence found in the following crimes sometimes indicates an occult motivation: trespassing, vandalism, theft, graffiti, arson, and animal mutilation and sacrifice.

Trespassing (Barry, 1987) related to occult activity usually involves individuals entering private areas such as wooded and forested lands, barns, and other old or abandoned buildings. The purpose for such trespassing is to worship either in the area as it is naturally arranged or to make it into an occult worship site with the appropriate altars and symbols. Occult-related trespassing of this nature is committed both by *true believers* and by *true criminals* who seek a private and isolated place to worship.

Vandalism (Crews and Montgomery, 1996) most often associated with occult crime includes cemetery and church desecration. The most common types of cemetery desecration attributed to occult groups are overturning, breaking, and/or stealing headstones; digging up graves; grave robbing; and tampering with human corpses or skeletons. The prevalence of cemetery desecration is unknown on either a national or statewide basis; more specifically, the prevalence of occult-related cemetery desecration is unknown. Most often committed by true criminals who use dabbling in the occult as an excuse to commit a crime, church desecration includes the following actions: destroying Bibles, urinating and defecating on holy objects and furniture, tearing crucifixes off walls, and destroying rosaries and crucifixes.

Thefts (Mueller, 1992) from Christian churches, Jewish synagogues, hospitals, morgues, medical schools, and funeral homes are often linked with occult crime. Items that are most often taken include cadavers, skeletal remains, and religious artifacts from churches and synagogues that are considered sacred: crucifixes, communion waters, wine, chalices, etc.

Graffiti (Crews et al., 1996) is one of the most common crimes related to the occult. While a small amount of graffiti is probably related to other occult groups, many argue that the vast majority is directly related to involvement in Satanic groups.

Arson (Johnston, 1989) is another crime that is almost always attributed to Satanists, especially youth subculture Satanists. Among the most common places for occultists to commit arson are churches and synagogues in which particularly holy sections or artifacts are burned and houses or buildings where damaging evidence could be uncovered by investigators.

Although *sacrificing animals* for religious rites (Petropoulou, 2008) has a long and significant history in many nations, it is not common practice in the United States. As the number of Latin American arrivals to the United States increased, so do the number of believers in Afro-Caribbean religions that practice animal mutilation and sacrifice. These are primarily the actions of true believers, primarily Santerians, who sacrifice animals as part of rituals designed to please their gods and to invoke some kind of magic.

This list is in no way attempting to indicate that all of these types of crimes are connected to occult practitioners or that all occult practitioners involve themselves in such crimes. Investigators simply need to realize that there is often a connection.

Questionable Crimes

Currently, at least four other crimes (Bromley and Shupe, 1981; Bromley, 1991) have been linked to the occult by some criminal justice professionals: suicide, kidnapping, murder and human sacrifice, and ritualistic abuse. But others disagree with such alleged linkages. *Alleged* is a key word because although many law enforcement officials believe these crimes are occurring and some people who have left occult groups claim they are common, very little physical evidence exists to substantiate such claims.

Occult-related suicide (Richardson et al., 1991b) appears to be the primary domain of youth subculture Satanists who are often true believers, but sometimes dabblers. Indeed, Satanic-related teenage suicide is a major concern among many criminal justice practitioners and therapists.

Kidnapping (Sharp, 1987) people of all ages, but especially children, is thought by some to be a prevalent crime among some occult practitioners. Especially accused are traditional/cult Satanists who are said to kidnap victims needed for ritual sacrifice, self-styled juvenile Satanists whose dabbling has taken them "to the point of no return," and Mayomberos, whose rituals require a human skull, often with the brains still attached, to add to their nganga (term for herbalist or spiritual healer).

Probably the most controversial crime allegedly committed for occult purposes is *murder* (Wedge, 1988) perpetrated for spiritual reasons and sometimes to provide a human sacrifice. Sacrificing a human being and cannibalizing human remains have occurred throughout history. Some early pagan rites included both animal and human sacrifice. Unsubstantiated rumors of murder and cannibalism have fueled many panic and hysterical outbreaks in many communities.

"Types" of Individuals Involved

Although the vast majority of occultists are law-abiding practitioners, some do commit criminal acts. Since this topic is so controversial and no universal definition or agreement exists, they are usually described in one of two ways (Mueller, 1992): either by *their method of operation* or by *their motive*. The typology that utilizes methods to describe occult crime perpetrators generally identifies two distinct categories: *dabbling* and *ritualism*.

Dabbling (Crews, 1996) involves people who are intermittently and experimentally involved in occult activities, while dabbling in supernatural belief systems involves non-criminal activity that generally stems from a vague, curious interest. Some dabbling does involve intense preoccupation that culminates in criminal behavior. Such perpetrators most often act alone or in small loosely organized groups. Dabblers usually make up their own belief system based upon some occult ideology and perpetrate criminal activity that conforms to that ideology.

Ritualism (Lanning, 1989) involves people who commit criminal activities characterized by a series of repeated physical, sexual, and/or psychological assaults combined with a systematic use of symbols, ceremonies, and/or machinations. The need to repeat such acts can be cultural, sexual, economic, psychological, and/or spiritual. Membership in either group is not mutually exclusive. Indeed, dabblers may commit ritualistic crimes and ritualists may also dabble in the occult.

The typology that utilizes *motives* (Perlmutter, 2003) to describe occult crime perpetrators also identifies two distinct categories: *true believers* and *true criminals*. *True believers* are occult practitioners who commit crimes because such acts fit into and/or are required by their particular belief systems. These persons are involved in crime primarily because the ideology, rituals, and behavior patterns related to their occult beliefs motivate and require them to do so. Because their criminal actions are dependent upon an occult belief system and include some form of spiritual ritual, true believers are often called spiritual ritualists. True believers either commit crimes for theologically evil purposes or for theologically good purposes.

True criminals (Crews, 1996), on the other hand, are persons who use the occult as an excuse to justify or rationalize their criminal behavior. They act individually or within occult groups that can and do "act as a social binding mechanism for some people to do what they want to do." True criminals both dabble with the occult and are involved in rituals that fit their particular physical, sexual, psychological, social, economic, and/or spiritual needs; they are committed not to the belief system, but to the criminal action.

Levels of Involvement

Since the 1980s, police officers have been taught that there are three levels of involvement for those involved in occult, Satanic, or alternative belief systems (Toth et al., 2008). Academics (Crews and Montgomery, 1996) studying the topic have added a fourth level starting in the 1990s. The initial three were *dabblers, traditional or religious practitioners*, and *self-styled practitioners*. The most recent or the fourth is the *youth subculture* in general.

The *dabbler* (Bromley, 1991; Crews, 1996) is almost always a juvenile who is beginning to explore one or more belief systems. They will generally experiment with the belief along with studying the belief. They will often learn of the belief from friends, Internet, library books, and movies/videos. They may actually go to one or more meetings associated with the group. All of these actions can be dangerous to himself or herself or others because he or she is trying to appease the group and prove himself or herself worthy.

Another type is the *traditional or religious practitioner* (Crews and Montgomery, 2001) who is very deep into their belief and makes their belief become their way of life. They tend to look, act, and go about their daily business like regular folks. These individuals often slip into their "life style" during their meetings and happenings.

The type that is most identified with criminal and antisocial behavior (Crews, 1996) is the *self-styled practitioner*. This is an individual and/or group that actually creates their belief system. They begin to make the belief become a part of their life and will generally experiment with the belief along with studying the belief. They often flaunt their affiliation by dressing a certain way, wearing associated jewelry, listening to music associated with the group, etc.

The final and most recent type of involvement (Crews and Montgomery, 1996) is named by many as simply the *youth subculture*. Some juveniles simply become involved with an alternative belief system out of excitement or boredom. This can often take the form of a cult or an occult-based belief system. It is often a combination of belief systems (e.g., vampire, Satanic, and black magic). The combination of beliefs and leadership makes these groups sometimes very dangerous as well as inviting. Many aspects of the occult and Satanic beliefs are mocked or "played with" by many youth. Many new fads involve occult and Satanic "themes." Many bands use occult and Satanic themes in their lyrics. Many movies, TV shows, and video games use same themes.

The reason (Osterburg and Ward, 2013; Brandl, 2014) for the criminal investigator to be familiar with these levels of involvement is to evaluate motive and mode of operation as with most investigations. Crime scenes, victims, suspects, and evidence must be examined carefully. Knowledge of the possible level of involvement of an individual and what it could mean can sometimes be vital.

Satanic Tourism and Legend Tripping

There are two relatively recent types of behavior that the criminal investigator needs to consider when examining juvenile involvement in potential occult-related crime. These concepts are *Satanic tourism* and *legend tripping* (Fine and Victor, 1994). Some believe that these are two types of "crimes" and/or activities that lead to criminal behavior. Most researchers and juvenile delinquency experts argue that the vast majority of these types of juvenile behavior are simply fads and activities exhibited for excitement and dabbling at best.

Gary Fine and Jeffrey Victor (1994) defined "Satanic tourism" an inherently delinquent juvenile activity at geographic sites associated with some tragic event, rumored to be supernatural or related to the occult. They offered a type of "legend trip" characterized by juvenile involvement in pseudo-Satanic/occult behavior such as drawing pentagrams, writing epithets, and burning candles. During this, a juvenile may visit a geographic location such as an abandoned church, historic graveyard, or reputedly "haunted" site and engage in mischievous, destructive, or "ritualistic" behaviors as "rites of passage." They argue that these activities, which often are relatively harmless and conducted primarily for juvenile thrills, may be perceived by law enforcement and the larger community as threatening and dangerous.

The concept of "legend tripping" is at least this old as Mark Twain's *The Adventures of Tom Sawyer* (1876). In this book, there are several accounts of adolescents visiting allegedly haunted houses and caves said to be the "lairs of criminals." *Legend tripping*, a name recently bestowed by folklorists and anthropologists, is considered an adolescent rite of passage in which a usually secret nocturnal pilgrimage is made to a site that is alleged to have been the scene of something tragic, horrific, and possibly supernatural or haunting.

These activities have been known to cause a great deal of panic and hysteria in communities across the United States. One of the biggest reasons for this is where the activities take place. Juveniles often meet and congregate in areas that are not normal gathering locations. Juveniles often meet and visit in the following areas (Fine and Victor, 1994):

Abandoned Buildings/Factories	Graveyards	Playgrounds	State Parks
Bridges	Historical landmarks	Ranger outlook stations	Train tunnels
Caves	Nightclubs	Roads/underpasses	Warehouses
Churches	Open fields	Rock quarries	Woods

Investigators should consider these concepts when examining potential occult-related criminal behavior. It can never be overstated that the extremely harmful impact misinformation, unsubstantiated assumptions, and hysteria can cause to a community. Many investigations have damaged communities and individuals around the world. Most if not all of these could have been corrected if only an investigator had taken a step back to fully examine each piece of evidence in a clear and consistent manner.

Factors Involved in the Identification and Investigation of a Possible Cult, Occult, Alternative Belief Crime Scene

The following is an overview of traditional materials that are taught to police officers to help them identify and investigate possible cult, occult, or various other types of alternative belief crime scenes. These materials have been used since the late 1960s, albeit generally false and misinformed. When information is presented to a "learner" in a "list format," it becomes very tempting to use them as a "check list" of sorts. A major problem that developed over the decades is that educators, parents, and law enforcement have been given lists that they were to keep in mind as *indicators* of a certain things, not *predictors*. These things were most often misused to seek individuals being involved in a behavior or a crime scene. Unfortunately, they often ultimately led to individuals being automatically linked to a certain type of behavior. Care must be taken by the investigator to use this information as additional tools to help them in doing their jobs, not a guaranteed list of indicators.

Investigating Occult-Related Crime

As with any type of crime scene investigation (Mueller, 1992; Osterburg and Ward, 2013; Brandl, 2014), great care must be taken in order to protect evidence, victims, witnesses, the public, and oneself. While greatly exaggerated for many years, there have been some occult-related crime scenes that were actually "booby trapped" with explosives and other items. Some of these actions were taken to protect a location from any intruder or even a first responder if officials notified of its location. Investigators should not enter the perimeter of occult crime scene until advised to do so by those in charge of securing a scene. Also, no substance at a ritual site should be touched without wearing gloves, eye protection, and masks in that poison can sometimes be used during ritual ceremonies.

Many in law enforcement are unclear about how to actually handle an alleged occult crime case (Barry, 1987; Clark, 1988; Hicks, 1990). They will have questions about whether investigators should handle the crime differently than other crimes and what resources should be devoted to training officers and providing specialized knowledge about this type of crime. Ultimately, whether comfortable or not, they will have to deal with an issue that is highly emotional and spiritual in nature, but they cannot afford to let their emotions or spiritual convictions enter into the lawful response required by their profession. Law enforcers must focus their attention on the criminal act, not on the perpetrators belief system. In short, he or she must listen to complainants, not automatically believe them.

Any crime requires an objective assessment, and occult crime is no exception. Nonetheless, few contemporary issues have so confounded and divided the law enforcement community than that of occult crime. Thus, they should "stick to the constitutional basics" by "investigating irregular behavior based on a well-founded and legally defined reasonable suspicion and arresting based on probable cause."

Since occult crime (Crews and Montgomery, 1996) has only relatively recently become a specialized area of criminal activity, law enforcers are gradually learning how to approach an investigation. Thus, there are some important points to keep in mind prior to conducting any investigation. First, investigators are obligated to address the issue of the perpetrators occult affiliation only if it is clear that the crime was committed in direct relation to his or her belief system. Second, as some have stated (Wedge, 1988; Perlmutter, 2003), traditional investigative responses do not always provide clear-cut answers in true occult crime cases.

Recognizing Occult Symbols and Rituals at the Crime Scene

If an investigator is called to an alleged occult crime, there are several important points he or she must keep in mind in order to be effective. First, at least one crime scene investigator should be familiar with the outward, physical symbols used in various occult rituals. If no one in the department has investigated an alleged occult crime, the participation of an outside law enforcement consultant should be obtained. It should be remembered that the investigator is not initially responsible for interpreting the meaning of any symbols; he or she only records their existence at the crime scene.

Occult Crime Scene Clues

Law enforcers (Wedge, 1988; Rimer, 2009) who have investigated occult crimes have developed many lists of general clues that could indicate the possibility that some kind of occult ritual may have been involved in a crime. While an alleged occult crime scene should not be handled any differently than other crime scene, special evidence may be found and must be processed.

At the scene of any crime (Wedge, 1988; Blood, 1994; Rimer, 2009), the following items and symbols may provide clues to possible occult involvement. The criminal investigator must remember that some criminals have actually used this same list and others like it to mislead an investigation. Much of this misleading is to derail an investigator into believing that an occult motivation existed when it did not.

Animal bodies that have been mutilated	Bottles of small vials of what may appear to be blood, found in refrigerator
Human bodies that have been decapitated, mutilated, or branded with symbols	Hypodermic needles used to remove blood from animals and humans
Human and animal organs that have been removed, such as the head, heart, tongue, eyes, and digits	Animal or human body parts, found in freezers Occult books
Human and animal bodies that have been drained of blood or cannibalized	Handwritten occult essays or poetry/messages written in blood
Waxes, powders, oils on or around a body or crime scene area	Writings in a nondiscernible alphabet
Religious artifacts such as altars, candles, chalices	Handmade drawings of occult symbols
Symbols such as inverted crosses, pentagrams, inverted pentagrams	Drawings or photographs of victims
A circle, 8 ft. in diameter, which may or may not contain a pentagram	Calendars with peculiar days marked
Graffiti and the use of specific colors included in any symbols	Computer bulletin boards tied to the occult

Other Potential Questions That Should Be Considered

The following questions (Barry, 1987; Wedge, 1988; California Office of Criminal Justice Planning, 1993; Rimer, 2009) should be addressed in an alleged occult-related homicide. As with any investigation, pictures and notations should be taken of anything that is considered significant.

What is the location of the cadaver? Missing body parts?	Has the cadaver been branded or burned and is there a particular pattern?	Are there any candle wax drippings on or near the cadaver? In any particular location, color, and number?	Is there any sign of semen on or near the cadaver?
What is the physical position of the cadaver?	Are there any jewelry, charms, stones, talisman, or amulets on or near the cadaver? Are there any occult ritual items or artifacts on or near the cadaver?	Are there any animal or human feces on the upper part of the cadaver, and is there any evidence such substances have been consumed?	Are there any oils, incense, perfumes, or potions poured or rubbed on the body? Wax dripping on the body?
Is the cadaver dressed or undressed?	Is there any evidence that jewelry is missing from the cadaver?	Is there evidence that hands or feet have been tied or shackled?	Is blood absent from the cadaver?
Does the cadaver have any cuts, slashes, teeth marks, or stab wounds? How many? Is there a particular pattern?	Oils or incense on the body?	Is there any sign of semen in the cadaver?	Symbols carved into the flesh? Past scarring?
Is there evidence that smoke, water, or blood has been collected in the lungs?	Has the cadaver been painted with any substance or spray paint and is the paint a particular color?	Are there any tattoos or ink marks on the cadaver and are they any particular pattern or color?	Is there evidence of urine, feces, drugs, wine, or other substances having been ingested?

Traditional Materials Used by Criminal Investigators

The following are lists of traditional information questions (Barry, 1987; Wedge, 1988; California Office of Criminal Justice Planning, 1993; Rimer, 2009) taught to and used by law enforcement since the 1980s. Great care must be used when examining this material in that much of it has been the catalyst for misdirection of many police investigations. The reason to review this material is that it has been disseminated by so many to so many for so many years that it has become part of American culture. Many young people wishing to become involved in any type of antisocial behavior often mimic it, while many wishing to derail law enforcement investigations use it to cover up the true motive of their crimes. Either way, it is definitely materials that the investigator should be familiar with and have access to as they conduct their investigations.

Occult Crime Scene Identifiers

There are myriad lists questions (Barry, 1987; Wedge, 1988; California Office of Criminal Justice Planning, 1993; Rimer, 2009) of "indicators of an occult crime scene" developed since the early 1980s. The following is a compiled list of the information provided in this lists. As stated prior, care must be taken in how this list is used by the investigator. While these have been found at many crime scenes and the in possession of criminal offenders, they are also used by many in their personal law-abiding lives. Just because one or more of these items are present that does not necessarily mean criminal involvement and could very well mislead an investigation. The wrong suspects or motives or evidence could be pursued and valuable time wasted. Moreover, more damage that good could be done to a community by a criminal investigation.

The identifiers are as follows:

Absence of blood on ground/floor	Bones: human or animal	Fire pit	Nonsensible (nondiscernible) alphabet or writings	Skulls with or without candles
Altar and items for worship	Books, games, movies, or music with occultic themes	Items from a grave robbery: coffin, tombstone, or dirt	Occult symbols	Small bowls of powder, salt, drugs, and herbs
Animal mutilations, including the removal of specific body parts (e.g., eye, anus, heart, tongue, kidney, and left leg)	Candles (e.g., black, white, and red) and candle drippings	Jewelry with occult symbols	Robes: black, white, or red	Unusual drawings or symbols (e.g., inverted pentagram, pentagram, inverted cross) on walls, floors, etc.
Ashes	Evidence of sexual activities	Literature and books related to subjects such as Satanism, magic, role-playing games, card games, witchcraft, and photographs pertaining to areas such as the preceding	Rooms painted red or black	Voodoo dolls
Blood: human or animal	Face/body paint	Mockery of Christian symbols	Silver implements	Whips, chains, handcuffs, or ropes

Occult Holidays

Various lists of "occult and Satanic holidays" questions (Barry, 1987; Wedge, 1988; California Office of Criminal Justice Planning, 1993; Lewis, 2001; Rimer, 2009) have been disseminated for many years. Beginning in the late 1970s, police training and seminars began distributing lists such as the one given in the following as another tool for investigators to use in determining whether a crime was "occult related" or not. Any unusual crime scene that was discovered within a day or two of one of these dates was to be examined further for potential occult connection. While many of these dates have their genesis from ancient pagan calendars, many have simply been made up by overzealous supposed occult experts over the years.

Sabbat: Holidays of the Occult Calendar (items marked with an asterisk (*) are the eight major holidays)

January 1	Druid Feast Day
January 17	Satanic Revels
February 1	Imbolc (first full moon)
February 2*	Candlemas (sabot)
March 20–21*	Spring Equinox (feast)
April 19–26	Preparation for Sacrifice
April 30 *	Walpurgis Night (great sabot)
May 1*	Beltane
June 21–22	Summer Solstice (feast)
July 1	Demon Revels
August 2*	Lammas (great sabot)
August 3	Satanic Revels
September 7	Marriage to the Beast Satan
September 20–21*	Fall Equinox (feast)
October 29	All Hallows Eve
October 31*	Samhain (great sabot—holy day)
December 22*	Winter Solstice (feast)
December 24	Satanic Revels
Person's birthday	Highest of All Holidays

The potential importance of this list to investigators in the twenty-first century is that many young "dabblers" use this list for dates to plan their activities. Some youth will try to shock their parents, teachers, and friends with activities or behaviors around these "holidays."

Potential Indicators of Dangerous Occult-Related Behavior

There have been myriad lists (Barry, 1987; Wedge, 1988; California Office of Criminal Justice Planning, 1993; Rimer, 2009) made for parents to use to "identify" if their child is involved in the occult or for teachers to identify if their student is a Satanist and for law enforcement to use to identify a potential suspect. The following is a compiled list of the most common characteristics found in an examination of the material.

A mutilation theme dominates playtime.	Aggressive play that has a marked sadistic quality.	Alienation from family.	An obsession with occult books, games, music, and movies.
Behavior is disruptive, disrespectful, and disobedient.	Bizarre cruelty; displays/ cruelty to animals.	Characteristically resorts to name calling, cursing, or abusive language.	Confidential phone calls.
Consistently prefers TV shows, movies, or music expressing violent themes and acts.	Discussion of participation in a "religious ceremony."	Drug and alcohol abuse.	Family pets or other animals are harmed.

Fascination with death/preoccupation with death.	Fascination with weapons.	Frequent runaway.	Habitually makes violent threats when angry.
Has a background of drug, alcohol, or other substance abuse or dependency.	Has a background of serious disciplinary problems at school and in the community.	Has a history of tantrums and uncontrollable, angry outbursts.	Has been bullied and/or bullies or intimidates peers or younger children.
Has little or no supervision and support from parents or a caring adult.	Has previously been truant, suspended, or expelled from school.	Has previously brought a weapon to school.	Has threatened or attempted suicide.
Has witnessed or been a victim of abuse or neglect in the home.	High truancy rate.	Is involved with a gang or an antisocial group on the fringe of peer acceptance.	Is often depressed and/or has significant mood swings.
Is on the fringe of his or her peer group with few or no close friends.	Is preoccupied with weapons, explosives, or other incendiary devices.	Jewelry, makeup, and clothing reflect an occultic theme.	Mysterious new friends.
Numbers or letters written backward, characteristic of the "Devil's alphabet."	Obnoxious and antisocial.	Occult symbols drawn on walls, books, and clothing.	Prefers reading materials dealing with violent themes, rituals, and abuse.
Preoccupation with the devil, magic, potions, and spells.	Reference to people dressed in costumes, robes, and masks.	Reflects anger, frustration, and the dark side of life in school essays or writing projects.	Refusal to participate in the family religious affiliation.
Secret messages/diary.	Self-mutilation.	Songs and chanting that are sexual or bizarre.	Suicide/attempted suicide.
Symbols carved, burnt, or tattooed on the child's body.	Tends to blame others for difficulties and problems that he or she causes himself or herself.	Violent and aggressive behavior.	

The caution that needs to be taken here is obvious. Many of these are also characteristics exhibited by children who have suffered bullying, neglect, or mistreatment. These children are in no way connected with the occult and to deal with them from that perspective will do more damage than good. Moreover, the investigator must remember that many of these "characteristics" are part of adolescent interests and exhibited by most young people at one time or another across the world. Plus, occult themes (Toth et al., 2008) have become part of the contemporary culture and permeate art, tattoos, music, dress, and appearance. They are seen by most as fashion, not a sign of personal belief or practice.

Symbols of the Occult and Alternate Religions

A comprehensive list of all potential symbols of the occult and alternative belief systems is beyond the scope of this chapter. Many sources questions (Barry, 1987; Wedge, 1988; California Office of Criminal Justice Planning, 1993; Rimer, 2009) dealing with symbols and their use exist for the investigator to use in order to define/identify an object, marking, or writing found at a crime scene. The following is a brief list of some of these symbols commonly used (whether appropriately or not) by some occult groups and individuals.

666/FFF	Anarchy symbol	Ankh	Anti-Christ	Anti-justice	Baphomet
Black mass indicator	Circle	Cross of confusion	Cross of Nero	Diana and Lucifer	Double lightning bolts
Eye in pyramid	Eye of Horus	Hexagram	Horned hand	Pentagram	Satanic moon
Seal of Solomon/ Star of David	Spiral	Swastikas	Talisman or amulet	The blood ritual symbol	The inverted cross of Satanic justice
The sexual ritual symbol	Trail markers	Triangle	Unicursal hexagram	Yin/yang	

The major thing that must be remembered by the criminal investigator is that the meaning of any symbol is in the "eye of the beholder." That is to state that the true meaning of a symbol is in the mind of the person using it in any manner. While many of these symbols have universal and/or historic meaning, they are still used by many for completely opposite reasons. The investigator should be aware of the general meaning of a symbol but should be vigilant in determining how its author views it and intended its use.

Developing Probable Cause for a Search Warrant

Putting together a comprehensive search warrant (Osterburg and Ward, 2013; Brandl, 2014) that may provide desperately needed physical evidence is key to a true occult crime investigation. Investigators must be sure to validate the need for every item prior to the search. While the following items should be included on a search warrant, it is again important to emphasize that when interpreting the actual occult connection between the evidence that is seized and an occult crime, other professional expertise should be obtained (Barry, 1987; Wedge, 1988; California Office of Criminal Justice Planning, 1993; Rimer, 2009).

Clothing and Jewelry

- Black satin or velvet right-handed glove
- Robes, detachable hoods
- Costumes and masks
- Martial arts clothing
- Medallions with Satanic symbols
- Large ruby or red-stoned ring

Games, Books, Wall Hangings

- Occult games
- Occult books
- Handwritten diaries
- Writings in nondiscernible alphabet
- Posters of heavy metal rock stars, mythological beings, nightmarish pictures, sadomasochistic sex

Weapons

- Heavy wooden staff
- Sword
- Knives or athame, a handmade knife with a black handle and etchings
- Bull whip, cat o' nine tails, ligatures
- Martial arts weapons

Ritual Items

- Altar, wooden stand, and marble slab
- Crosses
- Candles and candle holders
- Chalice, goblet, and cruet
- Gongs, drums, and bells
- Hair and skeletal remains
- Coffin and coffin nails
- Ashes from fire pits, fireplaces, and wood stoves
- Phallus and serpent symbols
- Incense and incense burner
- Body paint and face paint
- Feathers
- Mirror
- Twine string
- Herbs, especially salt, bay leaves, and garlic
- Caldron or iron pot
- Coins, statues, stones, and jewels

Barriers to Effective Law Enforcement Involvement in Occult, Satanic, and Alternative Belief System Crime

There are myriad barriers and obstacles (California Office of Criminal Justice Planning, 1993) to the effective investigation of suspected occult-related crime. Most if not all of these can be overcome with logic, open-mindedness, and common sense. Before any law enforcement officer comes face to face with allegations or actual instances of occult-related crime, he or she should be aware of the wide array of barriers discussed in the following, which can and often will confuse and even overwhelm law enforcement functions.

Barriers

First, many familiar with this type of crime (Richardson et al., 1991b; Victor, 1991a) will have major disagreements about many issues. Among the most debated points are the actual extent of occult crimes, the motives of occultists involved in criminal activity, and the veracity of self-professed "survivors." Not surprisingly, such disagreement will affect any law enforcement approach to an alleged occult-related criminal incident.

Second, traditional intelligence operations (Rimer, 2009) do not work very well with occultists. Because occult groups have been historically persecuted for their beliefs, most ceremonies and rituals are highly secretive and, therefore, difficult to penetrate. However, the biggest barrier to traditional intelligence is that most occultists require all group members to participate in their rituals. In most cases, law enforcers would be morally and legally prohibited from such participation.

Third, many people (Crews, 1996) both within and without law enforcement circles either are skeptical about the existence of occult activities or absolutely deny the existence of any criminal links. While a certain amount of skepticism may actually be beneficial to an investigation, such skepticism can also prohibit an investigation from getting "off the ground." Fourth, the law enforcer's own personal and spiritual belief system may inhibit an objective handling of the case, investigating crimes that are both morally and spiritually repugnant.

Fifth, law enforcers (Fine and Victor, 1994) who receive specialized training in occult crime may become what some people have called "oversensitized" to this type of criminal activity. The possibility increases that he or she will expect an occult encounter and, when confronted with unexpected or inexplicable information, may interpret it along the new lines of expectations. Sixth, law enforcement investigators may spend a great deal of time linking the commission of a crime to an occult belief system, only to find the prosecutor and/or an expert witness recommending the link be ignored or discredited in a jury trial. In many cases where occult links have been alleged, prosecutors are not presenting such ties to the juries, arguing such evidence is circumstantial at best and that juries simply will not accept the existence of such evil-minded crimes.

Overcoming Barriers

As with any type of investigation (Osterburg and Ward, 2013), officers must be prepared to follow any lead no matter where it goes. Any investigator faced with an alleged occult crime must be prepared to face these barriers and to devise some sort of strategy to overcome each hurdle as it arises. To help counter the effects of these investigatory problems, the following procedural guidelines are offered.

First, as with all investigation (Brandl, 2014), document all evidence as soon as it is received. This should occur (California Office of Criminal Justice Planning, 1993) through the working as a team in which the roles of each team member are clearly defined. Recognize that the perspectives of each team member will differ, but this is a positive rather than negative factor that encourages a broader base for sharing and analyzing information. The team should be open to new theories, should review the case often, and should not eliminate any factors unless they are conclusive. Teams should be composed of individuals with needed specialized knowledge. At least one investigator should be assigned as a liaison with non-law-enforcement groups that may be involved in a particular case (i.e., parents, educators, community members, and the media).

Given the controversy with many of these types of crimes (Mueller, 1992), investigators should involve the district attorney/prosecutor in the early stages of any investigation. It goes without stating (Osterburg and Ward, 2013; Brandl, 2014) that they must keep all investigative information confidential for as long as possible. As with any investigation, the investigator should execute search warrants as soon as needed, but not short of probable cause. They should follow careful, well-documented interview procedures with any involved.

Most importantly, the investigator must keep in mind when examining the evidence and interview results whether they can determine if the crime was occult related or not. Also, was it part of a belief system identified with a particular group or was it an individualistic belief system. Cases must be built on physical evidence, not circumstantial conjecture.

Conclusion

Few types of behavior bring about more controversy, panic, and hysteria than that which is potentially occult related. Because this new "field" of crime has been pioneered by people with wide-ranging spiritual convictions, professional objectives, political agendas, and emotional commitments, it is a difficult situation. The real problem is that everyone has a valid perspective; but the valid perspectives are all too often based upon fears, emotion, spiritual beliefs, and hearsay.

Law enforcers face many legal, spiritual, and emotional hurdles when confronted with an alleged occult crime. While there are no simple solutions for overcoming these hurdles, most criminal justice professionals recognize the answer lies somewhere within the educational realm. Indeed, law enforcers must clearly understand the belief systems of occultists and know when practicing such beliefs are within legally protected constitutional boundaries and when such practices step over the line into clearly criminal conduct.

Additionally, law enforcers must have a clear comprehension of the barriers they will face when investigating an alleged occult crime and must be able to formulate a plan for overcoming such obstacles. They must understand and be prepared to act upon orders to perform in any of the three capacities required of occult-related law enforcement (i.e., maintaining order through a protection role, providing services through a public relations role, and enforcing the law through an investigative role).

And perhaps most importantly, those assigned the task of investigating an alleged occult-related crime must be prepared to recognize occult symbols and rituals at the crime scene or call for a professional opinion from another source. This requires that police officers must be the recipients of objective information about the occult presented by objective and experienced instructors. Second, they must conduct occult-related investigations by objective law enforcers who base their actions upon firm educational knowledge and sound intelligence about occult groups and activities within their jurisdictions. Third, they must stop dwelling on the controversy surrounding the extent of occult crime and deal with the problems presented by law enforcement and community perceptions of occult activity and occult crime.

Questions for Discussion

15.1 Discuss the impact of the First Amendment of the U.S. Constitution upon the investigation of possible occult-related crimes.

15.2 Define the terms "cult cops" and "ghostbusters" and their impact upon the investigation of possible occult-related crime.

15.3 Explain the impact that "Satanic panic" and the "CSI effect" upon these types of investigations.

15.4 Describe the types of individuals involved in these types of behaviors and their characteristics.
15.5 Discuss the factors involved in the identification and investigation of a possible cult, occult, and alternative belief crime scene.
15.6 Discuss the possible barriers to effective law enforcement involvement in occult, Satanic, and alternative belief system crime.

References

Anti-Defamation League. (2012). *Primer on the First Amendment & Religious Freedom: How Does the U.S. Constitution Protect Religious Freedom?* New York: Anti-Defamation League.

Barry, R. J. (1987). Satanism: The law enforcement response. *The National Sheriff*, XXXVIII(l): 39.

Blood, L. (1994). *The New Satanist*. New York: Warner Books.

Brandl, S. G. (2014). *Criminal Investigation*. Los Angeles, CA: Sage.

Bromley, D. and Shupe, A. (1981). *Strange Gods: The Great American Cult Scare*. Boston, MA: Beacon Press.

Bromley, D. G. (1991). Satanism: The new cult scare. In *The Satanism Scare*, Richardson, J. T., Best, J., and Bromley, D. G. (eds.), pp. 49–72. New York: Aldine de Gruyter.

California Office of Criminal Justice Planning. (1993). *Occult Crime: A Law Enforcement Primer*. Dane Publishing Company. Sacramento, CA: Dane Publishing Company.

Clark, J. R. (1988). The macabre faces of occult-related crime. *Law Enforcement News*, XIV, 279–280.

Coleman, L. (1986). Therapists are the real culprits in many child sexual abuse cases. *Augustus*, IX(6), 7–9.

Crews, G. A. (1996, Spring). Adolescent satanists in America: Religious commitment or developmental stage? *What Police Know: The Road to Public Safety*, 8–9.

Crews, G. A. and Montgomery, R. H., Jr. (1996). Adolescent satanist: A sensible law enforcement approach. *Journal of Police and Criminal Psychology*, 11(1), 13–18.

Crews, G. A. and Montgomery, R. H., Jr. (2001). *Chasing Shadows: Confronting Juvenile Violence in America*. Upper Saddle River, NJ: Prentice Hall Publishing Company.

Crews, G. A., Montgomery, R. H., Jr., and Garris, W. R. (1996). *Faces of Violence in America*. Needham Heights, MA: Simon & Schuster Publishing.

Fine, G. A. and Victor, J. (1994). Satanic tourism: Adolescent dabblers and identity work. *The Phi Delta Kappan*, 76(1), 70–72.

Finkelhor, D., Hotaling, G., and Sedlak, A. (1991). The police model of satanic crime. In Richardson, J. T., Best, J., and Bromley, D. G. (eds.), *The Satanism Scare*, pp. 175–189. New York: Aldine de Gruyter.

Frankfurter, D. (2008). *Evil Incarnate: Rumors of Demonic Conspiracy and Satanic Abuse in History*. Princeton, NJ: Princeton University Press.

Heinrick, J. (2006). Everyone's an expert: The CSI effect's negative impact on juries. *The Triple Helix*, Fall, 59–61.

Hicks, R. D. (1990). *In Pursuit of Satan: The Police and the Occult*. Buffalo, NY: Prometheus Books.

Johnston, J. (1989). *The Edge of Evil: The Rise of Satanism in North America*. Dallas, TX: Word Publishing.

Lanning, K. (1989). Satanic, occult, ritualistic crime: A law enforcement perspective. *Police Chief*, 56(10): 62–84.

Larson, B. (1989). *Satanism: The Seduction of America's Youth*. Nashville, TN: Thomas Nelson.

Legal Information Institute. (n.d.). *The First Amendment*. New York: Cornell University Law School. Retrieved from http://www.law.cornell.edu/constitution/first_amendment. Accessed February 2, 2015.

Lewis, J. R. (2001). *Satanism Today: An Encyclopedia of Religion, Folklore, and Popular Culture*. Santa Barbara, CA: ABC-CLIO Incorporated.

Lyons, A. (1988). *Satan Wants You: The Cult of Devil Worship in America*. New York: Mysterious Press.

Mueller, L. E. (1992). Occult crime scene technology. *Law and Order*, 40, 35–38.

Osterburg, J. S. and Ward, R. H. (2013). *Criminal Investigation: A Method for Reconstructing the Past*, 7th edn. Cincinnati, OH: Anderson Publishing.

Perlmutter, D. (2003). *Investigating Religious Terrorism & Ritualistic Crimes*. Boca Raton, FL: CRC Press.

Petropoulou, M. (2008). *Animal Sacrifice in Ancient Greek Religion, Judaism, and Christianity, 100 BC to AD 200*. Oxford Classical Monographs. Oxford, England: Oxford University Press.

Religious Tolerance. (n.d.). *The Occult: Conservative Christian Beliefs*. Retrieved from http://www.religioustolerance.org/occult2.htm. Accessed February 2, 2015.

Reynolds V. United States. (October 1878). Supreme Court of The United States, 98 U.S. 145.

Richardson, J. (1991). Satanism in the courts: From murder to heavy metal. In Richardson, J. T., Best, J., and Bromley, D. G. (eds.), *The Satanism Scare*, pp. 205–217. New York: Aldine de Gruyter.

Richardson, J., Best, J., and Bromley, D. (1991a). Satanism as a social problem. In Richardson, J. T., Best, J., and Bromley, D. G. (eds.), *The Satanism Scare*, pp. 3–17. New York: Aldine de Gruyter.

Richardson, J., Best, J., and Bromley, D. (1991b). *The Satanism Scare*. New York: Aldine de Gruyter.

Rimer, D. (2009). *Ritual Crime & the Occult: The New Youth Subculture*. Virginia Beach, VA: Unpublished Manuscript.

Roane, K. (2005). The CSI effect on TV: It's all slam-dunk evidence and quick convictions. Now juries expect the same thing, and that's a big problem. Washington, DC: U.S. News and World reports.

Sharp, A. G. (April 1987). Cult investigation: A devilish problem. *Law and Order*, 35(4), 56–60.

Sills, D. (1990). Bedeviling questions about workshops. *Law Enforcement News*. December 15, 1990.

Smith, M. and Pazder, L. (1980). *Michelle Remembers*. New York: Congdon and Lattes.

Toth, R. C., Crews, G. A., and Burton, C. E. (eds.). (2008). *In the Margins: Special Populations and American Justice*. Upper Saddle River, NJ: Prentice Hall Publishing Company. ISBN: 0130284319/9780130284310.

Twain, M. (1876). *The Adventures of Tom Sawyer*. Hartford, CT: The American Publishing Company.

Victor, J. (1989). A rumor-panic about a dangerous satanic cult in western New York. *New York Folklore*, XV(1–2), 23–49.

Victor, J. (1993). *Satanic Panic: The Creation of a Contemporary Legend*. Chicago, IL: Open Court Publishing Company.

Victor, J. (Spring 1991a). Satanic cult 'survivor' stories. *The Skeptical Inquirer*, 15(3), 274–280.

Victor, J. (Spring 1991b). The spread of satanic-cult rumors. *The Skeptical Inquirer*, 14, 287–291.

Warnke, M. (1972). *The Satan Seller*. Commerce City, CA: Bridge Publishing.

Wedge, T. (1988). *The Satan Hunter*. Canton, OH: Daring Books.

All-Purpose Practices and Lessons for Investigations

V

Practical Aspects of Interviewing and Interrogating Witnesses and Suspects

16

MATHEW O'DEANE

Contents

Chapter Objectives	256
Introduction	256
Technique	256
Reluctant Witness	257
Recanting Witness	257
Recording Interviews	257
Talk to Me	258
Lies, Lies, Lies	259
Types of Suspects	259
Be Prepared	260
Deception	260
Behavioral Analysis	260
Eye Contact	261
Facial Expressions	261
Watch Their Hands	261
Watch How They Sit	262
Environment	262
The Law	262
Primary Exceptions to Miranda	264
Public Safety Exception	264
Rescue Doctrine	265
Subject Reinitiates Questioning	265
Subject Released from Custody	265
Subject Invoked His "Right to Remain Silent" Only	265
Anticipatory Invocation	266
Interviews in the Field	266
Step by Step: Fill in the Blanks, Be Complete, and Leave Nothing Blank	268
Interview All Parties	273
Conclusion	274
Questions for Discussion	275
References	275

Chapter Objectives

After reading this chapter you should be able to do the following:

1. Understand the definitions and differences between an interview and an interrogation.
2. Understand the importance of proper use of interview and interrogation techniques.
3. Understand some of the common characteristics of successful police interviewers and interrogators.
4. Evaluate the different environments in which interviews can take place, such as field versus custodial settings.
5. Identify the common techniques used by police to solicit information from suspects and the common defensive mechanisms used by suspects to avoid responding.

Introduction

Perhaps the most critical skill for any detective, working anywhere, is the ability to talk to people, the ability to communicate, and the ability to extract information needed to make the case. This can be a challenge as detectives often contact reluctant, scared, or lying people, or those with self-serving interests. As a police detective, you will likely conduct interviews and interrogations on a regular basis. For example, you may be assigned to work homicides, robberies, domestic violence, gang cases, narcotics cases, vice investigations, auto theft, fraud, elder abuse, etc. The wide array of police assignments bring along with them a variety of people and situations that require speaking to people in very trying and traumatic situations.

An "interview" is essentially the meeting of two or more people for the purpose of gathering information. The key to a successful interview is asking the correct questions; don't expect to get the answers you need if you don't ask the correct questions. An "interrogation" is defined as any "words or actions" by the police that the police knew or should have known are reasonably likely to elicit an incriminating response. It is a formal and adversarial meeting between two people controlled by the interrogator and is designed to resolve an issue and obtain an admission or confession.

Technique

An effective interviewer is a professional. Like any conversation we have in our lives, the first step is to introduce yourself and explain the purpose of the interview. For example, you may tell the person you are investigating a robbery that happened last night at the gas station on the corner and that you would like them to tell you anything they know about the incident.

It is also very important to establish rapport with people, establishing a common goal. The manner in which you approach an interview with a victim who has been repeatedly calling the police demanding her husband be arrested will be very different from the way you will approach a victim who has just been released from the hospital and, despite brutal injuries, insists that nothing happened. It is impossible to utilize a single interviewing style that will work across the board in all situations; often some modification of technique will be required. It is, however, possible to categorize a few major types of witness and different interviewing styles and strategies to employ with the various types of witnesses.

Reluctant Witness

Victims may be reluctant to cooperate or talk to the police for a variety of reasons, such as they have a relationship with the suspect, they are afraid of the suspect, or they simply don't want to get involved. As such, detectives involved in such cases are encouraged to build trusting relationships with victims as early in the case as possible to facilitate cooperation in the interview process. While a reluctant witness may be hesitant to take the stand and possibly be hard to locate and subpoena for court, they will not necessarily be untruthful in court. But since minimization and "forgetfulness" are valid concerns, the sooner a detective can get a statement from a reluctant witness the better.

Recanting Witness

As any domestic violence prosecutor can attest, the recanting witness is by far the most common type of witness in such cases. Recantation is usually accompanied by a claim or admission that the witness previously lied to the police or that the law enforcement officer "put words in my mouth" or must have "gotten the story wrong." For obvious reasons, the 911 call as well as the initial interview conducted by the first responder will be two critical pieces of evidence in a case involving a recanting witness. A heads-up that a victim plans to recant will likely change the entire approach to the victim interview a prosecutor may choose to conduct. Keep in mind that a recanting victim will often claim on the stand that the prosecutor attempted to coach her to testify a certain way. While witness interviews should always be done with an investigator present experience with recanting witnesses really drives home the rationale behind such a rule.

Recording Interviews

Most states and departments do not mandate the detective record interviews; however, many times the detective would need to be prepared to explain why they chose not to record. In addition, video and audio are oftentimes powerful in court as the jury can hear the words spoken by the suspect. If you do choose to record, record all gaps on the record, say the date and time if the tape is going to be turned off and do the same when you turn it back on. In addition, keeping interview notes is not required in all jurisdictions as the report you write from the notes is the records of the interview; however, be prepared to explain to the defense why you destroy notes after writing your report. The key is to be consistent and comply with the law in your state and your department's policy on the issue.

Talk to Me

As with everything police officers do, it's important to act in an ethical manner when conducting an interview. It's important to not approach an interview thinking that a crime is a "slam dunk." Even in cases where the evidence that you have the right suspect seems overwhelming to you, it's still important to obtain a statement and lock the suspect into a version of events if you can. A confession is useless if not legally obtained; therefore, a Miranda advisory, along with the rest of the interview, should be videotaped and audiotaped whenever possible so a complete transcript of the interview can be created later. The video will serve as a record of what was said, and it can show the nonverbal cues that can help determine the culpability of the suspect.

Take extra precautions with suspects that are mentally slow, drunk, injured, or criminally unsophisticated. It's a requirement that the person you are speaking to understand and voluntarily waive rights before talking to you. The statement you obtain must be the product of free and deliberate choice rather than coercion, intimidation, or deception. Factors that detectives need to be aware of include the suspect age, criminal experience, education level, background, intelligence, and capacity to understand the warnings.

When the suspects do decide to talk, it's important to let them give a free narrative of the event. Be a good listener; when the person is talking, you should be developing a strategy and formulating follow-up questions you will ask once they have exhausted their free narrative of events. Many detectives use open-ended questions to probe the significant areas of the story you were provided. For example, "You mentioned that X occurred; please explain what you meant." Have them explain further; provide a greater degree of detail, to get more specific as you want to reprobe significant areas of the story, such as tell me more about X; describe for me who, what, when, where, etc.; and ask for clarification and all critical details. The more details they give the better. The purpose is to get as much information as possible before you change from "nice guy" to someone who's confronting them and possibly even calling them a liar. Once you get the maximum amount of detail you think you're going to get, challenge their story.

Many times the suspect will try to explain why physical evidence like DNA or prints may be at the scene of the crime. They'll attempt to outsmart investigators, negating potentially damaging evidence by providing plausible explanations as to why it may be at the scene. Once we have a version of events and a story, we can then compare this to what we know of the physical evidence and witness statements.

Start chipping away at the details. Make contact with people with whom they said they were with, and confirm where they were. Is there any proof? Do they have any way to verify they were in a certain area? Ask for receipts or conduct cell phone tower searches to either corroborate or debunk their story.

It's legal for you, as an officer, to lie to someone to put pressure on them, but caution must be taken. Being highly confrontational can result in false confessions from suspects. Using aggressive scare tactics can increase the risk of a false confession. Take care to be only as confrontational as necessary by keeping the stress level low and by attacking details. Suggesting a defense is also a common technique, but be careful. This should be considered more of a last-ditch technique since what you suggest may be the defense that the suspect did not think of, and they adopt the defense based solely on your suggestion. Still, don't avoid what really could be a defense. Search for the truth at all times.

Lies, Lies, Lies

One of the keys to understanding when a person is lying to you is recognizing the level of stress the suspect is under when they tell a lie. Some people can show signs of stress even when they're telling the truth, and of course some people can lie about significant events without showing any signs of stress. This is why no two suspects or interviews are identical. It's critical that investigators have a solid understanding of psychology and human behavior to know which techniques work in which situations.

Before getting into specifics with your gangster suspect, it's important to establish rapport, much like you would do if talking to a suspect on the street during a field interview (FI). You need to establish a baseline. How stressed are they before the interview becomes confrontational? What are they like in a relaxed state? This can be done by giving them a soda or coffee while getting basic, nonthreatening information, such as details about their life that they'd unlikely lie about.

Concentrate on when a suspect tries to oversell you on their version of events, or they feel the need to qualify their responses. When a person says "honestly" or "I wouldn't lie" or "I swear on my mother," these are cues that they're most likely lying to you. The same is true when you ask a specific question and get an indirect answer.

Types of Suspects

When interviewing a gang member in an interview room at the police station, for example, the rules may change somewhat from an FI. The gang member is now likely the subject of a serious case, they know they may be arrested if they admit involvement, and they'll require more skill to interview compared to a street interview. The following are a few examples of typical gang member interviews and a suggestion on how to deal with individual types of gang members:

The denier: The least sophisticated suspect will deny their involvement in the crime you're investigating. This individual will say things such as "You got it wrong," or "You have the wrong guy." When talking to you, they'll avoid making eye contact and won't want to be confronted on the details. The best way to deal with a basic denial is to confront the person and use time to your advantage. Over an extended period of time, you should be able to break this type of offender. Confront them and demand specific details as to where they claim to have been during the crime, who they were with, and who can confirm this. The more details you can lock them into, the easier it will be to catch them in a lie, get them to break, and give the real version of events.

The minimizer: This suspect is attempting to minimize the crime to justify their actions. This gang member will blame society and everyone else but themselves for their actions. It's suggested that you confront this person and use social referencing, such as "A lot of people have it bad and don't commit crimes of violence," or "Many people from gang-infested neighborhoods grow up and don't become gang members." By using social referencing, you can put responsibility back on the gang member and try to get a more accurate, less self-serving version of events. Also, by referencing their behavior, you may get them to admit what they did by playing along with their minimizations. No matter what they did, you can typically think of someone, somewhere that did something worse.

Many times getting them to put themselves at the scene and admit minimal involvement is the start to getting a full confession.

The avoider: This suspect will hide behind a lawyer. He or she may sit in front of you and say nothing or the lawyer may object to the questions. This person won't give a direct answer to any questions. It's important to get personal with this gang member. He or she needs to be confronted, have their ego attacked, and be challenged in order to provoke a response. It's important not to show emotion when talking to suspects, as it tends to show weakness. Stay in control. When a suspect starts talking, let them talk and don't interrupt them. Give them enough rope to effectively hang themselves. After they have given their story, go back and start to confront them on the details. Once you have received a version of the events, you can start chipping away at the details. You may make contact with people with whom they said they were with, and certainly attempt to confirm where they claimed to be at the time of the incident. Is there any proof? Do they have any way to verify they were in a certain area, such as credit card receipts or cell phone tower searches that can corroborate they were in the area they claimed to be in an attempt to confirm or debunk their story.

Be Prepared

The interviewer must project total belief in the subject. The primary goal of the interviewer should be to try lower levels of exhibited anger and fear. Failure to do so may affect the reliability of the information obtained. It can also impact the victim's and witnesses' ability to remember details. Most people exhibit some form of emotion when they knowingly lie about something important. This can include observable symptoms such as dryness of mouth, restlessness, excessive tension, sweating, changes in complexion, pulsating carotid artery, breaking of eye contact, or even evasive or aggressive behavior. When anger is displayed in an interview, you must differentiate the reason why they are angry and whether or not the anger is legitimate or feigned. When someone is fearful, it may result in a fight or flight response, or telling a lie, moving away from the interviewer, or by telling the truth if a suspect is convinced that they cannot escape, and they may escape the interview via a confession.

Deception

Deception is a common trait among persons of all ages in every culture. It is used when the individual feels incapable or unprepared to solve a problem by more desirable means; most people given the choice would rather tell the truth as deception is difficult. It is used as an avenue of escape from the consequences of their behavior. When questioned, the suspect is usually not in a position to run so they will seek to escape via lies and deception. As a detective, your job is to convince the suspect that escape is impossible and then offer them an acceptable solution, such as a confession.

Behavioral Analysis

Behavior analysis improves the skill of the interviewer or interrogator in determining the truthfulness or deceptiveness of the information being obtained. By analyzing behavior, the interviewer can confirm whether the approach they are using is effective. Matching appropriate techniques with your interview subject's responses will improve your success rate.

Nonverbal information is more accurate than the spoken word when it comes to determining how you feel about an issue. What is said verbally is usually modified, emphasized, firm, or contradicted by nonverbal behavior. Over half of all communication between people is nonverbal, for example, significant amounts of information or pastor eye contact, facial expressions, and gestures. Additionally, information is passed through tone of voice as well as the verbal content. The more pressure there is in a person, the more likelihood of there being a behavioral reaction in response to pressure. Body language is very important; sometimes it is more significant to evaluate what the suspect did not say as opposed to what they said.

Eye Contact

When most people have a conversation with someone, normal eye contact between the two people occurs on average between 30% and 65% of the time. When interviewing innocent subjects, they tend to look at you more than guilty subjects do. This is the result of the person having nothing to hide; guilty subjects tend to believe that their guilt can be seen during questioning and thus they avert their gaze. However, people that are overly shy may have poor eye contact, as do individuals from different cultures that may view direct eye contact as a sign of disrespect.

There is a difference between good eye contact and staring. Staring is unbroken eye contact; you want to avoid getting into a staring contest if you lose; you lose your advantage or dominance in the situation. Other common issues related to eye contact include things such as the suspect closing their eyes as a mental escape, or rapid blinking, which may be an indicator of extreme tension or anxiety, or narrowing of the eyes, which would be indicative of anticipating trouble, or squinting, which could indicate distress. Guilty people may have a penetrating stare, or loss of eye contact when answering certain questions that may be indicative of deception.

Facial Expressions

Smiling can be the most misleading of all facial expressions. It is important for the interviewer or interrogator to determine if it's a real or fake smile. A real smile looks natural and on time with the nature of the material being discussed. A fake smile usually looks turned on and often happens at inappropriate times, or the person may be smiling while the rest of their body shows signs of tension or other signs of deception.

Watch Their Hands

All cops are trained to watch the hands of people you encounter. During an interview or interrogation, finger tapping is common; the faster the tapping the greater the stress. At times suspects may point their finger at you, which indicates aggression. Some may make a fist as an antagonistic gesture or demonstrate a defiant or deceptive position by tightly clasping their hands together, which may be an indicator that the person is holding back information.

Watch How They Sit

How the person sits down and remains seated during the interview can tell you a lot about the person. When having a discussion, for example, with a person that slouches down in the chair, with shoulders slumped, looking downward with head down, and the body in the defeated position, it is typically an indicator of guilt.

A defiant person may sit with the chair tilted backward in their arms folded in front of them indicating disagreement or defensiveness. The way the person is sitting in a chair or if they move or reposition the chair, it may be an attempt to expand the distance between the interviewer or interrogator, a common defense mechanism. If the suspect assumes a nonfrontal alignment, meaning they are not sitting squarely in the chair, it may be an indicator of deception. The suspect may sit and look at you but their body is turned away from you, or they may lean toward the door, or they may change the position of the chair during the interview as a defense tactic.

Innocent subjects tend to sit upright in their chair, sitting directly in front of you with his or her feet flat on the floor. They are likely involved in the interview process and are attentive to what you're saying. Innocent subjects may lean forward toward you thereby decreasing the distance between the two of you. On occasion, they typically have square frontal alignment and smooth and fluid changes in posture and movements.

Environment

The farther you are from the person the easier it is to lie; the closer you are the harder it is to lie. It is very hard to lie when being touched. The environment in which the interview or interrogation takes place is critical; the need for privacy is important. You must be able to control the environment in order to derive maximum advantage. It has a direct relationship on the behavior of the subject. Make sure if you have them in your custody for an extended period of time, you give food and water and address basic comfort needs if appropriate. Don't forget about issues like room temperature and suspect attire as it may impact the level of cooperation you receive.

The Law

Having the skills to conduct an interview is critical, so too is the legal knowledge to know when and how these interviews and interrogations can be conducted so the information that is obtained can be used in a court of law. Police interrogation tactics will always be an issue in cases where a suspect has made incriminating statements, hence the safeguards of Miranda v. Arizona. Miranda's warnings and waivers were intended to afford custodial suspects an informed choice between speech and silence and prevent involuntary statements. In order to ensure that an in-custody criminal suspect is aware that he or she has a right not to incriminate him- or herself and that he or she is entitled to the assistance of an attorney during any interrogation, unless other fully effective means are devised to inform accused persons of their right(s).

A full *Miranda* admonishment and waiver should be the first choice of an interrogator, in that that is what the courts have asked us to do, and, in practice, almost guarantees the admissibility of any resulting statements from the suspect. The Miranda decision was premised upon the presumption that any interrogation in a custodial situation or incommunicado interrogation of an individual in a police-dominated atmosphere is inherently coercive. I am talking about "psychological" pressure, rather than "physical abuse," even if unintended. The court expressed concern that the use of psychologically coercive techniques, as well as the inherently coercive effect of incommunicado interrogation, would, in the absence of adequate safeguards, cause persons undergoing interrogation to incriminate themselves involuntarily.

For purposes of Miranda, a person is in custody when he or she has been "deprived of his (or her) freedom in any significant way." Whether or not a person is in custody for purposes of Miranda depends upon how a reasonable man or woman in the suspect's shoes would have understood the situation. "Custody" implies a situation in which the suspect would reasonably know that he or she is speaking with a government agent and does not feel, under the circumstances, that he or she is free to end the conversation. The initial determination of custody depends on the objective circumstances of the interrogation and not on the subjective views harbored by either the interrogating officers or the person being questioned.

- "You have the right to remain silent. Do you understand that right?"
- "If you give up the right to remain silent, anything you say may be used against you in a court of law. Do you understand that?"
- "You have the right to have an attorney present before and during any questioning. Do you understand that right?"
- "If you cannot afford an attorney, one will be appointed for you by the court at no cost to you. Do you understand that?"
- "Then, do you wish to talk to me?" (or "… answer my questions?") (or "… give me your side of what happened?")

Miranda requires that the police first remind the suspect of his or her right to remain silent, including the possible use of any responses he or she might make, in court, and the right to the assistance of an attorney before and during the answering of any questions, including the right to a free attorney, before and during questioning, if the suspect cannot afford one.

The three legal prerequisites: Before a "Miranda admonishment" must be given, there are three legal prerequisites, all of which must be present:

1. Suspect is "in custody."
2. An interrogation takes place.
3. Questioning is conducted by law enforcement (or an agent of law enforcement).

The term "Mirandize" refers to the process of administering an admonishment of applicable constitutional rights as described in the Miranda decision. For purposes of Miranda, a person is not in custody unless he or she has been formally arrested, or there exists a restraint on freedom of movement of the degree associated with a formal arrest.

An individual is in custody for Miranda purposes when, under the totality of the circumstances, the suspect's freedom of action is curtailed to a degree associated with formal arrest.

If a reasonable person (not necessarily the suspect) would have felt that under the circumstances he or she was being formally arrested, or at least subject to immediate arrest, then he or she is in custody and must be advised of their rights prior to questioning. Custody implies a situation in which the suspect would reasonably know that he or she is speaking with a government agent and does not feel, under the circumstances, that he or she is free to end the conversation.

If a subject is not to be questioned, no admonition is necessary, with the exception of juveniles by statute who must be admonished whether questioned or not, and you decide to speak with them per Welfare and Institutions Code 625 if you reside in California. In the absence some tactical or department policy reason for not doing so, there is typically not many good reasons why a peace officer, who takes a criminal suspect into custody would not to admonish the suspect, and upon a waiver attempt to question him or her concerning the subject of the arrest. This is very true in gang cases, sometimes an admission, partial admission, or even the fact that they may have put themselves at the scene or involved in the fight, or they may provide an alibi that you can prove or disprove at a later time. The case typically only gets better when the gangsters talk to you.

Also if the suspect shows up to talk to you with a lawyer present, a Miranda admonishment is not necessary where counsel accompanies the suspect. The U.S. Supreme Court has indicated that the presence of counsel would be the adequate protective device necessary to make the process of police interrogation conform to the dictates of the privilege.

One way to inform the suspect that they are not in custody is to administer a "Beheler admonishment", or a simple advise telling the person that they are not in custody and re free to leave at any time, this effectively takes the custody out of the interrogation. No reasonable person would believe he or she is about to be arrested when told that he or she is free to terminate the questioning and walk away. The key is that they are really free to leave; you are not blocking the door or have your car blocking their car, or they are in a secure facility, and when you give the admonishment, the situation must match your words.

Primary Exceptions to Miranda

The following is an update on each of the "big six" lawful exceptions to the general rule of Miranda, which, in the absence of one of the exceptions, precludes the use of the defendant's statements in the people's case in chief and any recent relevant case law:

Public Safety Exception

It is universally accepted that questions asked of an in-custody suspect for the purpose of relieving a situation that poses a threat to the public safety do not require a Miranda admonishment or wavier to make the responses admissible. This exception applies whether or not the subject has even been advised of his rights as well as in the face of an invocation. Most commonly, the public safety exception involves situations where a suspect has discarded a gun that the officer reasonably feels needs to be located and secured before someone else finds it and either uses it or hurts himself. It can also include when an officer needs to determine in a hurry whether other suspects in a violent crime are at large out of concern for the officer's own safety.

Rescue Doctrine

Closely related to the "public safety exception," it has been held that questions necessitated by the need to save a victim from death or serious harm need not be impeded by a Miranda admonishment. Typically, a kidnapping suspect is arrested under circumstances where his victim is missing and concerns center on whether the victim is still alive and can be saved. As noted by at least one state court, "When life hangs in the balance, there is no room to require admonitions concerning the right to counsel and to remain silent."

Subject Reinitiates Questioning

A suspect who has invoked his Miranda rights may certainly reinitiate questioning, if he chooses to do so. But once the subject has invoked, his decision to reinitiate the conversation with police must be "clearly and unequivocally" indicated, with a heavy burden being placed on the prosecution to show that no one pressured the subject into doing so. Therefore, it is strongly suggested that when an in-custody suspect recontacts his interrogators telling them that he has changed his mind, that he now wants to waive his rights and talk with the police, at a minimum, a new Miranda admonishment must be given and an express waiver obtained. After making it perfectly clear that it is the suspect's idea to reinitiate questioning and not the result of any pressure or law enforcement trickery, an interrogation may begin anew.

Subject Released from Custody

The whole purpose of requiring a Miranda admonishment and waiver is to relieve or minimize the inherent coerciveness or pressure on an in-custody suspect of an incommunicado—sometimes referred to as a "station house" interrogation. For this reason, it has been held that releasing the suspect from custody, giving him or her the opportunity to contact and seek the advice of friends, relatives, and counsel, as well as consider their own predicament, opens them up to another attempt at interrogation.

Subject Invoked His "Right to Remain Silent" Only

When an in-custody suspect invokes his "right to remain silent" (as opposed to his fifth amendment "right to an attorney"), police officers may sometimes reinitiate questioning themselves. The law is clear that officers may return on their own initiative, instead of waiting for the suspect to reinitiate questioning himself, and attempt to question him (after a new admonition and waiver) about any other case other than the case for which he has already invoked. But this rule only applies when the right invoked was his right to silence. If in invoking he specifically asks for the assistance of an attorney, he is off-limits to any further questioning about that case or any other case, so long as he remains in custody.

There are two separate rights involved in a Miranda admonishment:

1. "Right not to incriminate oneself": expressly provided for under the fifth amendment
2. "Right to the assistance of an attorney": impliedly provided for under the fifth amendment

Invoking one's right to not answer questions (i.e., incriminate oneself) may be accomplished through the use of any words or conduct that are inconsistent with a present willingness to discuss the case freely and completely. The right to counsel can only be invoked by a clear and express request for an attorney. Any ambiguous attempts to ask for an attorney will be held to be ineffective. Once warnings have been given, if the individual indicates "in any manner and at any stage of the process," prior to or during questioning, that he wishes to remain silent or to consult with an attorney, his request to terminate the questioning or obtain counsel must be "scrupulously honored."

Anticipatory Invocation

Any attempt by a suspect to invoke his rights under the Miranda decision prior to that point in time where he is both (1) in custody and (2) an interrogation is either in progress or is imminent is ineffective. This is because it is a rule of law that most rights must be asserted when the government seeks to take the action they protect against.

Interviews in the Field

Interviews done in the field or out on the streets are often referred to as "field interviews (FIs)." FIs are most oftentimes used to identify subjects in the community that may be involved in some sort of potential criminal activity or to document a police contact that did not result in an arrest being made. FIs are a significant tool for detectives that work in the community, such as gang detectives, vice detectives, and narcotics detectives. They are also tremendously important to detectives that work sex crimes or burglary as they document the presence of a person in an area that may have relevance to the investigation you are conducting.

When interviewing gang members, for example, it is extremely common for them to minimize the crimes they are involved in. Many gang members tend to minimize their role in the crime and they commonly justify their actions by saying things like "I didn't mean to do it." The gang member sees himself as the victim of circumstances and claims the crime was not really their fault; society made them do it. Some justify particular crimes by claiming "Nobody got hurt." The gang member maintains that no one was harmed by the act (property crime, auto theft, or they shot and missed, etc.). Some justify their crimes because they feel "They had it coming." The gang member was not wrong given their view of the situation (such as a rival came to their turf, crossed out their graffiti). Some just feel "Why is everybody picking on me?" The gang member may displace guilt by saying that justice is biased failing to take responsibility. Some claim that "I did it for my friends." The gang member may claim that it is more important to be loyal to his or her peer group (gang) than to a society that does not want them to exist.

Through field contacts and observations, detectives can supply confirmation of an individual's gang membership. FI cards are commonly utilized to link suspects to specific vehicles, addresses, and associates and to document subjects as gang members with a particular gang. A properly completed FI card can be instrumental in officially documenting a street gang member or updating the current status of a documented gang member or associate. Two things must occur for the information contained on an FI card to be of use.

First, an officer must take the time and initiative to fill out the FI card, and second, the card must be accurately and completely filed out. The detectives in the field can do things to make their contacts more productive. Several interview techniques can be applied across most street gangs, regardless of ethnicity. Gang members uniformly demand respect, whether they are entitled to it or not. This can usually be addressed by having a fair but firm attitude and demeanor with gang members. Many experienced officers are very good at developing a rapport with the gang members on their beat. The only way that is going to be accomplished is by getting out of your car and making contact with the gang members. It is important that the gang members know the officer on the beat knows who they are.

It gives the police the psychological advantage. The gang members know they have been identified, they are not just an unknown face in the crowd, and the police do not fear them and will not hesitate to contact them. They know they are now more likely to be held accountable for their actions, arrested, and prosecuted as a gang member after being contacted by police who completed an accurate and complete FI. It also allows for the opportunity to conduct intelligence gathering and establish potential sources of information within the gang. Many times gang members will develop a basic level of respect for a particular officer that may have helped them, helped a family member, or showed them respect. Some may make good candidates to be cultivated into informants to help solve more serious gang crimes as they occur. The psychological key to an FI is that individual gang members need to know that they are not a part of a mysterious gang operating with anonymity and impunity.

To help establish rapport and respect between officers and the gang members, several techniques can help. If you are talking to a gang member about something significant, such as information about specific crimes or other gang members, do it in an area where other gang members cannot hear your conversation. When you receive the information you needed, do not do anything that will let the other gang members know that the subject was cooperative with you. Do not lie to a gang member unless you are certain that you can get away with it. If you tell a gang member that you are going to arrest him if he does not stop some activity, and then they do it again, you need to arrest them. If you fail to follow through with what you say, the gang will continue to challenge your authority and not respect you.

When interviewing a group of gang members, it is oftentimes beneficial to start with the youngest or most inexperienced member that may have a higher likelihood of talking to you. That member may provide you with enough factual information that you can make it appear to the older members that you know more than you do. It is also very important to isolate gang members suspected of being involved in a crime immediately so they do not have the opportunity to get their stories straight. If you do place gang members together, sometimes a surreptitious recording, such as a conversation in the back of a police vehicle or holding cell, may net some very useful and incriminating conversations as they quickly try to get their stories in line before being brought to the police station to be interviewed.

Each department may have different report forms or gang cards that contain varying formats for the field interview information. Regardless of what the card looks like, the purpose is the same. FI cards should contain factual information and not include unsupported conclusions and should provide as much specific detailed information as possible. Officers can make these gang member contacts or FIs more useful to investigators and prosecutors by following the guidelines listed in this book.

It is also important to remember that gang members will often discard any contraband on them when they see an officer approaching them, or they will have weapons and other contraband close by hidden in an area where it is accessible, but not in their possession should they get stopped. For this reason, it is important to check the area surrounding the contacted gang members for abandoned weapons, drugs, or other contraband. If any are found, the contact may become a detention while you investigate who the items belong to. Even if the contraband cannot be linked to an individual, they no longer have it in their possession and it can be disposed of per your department's policy. Many times guns or baggies of drugs may be found and can be processed for fingerprints. That may lead to a future arrest if the prints match the gang member you found standing next to the item that said they have never seen it before.

While you are talking to the subject/s and obtaining their biographical information, be professional and mindful of the fact that most gang members are very conscious of what they believe to be "respect." If you disrespect a gang member in front of his "homeboys" or female friends, they are less likely to tell you anything about themselves or the gang. The disrespect does not have to be real, only perceived by the gang member. Occasionally the "dissed" gang member will become confrontational or violent toward the officer to save face with his friends, which can escalate the contact. After you have established open communication with the suspected gang member because of your command presence, inquire about their gang affiliation and moniker, or street name.

Each officer will do this in a different way. Develop a method that works well for you and build upon that. It will benefit you immensely during these contacts if you are familiar with the gangs in your area, who the local gang members are, and what areas they "claim" or hang out in. If the subject is hesitant to claim, ask them about their clothing, belt buckles, tattoos, or any other indicators of gang involvement you have noticed during the contact to get them to acknowledge their affiliation with the gang.

Step by Step: Fill in the Blanks, Be Complete, and Leave Nothing Blank

The agency information is very important to track down the officer or related reports for use later in court. Dates of events are obviously very important for tracking gang-related incidents by date and time in addition to location. That can help determine what hours antigang operations should take place, such as sweeps or other operations, based upon the dates and times the gangs in the area seem most active. With limited resources, we have to work smarter not harder and must adapt, including alternating our work schedules if the gang's activity dictates we do so.

Make sure that the FI location and time are the same on every FI; this will help in linking them together in later investigations and computer checks. Many times five or six officers can be contacting a large group of gang members. The officers on one side of the corner may put 1200 Main Street, while officers just 20 ft. away may put 100 Elm Street. This makes later computer checks a little more difficult and may make it look like the group was not all together.

When conducting an FI of a gang member, many will pretend to be ignorant of the English language; and some may even lie to a police officer about their name (say it isn't true). Many gang members of Hispanic decent, for example, use two last names, a Spanish concept involving the use of paternal and maternal last names. For instance, the name Juan Manuel Garcia-Flores is composed of four elements: Juan is the first name, Manuel is the middle name, Garcia is the paternal last name and the legal name, and Flores is the maternal last name. The names are traditionally joined by a hyphen, the conjunction Y, or nothing. The last name of Spanish females changes after marriage. If Rosa Garcia Rodriguez marries Juan Gonzalez Villa, she is known as Rosa Garcia De Villa. Should her husband die, she will be known as Rosa Garcia Viuda De Villa ("viuda" means "widow of"). It is important to recognize both last names and record them accurately in criminal records. Failure to properly document an individual by his or her last name will result in confusion. It is also important to check the subject in various law enforcement databases switching the paternal and maternal last names, basically running their name twice. Many gang members use both versions of their name.

Sophisticated offenders are aware of this confusion and will attempt to hinder law enforcement, especially when dealing with Hispanic and Asian gangs, when in fact most know enough to realize what is being said and what actions are about to be taken. They will profess their innocence, frequently using the phrases like "No problem" or "No entiendo" hoping to make the officer lose interest and record the false information.

Take time to investigate a moniker. Many times gang members possess what is sometimes called "pocket litter." It refers to the personal items they have in their possession that may help you in your gang investigation; do they have an address book on their person with gang names on it that can tell you their moniker and the moniker of their companions? Do they have graffiti on their hats, belts, shoes, etc., that may tell you their moniker? If they do have an address book containing phone numbers and monikers, record that information for gang investigators. Many times the gang members will have personal photos in their wallet, maybe of friends and family. It has been beneficial to look at the back of the photos and read any personal messages that may be addressed to a specific moniker. The reality is when many gang crimes occur, the victims may know only that it was "Speedy" or "Flaco" that was responsible; they do not know the real name. Obtaining a moniker is very important.

Phone numbers are also becoming much more critical. It is important to include an area code of the number and to get the number of any cell phones or pagers on their person. If possible, review the numbers they have called recently and stored in their cell phone directory, and make note of which service provider they have. All of this may become very important in gang investigations at a later time should you want to conduct a wire tap or request a jail or prison facility monitor their phone calls.

An essential part of your contact with the gang member is taking a photograph of the subject. When taking photographs of gang members in noncustodial situations, it is important for the officer to articulate the need for the photo, such as identifying or eliminating the individual as a suspect in a crime or the prevention or suppression of gang violence. It is important to understand that photographs are critical to the gang documentation process, but there are legal issues that officers must be aware of when photographing subjects during FI contacts.

The photograph you take may be used to identify the person as a suspect in a serious case down the road and can be a decisive factor in court. A photograph obtained as a result of an illegal detention can be suppressed in court as any identifications made of the suspect by the victims and witnesses utilizing that photograph. A person who exposes their facial features, and/or body in general, to the public, in a public place, has no reasonable expectation of privacy in their appearance. It is not therefore a constitutional violation to photograph them, so long as they are not detained for that purpose. Basically, you can photograph a subject during an FI situation if the subject gives consent or if the photograph was obtained during a lawful detention. In general, most department policies prohibit officers from physically forcing anyone to be photographed in a noncustodial situation. Therefore, minus any probable cause to arrest the individual, it may not be possible to get a photograph.

When you do take a photo, make sure it is a good quality photograph. A digital camera is great in the field and all detectives should have a camera handy. Officers should find a good background prior to taking a photograph. Typically the photograph should be taken against a light-colored background and should show the subject from mid chest up, or from the same distance each time you take them to be consistent department-wide to give you a large pool of photos for lineups that are consistent. Have the gang members remove hats and sunglasses and have them look straight ahead and not smiling. To avoid having them blink giving you a photo with their eyes closed, I usually tell them to close their eyes, and then open them just prior to my taking the photo. This usually gives you a good photo on the first attempt.

If the subject is wearing a hat or glasses, you can take a photograph with and without the items if clothing is going to be an identifying issue, such as the suspect matching the description given by a victim or witness; if so you may want to take a full-length head-to-toe photograph as well. All photos of gang members must be properly labeled to make them useful and will need to fit into your lineup format. As such, you may want to leave enough extra space above the head (approx. 1/2 in. on the photo) to allow for adjustments in a photographic lineup folder if you use those. If the photo is taken too close the subject's face, it will not fit properly in a lineup folder, and if the photo is taken too far away, the face will be too small. If you use an automated photo lineup program, using a digital camera saves time and effort and eliminates the need to scan photos before using them in the lineup.

If you can take a group shot of all the home boys throwing up gang signs all gathered in a group, it is great evidence down the road when the gangster says that he or she is not a gang member. I have usually gotten the group to allow me to take their photo by telling them they can have a copy for them to keep. I keep my copy and then give the group one or two copies depending upon my available film supply. I have taken a digital photo of a group of Asian gang members and actually got them to give me their e-mail address so I could e-mail them their free copy. Many times the photos they walk away with will be found during a probation or parole search down the road by the next officer that encounters the gang members.

It is critically important to record all tattoos and other scars and marks; make them lift shirts (if appropriate) to expose their back, stomach, and chest. Do not take their word for it that they do not have tattoos and be as comprehensive as you can. If they have a picture tattoo, describe it with as much detail as possible and take a photograph if possible. Specific clothing is also very important; it may match clothing of crimes that had previously occurred or it may help document the gang member if the clothing is associated with a specific gang. When all photos have been taken, it is important to make the appropriate comments on the photograph.

The subject's full name, subject's DOB, circumstances of photo (arrest, detention, consent, evidence, or investigation), case or FI numbers, officer's name, officer's identification or badge number, and the date and time of the photograph should all be written on the back of the photo. This information is critical if the photograph is to be used in a photographic lineup or as evidence in a future court proceeding, and it is required before photos can be uploaded into most automated gang file systems.

Vehicle information is also a critical element. It is very common for gang members to drive cars not registered to them. Your FI may be the only way to link a specific gang member to a specific vehicle. Write the license plate, state, registered owner info, color, and vehicle description down on the contact card or FI. Record any damage to the vehicle that may help identify it down the line and if possible take a photo of the car they were driving as well.

The most critical part of the FI is why the person was stopped, what happened to lead the police officer to stop the gang member, what specific criteria did they violate, what they said, what they were doing, who were they with, etc. Were they looking into car windows, running from the scene of a gang fight, or just loitering in front of a store? The crime potential section clearly indicates on the FI that it is gang related by putting "Gang Related," "186.22 PC," "999," or whatever code or section that is used by your department's gang unit in the crime potential section or narrative box. This will help ensure that the FI gets sent to the gang unit where it belongs. It is also highly recommended to add the section of law that they were violating when you made contact with them to help justify the FI. Put the documentation criteria in the narrative, such as admitted gang member, wearing gang hat, and was with two other admitted gang members; "Documentation criteria is essential." The criteria should be explained in as much detail as possible, and the usual criterion consists of the following:

Criteria # 1 is pretty straightforward and is the strongest evidence of gang membership. This occurs when a subject you are talking to tells you that they are a member of a specific gang. If they claim to be a "Crip" or "Blood" gang member, make sure to ask what "set" they claim. The narrative should say something like "Subject admitted to being a West Coast Crip for the past four years." Their admission is strong evidence of gang membership. While they are talking about being in the gang, get their moniker, or gang name, and find out how long they have been a member of the gang. Gang members have become more aware of the penalties being used more often against gangs, and many have become more and more hesitant to "claim" their gang membership to law enforcement. Many however will still admit if the officer is skilled and knowledgeable.

Criteria # 2 is met when a subject has "gang-specific" clothing, tattoos, or "paraphernalia" that is only associated with a specific gang. The important factor with this criterion is that the items are clearly related to a specific gang. Gone are the days of being able to call a subject a gang member because he is wearing baggy clothes, a Raiders jacket, and blue bandana and has a tattoo of three dots on the web of his left hand. For example, if the subject had a belt with the chrome buckles "M," "T" attached to it, "Menudo" embroidered on his bandana, and "MTL" tattooed on his forehead, these would be valid indicators that he is associated with the Menudo Town Locos street gang. Listing "numerous" under the tattoos section doesn't help us at all unless the subject has the word "numerous" tattooed on his body. Be specific and list all of the identifying tattoos the subject has. If you need more space to document the tattoos, use the remarks section or continue to list them on the back of the FI. We want the gang file for the gang member to accurately depict every tattoo on their body to help with future investigations.

Other frequently overlooked examples of gang paraphernalia are the writings a person may have on their personal belongings (wallet, phone lists, school notebook, etc.) and any gang-related photographs they might have with them. If a subject has any gang graffiti or rosters written in their property and they are in custody, photocopy the items and attach the copies to the arrest report or FI. Do the same with gang-related photographs depicting gang members "throwing" hand signs or displaying weapons. These items are commonly encountered during searches of gang homes and are excellent evidence of gang involvement.

Criteria # 3 covers circumstances where a subject is arrested for "delinquent/criminal activity" with another known gang member. This means that the companion must have claimed their gang membership at the time of the contact, or they are already documented as a gang member. What does "delinquent/criminal activity" mean? This covers anything an adult can be arrested for and also provides for the miscellaneous "status offenses" committed by juveniles (curfew violation, truancy, etc.). List the specific crime section they violated to help establish the FI as being conducted a lawful detention versus a consensual encounter.

Criteria # 4 is used to document "associates" of gangs who may not (yet) be members of the gang but frequently associate with known members. These criteria can also be used when a suspected member of the gang will not claim their membership to law enforcement but commonly hangs out with fellow gang members. FI reports listing companions are very important when it comes to documenting a gang member using these criteria.

Criteria # 5 is met when we receive information from a "reliable informant" identifying the subject as a gang member. This criterion is rarely used to initially document a subject as a gang member, but can be helpful to support and maintain a subject's current documented status as a member of a gang. A "reliable informant" can be anyone who would have true knowledge of a subject's membership in a gang. These can be family members, other members from the subject's gang, other law enforcement sources, etc. The key issue here is that the informant be a person who would "know" that the subject is a gang member.

In order for a subject to be initially "documented" as a gang member, we must have at least a total of three of the aforementioned criteria met, which may vary from department to department or between the United States and a foreign country. This can be done in one contact (i.e., subject is arrested with other gang members while wearing a "Menudo Town" hat and has "MT" tattooed on his wrist) or three separate contacts (i.e., subject is hanging out with "MT" gang members on each occasion); that requirement also varies from department to department. The only exception to this is an individual that self-claims his gang membership to an officer during a jail classification interview, which is one criterion, and this can be enough to document that person as a gang member in many departments.

There are many other indicators of gang involvement that can be used to support a person's current documentation status. Some of these are witnessing the subject "throwing" gang-related hand signs, the subject's name/moniker and/or phone number appearing on a gang list, the subject corresponding with a known gang member in custody and discussing gang activities, the subject using gang language, etc. Any of the previously mentioned criteria for documenting gang members or other gang involvement indicators located during an arrest or FI should be indicated in the narrative of the report. If you obtain substantial gang information during a contact or arrest, write a separate report detailing the facts and forward it to the gang unit.

Always confirm the information given. Does the address exist? Call the phone number. Is it really their house? Take time to get complete and accurate information. I always assume the gang member has lied to me until I prove otherwise. Quiz them on the information that they have provided. If you are not satisfied, have an additional unit check the address they provided and see if the people know the subject or can help identify him or her while you have the subject to confirm the information, or have your dispatcher verify the information provided in a database, or by making phone calls if necessary. Finally, make sure the officer's name and beat are recorded so if/when the FI will be used in court to prove a gang enhancement, the officer can be located to come to court and testify about the contact.

Interview All Parties

Interview victim and witnesses separately, including any children who may have witnessed the incident or any prior incidents. **Do not ask the victim whether he or she wishes to press charges**. The decision to prosecute is made by the district attorney or the city attorney. The victim and suspect should be advised that he or she has no control over the decision to prosecute.

1. *Victim*: Note and document the following:
    a. The victim's physical condition, including
        i. Any injuries—describe in detail.
           Determine if medical treatment is necessary and seek appropriate care.
        ii. Torn clothing.
        iii. Smeared makeup.
    b. The victim's emotional condition.
    c. Any evidence of substance/chemical abuse by the victim.
    d. Determine victim's relationship to the suspect.
    e. Record any spontaneous statements of the victim.
    f. Obtain emergency contacts, telephone numbers, and pager numbers for the victim.
    g. Note any statements made by the suspect to the victim during the incident.
    h. Ask the victim if he or she wants to be notified when the suspect is released from jail.
2. *Witnesses*
    a. Interview all witnesses separately and record names, addresses, phone numbers, and emergency contacts.
    b. List the names and ages of children present.
    c. One of the keys to understanding when a person is lying to you is recognizing the level of stress the suspect is under when they tell a lie. Some people can show signs of stress even when they're telling the truth, and of course some people can lie about significant events without showing any signs of stress. This is why no two suspects or interviews are identical.

      d. Record names and addresses of emergency personnel.

      e. Interview neighbors (earwitnesses).

      f. Determine from witnesses if they are aware of a history of abuse.

3. *Suspect*

      a. Describe suspect's location on arrival.

      b. Describe suspect's physical condition.

      c. Describe suspect's emotional condition.

      d. Document evidence of substance/chemical abuse by the suspect, conduct examination, and add charge if appropriate.

      e. Record spontaneous statements.

      f. Document, describe, and photograph any injuries.

      g. Inform the suspect that abuse is a crime and obtain a waiver.

      h. Interview the suspect.

4. *Evidence*

      a. Describe the crime scene. Note signs indicating struggle such as overturned furniture, hair that has been pulled out, blood, broken fingernails, holes in walls, and damaged telephones.

      b. Photograph the crime scene if applicable.

      c. Ensure that the victim's and suspect's injuries are photographed clearly.

      d. Impound and photograph all weapons and other evidence including all instrumentalities of the crime (i.e., belts, phone cords, hangers, gas cans, lighters, broken lamps).

      e. When using digital cameras, follow established departmental guidelines for the storage and transfer of digital images.

5. *Medical treatment*

    If medical treatment is necessary,

      a. Transport or have the victim transported to the hospital.

      b. Obtain names, addresses, and telephone numbers of ambulance or paramedic personnel treating the victim.

      c. When reasonably practical, try and photograph the victim's injuries before the victim is transported to the hospital.

      d. Obtain signed medical release from victim.

      e. Obtain a copy of the medical treatment form including doctor's name, address, and telephone number.

      f. Interview treating physician and confirm nature and severity of injuries.

      g. Document whether the victim made statements to treating personnel regarding injury, incident, or prior abuse.

Conclusion

There's a lot to consider before conducting an interview or interrogation. But the more information you are able to gather, the more you have—either to use against them or to use to corroborate your case. Work with your department and your officers to ensure that the investigative interviews you perform are done so in accordance with the law.

Questions for Discussion

16.1 Define the terms interview versus interrogation.
16.2 Discuss Miranda and understand when it is and is not required.

References

Miranda v. Arizona (1966) 384 U.S. 436, 445 [16 L.Ed.2nd 694, 708].
California v. Beheler (1983) 463 U.S. 1121 [77 L.Ed.2nd 1275].
Rhode Island v. Innis (1980) 446 U.S. 291, 300–302 [64 L.Ed.2nd 297, 307–308].

Detectives and the Criminal Investigation Process

17

CASILDA E. ROPER-SIMPSON

Contents

Chapter Objectives	278
Chapter Outline	278
Justice is Not Blind	278
Criminal Investigation	278
Detectives	278
Crime Scene	279
Detective File Folder	280
Evidence	280
Warrants	281
Fingerprints	281
Bloodstain Pattern	282
Chain of Custody	282
Players in a Criminal Investigation	283
Prosecutor	283
Lead Detective	285
Defense Counsel	285
Rosario Disclosure	286
Judge	287
Private Investigators	288
Detective's Relationship with the Prosecutor and Defense Counsel	288
Fourth Amendment	289
Testimony	290
Police Misconduct	291
Profiling	291
Brutality	291
Planting Evidence	292
Defendant's Constitutional Rights	292
Fifth Amendment	293
Sixth Amendment	293
Conclusion	294
Questions for Discussion	294
References	294

Chapter Objectives

After reading this chapter, you should be able to do the following:

1. Identify the detective's role during a criminal investigation.
2. Identify the players and their roles and responsibilities during a criminal investigation.
3. Understand the interaction of the detective with the prosecutor and defense attorney.
4. Know the significance of evidence in a criminal investigation.
5. Understand the impact of the detective testifying on jurors—the trier of facts.

Chapter Outline

Criminal Justice System
Criminal Investigation
Evidence
The Players in a Criminal Investigation
Detective's Relationship with the Prosecution and Defense Counsel
Police Misconduct
Defendant's Constitutional Rights

Justice is Not Blind

When learning or reviewing the criminal justice system, one must lead with the assumption that justice is not blind; justice is not impartial. Detectives, law enforcement, prosecutors, defense attorneys, judges, jurors, court officers, and court clerks have pivotal roles within the criminal justice system. Yet, these players operate within the justice system harboring their own biases, life experiences, and prejudices. Inevitably, these biases permeate the justice system when these players operate in the criminal justice system. As a consequence, these biases suggest that Lady Justice peeks. Lady Justice with her blindfold "symbolizes the fair and equal administration of the law" (Gomez, 2005). Nevertheless, her blindfold is lifted more times than we want to admit and acknowledge—justice is not blind.

Criminal Investigation

Detectives

Lead detectives and police officers are often the first players within a criminal investigation; they are believed to "get the ball rolling" with the criminal investigation. Within a criminal investigation, they are tasked with the duty to investigate and obtain evidence. They are tasked to find the "truth," arrest a suspect, and assist the prosecution with the defendant's conviction. Detectives are essentially promoted police officers. As police officers, they were required to "walk the beat," make arrests, patrol neighborhoods, respond to crimes, secure crime scenes, and apprehend suspects. Once promoted, detectives are trained in the police academy and are required to have ongoing training; their ongoing training includes studying forensics and legal theories. The police academy trains its detectives on the methodology of conducting a criminal investigation; the methodology includes how evidence should be collected and the art of interrogation. Interestingly, detectives are sometimes taught to hypnotize a complainant—the victim of the crime. When hypnotized, a victim of a crime may mentally return to an incident and focus on identifying the perpetrator. Additionally, detectives are often tasked to investigate their fellow officers when misconduct occurs. There too, the detectives investigate and collect evidence to determine whether a fellow officer violated the law or acted beyond the scope of his duties.

How a lead detective investigates a crime is contingent upon the classification of that crime. Crimes are either classified as major or minor.

Minor crimes. Minor crimes are usually nonviolent. Examples of minor crimes are snatching a woman's pocket book, shoplifting, and embezzlement. Nonviolent crimes are processed by a patrol officer who takes a complaint and speaks with a victim. Usually there are no crime scenes when a minor crime is committed. With technological advances, police officers are able to locate surveillance cameras, which allow them to easily collect evidence in minor crimes; the collected evidence may even include the suspect's identification.

Major crimes. Violent crimes are generally deemed major crimes. Examples of major crimes are murder, burglary, arson, rape, and kidnapping. At the scene of a major crime, the lead detective along with the first-responding police officer must preserve the crime scene. The crime scene is preserved to deter and avoid the contamination of the crime scene. If a crime scene is contaminated, an entire criminal investigation and thus criminal case against a suspect may be challenged and/or dismissed. As a consequence, the first-responding officer has essential duties at a crime scene: (1) preserve life; (2) apprehend the suspect, detain witnesses, and interview the victim; and (3) preserve the crime scene to avoid contamination.

A major crime is investigated with the assistance of the Crime Scene Unit (CSU). The CSU is a division within a police department, which is dispatched to the scene of a major crime. The CSU is responsible for collecting evidence during the investigation of a major crime. Once CSU arrives at the scene, any and all crucial evidence that would assist in obtaining the "truth" must be meticulously collected. Once collected, the evidence is transported to a lab for examination and eventually transcribed into a report.

Crime Scene

Essentially, a crime scene is where a crime occurred. A crime scene should provide crucial evidence that would lead to the "truth" as it regards a crime. To ensure that valuable evidence is located and collected at a crime scene, the scene must be secured, analyzed, and free from taint or contamination. For example, a crime scene may be contaminated when an EMS worker attempts to resuscitate a seriously injured victim. At a crime scene, preserving life is the utmost concern. Whether a crime scene is contaminated or evidence is lost during life-saving efforts is merely secondary.

Lead detectives or police officers speak to as many people present at a crime scene as possible. More importantly, they speak to victims and witnesses. Lead detectives or police officers even attempt to speak to dying victims with hopes that the victim may identify their assailant. A statement made by persons who were under the belief that their death was imminent, whom are presently unavailable, and their statements concern the circumstances or causes of their imminent death is called a dying declaration. Federal Rules of Evidence 403 states, a dying declaration is admissible during trial as an exception to hearsay. The lead detective or police officer who heard the dying declaration may testify at trial as to the victim's statement. Overall, lead detectives or police officers speak to victims and/or witnesses at a crime scene in order to seek facts and the truth.

Detective File Folder

A case file folder prepared by the lead detectives in conjunction with the arrest of a suspect signifies the end of the criminal investigation. The file folder is usually given a number, signed off by either a sergeant or lieutenant, logged within the precinct, and filed within the precinct's filing system. The prosecutor assigned to the case receives the lead detective's entire file folder, since the file contains all the facts and crucial evidence obtained during the criminal investigation; the prosecution utilizes the file to prepare the case for trial. When the case against a suspect is ready for trial, then the entire folder is retrieved and brought into court to aid the testimony of the lead detective.

The lead detective's file folder will contain DD5s, the complaint follow-up forms where the detectives details their investigative actions, findings, interviews/interrogations and also the final action whether an arrest was made. In addition, the file folder will contain a list of recovered evidence, ballistic reports, fingerprint reports, statements, the identify of the first-responding officer, any photographs taken at the crime scene and any evidence that is subject to the Rosario Rule. In People v. Rosario (1961), the New York Court of Appeals held that in a criminal prosecution "the prosecution must disclose to the defense all of a prosecution witness' prior recorded statements as long as they are material to that witness' testimony." Upon receipt of the detective's file folder, the prosecutor should redact certain material in the file and turn over its contents to the defense counsel; redacted means that personal and confidential information about the witnesses are blocked or deleted out of the materials provided to the defense. Therefore, addresses of the victims and witnesses are redacted. The names and addresses of informants are also redacted. Essentially, the folder is turned over to defense counsel to allow them to prepare an adequate defense for their client.

Evidence

What makes or breaks a criminal case is the abundance or lack of evidence. Essentially, evidence is anything that a judge or juror examines related to a case; the evidence may be a tangible or intangible object or statements that are admissible in court. Evidence can be direct or circumstantial. Direct evidence is clear and does not require anyone to make any inferences. Circumstantial evidence requires that an inference or a logical conclusion is made from the facts provided. An example of circumstantial evidence is if Shaunie walks in with a wet umbrella, then Jayden may reasonably infer that it is raining. Ultimately, evidence is pivotal during a criminal case, since such evidence may prove innocence or guilt.

A lead detective defines evidence as anything that will assist with seeking the "truth" within a criminal investigation. The facts obtained in a criminal investigation are evidence. Questions that lead detectives should ask themselves in order to check their fact-finding are the following: What happened that led to the crime? What did the suspect do that day? Were there any witnesses to the occurrence? What evidence suggests the suspect's guilt? On the other hand, the prosecutors would ask: With the evidence collected, how could the defense argue or suggest reasonable doubt? Former prosecutor Alan Ross stated that he approached every case by attempting to visualize the entire picture regardless of how it affected the case (A. Ross, personal communication, July 9, 2014). At trial, Attorney Ross would present the case, so that any conviction would be based on the "real facts and not on a tidied up or smoothed out version of them" (A. Ross, personal communication, July 9, 2014).

In a nutshell, anything can potentially be evidence. Evidence may be found on the body of a deceased victim, the clothes on an assault victim, or the area where a crime occurred. If the victim was punched in the face, then the photographs of the injuries would be evidence. If the victim was punched with a ring and an indentation is evident on the face, then a photograph will assist in identifying the type and shape of the ring. Basically, "all products made in this country are kept for investigation" or may be deemed evidence (G. Weatherspoon, personal communication, July 15, 2014).

Warrants

To obtain evidence from a specific place, a lead detective of a criminal investigation must apply for a search warrant. "Without a search warrant, police officers may not search a place without its owner's consent" (Search Warrants, n.d.). Usually, a lead detective applies for a search warrant when the detective suspects or is provided information from a reliable confidential informant that evidence of a crime would be found at a certain location. In order to obtain a search warrant, a lead detective must file an affidavit providing "that there is probable cause to believe a search is justified" (Search Warrants, n.d.). The affidavit must provide the specific place to be searched or specific item to be seized.

A lead detective must also apply for an arrest warrant to apprehend a suspect. The detective must have sufficient evidence to prove that the suspect identified in the warrant committed the crime to be charged and thus should be arrested to stand trial for such crime. Ultimately, both warrants are issued by a judge when the lead detective shows sufficient evidence that such warrant is necessary to effectuate evidence gathering or prosecution of a suspect.

Fingerprints

There are various types of evidence collected at a crime scene, but fingerprints are a heavily sought-after type of evidence. Fingerprints are usually lifted from anything that a suspect came in contact with, which may include a body, an object, or a structure near to where the crime was committed. Fingerprints lifted from a crime scene are sent to a lab for analysis and compared to fingerprints that are located within a national criminal database. If fingerprints found at a crime scene match those of a person within the criminal database, then the person's report is transferred to the assigned lead detective; the detective may bring the person in for questioning, further investigate and seek an arrest warrant, or request a lineup from a witness. Nevertheless, the fingerprint match is merely a fact, and the lead detective uses such information to seek the truth.

At trial, both the prosecution and defense use fingerprint evidence; yet, they use the fingerprint evidence differently. If fingerprint evidence found at the scene of a crime matches the defendant, then the prosecution seeks to place the defendant at such scene. By placing the defendant at the crime scene, the prosecutor suggests to the jury that not only was the suspect at the scene of the crime but also that the suspect is responsible for such crime. However, the defense will challenge the fingerprint evidence. The defense counsel will suggest to the jury either that the fingerprints are the result of a shoddy investigation or that the suspect was at the scene of the crime at some earlier time; being at the scene of the crimes does not necessarily mean that you committed the crime. Thus, the defense will seek to discredit the fingerprints and the criminal investigation in its entirety.

Bloodstain Pattern

At a murder scene, bloodstain patterns are extremely crucial evidence. Bloodstain patterns provide a piece of the puzzle that may eventually solve the crime. Blood found at a crime scene is collected and tested for DNA; DNA analysis looks for a "substance that carries genetic information in the cells of plants and animals" (DNA, n.d.). DNA analysis assists in determining whether the suspect or victim was running from the crime scene, stationary, or moving. Analyzing blood found at a crime scene is deemed evidence if the blood belongs to the victim or even a suspect. If analyzing the blood reveals that the blood belongs to the defendant, then the blood evidence merely provides the "fact" that the suspect or defendant was at the crime scene. Additionally, if the suspect or defendant is located immediately near the crime scene, then the blood on his or her clothing is compared to determine if the blood matches the deceased victim.

Similar to fingerprint evidence, the prosecution and defense utilizes blood evidence differently. At trial, the prosecution attempts to use blood evidence to place the defendant at the scene of the crime when it was committed. The prosecution may even attempt to show the jury photographs of the bloodstains found at the scene. However, such presentment to the jury could be highly prejudicial to the defendant, since the photograph could be inflammatory, misleading, or shock the jury's conscience. Evidence is prejudicial "if its probative value is substantially outweighed" by its prejudicial value (Fed. R. Evid. 403). Essentially, the defense will argue that the photograph of the blood evidence should be kept away from the sight of the jury. With prejudicial evidence, a jury may reach a verdict based on sympathy or any other reason besides the evidence provided to the jury. Prior to jury deliberation, a judge must instruct the jury to reach a verdict purely on the evidence presented—called charging a jury; charging the jury occurs when the judge informs and instructs the jurors of the law as it applies to the case.

Chain of Custody

Evidence collected at a crime scene must be collected, analyzed, and stored to sustain its integrity at all times. Once evidence is collected, a lead detective will complete a voucher that is handed to a desk officer. The names of the lead detective and desk officer are placed on the voucher along with an identification number. Next, the lead detective submits the evidence for analysis within an envelope with a description of all the envelope's contents.

Evidence or property recovered from a suspect or defendant must be vouchered and logged with the property clerk. To analyze the suspect or defendant's property, such property is sent to an appropriate lab and tested; a suspect or defendant's property may include narcotics, weapons, or even fingerprints. The results of the testing are transcribed in a report, logged, and provided to the assigned lead detective. In preparation for trial, the lead detective will retrieve all vouchered and logged evidence and transport the items to the court on the day scheduled for the detective's testimony. During trial, the lead detective will testify as to how the evidence was collected and any test results contained within the lab reports; only the lab technician can testify as to the testing and analysis of the collected evidence.

Players in a Criminal Investigation

Prosecutor

A prosecutor assigned to a criminal investigation is responsible for advising, investigating, prosecuting, advocating, reforming, investigating, supporting, and/or negotiating. Like detectives, a prosecutor handles cases according to the type of crime charged—major or minor. In some states, a prosecutor handling a major crime will immediately dispatch to the crime scene after the commission of a crime. In New York City, a prosecutor who goes to the crime scene is called a "riding assistant district attorney/prosecutor" (ADA). If an ADA "rides," then the ADA is carrying out the investigatory function, and thus working the crime scene investigation with the lead detective.

In the investigatory function, the prosecutor will obtain statements from the victim and witnesses. A prosecutor will advise the lead detective as to what type of evidence should be collected at a crime scene, and what type of evidence should be sought throughout the criminal investigation. On occasions, the prosecutor will also participate in lineups of the suspects; a lineup occurs when the victim or witnesses are asked to pick out the suspect from a lineup of individuals in a police station. A photo lineup requires a witness to pick the suspect from a group of photographs known as a photo array. Lineups must not be prejudicial to a suspect. The individuals in a lineup must have the same characteristics as the alleged suspect, so as to not appear suggestive. During a lineup, both the detective and prosecutor must be careful not to taint the identification process. Accordingly, the detective or prosecutor should only ask the victim or witness whether they recognize an individual within the lineup and how do they recognize such individual; no other discussions are necessary, since detectives and prosecutors must be cautious to not sway a witness or victim into identifying a suspect.

In the prosecutorial role, the prosecution has a duty to protect and defend the constitutional rights of all state citizens. People v. Bailey (1983) provided that the prosecutor's sole intent cannot be placed on prosecuting the case. The prosecutor "must never lose sight of the fact that a defendant, as an integral member of the body politic, is entitled to a full measure of fairness" (People v. Bailey, 1983).

Notwithstanding Bailey's tenets, prosecutors can become overzealous in their quest to convict. As a result, prosecutors have been found to violate a defendant's constitutional rights and fail to fulfill their prosecutorial obligations. Gilbert Parris, a former prosecutor and now practicing defense attorney, stated that the "prosecution must seek the truth." When a prosecutor suspects that a lead detective has provided false information, then it becomes the prosecutor's duty to seek the "truth" and even confront the detective. Veteran prosecutors are trained to always seek the truth first and not align themselves too closely with a detective; the goal is to never lose sight of their roles as truth seekers. For this reason, prosecutors must interview a lead detective during a criminal investigation as to why the detective believed the person committed the crime and if they had probable cause to inquire or detain such person. Seeking the truth requires the prosecutor to represent both the victim and the person accused. Hence, the accused's innocence must be exhausted before the prosecutor can even move on with a criminal case.

The Drug Treatment Court provides an alternative to incarceration; if a defendant's rap sheet in conjunction with evidence collected reveals that a defendant has an addiction, then a prosecutor may recommend drug treatment. In this vein, the prosecutor hopes to support the defendant's quest for treatment and rehabilitation. The prosecutor will review the detective's report and determine whether the drug treatment part is the proper place for a defendant. If so, the defendant's case will proceed in the Drug Treatment Court. Defendants, their family, and defense attorneys, including myself, are always happy to interact with the prosecutors in this part. Here, prosecutors use collected evidence to support a defendant's road to rehabilitation and treatment—not to convict and incarcerate.

Unlike defense attorneys, prosecutors have a higher duty. In the prosecutorial role, prosecutors have a duty to disclose information to the defense that may strengthen or weaken the prosecutor's case. For example, if Janice admits that she is only 80% sure that she correctly identified the suspect in a lineup, then the prosecution must turn over such admission. Clearly with only 80% certainty, a defense counsel could argue that reasonable doubt exists. The type of evidence that may weaken a prosecutor's case, but still have to be disclosed to the defense, is called exculpatory evidence. Exculpatory evidence is any information obtained during a criminal investigation that could prove that the defendant did not commit the crime.

In their capacity as advisors, prosecutors must maintain a professional and cooperative but distant working relationship with law enforcement. Prosecutors must advise lead detectives on what type of evidence is necessary for a charge, indictment, and conviction. Prosecutors must advise lead detectives on what type of evidence to collect at a crime scene. Furthermore, prosecutors must advise whether their acts within a criminal investigation were lawful, and not in violation of the defendant's rights. At times the advising role is not easy for a prosecutor. When detectives are questioned as to the validity of evidence that they collected, they often become adversarial to the prosecutor.

Former prosecutor and now criminal defense attorney Audrey Thomas during her tenure as a prosecutor has encountered detectives who became angry when confronted and questioned about evidence. When prosecutors are not experienced, they present the questionable evidence and information received from the detectives to their supervisor; the supervisor would then confront the detective. Often, prosecutors are cautious as it regards their interactions with investigators, especially when they are uncertain about whether the detective is being forthcoming. Prosecutors may have worked with the same detective for years and don't want to complicate their working relationship; any complications may affect the other cases the prosecutor has or will have with the lead detective. Essentially, prosecutors must confront detectives with caution. Prosecutors must seek the truth, especially when any doubts exist that detectives abused their authority, planted evidence, or changed their presentment of the facts during an interview.

Prosecutors are cautioned against getting too cozy with detectives. During my tenure in a New York City district attorney's office, the detectives and the prosecutors socialized together; does the coziness between the prosecutors and detectives affect the duties and responsibilities of either? Would a prosecutor be subjected to the "blue wall of silence" within the detective's world? The "blue wall of silence" is when police officers or detectives protect only those who serve within a police department. Would a detective conform to the prosecutor's world if that prosecutor thought that there was corruption within the police department? Either way, the coziness between prosecutors and detectives may be a damaging effect upon a criminal investigation; seeking truth and justice is truly problematic in such a situation.

Lead Detective

Even though prosecutors and detectives must rely upon reciprocal cooperation and service, their roles within a criminal investigation may appear blended. Yet, detectives are responsible for investigating and arresting. Whereas, the main responsibilities of prosecutors are to seek the truth, prepare for trial, and obtain justice. Retired Detective Graham Weatherspoon illustrates the relationship between prosecutors and detectives within a criminal investigation as "I'm the chef and you're the waiter...I conduct the investigation and you do the trial" (G. Weatherspoon, personal communication, July 15, 2014). Once the "chef" provides the "waiter" with the criminal investigation file folder, the prosecutor reviews the paper work. As the prosecutor prepares for trial and additional evidence is required to make its case, the detective will be notified as to what further evidence should be acquired. Det. Weatherspoon understood what it meant for prosecutors to require additional evidence, because their burden is quite high—they have to prove each element of a crime to the jury beyond a reasonable doubt.

According to retired Det. Weatherspoon, a detective is the "seeker of truth and not fact" (G. Weatherspoon, personal communication, July 15, 2014). In illustration, suppose a weapon is recovered at a crime scene. Fingerprints are lifted from the weapon, and Elaina's fingerprints are a match to what was found on the weapon. Therefore, it's a proven fact that the prints lifted from the weapon belonged to Elaina. Yet, this fact merely indicates that at some point Elaina handled the weapon; Elaina would be deemed suspect number one. However, does the fact that Elaina handled the weapon at some point conclusively prove that she fired the weapon on the date and time at the scene of the crime? No, this proves that the lead detective must now further the criminal investigation to seek the truth beyond the mere fact that her prints were on the weapon. Hence, Det. Weatherspoon argues that a lead detective has the essential role to seek the "truth" beyond the mere facts that are collected and examined during a criminal investigation (G. Weatherspoon, personal communication, July 15, 2014).

Defense Counsel

Why would you defend criminals? Most defense attorneys are asked that question at some point throughout their career. However, a criminal defense attorney's role is not to defend "criminals." The role of a defense attorney is to assure that the constitutional rights of all clients are protected. The defense attorney is tasked with the duty to defend clients from the criminal investigation stage through to trial. Even when a defense attorney has evidential reason to conclude that a client might be guilty, the attorney must zealously defend the client. While zealously advocating for a client, the defense attorney must still conform to ethical standards.

Unlike the prosecutor, defense attorneys do not have the full cooperation of the lead detective in a criminal investigation. During the criminal investigation and prior to trial, detectives rarely speak with defense attorneys. Lead detectives do not assist the defense with trial preparation. More common, the detective interacts with the defense counsel at trial only. Generally, the initial interaction between the defense counsel and the lead detective is while the investigator testifies about the investigation at a hearing or trial. During the lead detective's testimony, the defense attorney's duty is to discredit as much as possible the detective's handling of the criminal investigation. The defense attorney must ensure that the prosecution does not prove the defendant's guilt beyond a reasonable doubt. In essence, the defense attorney must create doubt within the minds of the jury—all it takes is creating reasonable doubt as it regards one element of a charge. Hence, when a criminal defendant is found not guilty, that does not necessarily mean that the defendant was proven innocent. In essence, a not guilty verdict signifies that the prosecution failed to prove its case beyond a reasonable doubt to the trier of the facts—the jury or judge.

Rosario Disclosure

In most states, the defense is provided with a copy of the criminal investigation file that the lead detective turned over to the prosecution. In few states, the district attorney's office and the defense counsel enter into a voluntary disclosure agreement. With such an agreement, defense counsel avoids motion practice requesting specific evidence that should have been provided by the detective in the file. However, after defense counsel reviews the disclosure documents received from the prosecutor and notices that the file is lacking certain documents, information, or evidence, the defense counsel must make a record and engage in motion practice. Certainly, late disclosure of essential discovery prevents the defense counsel from adequately preparing a client's defense. Criminal defense attorney Joyce David recalled a federal trial where the judge reviewed the U.S. attorney's entire file, provided her with all the paper work that the prosecution failed to disclose, and adjourned the trial; David was provided the time to adequately prepare a defense (J. David, personal communication, July 3, 2014).

Some judges do not provide any time or provide a short period to receive and review Rosario materials not turned over prior to trial. During an assault case, a detective testified and referred to documents and materials in his file that were not provided to me prior to his testimony. I immediately objected, and the court inquired of the prosecutor as to why the detective's paper work was not provided. The court adjourned the case and only gave me until after lunch on that day to obtain the excluded paper work, review the paper work, and continue with the trial. Fairness dictates that a judge should allow a defense counsel extra time to prepare an adequate defense should the prosecution violate the Rosario tenets. Yet, most judges neither provide extra time to the defense nor impose sanctions upon the prosecutor for failure to disclose.

Without adequate Rosario disclosure, defense attorneys are not able to properly advise a defendant on whether to accept a plea or go to trial; these are the only two options a defendant has in a criminal case. In order to advise the defendant, the defense counsel must determine whether the case against the defendant is strong or weak. Recall, it's not about whether the defendant is innocent, but whether the prosecution can prove each element of the crime charged. If the prosecution lacks sufficient evidence to prove an element or elements of a crime, then a case against the defendant is probably weak. If the prosecution has sufficient evidence to prove each element, then the case against the defendant is probably strong. The only way for the defense to make this determination is to be aware of what evidence the prosecution has within its possession; this is why the Rosario disclosure is so very important and essential to the defense.

Defense Attorney Howard Schwartz recalled being told by prosecutors, "we are not wasting time providing paperwork—your client knows whether or not they did the crime" (H. Schwartz, personal communication, July 2, 2014). When the prosecution withholds Rosario, whether intentionally or not, is the defendant being "bullied?" Experienced defense attorneys will agree that prosecutors with confidence in their cases don't play "discovery games." Thus, when discovery games are played by the prosecution, there's a possibility that the case against the defendant is rather weak.

While faced with discovery games, inadequate disclosure by the prosecutors, and uncooperative lead detectives, defense attorneys must still formulate an effective defense theory or defense strategy. Defense attorney Ellen Edwards agreed that detectives are generally not helpful to defense counsel (E. Edwards, personal communication, June 14, 2014). However, a detective not being helpful must not affect the defense's theory and preparation for trial (E. Edwards, personal communication, June 14, 2014). For Attorney Joyce David, her main tactic is to impeach and discredit the lead investigator at trial with contradictory information that was found by her private investigator (J. David, personal communication, July 3, 2014). In addition, Attorney David discredits the investigator by establishing the uncooperative nature of the detective by revealing on cross-examination that she made several attempts to speak with the detective prior to trial, but to no avail (J. David, personal communication, July 3, 2014). By discrediting and impeaching the detective, Attorney David may skillfully argue during her closing arguments (J. David, personal communication, July 3, 2014). During her closing argument, Attorney David may create and suggest doubt in the juror's minds by alluding to the prosecution's lack of evidence, the detective's "shoddy" investigation of the crime, and the lack of cooperation by the lead detective (J. David, personal communication, July 3, 2014).

Judge

Judges play very little role in the criminal investigation process. Their involvement is limited to the issuance of warrants upon the application by a detective or prosecutor. Recall that an issued warrant must be limited in scope—specific person, place, or thing. Judge Mark A. Scott notes that "search warrant standards are governed by both the U.S. Supreme Court and state court interpretation of their respective constitutions. Judges try to apply the applicable standard and remain fair to both sides" (M. Scott, personal communication, July 30, 2014).

Judges are also involved in the criminal investigation process as it regards deciding motions or hearings prior to trial. A common motion made by the defense is a motion for a directed verdict. A directed verdict requests that the judge evaluate the evidence and dismisses the case against the defendant for the prosecution's failure to satisfy their burden; recall that the prosecution has a burden to prove each element of a crime beyond a reasonable doubt. Judge Mark A. Scott states that judges "must still be attentive to the quality of the investigation in order to handle motions for directed verdict, which includes an evaluation of the evidence (M. Scott, personal communication, July 30, 2014). It is only when a shoddy or an inadequate investigation is done that the public becomes aware, because the advocates tend to make a big deal out of their position which puts the judge in the unenviable position of having to make a decision which he or she may not care to make…. It is only when those investigatory standards fall below acceptable standards that the results are called into question… that is rare" (M. Scott, personal communication, July 30, 2014).

Private Investigators

Private investigators are hired by the defense during a criminal investigation to assist with trial preparation; investigators are only hired if a defendant can afford their services. Private investigators are often retired detectives or law enforcement officers. They assist the defense by investigating the evidence and charge against the defendant. The investigator visits the crime scene and attempts to speak to the victim; they are often not successful. Although prosecutors should not tell the victim to not speak to the defense, prosecutors on occasions advise the victim of that anyway. As a result, private investigators rarely speak to a victim.

During their investigation, private investigators canvass the crime scene for witnesses and obtain signed statements when witnesses are located. These statements allow the defense attorney to question the victim and witnesses at trial based on the information provided in the statements; the defense may also impeach the victim or witnesses should there be any inconsistencies found within the signed statements or lead detective's report. To impeach means to attack the credibility of a witness on the stand. Ultimately, a successful impeachment of a witness during trial may establish that doubt exists as to the charges against the defendant.

Detective's Relationship with the Prosecutor and Defense Counsel

The detective's interactions and relationship with the prosecutor is quite different than with the defense counsel. Once a suspect is identified, charged, and arrested, then the suspect is arraigned according to the charges; an arraignment is the formal hearing where the defendant is formally read the charges brought against him or her. The defendant is expected to reply to the charges with either guilty or not guilty.

During intake of the criminal case, the prosecutor assesses whether the evidence collected will prove the elements of the crime to which the suspect was charged. Recall that the prosecution has a heavy burden to prove all elements of a crime beyond a reasonable doubt. For all crimes, the prosecution must prove the elements of mens rea and actus reus. Mens rea speaks to the defendant's mental capacity and establishes a defendant's intent to commit a crime; there are some crimes where intent is not required, that is, strict liability crimes. Actus reus requires that the defendant commits an illegal act or fails to act, which causes the victim harm; failing to act requires that the defendant had an affirmative duty to act, that is, parent to child.

Upon review of the file, if the prosecutor finds that the evidence collected does not satisfy one of those elements, then the case against the defendant should be dismissed. Another example is the case against Staci. Detective CJ arrested and charged Staci with assault. After review of the surveillance camera, the coverage revealed that Staci was involved in the fight while under the influence, because someone put drugs in her drink. As such, the prosecutor would have difficulty satisfying the beyond a reasonable doubt burden at trial, since the mens rea element would not be satisfied; the suspect could not formulate intent, since she was involuntarily under the influence. In this example, Prosecutor Camille would review the case with her supervisor and recommend that the district attorney's office decline to prosecute Staci; the district attorney's office should not prosecute Staci, since the likelihood of obtaining a conviction based on the "facts" provided by Detective CJ is slim.

Fourth Amendment

The fourth, fifth, sixth, and eighth amendments of the U.S. Constitution are heavily utilized to challenge the constitutionality of criminal investigations, arrests, trials, and imprisonment. By far, the fourth amendment is probably the most coveted challenge. If a fourth amendment challenge is successful, then a defendant will have the evidence collected against him or her suppressed; suppressed means that the prosecution is unable to utilize such evidence to prove the elements of the crime charged against the defendant. The evidence suppressed can include statements made by the suspect or tangible items such as drugs and stolen property. On occasions, successful fourth amendment challenge can potentially eliminate all charges against a suspect.

The fourth amendment to the U.S. Constitution provides that

> the right of the people to be secure in their persons, houses, papers, and effects, against unreasonable searches and seizures, shall not be violated, and no Warrants shall issue, but upon probable cause, supported by Oath or affirmation, and particularly describing the place to be searched, and the persons or things to be seized. (U.S. CONST. AMEND. IV)

The fourth amendment prohibits unlawful searches and seizures by law enforcement. Further, the fourth amendment requires that any warrant issued to a law enforcement officer for the arrest or search of a person or place be supported by probable cause and signed by a judge; probable cause is whether at the specific "moment the facts and circumstances within their knowledge and of which they had reasonably trustworthy information were sufficient to warrant a prudent man in believing that the petitioner had committed or was committing an offense" (Cook, 1970).

In addition, the fourth amendment mandates that a warrant issued by a judge shall be limited in scope—specific person, place, and/or thing. As with most constitutional mandates, there are exceptions to the Fourth Amendment warrant requirement, such as pure and present danger, plain view, automobile exception, exigent circumstances, hot pursuit, and consent.

In practice, any evidence obtained by a law enforcement officer as a result of an illegal search, arrest, or stop is referred to as "fruit of the poisonous tree." The evidence obtained from the officer's illegal actions are excluded and suppressed. For example, Prosecutor Coreen when reviewing a criminal investigation notices that the gun found on Lionel by detectives was illegally obtained. The investigation revealed that the detectives did not have probable cause to stop Lionel as he was walking home. Accordingly, Prosecutor Coreen could proceed with the case where she faced the possibility that the case would be dismissed, since the illegal evidence obtained from Lionel would be deemed "fruit of the poisonous tree." Similarly, if a judge determines that probable cause did not exist and law enforcement should have obtained a search warrant, then any evidence collected would be suppressed after a Dunaway hearing. A Dunaway hearing is conducted to challenge how probable cause was obtained to justify a stop.

As previously mentioned, there are special rules as it regards automobiles. In Arizona v. Gant (2009), the Court held that law enforcement shall not search a vehicle incident to arrest without a warrant when the crime scene is secure. The crime scene is secure if the arrestee is no longer a danger to the officer and/or in a position to destroy evidence (Arizona v. Gant, 2009). Accordingly, if during a traffic stop the law enforcement searches your trunk and finds a gun or narcotics, then such evidence would be deemed inadmissible if the trunk was closed and the individual in the stop had no reachable access to the trunk.

Recall that plain view is an exception to the warrant requirement. Law enforcement officers are not required to have a search warrant to obtain evidence that is in "plain view." Plain view is described as any evidence that is observed openly; the caveat of plain view is that the officer must be lawfully in the location where the evidence is viewed. Therefore, the officer may not use the plain view exception to the warrant mandate if the officer entered the home without a warrant or consent. As an example, suppose that a suspect consents to an officer interviewing him at his home—the officer is lawfully there. When interviewing Ana about a burglary, the detective observes an open box with gems on Ana's piano. The box that the gems are in has the logo of the store that was burglarized 2 days ago. Under the plain view exception, the gems found inside Ana's home could be seized, and she is arrested without violating her right to be free from illegal search and seizure.

Testimony

Voir dire is when the prosecution and defense get the opportunity to question potential jurors to rule out those persons who are biased, have a conflict of interest, or are unable to deliberate without prejudice. During voir dire, most jurors are confident that lead detectives or officers in the criminal investigation are credible during their testimony. The level of confidence depends on where a case is occurring and whether such locale is known for police corruption. However, the credibility of a testifying detective should be based on the "facts" used to seek the "truth." Most jurors view detectives and police officers as being honest during their testimony. Generally, this view occurs because most jurors already have preconceived thoughts about a defendant—as a criminal who has credibility issues and is less trustworthy when compared to law enforcement.

In a New York Times editorial, Professor Michelle Alexander provided commentary on this issue of preconceived thoughts about a defendant and the law enforcement at trial. In the editorial, she articulated that law enforcement officers are often not forthcoming during their testimony (Alexander, 2013). As a result, some defendants plead guilty, because "the odds of a jury believing their word over a police officer's are slim to none" (Alexander, 2013). She warned that jurors should take into consideration that "because the police have a special inclination toward confabulation… disturbingly, they have an incentive to lie" (Alexander, 2013). Professor Alexander argued that the law enforcement may be induced not to be honest during their testimony, because the "police departments have been rewarded in recent years for the sheer number of stops, searches and arrests" (Alexander, 2013). Apparently, "federal grant programs like the Edward Byrne Memorial Justice Assistance Grant Program have encouraged state and local law enforcement agencies to boost drug arrests in order to compete for millions of dollars in funding" (Alexander, 2013). In addition, Professor Alexander observed that "even where no clear financial incentives exist, the 'get tough' movement has warped police culture to such a degree that police chiefs and individual officers feel pressured to meet stop-and-frisk or arrest quotas in order to prove their productivity" (Alexander, 2013). She noted that quotas are illegal under state law in New York; "Police Commissioner, Raymond W. Kelly, denies that his department has arrest quotas" (Alexander, 2013).

Police Misconduct

Profiling

Ideally, most law enforcement officers take their oath seriously—serve and protect their citizens. In some communities, citizens wonder who are they (law enforcement) protecting and serving? There have been too many examples of citizens being profiled and stopped unjustly by law enforcement; these citizens are profiled and stopped because of their race, gender, sexuality, or age. If there is a small percentage of police profiling, abuse of authority, and brutality, does that mean that a systemic problem exists? Minority communities argue that profiling is pervasive in their communities by white officers. Actually, NYC Liberties' data shows the statistics suggest that minority communities experience high rates of illegal stops and frisk. According to a recent study in New York City, 54% of the population stopped and frisked by the police was black; 12% of those stopped and frisked by the police were white, and 29% were Latino. A stop and frisk occurs when law enforcement officers allege that they found a specific individual to be suspicious. As a result, the individual is stopped and searched. Sometimes the individuals might have illegal substances on his or her person or have outstanding warrants. Yet, when profiling occurs the offender is not the black or white officer. The offender is the "blue officer." The "blue officer" can best be described as the systematic discrimination within a police department. Race and culture are the predominant characteristics used to profile individuals by white officers. For African-American officers, they tend to profile people of their own color.

The "blue wall of silence" is also used to protect officers who find themselves the subject of a criminal investigation. Even when detectives are required to investigate "their own," the criminal investigation still requires obtaining the facts and ultimately the truth. Often, the "blue wall of silence" impedes a criminal investigation of a fellow officer, since the officer's friends (fellow officers) may become uncooperative, destroy evidence, fail to give truthful statements, or evade the investigation for fear of retaliation by other officers. Consequently, investigating and prosecuting officers for their misconduct is problematic unless that "blue wall of silence" tumbles. Oftentimes, the truth as to what transpired between an officer and citizens is now captured on amateur videos. With the advancement of technology and numerous cases of police brutality, citizens now use their cell phones, iPads, and other devices to document instances of police misconduct. These citizens are able to provide the truth without the problematic "blue wall of silence" covering up such evidence.

Brutality

In New York, what has been deemed "one of the worst cases of police brutality" and misconduct was the Abner Louima incident. Initially, Mr. Louima was represented by attorneys Carl Thomas, Brian Figueroux, and Casilda E. Roper-Simpson (myself). We represented Mr. Louima in both the civil and criminal matters. In August 1997, Mr. Louima was assaulted by police officers in the back of their vehicle and in a precinct bathroom while arrested. Police officers Justin Volpe, Charles Schwarz, Thomas Bruder, and Thomas Wiese were charged with violating Mr. Louima's civil rights. Another police officer, Michael Bellomo, was charged with obstructing justice when he lied to cover up the brutality—there's the blue wall. Mr. Louima sustained serious mental, physical, and emotional injuries.

Fearing that Mr. Louima would fall victim to the "blue wall of silence" and other biases, our team of attorneys immediately expressed our lack of confidence in the then Kings County District Attorney's Office. The district attorney's office stepped aside from the case, and the prosecution of the police officers' misconduct and brutality was assigned to Assistant United States Attorney (AUSA) Ken Thompson. AUSA Thompson led a fierce and impartial criminal investigation of the police misconduct and brutality that Mr. Louima sustained. Ultimately, the officers pled guilty and were sentenced to time in jail. In the civil case, Mr. Louima was awarded $8.75 million dollars. Currently, Justin Volpe still remains in jail, since he was sentenced to 30 years in prison without the possibility of parole (Fried, 1999).

Planting Evidence

In New York, Detective Jason Arbeeny was convicted of planting drugs on a woman and her boyfriend after a bench trial (Stellch, 2011). A bench trial is when a defendant waives a jury trial and opts for a trial where the judge is the trier of facts and law. In a jury trial, the jury is the trier of facts, and the judge is the trier of the law. Mr. Arbeeny was a former detective previously assigned to the Narcotics Division (Stellch, 2011). At Mr. Arbeeny's trial, Mr. Stephen Anderson testified (Stellch, 2011). Former detective Anderson was also charged and pled guilty to misconduct in a different case (Stellch, 2011). During his testimony, Mr. Anderson testified that the illegal conduct of Mr. Arbeeny was not "limited to a single squad" (Marzulli, 2011). He further testified that "it was something I was seeing a lot of, whether it was from supervisors or undercovers and even investigators" (Marzulli, 2011).

Judge Gustin L. Reichbach, the State Supreme Court Justice who issued the guilty verdict against Mr. Arbeeny, stated, "I thought I was not naïve…but even this court was shocked, not only by the seeming pervasive scope of misconduct but even more distressingly by the seeming casualness by which such conduct is employed" (Stellch, 2011). When law enforcement find it acceptable to "plant evidence" on an innocent person who might have a criminal past, we must keep in mind that "injustice anywhere is a threat to justice everywhere" (Gottlieb, 2003, p. 18); this powerful statement was eloquently stated by Dr. Martin Luther King as the nation was addressing the civil rights issues during the civil rights movement. Currently, this statement resonates as we have to be concerned about those who are hired to protect and serve.

Defendant's Constitutional Rights

As a criminal investigation is underway, all parties within the criminal justice system must protect and uphold the defendant's constitutional rights. Recall that the fourth, fifth, sixth, and eight amendments are heavily used by defendants to challenge the constitutionality of a criminal investigation through imprisonment. Upon arrest by law enforcement, Miranda warnings must be given to the defendant. The Miranda warnings provide that the defendant has a right to remain silent and an attorney (Miranda v. Arizona, 1966). If a defendant cannot afford an attorney, then one will be appointed to them (Miranda v. Arizona, 1966). Further, anything the defendant says can and will be used against him or her in a court of law (Miranda v. Arizona, 1966). The Miranda warnings are a blend of the constitutional components found in various amendments. Ultimately, the fifth and sixth amendments to the constitution when enforced have the effect of protecting individual rights.

Fifth Amendment

No person shall be held to answer for a capital, or otherwise infamous crime, unless on a presentment or indictment of a Grand Jury, except in cases arising in the land or naval forces, or in the Militia, when in actual service in time of War or public danger; nor shall any person be subject for the same offence to be twice put in jeopardy of life or limb; nor shall be compelled in any criminal case to be a witness against himself, nor be deprived of life, liberty, or property, without due process of law; nor shall private property be taken for public use, without just compensation (U.S. CONST. AMEND. V).

Under the fifth amendment, defendants have the right to remain silent. Defendants do not have to provide any evidence (tangible or intangible) that would incriminate them. However, if defendants provide a statement or confession, then such statements can be used against them in the prosecution's case-in-chief and admitted as an admission.

Sixth Amendment

In all criminal prosecutions, the accused shall enjoy the right to a speedy and public trial, by an impartial jury of the state and district wherein the crime shall have been committed, which district shall have been previously ascertained by law, and to be informed of the nature and cause of the accusation; to be confronted with the witnesses against him; to have compulsory process for obtaining witnesses in his favor, and to have the assistance of counsel for his defense (U.S. CONST. AMEND. VI).

Under the sixth amendment, defendants have the right to obtain counsel to protect their constitutional rights once an arrest or detainment occurs. If the defendant is unable to afford an attorney, then an attorney is appointed. Usually, the appointed attorney is from legal aid or an institutional provider for indigent defendants. Once the defendant requests counsel, interrogation of the defendant must cease. However, if a defendant decides to make a statement without any further questioning from detectives or law enforcement, then the statement would be deemed admissible. For example, in Brewer v. Williams (1977) the court held that the defendant's statement was admissible after he exercised his right to counsel, because he provided the detectives with the location of a child's body. Here, the detectives did not continue to question the defendant, since they were having a conversation among themselves as they were transporting the defendant (Brewer v. Williams, 1977). In addition, the Supreme Court has held that detectives and law enforcement officers are allowed to use "mere strategic deception" or trickery to obtain incrementing evidence (Illinois v. Perkins, 1990). There, an undercover officer posed as an inmate to solicit incriminating evidence from a suspect. The court reasoned that Miranda warnings seek to protect suspects from being coerced by officers into providing incriminating evidence. The coercive nature is definitely an issue when an officer speaks to a suspect—"police dominated atmosphere" (Illinois v. Perkins, 1990). Yet, the coercive nature is not necessarily present when a friend speaks to a purported friend; here, it was an inmate to an inmate.

Conclusion

The criminal investigation process is so essential to the criminal justice system. If all players within the criminal investigation process remain in their respective roles and conform to their duties, responsibilities, and constitutional mandates, then the process will work effectively without taint. As a criminal defense attorney for many years, it's rather unfortunate that I have had to remind and convince many of my adversaries that a defendant is innocent until proven guilty; in our justice system, this basic tenet of criminal justice can never be forgotten or disregarded. The assistant district attorney or prosecutor must seek to obtain justice. The detective must lead an investigation with the goal of seeking facts and the truth. Further, detectives must "protect and serve" their citizens throughout the entire criminal investigation process; their citizens must include suspects and defendants. The defense counsel must zealously advocate for their clients. Consequently, the prosecutor, defense attorney, detective, and judge, should all remain in their respective roles and conform to their duties and responsibilities. Neither should be singularly the judge, jury, or prosecutor during the criminal investigation or the criminal justice process.

Questions for Discussion

17.1 Discuss the assigned lead detective's role in a criminal investigation.
17.2 Discuss the importance of the detective file folder and its impact, if any, on the defendant.
17.3 Is the collection of evidence significant in a criminal investigation?
17.4 What are the prosecution, defense, and judge's role during the criminal investigation process?
17.5 Compare and contrast the relationship between the detective, prosecution, and defense counsel.

References

Alexander, M. (2013, February 2). Why police lie under oath. The New York Times. Retrieved July 27, 2014 from http://mobile.nytimes.com/2013/02/03/opinion/sunday/why-police-officers-lie-under-oath.html?pagewanted = all&_r = 1.
Arizona v. Gant, 162 P. 3d 640 (2009).
Brewer v. Williams, 430 U.S. 387 (1977).
Cook, J. G. (1970). Probable cause to arrest. Vand. L. Rev., 24, 317.
DNA. (n.d.). Merriam-Webster. Retrieved from http://www.merriam-webster.com/dictionary/dna.
Dying Declaration. (n.d.). Legal Information Institute (Cornell University Law School) online. Retrieved July 27, 2014 from http://www.law.cornell.edu/wex/dying_declaration.
Fed. R. Evid. 403.

Fried, J. P. (1999, January 14). Volpe sentenced to a 30-year term in Louima torture. *The New York Times*. Retrieved July 27, 2014 from http://www.nytimes.com/1999/12/14/nyregion/volpe-sentenced-to-a-30-year-term-in-louima-torture.html.

Gomez, F. T. (2005). Perils of judicial notice: An argument in opposition of rule 201 (c) of the federal rules of evidence and rule 11 of the Puerto Rico rules of evidence. *The. Rev. Der. PR*, 45, 213.

Gottlieb, R. S. (2003). *Liberating Faith: Religious Voices for Justice, Peach, & Ecological Wisdom*. Lanham, Md: & Littlefield Publishers, Inc. Retrieved July 27, 2014 from https://books.google.com/books?id=6GHM_9ktdyoC&pg=PR3&dq=Liberating+Faith:+Religious+Voices+for+Justice,+Peace,+and+Ecological+Wisdom&source=gbs_selected_pages&cad=2#v=onepage&q=Liberating%20Faith%3A%20Religious%20Voices%20for%20Justice%2C%20Peace%2C%20and%20Ecological%20Wisdom&f=false.

Illinois v. Perkins, 496 U.S. 292 (1990).

Mazurilli, J. (2011, 13, October). fabricated drug charges against innocent people to meet arrest quotas. *Daily News*. Retrieved July 27, 2014 from http://www.nydailynews.com/news/crime/fabricated-drug-charges-innocent-people-meet-arrest-quotas-detective-testifies-article-1.963021.

Miranda v. Arizona, 384 U.S. 436 (1966).

New York Civil Liberties Union. (2014). Stop-and-frisk data. Retrieved July 27, 2014 from http://www.nyclu.org/content/stop-and-frisk-data.

People v. Bailey, 58 N.Y.2d 272 (1983).

People v. Rosario, 9 NY2d 286 (1961).

Search Warrants. (n.d.). Legal Information Institute (Cornell University Law School) online. Retrieved July 27, 2014 from http://www.law.cornell.edu/wex/search_warrant.

Search Warrants. (n.d.). Legal Information Institute (Cornell University Law School) online. Retrieved from http://www.law.cornell.edu/wex/search_warrant.

Stelloh, T. (2011, November 2). Detective is found guilty of planting drugs. *The New York Times*. Retrieved July 30, 2014 from nytimes.com at http://www.nytimes.com/2011/11/02/nyregion/brooklyn-detective-convicted-of-planting-drugs-on-innocent-people.html#.

Stop-and-Frisk Data. (2014). [Data is retrieved from the NYPD Quaterly Reports July 27, 2014]. *Stop-and-Frisk Data from the New York Civil Liberties Union*. Retrieved from http://www.nyclu.org/content/stop-and-frisk-data.

Interviewing and Communicating with Special Populations, Including Nonverbal Individuals, Persons with Mental Disabilities or Illness, and the d/Deaf

18

LAUREN M. BARROW

Contents

Chapter Objectives   297
Chapter Outline   298
Visible Disabilities   300
Invisible Disabilities   301
   Deafness   302
Cognitive Impairment   304
Intellectual Disability   305
Autism   306
Traumatic Brain Injury   308
   Mental Illness   310
References   313

Chapter Objectives

This chapter is intended to provide insight into some specific challenges facing individuals with mobility or communication disabilities who often find themselves involved with the criminal justice system as either a suspect, witness, or victim. Implementing necessary accommodations as identified by the specific disabling condition ultimately improves the experiences of the individual, law enforcement while improving the pursuit of equal justice. Specific goals include:

- Creating an awareness of the social struggle to extending equal justice to members of the disabled community.
- Identifying potential obstacles when interviewing suspects, witnesses or victims with mobility or communication challenges.
- Providing useful information and/or approaches for obtaining accurate information from suspects, witnesses or victims with mobility or communication challenges.

Chapter Outline

Introduction
Visible physical disabilities
Mobility
Wheelchairs
Canes/Walkers
Invisible disabilities
Persons who are d/Deaf
Cognitive Impairment
Mental Impairment
Autism
Traumatic Brain Injury
Mental Illness

Police force's sloppy investigations leave abuse of disabled unsolved (February 24, 2012).

http://www.news10.net/

The aforementioned headline suggests that police do not care about investigating crimes against persons who are disabled. But what this snapshot in time fails to demonstrate is that all members of society, police included, were thrust into a new reality after the deinstitutionalization movement of the 1970s placed vulnerable persons into mainstream society with promises of equality. That new reality did not come with an instruction manual. The result is that equal justice has proven to be an elusive concept for persons with disabilities—regardless of the disability. It is time now to accept the failure of good intentions and move instead toward an age of equality.

The primary goal of an investigation is to clear the case and bring justice to the victim. It is understandable under those circumstances that some officers may be zealous in their efforts. However, when the witnesses, victim, or even offender is an individual with a disability, the goal of police investigation must slightly shift toward conducting the investigation while preserving the welfare and/or well-being of the person with a disability. It is necessary to consider the possibility that an offender will not be caught or that the witness may not be able to testify, and therefore, the validity of law enforcement efforts may be called into question. It may help here to remember that offenders who do not get caught often offend again, so while the investigative efforts may not help in the instant case, they may prove invaluable in a future effort, and the act of simply pursuing justice does contribute to the restoration of the victim. With that in mind, this chapter will provide specific guidance and suggestions on how to best interview individuals with specific disabling conditions.

> A blind quadriplegic was assaulted three times and pulled from her wheelchair. She was told by police: "Don't bother calling us, [then]"—when she did call for help and said she could not visually describe her attacker.
>
> **(Stark, 2014)**

The aforementioned excerpt confirms the findings of Moriarity (2002:52) that crime victims generally felt that law enforcement officers were not sensitive to their needs and/or did not provide them with critical information in an ongoing investigation, and when the discussion shifted to vulnerable populations, those challenges presented an acute problem since most local communities did not have adequate resources, training, or support services (2002). There are several potential reasons for this failure, including the rigidity of the court system, or how the Court upholds and protects the rights of the accused, or the unique challenges posed to law enforcement when dealing with a crime that involves a person with a disability. Regardless of the reason(s), all members of society now have the right to live a safe and ordered existence, and that requires equal access to the justice system.

The question may be asked *why*? Or what is to be gained by interviewing persons for whom the legal system places questionable merit? The answer to that question is twofold: one is the more obvious, which is because they have been victims or witnesses of a crime and, as such, are entitled to seek justice in whatever capacity they can, and the second is that as the one harmed, they are often in the best position to provide useful and valuable information to an investigation. The challenge for the law enforcement community is to recognize that traditional methods of expression must be expanded to reflect the abilities of the interviewee, which may mean placing equal emphasis on body shifts, gazes, grimaces, utterances, etc., as are typically placed on words themselves. The methods employed to effectuate a useful and productive interview will vary according to the type of disability, but there are some universal approaches that can be implemented, which include the following:

- *Use "person-first" language that recognizes the person before the disability.* Historically, people with disabilities have been regarded as "individuals to be pitied, feared, or ignored... or as charity cases who must depend upon others" (arc. org). The "person-first" movement seeks to shift language away from the disability itself (disempowering) and focus instead on the person (empowering), thereby reversing the damaging labels that result in marginalization of the disabled community. This is important because labels have been used to define the value and potential of people (dmh.mo.gov), and given the "disability negative" (Baladerian, 1991) climate in society, it is not uncommon for one to make assumptions about an individual and their abilities upon simply hearing of a disability.

  Therefore, recognition of the disability *may* be important in preparing for accommodations *during* the interview, but if the disability is not germane to the investigation, do not mention it.

- *Do not pretend that you understand.* Regardless of the disability, individuals who have been criminally victimized or find themselves suddenly involved in the criminal justice system have lost control of their life for a period of time. They are experiencing greater than average levels of anxiety and confusion. This may very likely increase their difficulties in communication or thought organization—even absent a disabling condition. Therefore, if you do not fully understand what the victim/witness is attempting to say (either verbally or conceptually), do not hesitate to ask the victim to repeat himself or herself. It is also advisable to slowly read back what you have written to the victim after you have completed your notes. Some victims may be uncomfortable correcting an investigator (given the authoritarian role) and therefore may not offer verbal correction, so pay careful attention to body language as an indicator that the interpretation of responses is accurate.

- *The interview will require additional time and patience.* This may be due to several factors, including but not limited to discomfort with the language, difficulty speaking, use of assistive technology or interpreter, question order or complexity, and memory challenges. These issues will be discussed in greater detail later, but the important element at this point is to allot sufficient time to acquire the necessary information. If the interviewer fails to account for time, the resultant rush will produce invalid information that will ultimately delay or impede the investigation.
- *Be mindful that comorbid conditions can, and often do, exist.* Comorbidity refers to the presence of more than one distinct but unrelated condition in an individual. For example, a patient presenting with anxiety and schizophrenia would not be considered to have comorbid conditions since those diagnoses exist along the same continuum (Valderas et al., 2009). However, someone with an intellectual disability (ID) who begins showing evidence of posttraumatic stress disorder (PTSD) would be someone for whom a comorbid diagnosis is valid. The initial disabling condition often creates a situation wherein the victim may not fully disclose or even be aware of the existence of a comorbid condition. If a second condition should present itself during the investigation (i.e., emergence of anxiety, panic, fear), the investigator should be prepared for it to delay or slow down the interview.
- *Validate the interviewee.* Part of having a disabling condition is that one's personhood is often affected by the stigma and attitudes surrounding disabilities. The detective should look at and speak directly to the person being interviewed—even (and especially) if they have an interpreter or family member present. Do not assume that they do not wish to speak for themselves, wait until they request the intervention or support from the family member or interpreter.

Visible Disabilities

Visible disabilities are those conditions that are often immediately apparent upon observation. They include physical conditions that typically require assistive devices, such as a wheelchair, cane, and walker, and as such convey to a casual observer that a disabling condition exists. Be mindful that just as you observed an assistive device and surmised a disabling condition, an offender likely did the same. This realization is also known to the victim/witness and may play a role in how they choose to participate or answer the questions. Also, while a known physical condition does not dictate the existence of a mental condition, special accommodations (e.g., additional time and carefully worded questions) should also be considered prior to the interview. These are consistent with ensuring the individual's perceptions of safety while returning some level of control and independence to them in their daily living activities. Some considerations include the following:

- Do you know how the victim will arrive at the interview location?
  - If they rely upon public transportation, is the interview location easily accessed by the transportation routes?
  - If they rely upon private transportation services, make sure to plan the interview at least 12 h in advance, so that they can make necessary arrangements.

- If they have a vehicle, are there sufficient *accessible* parking spaces available at the interview location?
  - Is there a ramp or a step-free entrance? If not, have you made arrangements for an alternative location?
  - Are there accessible restrooms at the interview location?
  - Is the intended interview room accessible? If located in a precinct house, does it ensure privacy? Confidentiality? (aaidd.org)
  - Ideally, the interview location should have an elevator, but in a retrofitted building, if there is a chair lift, make sure that someone who is trained in how to use the equipment is present at the time of the interview (and will remain throughout the interview time!).
- Wheelchair users
  - A wheelchair is part of a person's personal space; therefore, leaning or hanging on it is inappropriate.
  - It is considered rude to push someone who does not ask for help.
  - If a lengthy conversation is expected, make arrangements to sit at eye level—perhaps at a table.
- Canes/walkers
  - A cane or a walker could convey a chronic condition or a challenge to mobility. It can also designate a visual impairment that occurs along a continuum from blurred vision to total blindness. One simply cannot make assumptions as to what the nature of the condition is simply from the existence of the mobility aid.
  - If the cane or walker is used as a mobility aid, then see the section earlier regarding accommodations at the interview location.
- Vision impairment
  - If the cane or walker is used due to visual impairment, then detectives should consider the following:
    - Make sure that all lighting in the room works—replace any blown light bulbs or bring in additional lighting to enhance the room's illumination.
    - Make sure to position yourself directly in front of the victim. Visual impairments have different characteristics, such as limited to no peripheral vision.
    - Avoid changing position or location during the interview and do not make sudden movements.
    - Clearly identify yourself and any other person in the room. It is also a good idea to indicate where the other persons are sitting/standing and ask if the victim/witness wants them to move to another location. Part of the identification of the individuals should include what their role in the investigation is and why they are present in the room.

Invisible Disabilities

An invisible disability refers to any condition that limits daily activities but may not necessarily be immediately identified by casual observation. This type of disability can often be associated with *malingering* in as much as the diagnosis or presence of a disability can be called into question. (NB: This is more likely when the witness is also a potential offender.) It is important to remember that from an investigator's standpoint it is less important whether or not the individual is faking and more important to gather details related to the offense. Given the nature of these disabilities, investigators may need to adjust quickly to unexpected situations. For example, it is likely that they will know ahead of time that the interview process will require an interpreter if the individual is d/Deaf, but the tone of the interview may differ depending upon whether the individual is deaf or Deaf.

Deafness

The distinction is significant in that Deaf (capital D) identifies individuals who are medically incapable of hearing (often prelingually) and are active participants in the Deaf subculture; they are proud of their deafness, rely mainly on American Sign Language (ASL) to communicate, and employ no medical aids to facilitate hearing. Persons who identify as deaf (lowercase d) may also be medically incapable of hearing but may choose to attempt to mitigate or cure their deafness through medical innovations, do not rely solely on ASL to communicate, and are often shunned by the Deaf community (Barrow, 2007). An investigator's awareness of this key difference signals to the individual an awareness of and sensitivity to their cultural practices and a comfort that the best interpreter for them will be secured, i.e., licensed interpreter, CODA, etc.

Another challenge for law enforcement is that depending upon the urgency of the situation, officers/investigators tend to rely heavily upon family members to act as interpreters. This can present several unforeseen challenges to the investigation. The first risk is that the family member may be the offender, and therefore, relying upon them to gather information may result in a poor investigation and place the victim at greater risk for harm. The other significant risk is that unwittingly, by relying upon family members to interpret for the victim, officers/investigators may actually be creating secondary victims if they are unaware or unprepared for what they may learn during the course of interpreting.

Finally, depending upon the nature of the first encounter, officers/investigators need to be aware that the individual may simply not be able to hear the commands being issued to them. In the current climate of policing and the very real threats facing law enforcement, an individual's appearance to be ignoring commands may be construed as disrespect, as illustrated in the following:

> Pearl Pearson, a 64-year-old deaf and diabetic man, was brutally assaulted by police during a routine traffic stop. When an officer shouted instructions, he attempted to show the patrolman that he was deaf. That's when the officer punched him in the face and pulled him from his car. According to Pearson, police beat him for not following verbal orders.
>
> **(Lohr, 2014)**

This scenario demonstrates why it is important for officers to take a moment to determine what the reality of the situation might be before taking definitive action. The U.S. Department of Justice (2006) recommends implementing these practical practices whenever possible in dealing with the d/Deaf community:

- Before speaking, *get the person's attention* with a wave of the hand or a gentle tap on the shoulder. If indoors, stomping your foot (creates vibration) or turning a light on and off can signal a desire to communicate. Do not assume that they are aware that you are speaking to them simply because you are present. They may be trying to communicate with someone else at the same time.

- *Face the person* and do not turn away while speaking. In the Deaf culture, it is rude to turn away from them when speaking. This presents a significant challenge for law enforcement since they are often trying to observe multiple situational factors, collect testimony, and manage a crime scene simultaneously.
- Try to *converse in a well-lit area.* Remember, d/Deaf individuals place equal emphasis on body language and facial expression to interpret and communicate.
- *Do not cover your mouth or chew gum.* Some d/Deaf individuals supplement their understanding with lip reading. While this is generally listed at 40% effective, it is still a coping mechanism that is often employed. Covering your mouth, chewing gum, and even a mustache can limit or impede communication.
- If a person is wearing a hearing aid, do not assume he or she can hear you well. Hearing aids are simply tools—they are not intended to cure deafness. Therefore, their effectiveness might be minimal.
- *Minimize background noise* and other distractions whenever possible. This is especially true if hearing aids are used.
- When you are communicating orally, *speak slowly and distinctly.* This may include using shorter sentences and simple words. Use facial expressions to reinforce what you are saying.
- *Use visual aids* whenever possible such as pointing to printed information on a citation or other document.
- When communicating in writing, keep in mind that some individuals who use sign language may lack good English reading and writing skills. This is not because they are not intelligent, but rather because ASL syntax differs from spoken English and many words do not have corresponding symbols in ASL.
- If someone with a hearing disability cannot understand you, write a note to ask them what communication aids or services are needed. Do not assume that just because you have provided an interpreter, the communication will be easy. Different regions have different dialects, use different slang, and perhaps, different styles. While ASL is the more familiar language, many non-formally trained speak Signed Exact English (SEE), which is more consistent with English syntax.
- If a sign language interpreter is requested, be sure to ask which language the person uses. ASL and SEE are the most common.
- When you are interviewing a witness or a suspect or engaging in any complex conversation with a person whose primary language is sign language, a qualified interpreter is usually needed to ensure effective communication. Make sure that any unfamiliar words, titles, or locations are finger-spelled for the witness.
- When using an interpreter, *look and speak directly at the person who is d/Deaf* and not the interpreter. This represents a cultural courtesy.
- *Talk at your normal rate or slightly slower* if you normally speak fast, and use short sentences and simple words. Remember, lip reading is only 40% effective, and if an interpreter is being used, they have to be able to keep up. Speaking too slow implies that you think the person is not smart.
- Only one person should speak at a time—a cultural courtesy.

Cognitive Impairment

Cognitive impairment is defined as a decline in at least one of the following domains: short-term memory, attention, orientation, judgment and problem-solving skills, and visuo-spatial skills (Carr et al., 2006). While this often translates into resistance on the part of investigative staff to rely upon these individuals as witnesses, individuals with cognitive disabilities can have excellent recall of traumatic or special events in their lives (OVC, 2011:7). It is important for the investigator to accept that a cognitive disability is *not* related to the ability to differentiate between a truth and a lie, which is a developmental milestone often achieved in childhood, and it is *not* related to the reliability of one's memory—key events and specifics are often able to be recalled much better than routine activities or unimportant details (OVC, 2011:9).

The assumption that an individual with cognitive impairment may not make a good witness may be due to the challenges they face in articulating what happened or in the amount of time necessary for them to express themselves. These are challenges that can be overcome with preparation and patience *on the part of the investigator*. It is important to note that while the mode of communication used by the victim/witness is new to the investigator, it is not new to the victim or witness. Therefore, the responsibility to learn how to effectively exchange information falls to the investigator in this case. So how does one go about accessing their information and using it successfully in a prosecution?

Investigators need to allot sufficient time to the interview process given the challenges of communication (not recall) for the victim/witness. Just as in mainstream culture, if an individual senses impatience or displeasure on the part of the investigator, they will likely become more anxious, which will only lengthen the process and create an uncomfortable environment for both parties. Remember, as a law enforcement representative, the detective already enjoys a position of power and authority in this exchange. That is stressful for any person, especially so for the person with a disability. It may help to remind them that you are there to facilitate their search for equal justice so that they can orient their thinking to your role as their advocate rather than their adversary.

Again, the responsibility is on the investigator to do some deep preparation for the interview, perhaps internally. The assumption that an investigator "caught" this case and therefore needs to complete the investigation may not be the best approach when dealing with persons with disabilities. Reliance on "person-first" language as discussed earlier will help to remind the investigator that the person with a disability is first and foremost a person—not a disability. If the lead investigator is unable or unwilling to see past the disability itself, the case should be reassigned.

The Department of Justice, Office for Victims of Crime (2011) recommends using all sources available to effectuate the best interview conditions (calm and organized environment) for the victim/witness as possible. They suggest referring to any public records (caseworker, advocate notes, etc.), but also asking family members or care providers for recommendations on how to best communicate with the individual being interviewed. As noted earlier, use caution when using people close to the victim/witness because of the risks of either creating a secondary victim or inadvertently interviewing the perpetrator. Additionally, the best interviews are generated when there is mutual trust that can be achieved if the victim/witness feels validated in their role and potential contribution to the case. Simply asking the victim/witness how they wish to be questioned (e.g., paper, orally, videotape) is the most effective way of empowering the victim/witness and building trust with the investigative process.

Where the interview is to take place should be a major consideration for the investigator. The location should be a place that is familiar to the victim/witness but that offers a place for confidential communication (perhaps a library with a conference room). If the decision is to have the interview in the police department, the location of the interview should *not* be an interrogation room with stark walls and recording equipment, but rather in a comfortable conference room where the victim/witness does not feel discomfort. Decisions regarding the location of the offense should be made on a case-by-case basis. If a *diorama* of the crime scene is possible, it may help the victim/witness to visualize the space and answer questions more effectively without placing them at risk of emotional harm. In rare cases, however, victims/witnesses may need to return to the crime scene to solidify memory recall or to effectively explain what happened. In these circumstances, all possible steps should be taken to ensure the safety and well-being of the victim/witness.

Intellectual Disability

Intellectual disability (ID) represents a distinction for persons with a below-average cognitive ability who manifest three specific characteristics:

1. Intelligence quotient (IQ) is below 70.
2. Significant limitations in adaptive behaviors (the ability to adapt and carry on everyday life activities such as self-care, socializing, communicating).
3. The onset of the disability occurs before age 18 (www.thearc.org).

Intelligence refers to general mental capability and involves the ability to reason, plan, solve problems, think abstractly, comprehend complex ideas, learn quickly, and learn from experience. Studies show that somewhere between 1% and 3% of Americans have intellectual disabilities. There are many causes of intellectual disabilities, including physical, genetic, and/or social. The most common syndromes associated with intellectual disabilities are autism, Down syndrome, fragile X syndrome, and fetal alcohol spectrum disorder (FASD).

Perhaps one of the greatest challenges facing law enforcement is the increasing encounters with persons with intellectual disabilities and the resultant determination of their mental capacity as a witness. It is important at this juncture to note that one's ability to testify (i.e., competency requirements) is separate from questions of reliability or credibility. Specifically, one's mental capacity is to be determined by a trial judge, whereas one's reliability or credibility is determined by a jury in terms of how much weight they attach to the testimonial evidence (Gudjonsson and Joyce, 2011). This does not remove the burden carried by law enforcement when they must interview a person with ID, but perhaps it will help to focus on what the goal actually is (or should be), which is to extend equal justice to all persons.

An ID (previously referred to as mental retardation) occurs along a continuum from mild to severe. Specific symptoms include (but are not limited to)

- Lack of or slow development of motor skills, language skills, and self-help skills, especially when compared to peers
- Failure to grow intellectually or continued infant-like behavior
- Lack of curiosity
- Problems keeping up in school
- Failure to adapt (adjust to new situations)
- Difficulty understanding and following social rules (www.nlm.nih.gov)

Autism

Autism or *autism spectrum disorder* (ASD) is presented here as a separate section because when dealing with a person along the autistic spectrum, investigators need to be aware of very specific characteristics. While it is a neurologically based developmental disability, it is not necessarily a cognitive impairment or mental illness. It does, however, significantly impair one's ability to communicate and to interact in a socially appropriate manner (www. asmonline.org). It is not uncommon for people to mistake persons with autism with someone under the influence of drugs or alcohol, or with someone who is acting "suspiciously," or with someone who is intentionally being evasive or deceitful. As a result, individuals with autism are *seven times more likely* to come into contact with law enforcement (www.asmonline.org).

While here is no specific "type" for identifying someone who has autism, statistics suggest that the disorder is found in males five times more than females, and there are some common characteristics found in the adult population. Those characteristics can be grouped into three separate categories: social communication, social understanding, and flexibility of thought (www.nami.org). A more specific listing of symptoms is presented in the following:

Social communication

- Difficulty understanding gestures, body language, and facial expressions
- Unaware of what is socially appropriate and have difficulty choosing topics to talk about
- May not be socially motivated because they find communication difficult
- May not have many friends and may choose not to socialize very much

Social understanding

- Difficulty in group situations
- Finding small talk and chatting very difficult
- Problems understanding double meanings
- Not choosing appropriate topic to talk about
- Talking about people say very literally

Flexibility of thought

- An obsession with rigid routines and severe distress if routines are disrupted
- Problems making plans for the future and having difficulties organizing your life
- Problems with sequencing tasks

When conducting an investigation, detectives must be aware of these specific behavioral and cognitive characteristics since they will dictate the nature and success of the investigation. Those who are close to persons with autism report that they often fear for the safety of their loved ones when/if they would encounter the criminal justice system. Unlike persons with cognitive impairment, persons with autism tend to recoil from contact and demonstrate behaviors consistent with someone who is attempting to evade or deceive law enforcement. Investigators must be very cautious when approaching and engaging a person with autism, and they must remember that the individual, if alone, will react in a manner consistent with their disability. For example, persons with autism do not like physical contact; in fact, they may hate it. Therefore, if an investigator attempts to handcuff or detain an individual, the situation can escalate quickly into a physical confrontation. The problem is when the individual is reacting from an instinctive, conditioned response, and the investigators are responding from an assumption of evasion or combat. Given the invisible nature of autism, the true motivations of the individual may not be immediately clear.

> Ernest, 57 years old, had autism and lived with his family in their neighborhood. When police saw him walking down the street with a toy rifle they started shouting at him to put down the 'weapon.' Ernest was scared and confused by the police officers and hesitated just long enough for those police officers to shoot and kill him.
>
> http://www.disabled-world.com/editorials/cops.php

Parents of persons with autism posed the question "What is the one thing you would like your local police officers to know about your ASD loved one?" and received several responses from family members/friends that should be considered whenever investigators need to interview persons with autism (www.facebook.com). Some of the main suggestions include the following:

- *"Take their time when they approach. Slow is best. Some don't like loud noises so maybe turn radio down when approaching as we'll."* (April 28, 2014)
  This request is consistent with the recognition that persons with ASD are very sensitive to loud noises, bright lights, and strong smells. Any of these factors can quickly increase their comfort level and result in agitated behaviors.
- *"That questions make him very nervous."* (April 28, 2014)
  Persons with ASD typically have processing delays and, as a result, need extra time to respond to questions or instructions. If they are unprepared for the questions or the number of questions, they may become anxious.
- *"That my boys stims come in the form of sudden (and loud) movement... please keep your weapon holstered so you don't react reflexively."* (April 28, 2014)
  This is a consistent theme in focus groups with parents of children with ASD. They fear that law enforcement will react to *stimming* behaviors (self-stimulating behaviors such as rocking back and forth, flicking fingers) and take action without realizing that the behaviors are a way for individual with ASD to calm their system down internally. The result could be catastrophic and anecdotal reports support these concerns.
- *"...If you add an increased volume, impatience tone or confrontational tone often it shuts down our kiddos, they freeze in fear and often flips the switch to put them in a flight or fight response..."* (April 28, 2014)

Some individuals on the ASD are nonverbal and use an alternative method of communication or instinctive behaviors to exit unpleasant situations.

- *"Don't touch. Talk to him."* (April 28, 2014)

  Individuals along the ASD often dislike being touched, especially if they are touched suddenly and without warning.

- *"Questioning an officer about why a request is made isn't meant as questioning his or her authority. Many people on the autism spectrum, especially those with high functioning autism, have an almost obsessive need to know the why of a request when they are anxious or immersed in an unfamiliar situation."* (April 28, 2014)

  Persons who are high functioning may appear to be cognitively functioning, due to their extensive vocabulary, language skills, and intelligence. In reality, they are functioning at a much lower social and developmental level than their peers and need a greater amount of information to adequately process information.

- *"He will go for your weapon."* (April 28, 2014)

  Individuals with ASD do not understand many unwritten social rules, such as maintaining appropriate body spacing, and their behaviors are often misinterpreted as rude or inappropriate.

- *"Don't throw too many questions at him at once—you'd get him confused and likely to admit to every crime in country. Listen to what he's saying and how he says it—he might be explaining things not admitting to anything or he might not see why what he did was wrong if it not explained to him."* (April 28, 2014)

  Individuals with ASD tend to interpret information very literally and may not fully understand instructions unless they are concise and clear.

Traumatic Brain Injury

Traumatic brain injury (TBI) is generally defined as "a disruption of normal brain function that occurs when the skull is struck, suddenly thrust out of position, penetrated or struck by blast pressure waves" (CDC, 2009). If the injury results in long-term or permanent damage, the individual is often diagnosed with "acquired brain injury" that signifies an "insult to the brain that has occurred after birth, for example, TBI, stroke, anoxia." The severity of such an injury may range from "mild," with a brief change in mental status or consciousness, to "severe," with an extended period of unconsciousness or amnesia after the injury (Spearman, 2007). Further, a related but different diagnosis has emerged to better identify returning veterans who have suffered significant brain injury and have experienced altered behavior and/or perceptions as a result—"blast injury."

Implications for law enforcement are significant if the injury is classified as "closed head" because there are no obvious external signs of injury. This is often the case in motor vehicle accidents, child abuse situations, or returning veterans. The Centers for Disease Control and Prevention (CDC) reports that every year 1.7 million people sustain a TBI with 80,000 people experiencing long-term disability as a result (Faul et al., 2010).

With figures such as these, law enforcement and investigative personnel have an obligation to research and adapt their practices. When an investigation is ongoing, it places a greater obligation on those representatives who are seeking the truth and/or justice to be aware of and respond to the needs and rights of those may be disabled, especially since community personnel and resources are generally not designed to address their unique needs. Sadly, members of the disabled community face a roughly 4–10 times greater risk than the general population for physical or sexual (assault http://www.CDC.org).

An immediate challenge for law enforcement or investigators is to determine whether or not they are dealing with an individual with a TBI or not. The following chart illustrates symptomologic similarities between TBIs and alcohol or drug consumption, and it should be further noted that Substance Abuse and Mental Health Services Administration (SAMHSA) has recently reported a very high correlation between substance abuse and TBI, which increases the ability of the officer to accurately identify the best course of action to employ.

TBI (www.samhsa.gov)	Drunk (www.rightdiagnosis.com)	High (www.phoenixhouse.org)
Physical symptoms		
Dizziness, light-headedness, or vertigo; gait disorders	Uncoordinated movements	Slowed or staggering walk; poor physical coordination
Sensory impairments (blurred vision, light sensitivity, ringing in ears, noxious smells/taste)		
Spasticity/tremors	*Only in withdrawal*	Tremors or shakes of hands, feet, or head
Speech	Slurred or incoherent speech	
Fatigue/lethargy or weakness	Progressive lethargy, low energy	Unusual laziness
Seizures	*Only in withdrawal*	
Behavioral/emotional symptoms		
Severe depression		
Social skills problems		Paranoia
Mood swings (anxiety)	Mood changes	Moodiness, irritability, or nervousness
Problems with emotional control		Sudden oversensitivity, temper tantrums, or resentful behavior
Inappropriate behavior(s)	Uninhibited behavior	
Inability to inhibit remarks		
Inability to recognize social cues	Poor judgment, loud talking, and inappropriate laughter	Excessive talkativeness
Reduced frustration tolerance	Flare-ups, irritability, and defensiveness	

The responsibility to quickly and accurately diagnose the cause of the immediate behavior places an unfair burden upon the investigator as it may not be immediately clear what condition they are dealing with, and most law enforcement personnel do not have the necessary medical training (or time) to differentiate between the possible causes of a specific behavior. This is not to say that they are not trained, simply that the majority of their training is geared toward managing the immediate situation, not diagnosing or treating chronic medical conditions. In this circumstance, it may be necessary to ask close friends or family members whether or not the individual suffers from a chronic condition. Often times, if the individual has a TBI, they will disclose that during the initial contact; but it is certainly not inappropriate to ask the individual as long as they understand that the information is needed to best manage the situation. However, if the behavior manifested presents a risk to either the individual or the investigating officer, then the detective may need to call upon additional training methods to properly control and/or complete the interview.

Recommendations for interviewing individuals with traumatic brain injuries are similar to those listed earlier and include the following:

- Since attention deficit is a consistent comorbid condition with TBI, it is best to *interview the individual in a place with little to no environmental distractions*, to allow for extra time for the individual to process and respond to the question, and even ask them to repeat the question back to you or write it down so that you know they understood the content of the inquiry.
- Another consistent challenge is the short-term memory deficits that accompany TBI. In this circumstance, it is best to *explain each of the separate elements of the question*, provide specific examples of what you are looking for (better to have these prepared and not related to the incident at hand), or ask the individual for examples of what they think you are asking. It is also helpful if you provide support and encouragement early in the interview for the individual to ask for clarification if they need it.
- Because delayed speech and physical movement exist as a possibility, *allot additional time* to the interview and realize that failure to immediately respond to even "simple" commands should not be considered defiance or challenges to authority. Doing so can erode the relationship and impede the investigation.
- Individuals with TBI can become suddenly irritable or angry. *If a line of questioning is creating agitation, stop and redirect.* Return to that later using a different approach or format. Reassure the individual that you are seeking to help them achieve justice and offer positive reinforcement when they are able to regain control, that is, "This is good; we are working together again. Thank you for staying with me on this."
- Impulsive or inappropriate actions may take place during the interview. If pointing out that you find these behaviors counterproductive to your efforts is unsuccessful, it may be best to end the interview for a period of time and return to it later. It is important to remember that biases not become a part of this interaction. For persons with TBI, such behaviors are not controllable, so even if they might appear to have contributed to the criminal incident, no one deserves to be victimized (http://www.tbiwashington.org).

Mental Illness

Mental illness is defined as a mental, behavioral, or emotional disorder, exclusive of developmental or substance use, that has existed long enough to meet the diagnostic criteria outlined in the Diagnostic and Statistical Manual of Mental Disorders (DSM). The disorders can range from mild to severe and include conditions such as obsessive–compulsive disorder (OCD), PTSD, bipolar disorder, depression, and/or schizophrenia.

The National Institute of Mental Health (NIMH) reports that approximately 61.5 million Americans (one in four adults) experience mental illness in a given year, with approximately 5 million of them suffering from severe mental illness (SMI), such as bipolar disorder and schizophrenia. It is relatively undisputed that given these figures, police officers across the United States are finding themselves playing a dual role of law enforcers and psychiatric social workers. County jails and state prisons have become de facto mental institutions since the deinstitutionalization of the 1970s and the subsequent withdrawal of mental health spending that has occurred through the 1990s (Santos and Goode, 2014). But what is interesting is that most of the literature that exists on this topic exists from the perspective of the person with mental illness as a suspect, not as a potential victim or witness. Therefore, very few of the resources address the very specific needs of law enforcement and investigators regarding *how* to interview persons with mental illness with respect to their role as a witness versus an offender.

However, this appears to be changing with new awareness of the risk of victimization that faces persons with mental illness. In 2005, Israel passed new legislation aimed directly at extending equal justice to all members of society. The rationale included a legal understanding that "even if the witness's perception is inadequate, it does not mean that the admissibility of his or her testimony should be rejected" (Melamed, 2008). Melamed (2008) provides an example of a patient with mental illness possessing delusions of grandeur, leaving the hospital, walking to a bus stop, standing in line, and paying the driver. His ability to behave in such a way does not conflict with his belief that he is the Messiah. This illustrates that two worlds (the sick and the healthy) can coexist, and while it may be difficult to know which world is real, most patients live comfortably in that division. Using this example, it becomes the job of the court to conduct internal testing for logic, organization, and common sense, as well as to seek, even insist, upon external support for the testimony. According to Melamed, the movement to integrate individuals with mental illness into the community equates their status to that of the general public and so foists upon society the obligation of administering equal justice.

Since the focus of this chapter is to empower investigators in the process of interviewing vulnerable persons, the only noncrisis advice discovered was presented in Spring (2000) by the SAMHSA and includes the following:

- *Learn and use consumer's name.* This may de-escalate a situation and validate the individual's identity.
- *Be polite* when making statements or requests. As a member of the disabled community, individuals are accustomed to being disregarded or ignored. Being polite invites them into a dialogue and encourages them to cooperate.
- *Use a nonthreatening stance* and keep a leg's length between you. Body language is an important tool of law enforcement, but since some individuals with mental illness exist in a survival mode, aggressive stances can be quickly misinterpreted. However, do not mistake an agreeable demeanor for safety; impulsive and sudden behaviors/movements are consistent with mental illness.
- Keep your hands in sight and your palms up.
- Keep the tone of your *voice low and calm.*
- Avoid making promises you can't keep.
- *Do not agree or disagree with delusions.* Best to not acknowledge any reference to delusions. Look down or away if the individual attempts to involve you in their hallucination.
- Be patient.
- *Do not make threats or argue.* Doing so will alienate your witness and delay the interview.
- *Avoid continuous eye contact.* This is seen as aggressive and can result in agitation.

Posttraumatic Stress Disorder

> Icarus Randolph, 26, was shot and killed by police at about 1:30 p.m. after he went after an officer with a silver knife. The officer then shot Randolph at least three times in the chest, and the man was later pronounced dead. Various family members and neighbors told police that Randolph was a U.S. Marine combat veteran of the Iraq War and had been suffering from Post Traumatic Stress Disorder. Other preliminary information suggests that Randolph's violent behavior could have been triggered, or compounded by, firework blasts.
>
> www.jrn.com/kfdi/news, July 2014

PTSD is a mental condition that may develop "after an individual has been exposed to an event that involved the deaths of others, or an event that threatened death or serious injury to oneself or others and the person's response involved fear, helplessness or horror" (APA, 2000).

According to French (2013), a number of combat veterans suffer PTSD and do not receive treatment. He observed that a common mistake often made by officers is that they may verbally or physically force a veteran into a corner. By leaving him no way out of the encounter, the veteran battles because that is what he was trained to do, and in a moment, it is the only response he knows.

> Stewart's father, Michael Stewart, said his son may have felt threatened when police pounded on his door. He said his son works a night shift at a local Walmart and may have been sleeping when police arrived. The elder Stewart said his son suffers from post-traumatic stress disorder, anxiety and depression and may have been self-medicating with small amounts of pot. He said he believes his son may have been growing the weed himself.
>
> www.cbsnews.com, January 2012

One way to circumvent this challenge is to "set the stage" for an interview. A trauma survivor should be approached with respect, neither gingerly nor casually. It is not always an option for officers to control the environment in which they may encounter a person with PTSD; this is more likely when the interview takes place in a scheduled format. Nonetheless, whenever possible, every effort should be taken to accommodate the needs of the interviewee. Remember, depending upon the nature and timing of the trauma, the person may be in a daze, may be numb, may be easily startled, may be hypervigilant, or may be confused. Generally though, they can identify the setting that will suit them best, which may include a companion, an open door, or several breaks for self-composure (Ochberg, n.d.).

If the interviewee is someone who has suffered a non-combat-related trauma, the officer must remember that flashbacks are possible. This means that the timing of the interview may not affect whether or not the person has recovered from the immediate after effects. If you are asking questions regarding the traumatic event, their reaction may be consistent with a trauma that just occurred.

If the interviewee suffered a combat-related trauma, that can introduce greater tension between the officer and the veteran because of the similarities of their life experiences. Both populations believe that outsiders do not understand them, they are people of great honor and integrity, they like to be with other officers/veterans, and they will die for their convictions (French, 2013). French suggests using those similarities during an investigation and working toward achieving a level of trust with the veteran to facilitate an optimal resolution. It is an unfortunate reality that most crisis encounters involving veterans with PTSD end in the death of the suspect. Trust can often be achieved by asking very simple questions focused on recognizing their service to the country and stressing the camaraderie with law enforcement. Such questions include the following:

1. How long were you in the military?
2. Are you still on active duty?
3. What was your military specialty?
4. Were you ever deployed overseas?
5. How long have you been home?

Remember, the goal is to keep the questions simple and straightforward so that they are most likely to elicit a response. Once a dialogue has been established, it may be appropriate to move on to specific questions about the incident. Anecdotally, many veterans advise against asking questions that may remind the suspect about their combat experience as it is likely to increase the level of emotional instability and agitation.

Although officers are being urged to employ a more social order approach to managing suspects with PTSD and/or blast injury, the reality is that often times those encounters involve immediate crisis intervention and require extreme action to ensure the safety of the public. Veterans are often armed, as that is how they have been trained—and a further risk to law enforcement and the general public is that they have been trained to use those weapons to protect themselves. Many veteran organizations urge the law enforcement community to use nonlethal methods to de-escalate an escalating situation. Investigative officers should be aware of any local programs or veteran courts and use their resources. Given the lack of information specifically focused on interviewing persons with PTSD and the anticipated increase in this population as veterans return home, close collaboration with available military outreach programs and/or veteran courts is encouraged.

References

American Psychiatric Association. (2000). *Diagnostic and Statistical Manual of Mental Disorders*, 4th edn. Washington, DC: American Psychiatric Association.

Baladerian, N. (1991). Sexual abuse of people with developmental disabilities. *Journal of Sexuality and Disability*, 9(3), 96–101.

Barrow, L. (2007). *Criminal Victimization of the Deaf*. New York: LFB Scholarly Publishing, LLC.

Carr, D.B., Duchek, J.M., Meuser, T.M., and Morris, J.C. (2006). Older adult drivers with cognitive impairment. *American Family Physician*, 73(6), 1029–1034.

CDC Fact Sheet. (n.d.). Victimization of persons with traumatic brain injury or other disabilities. Retrieved from http://www.cdc.gov/traumaticbraininjury/pdf/VictimizationTBI_Fact%20 Sheet4Pros-a.pdf, April 2014.

Centers for disease control and prevention, National Center for injury prevention and control. (2009). *Traumatic Brain Injury*. Retrieved August 2014, from http://www.cdc.gov/traumaticbraininjury.

Faul, M., Xu, L., Wald, M.M., and Coronado, V.G. (2010). *Traumatic Brain Injury in the United States: Emergency Department Visits, Hospitalizations, and Deaths*. Atlanta, GA: Centers for Disease Control and Prevention, National Center for Injury Prevention and Control.

French, G. (2013). Tips for police interaction with combat veterans. Retrieved from http://www. policeone.com/Officer-Safety/articles/6190352-Tips-for-police-interaction-with-combat-veterans/, April, 2014.

Gudjonsson, G.H. and Joyce, T. (2011). Interviewing adults with intellectual disabilities. *Advances in Mental Health and Intellectual Disabilities*, 5, 16–17.

Lohr, D. (January 15, 2014). Police allegedly beat pearl pearson for disobeying orders he could not hear. *Huffington Post*. Retrieved August 2014 from http://www.huffingtonpost.com/2014/01/15/pearl-pearson-police-brutality_n_4603445.html.

Melamed, Y. (2008). Testimony by mentally ill individuals. *Journal of American Academy of Psychiatry Law*, 36(3), 393–397.

Moriarity, L. (2002). *Policing and Victims*. Upper Saddle River, NJ: Prentice Hall.

National Institutes of Health, National Institute of Mental Health. (n.d.). Statistics: Any disorder among adults. Retrieved from http://www.nimh.nih.gov/statistics/1ANYDIS_ADULT.shtml, May, 2014.

Ochberg, F. (n.d.). PTSD 101. Retrieved July 2014 from http://dartcenter.org/content/ptsd-101-2#.U-Q5s1xtfR0.

Santos, F. and Goode, E. (2014). Police confront rising number of mentally ill. *New York Times*, April 2, 2014, p. A1.

Spearman, R.C. (2007). Traumatic brain injury: Causes, impacts and implications for the criminal justice system. Retrieved from www.tbiwashington.org/professionals/documents/tbitrainingforlawenforcementandcorrections.pdf, May 2014.

Stark, J. (July 20, 2014). Disabled crime victims ignored by police. *The Age*. Retrieved July 2014 from http://www.theage.com.au/victoria/disabled-crime-victims-ignored-by-police-20140718-zujxr.html#ixzz39ZMNLiHJ.

U.S. Department of Justice, Civil Rights Division. (2006). Communicating with people who are deaf or hard of hearing—ADA guide for law enforcement officers. Retrieved from http://www.ada.gov/lawenfcomm.htm, May 2014.

Valderas, J.M., Starfield, B., Sibbald, B., Salisbury, C., and Roland, M. (2009). Defining comorbidity: Implication for understanding health and health services. *Annals of Family Medicine*, 7(4), 357–363.

Fourth Amendment

ROBERT WINTERS

19

Contents

Chapter Outline	315
Introduction	316
Historical Background of the Fourth Amendment	316
Legal Overview of the Fourth Amendment	317
Fourth Amendment Legal Terms	319
Evolution of Constitutional Law	320
Exclusionary Rule and the Warrant Requirement	321
Search Incident to a Lawful Arrest	323
Exigent Circumstances	323
Emergency Entry	324
Searches at or near the Border	324
Motor Vehicle Searches	324
Vessel Searches	325
Consent Search	325
Probable Cause and Reasonable Suspicion	325
Reasonable Expectation of Privacy	328
Fourth Amendment and the Home	328
Fourth Amendment and Motor Vehicles	329
Eavesdropping and Surveillance	331
Technology and the Fourth Amendment	331
Conclusion	333
References	333

Chapter Outline

Introduction
Historical Background of the Fourth Amendment Legal Overview of the Fourth Amendment Legal Terms
The Evolution of Constitutional Law
The Exclusionary Rule and the Warrant Requirement Probable Cause and Reasonable Suspicion
The Reasonable Expectation of Privacy The Fourth Amendment and the Home
The Fourth Amendment and Motor Vehicles Eavesdropping and Surveillance
Technology and the Fourth Amendment Conclusion
End Notes

Introduction

For nearly a century, the courts have worked to balance the interests of the individual and his constitutional guarantees with the need for effective law enforcement. That balance has swayed a little more in one direction or the other over the years as social and political circumstances changed, and the only guarantee is that it will continue to change and evolve in the coming years. Fully understanding what is and is not permissible for law enforcement under the Fourth Amendment means following the opinions constantly emerging from state and federal court systems and the U.S. Supreme Court. Here, we will survey the legal landscape as it currently stands, understanding that this is a law enforcement officer's overview, not the detailed study of the attorney.

Historical Background of the Fourth Amendment

The Fourth Amendment has the majority of its roots in English common law generally and in the reactions against certain acts that occurred in the colonies in the years leading up to the revolution specifically. However, the principle that an individual and his home enjoyed a certain inviolability dates back much further: under the Roman law, for example, a theft victim was not permitted to search the home of a suspect without specifically describing what items he would be seeking, and multiple witnesses had to be on hand during the search.[1]

Two major cases in England established the common law foundation for this principle. The first was *Semayne's case* in 1604. As a result of a dispute over inherited property, the sheriff of London entered the home of Richard Gresham by breaking down the doors. Although the sheriff had a valid writ, Gresham sued. Sir Edward Coke, the attorney general of England, ruled that "In all cases when the King is party, the sheriff may break the party's house, either to arrest him, or to do other execution of the King's process, if otherwise he cannot enter. But before he breaks it, he ought to signify the cause of his coming, and to make request to open doors…," thereby creating the "knock-and-announce rule." This ruling also became the source of a phrase most will recognize when Coke wrote that "the house of every one is to him as his castle and fortress, as well for his defense against injury and violence as for his repose."[2]

The second case arose in 1762. John Wilkes had been publishing various writings opposing King George III, his state officers, and various government policies. Although Wilkes himself sued in a closely related case, *Wilkes v. Wood*, 19 Howell's State Trials 1153 (C.P. 1763), the better known case is that of *Entick v. Carrington*, 19 Howell's State Trials 1029 (C.P. 1765), which arose when Nathan Carrington, the king's chief messenger, and three others forcefully entered the home of John Entick, an associate of Wilkes, with the intent to seize any publications or other documents related to Wilkes's writings. Chief Justice Lord Camden ruled the search illegal, in part because Lord Halifax, who had ordered Carrington to conduct the search, had no standing to order the search, but mostly because the warrant authorized the officers to seize *all* of Entick's documents, not just those related to the charges at hand, meaning there was insufficient probable cause. Charles Pratt, Lord Camden, made this statement as part of his ruling:

> By the laws of England, every invasion of private property, be it ever so minute, is a trespass. No man can set his foot upon my ground without my license, but he is liable to an action,

though the damage be nothing; which is proved by every declaration in trespass, where the defendant is called upon to answer for bruising the grass and even treading upon the soil. If he admits the fact, he is bound to show by way of justification, that some positive law has empowered or excused him. The justification is submitted to the judges, who are to look into the books; and if such a justification can be maintained by the text of the statute law, or by the principles of common law. If no excuse can be found or produced, the silence of the books is an authority against the defendant, and the plaintiff must have judgment.[3]

Over a century later, in *Boyd v. United States*, 116 U.S. 616 (1886), the U.S. Supreme Court referred to *Entick* as "one of the landmarks of English liberty" and "one of the permanent monuments of the British Constitution."[4] So popular were Camden's decisions (he ruled in favor of Wilkes as well as Entick) in the colonies that numerous towns and cities were named after him.[5]

Many of the issues addressed by the Bill of Rights were direct responses to abuses the Americans had suffered under British rule. Until the 1760s, British officials typically enjoyed the right to conduct a search of any person or their home at any time using a general warrant, and the Excise Act of 1754 gave broad search and interrogation rights to British tax collectors, including the widely hated general warrants called writs of assistance. In subsequently drafting the Virginia Declaration of Rights in 1776, George Mason was particular to address general warrants:

That general warrants, whereby any officer or messenger may be commanded to search suspected places without evidence of a fact committed, or to seize any person or persons not named, or whose offense is not particularly described and supported by evidence, are grievous and oppressive and ought not to be granted.[6]

Thomas Jefferson in turn relied heavily on the Virginia Declaration of Rights in drafting the Declaration of Independence.[2]

Legal Overview of the Fourth Amendment

One of the strengths of the U.S. Constitution and a factor that has given it the flexibility to adapt to changing times is the general nature of its statements. Because subsequent judicial review and interpretation have created many of the constitutionally based legal principles followed today, an examination of the legal aspects of the Fourth Amendment invariably must consider the historical context of the text and its origins, blurring the lines between historical and legal overviews.

The Fourth Amendment itself comprises only 54 words:

The right of the people to be secure in their persons, houses, papers, and effects, against unreasonable searches and seizures, shall not be violated; and no Warrants shall issue but upon probable cause, supported by Oath or affirmation, and particularly describing the place to be searched, and the persons or things to be seized.[7]

Taken at face value, those words seem straightforward enough. Historians generally agree that this amendment was intended to affirm the rulings in both *Entick* and *Wilkes*, as well as to reject the outcome of a 1760 case in Boston in which a group of 50 merchants represented by James Otis filed suit to overturn the writs of assistance issued in the name of King George III—and lost. The basic principles were that the government should not conduct a search of private property without substantial justification, that the objects of any such search should not go beyond that justification, and that general warrants should not be used to evade these common law rights.

It is also important, however, to consider what is not contained or implied here. First, the historical events that motivated the drafting of the Fourth Amendment did not involve conventional criminal acts—theft, murder, rape, and so on. Instead, the individuals who suffered as a result could more accurately be classed as dissidents (at least from the government's viewpoint). Second, the government actors in these cases were not police officers—in fact, at that time, no police forces in the modern sense existed in either England or America. There is no historical evidence that the framers of the U.S. Constitution were contemplating conventional criminal acts when they drafted the Fourth Amendment, and furthermore, no way that they could have considered how to regulate the actions of law enforcement when such agencies did not yet exist. Together, these two factors mean care must be taken when using the historical context of the amendment to support or attack its contemporary applications.[5]

The first clause, prohibiting unreasonable searches and seizures, is typically known as the "reasonableness clause." However, a moment's consideration will show that "unreasonable" is not defined, leaving the term open to interpretation. (This process of interpretation will be addressed in section "Evolution of Constitutional Law.") The second clause, the "warrant clause," requires that warrants be issued only upon probable cause and that they specifically define the location of the search and who and/or what is to be seized.

Note that the language does not link warrants and reasonable search and seizure. While it places limits on the issuance of warrants, it does not state that warrants must be obtained before a search or seizure is made. Based strictly on the language of the amendment, police could conduct any search or seizure without a warrant so long as it is reasonable—again, subject to how "reasonable" is defined. It is important to remember that given the historical experiences of the framers, warrants were weapons used by the government to circumvent the common law rights of citizens. Far from requiring the use of warrants to support search or seizure, the framers were concerned with *limiting* the government's use of warrants.[5]

Until the early twentieth century, the Fourth Amendment applied only to the federal government. Law enforcement at the local and state levels was not bound by its terms. Yet there was almost no federal law enforcement in existence at this time; the only agency was the U.S. Marshal Service, and there were no federal prosecutors. It was not until prohibition in the 1920s that a significant federal law criminal justice system began to develop.

In the first half of the twentieth century, there were three major developments involving the Fourth Amendment:

Exclusionary rule: This rule, which prohibits the use of evidence obtained in violation of the Fourth Amendment search and seizure limitation in a criminal trial, arose from the Supreme Court decision in *Weeks v. United States*, 232 U.S. 314 (1914).

Widespread use of warrants: Over time, warrants came to be seen as a means of limiting police power, given that the Fourth Amendment imposed strict limits on them, and thus came to be a generally accepted requirement.

Probable cause: The definition of a "reasonable" search or seizure came to be the existence of probable cause—generally speaking, that police could present good reason to believe that evidence of a given crime would be found in a proposed location to be searched.[5]

Two Supreme Court cases also extended the application of the Fourth Amendment to state and local law enforcement agencies:

Wolf v. Colorado, 338 U.S. 25 (1949): The U.S. Supreme Court (referred to hereafter for brevity's sake as Supreme Court of the United States [SCOTUS]) determined that the due process clause of the Fourteenth Amendment meant that state and local governments are prohibited from infringing individual liberties—including those protected by the Fourth Amendment—just as the federal government is.

Mapp v. Ohio, 367 U.S. 643 (1961): SCOTUS imposed the exclusionary rule on state and local criminal justice systems, putting the same enforcement mechanism behind the Fourth Amendment that already affected federal agencies—the exclusion of illegally obtained evidence from a criminal trial.[5]

The rapid rise in crime rates seen during the 1960s contributed to a social environment that created something of a backlash against increasingly strict regulation of police activity. The first significant reversal was *Terry v. Ohio*, 392 U.S. 1 (1968), which permitted the "stop and frisk" of suspects encountered on the street on the basis of reasonable suspicion, which is a lower legal threshold than probable cause. Although the *Terry* case specifically involved a potential robbery, given the nature of U.S. crime, the principle was soon extended to drug-related offenses.

From the 1970s through the 1990s, SCOTUS also tweaked the requirement for search warrants by creating or expanding exceptions. Searches of motor vehicles, searches incident to arrest, and inventory searches were all exempted from warrant requirements, although probable cause or reasonable suspicion still applied.[5]

In addition to the right "to be secure in their persons, houses, papers, and effects," the Fourth Amendment has been interpreted as a guarantee of the right to privacy, although such a right is not explicitly described in the Constitution. This additional principle has become an important component in the courts' interpretations of the Fourth Amendment, especially where various modern technologies are concerned. The expectation of privacy must meet both subjective and objective tests, which are defined next in section "Fourth Amendment Legal Terms."

Fourth Amendment Legal Terms

Words in a legal context have specific and defined meanings, so it is important to understand the terminology associated with the Fourth Amendment.

Search: An agent or employee of the government infringes an individual's expectation of privacy that is considered reasonable by society. Note that a private individual not acting in one of these capacities is exempt from Fourth Amendment restrictions.

Seizure (property): An agent or employee of the government interferes with an individual's possessory interest in a piece of property. A seizure is unreasonable when the property owner had a reasonable expectation of privacy regarding the item or items. However, the previous owner of a piece of abandoned property has no standing to claim unreasonable seizure.

Abandoned property: Property left behind in such a manner that the owner relinquishes possessory interest in it. Abandonment also ends that individual's reasonable expectation of privacy regarding the item or items.

Seizure (person): An agent or employee of the government (1) uses physical force to restrain an individual or (2) creates such a situation that a reasonable person experiencing the same or similar circumstances would not feel free to leave the scene.

Standing (formally, *locus standi*): The right to bring suit in a court regarding a given matter. For federal (and in particular constitutional) matters, an individual must have an actual dispute, having sustained or having the potential to sustain direct injury or harm; simply disagreeing with a federal law or government action is not sufficient. In Fourth Amendment matters, the plaintiff must have had a legitimate expectation of privacy at the searched location that was violated.

Subjective test of privacy expectation: The individual genuinely and actually expected privacy.

Objective test of privacy expectation: In similar circumstances, a reasonable person would have likewise expected privacy.

Probable cause: A reasonable basis exists to believe that a crime may have been committed and, in the case of a search, that evidence of that crime is likely to be present in the location to be searched.

Reasonable suspicion: Under a given set of circumstances and based on specific and articulable facts, a reasonable person would suspect that a crime may have been committed.

Evolution of Constitutional Law

More likely than not, you are familiar with **precedent**—the rulings of federal courts on various issues, including constitutional ones. Its historical basis is common law, which rather than a set of legislated statutes is the accumulation of past court decisions (in similar cases) that then guide the adjudication of current cases. Formally, this principle is known as *stare decisis*, Latin for "to stand by things decided." Precedent is most important for civil and constitutional law; criminal law is rarely affected because criminal statutes are fairly straightforward: if you do x, you have violated the law, and the penalty is y. Where precedent becomes important for law enforcement is in **procedural law**, which controls the investigation, arrest, trial, and incarceration of the accused.

As you might imagine, *stare decisis* can be complex and is governed by a set of rules that dictate when it applies and which courts must respect the decisions of which other courts. (While state court systems also rely on this principle, one of the aforementioned rules is that a court is bound to consider only decisions of the highest court *within that jurisdiction*, meaning decisions in state courts cannot determine Fourth Amendment issues nationally. They can, however, affect any law enforcement agency operating within their jurisdiction.) For our purposes here, the main concern is not the mechanics of precedent but rather how it affects constitutional law. The general public tends to equate SCOTUS with decisions on the constitutionality of laws passed by Congress, executive orders, or (most commonly) the rulings of lower courts—the process of **judicial review**. While it seems to make perfect sense that given the system of "checks and balances" that the framers intended this would be the primary responsibility of the high court assigned by the Constitution, the facts of the matter are quite different.

In reality, nowhere in Article III (which discusses the judicial branch) is the concept of judicial review even mentioned, let alone spelled out. Its origin lies with the case *Marbury v. Madison*, 5 U.S. 137 (1803), a name that might stir memories from a high school civics or American government class. Without going into detail here, suffice it to say that despite the shaky legal foundations of this case, the court's ruling established the authority of SCOTUS to review the constitutionality of laws and court rulings, and that authority has persisted and evolved.

Decisions in court cases—particularly in federal courts and most of all the U.S. Supreme Court—are the determinants of what is and is not permissible in constitutional terms.

Consequently, the legal landscape is ever-shifting, though fortunately it does not normally shift radically or quickly.

Exclusionary Rule and the Warrant Requirement

The exclusionary rule, which as noted earlier was created by the ruling in *Weeks v. United States*, 232 U.S. 314 (1914) and extended to jurisdictions below the federal level by *Mapp v. Ohio*, 367 U.S. 643 (1961), serves as the enforcement mechanism of the Fourth Amendment. Simply put, evidence obtained by a search or seizure not compliant with the Fourth Amendment may not be admitted as evidence in a criminal prosecution. The rule itself is fairly straightforward; the associated complexity arises from the multitude of exceptions to the warrant requirement.

While the exclusionary rule might seem harsh and unbending at first glance, keep in mind that it arose not from the language of the Constitution but from subsequent court opinions.

Writing for the majority in the fairly complex case of *Illinois v. Gates*, 462 U.S. 213 (1983), Justice Rehnquist noted, "The exclusionary rule is 'a judicially created remedy designed to safeguard Fourth Amendment rights generally,' and not 'a personal constitutional right of the party aggrieved,'" here quoting from *United States v. Calandra*, 414 U.S. 338, 348 (1974).[8] In other words, it is a tool the courts may employ to curb what they determine to be abuses of the government's power to search and seize, not an automatic penalty imposed on the prosecution.

At present, the courts continue to try to balance the protection of individual rights with the need for effective law enforcement. In *United States v. Leon*, 468 U.S. 897 (1984), the ruling stated in part, "The [exclusionary] rule is not an individual right and applies only where its deterrent effect outweighs the substantial cost of letting guilty and possibly dangerous defendants go free."[9]

There are three main types of warrants. The first is the **knock-and-announce warrant**, which imposes the requirement for officers to knock, announce and identify themselves, and provide the occupant time to answer the door. Interestingly, in 2006, SCOTUS ruled in *Hudson v. Michigan*, 547 U.S. 586 (2006) that the failure of law enforcement to knock or announce when relying on a knock-and-announce warrant does not automatically activate the exclusionary rule.

The ruling identified several interests protected by the knock-and-announce procedure:

> …human life and limb (because an unannounced entry may provoke violence from a surprised resident), property (because citizens presumably would open the door upon an announcement, whereas a forcible entry may destroy it), and privacy and dignity of the sort that can be offended by a sudden entrance.

However, Justice Scalia continued, "…the rule has never protected one's interest in preventing the government from seeing or taking evidence described in a warrant. Since the interests violated here have nothing to do with the seizure of the evidence, the exclusionary rule is inapplicable."[10]

The logical counterpart to the knock-and-announce warrant is the **no-knock warrant**. As the name suggests, these warrants allow law enforcement to enter a premise without prior notification. They are typically issued only when there is a reasonable expectation that the occupant could destroy the evidence sought in the time allowed by a knock-and-announce warrant.[11]

Least common is the **anticipatory warrant**, which is issued to authorize a search or seizure justified by a condition that does not yet exist but is reasonably expected to exist at some point in the future. SCOTUS upheld this form of warrant as not violating the warrant clause of the Fourth Amendment in *United States v. Grubbs*, 547 U.S. 90 (2006). In that particular case, police had obtained a warrant with an affidavit that explained that it would not be executed until a parcel—expected to contain child pornography that Grubbs had ordered from an undercover postal inspector—arrived at his residence.[12]

There are a number of exceptions to the Fourth Amendment warrant requirement for searches. Following are the major ones.

Plain view doctrine: No warrant is required for an officer to seize any item in plain view if the officer has probable cause to believe that the item is involved in a criminal act.[13]

Open-field doctrine: No warrant is required to search an open field or other outdoor area, even if such area is on private property, as there is no reasonable expectation of privacy in an open outdoor area. However, this exception does not extend to **curtilage**, which is the area immediately surrounding a private dwelling and is legally considered to be part of the dwelling.[13] Based on the Supreme Court ruling in *United States v. Dunn*, 480 U.S. 294 (1987), the courts consider four factors in defining what constitutes curtilage and what constitutes an open field (in legal terms, everything else):

- The proximity of the area in question to the dwelling
- Whether the area falls within an enclosure that surrounds the dwelling
- The customary use of the area
- What actions, if any, the resident has taken to protect the area from access or observation by passersby[14]

Adjuncts to the open-field doctrine are SCOTUS rulings holding that the erection of a fence (particularly one not specifically designed to provide privacy) in an open field does not create a reasonable expectation of privacy and that is permissible to shine a flashlight into a protected area even without probable cause.[15]

Search Incident to a Lawful Arrest

Upon making a lawful arrest, a police officer may search the arrestee's person and the area immediately around him without a warrant or consent.

Even if the officer mistakenly but in good faith arrests the wrong person and in the course of the post-arrest search discovers contraband, that evidence is permissible.[11]

Exigent Circumstances

This principle applies to situations in which obtaining a warrant is impractical, usually because of time constraints. There are two main variations. One is when an officer has reasonable belief that there exists an immediate danger to his life or that of others or to private property, or otherwise faces a compelling need to take official action, and in taking such action does not have the primary intent of arresting or seizing evidence, no warrant is required. Typical situations that fall into this category are the fresh pursuit (aka "hot pursuit") of a suspect, the need to prevent the escape of a suspect, and the need to protect public safety or welfare.[13]

The second is the need to prevent immediate destruction of evidence. This justification can embrace a vast range of possible circumstances and has even been used to justify warrantless, nonconsensual blood draws to determine the blood alcohol content of DUI arrestees since the body is constantly metabolizing alcohol and thereby destroying evidence. (That particular exigency was overturned in *Missouri v. McNeely*, 133 U.S. 832 (2013), for routine DUI cases.)[16]

A good examination of the exigent circumstance principle can be obtained from *Kentucky v. King*, 131 U.S. 1849 (2011). In October 2005, Lexington, Kentucky police officers were pursuing a suspect identified by an undercover officer who had just completed a drug buy from the individual and directed the uniformed officers to a specific breezeway of a nearby apartment complex. The officers heard a door slam in the breezeway just before they arrived and detected a strong odor of marijuana emanating from the back left door of the breezeway. They knocked on the door and announced themselves. The door was not opened, but the officers heard sounds from the apartment that led them to believe evidence was being destroyed. At that point, they forced entry, where they discovered several individuals in possession of drugs and drug paraphernalia. The original suspect was subsequently located in the apartment through the back right door of the breezeway.[17]

The exigent circumstance exception does not exist when it is police conduct that creates those circumstances, and this was the claim Hollis made in moving to suppress the evidence obtained after the warrantless entry. In affirming Hollis' claim, the Kentucky Supreme Court used a two-part test: first, whether police had deliberately created the exigent circumstances (which is an act of bad faith) and, if not, whether it was reasonably foreseeable that their conduct would do so. The Kentucky Supreme Court held in essence that the initial "knock and announce" by the officers created the exigent circumstances. In overturning this ruling, SCOTUS countered that the standard must be one of reasonableness, and if prior police conduct has been lawful—that is, not in violation or threatened violation of the Fourth Amendment—then it has not created the exigency.[18] This ruling finally clarified the confusion arising from various police-created exigency tests (such as the one applied by the Kentucky Supreme Court) that had arisen in various state and lower federal courts.[19]

Emergency Entry

If an officer enters a dwelling in the course of responding to an emergency such as a fire or medical emergency and discovers evidence of a crime in plain view (or in the course of actions reasonably necessary to that response), the Fourth Amendment has not been violated. The warrantless entry was made for reasons of public safety, not to procure evidence, and is therefore acceptable.

An interesting variation on this exception arose in Massachusetts in 2011 when a woman notified police of two dead dogs and a third "emaciated" dog in her neighbor's yard. Unable to obtain any response from the owner of the house, the officers climbed up on a snowbank in order to observe the yard over the privacy fence surrounding it and observed what the neighbor had described. They then contacted the fire department to remove the padlock on the gate so that they could enter the yard.

The owner was subsequently charged with three counts of animal cruelty. She filed to suppress evidence obtained by police entry into her yard on the grounds that it was a warrantless search, thereby raising the question of whether the emergency exception extends to the welfare of animals. The Supreme Judicial Court of Massachusetts ultimately ruled in *Commonwealth v. Duncan*, SJC-11373 (2014) that it does, although this precedent is valid only in Massachusetts.[20]

Searches at or near the Border

Although an extremely particular and geographically limited circumstance, the conduct of warrantless searches at the national border requires no additional justification, not even probable cause or reasonable suspicion. The ruling in *United States v. Ramsey*, 431 U.S. 606, 616 (1977), stated, "That searches made at the border, pursuant to the longstanding right of the sovereign to protect itself by stopping and examining persons and property crossing into this country, are reasonable simply by virtue of the fact that they occur at the border, should, by now, require no extended demonstration." Once an individual departs the border, however, even by a few miles, this exception no longer applies.[21]

Motor Vehicle Searches

An example of new technology not foreseen by the Constitution is that automobiles became a Fourth Amendment issue in the early twentieth century, particularly given their use for smuggling during prohibition. SCOTUS was fairly forgiving when it came to automobile searches. Because the mobility of the automobile provided a means to quickly remove evidence from police jurisdiction and possibly facilitate its destruction, obtaining a warrant for a vehicle search was seen as impractical. Because they are used on public thoroughfares in plain view, not generally used as a repository for personal items, and do not serve as a residence, the courts associate a reduced expectation of privacy with motor vehicles.[22] Given its significance and frequency of occurrence, this exception will be explored more fully in section "Fourth Amendment and Motor Vehicles."

Vessel Searches

With a rationale closely related to that of border searches, seagoing vessels may be stopped and boarded without a warrant even in the absence of any suspicion of criminal activity in order to inspect documentation. The extensive freedom of movement available to vessels—beyond even that of motor vehicles—is considered to justify this degree of latitude.[23]

Consent Search

If an individual agrees that the officer may conduct a search without first obtaining a warrant, such a consent search does not violate the Fourth Amendment.

Naturally, there are conditions: consent must be given intelligently, specifically, and unequivocally, and it must not arise from duress or coercion, whether implicit or explicit.[11] Also, since the individual has granted consent for the search, he has full authority over the location to be searched and may choose to limit the scope of that search.[24]

If the search involves a physical premise with two or more residents and one of them consents to a search but the other one objects, the objecting resident's rights take precedence, and no consent search may be conducted. However, if a consent search does take place and evidence that potentially incriminates another resident of the premises who was not present to give or withhold consent, that evidence will be admissible.[11]

Landlords are not entitled to grant permission to search a leased premise. Similarly, an employer may consent to a search of its place of business but is not entitled to grant permission for a search of spaces specifically assigned to an employee.[11]

Probable Cause and Reasonable Suspicion

Because these two concepts are key to a variety of search and detention actions, it is important that they be clearly understood. If we create a "degree of certainty" scale with 100 being absolutely certainty, probable cause falls somewhere between 45 and 55, and reasonable suspicion is in the neighborhood of 20–30.

Fundamentally, probable cause means that given the circumstances in question, a reasonable and prudent person would have cause to believe that (1) a crime has been committed and (2) that the subject of the detention and/or search is the one who committed that crime. Even if that assumption later proves inaccurate, the officer's conduct is permissible so long as it was reasonable based on the information available at the time.[25]

Stops and frisks based on probable cause are often called "*Terry* stops" and "*Terry* frisks" because the practices were upheld by SCOTUS in *Terry v. Ohio*, 392 U.S. 1 (1968). The opinion specifically differentiated a "stop" from an arrest and a "frisk" or pat-down from a full-blown search. To see the application of probable cause and the different levels of detention and search involved, the circumstances of the *Terry* case itself provide an excellent example.

A detective of the Cleveland Police Department with 39 years on the force was walking a downtown patrol beat that he had worked for some 30 years. He observed two strangers on a street corner who were behaving suspiciously. Alternately, each man would walk out and back along an identical route, stopping every time to stare into a specific store window, and when the walker returned to the corner, the two men would confer. McFadden, the detective, observed the men do this about 24 times. At one point, a third man joined the other two for a conversation, after which the third man left hurriedly.[26]

Suspecting that the two walkers were probably casing the store in preparation for a robbery, McFadden followed the two men when they left the corner and saw them rejoin the third man a couple of blocks away. At that point, he approached, identified himself, and asked the men for their names. Receiving only mumbled responses, McFadden turned one of the men, Terry, around, patted down his outer clothing, and identified a pistol in one coat pocket. He ordered the three into an adjacent store, removed Terry's overcoat, found a revolver in the previously identified pocket, and ordered all three to face the wall and raise their hands. He then proceeded to pat down the other two men, identifying another pistol in the overcoat pocket of one (Chilton). At that point, he placed Terry and Chilton under arrest for carrying concealed weapons.[26]

The court affirmed that McFadden had reasonably concluded that the men were acting suspiciously, which warranted his interrogation. For his own safety, he was entitled to conduct a pat-down, which is what uncovered the two weapons. The detective's search was limited—he patted down only the men's outer clothing and did not place his hands under the outer garments of Katz (the third man) since his initial pat-down identified nothing of concern, and he did not reach under Terry's or Chilton's outer clothing until after his initial pat-down identified a weapon. His initial interrogation and search did not constitute an arrest.[26]

It is important to understand that, as noted in the *Terry* opinion, McFadden's actions amounted to a "seizure" under the Fourth Amendment, since he accosted the men and restricted their freedom to walk away, and a "search" as well. However, the conduct of both without a warrant was justified by the circumstances; as the court put it, "The reasonableness of any particular search and seizure must be assessed in light of the particular circumstances against the standard of whether a man of reasonable caution is warranted in believing that the action taken was appropriate."[26]

The notion of the "reasonable person" can be misleading, however. A more accurate definition is this: "Facts or apparent facts viewed through the eyes of the experienced officer which would generate a reasonable belief that a crime has been or is about to be committed."[27] An officer is not the average citizen; he or she has specialized training, experience, and therefore an enhanced ability to identify criminal conduct.[28]

Because of the nature of probable cause, there is no hard-and-fast set of rules for determining when it exists. Rather, the "totality of circumstances" or accumulation of facts at some point becomes sufficient to constitute probable cause. A sound definition along these lines comes from another ruling: "Probable cause is the sum total of layers of information and synthesis of what police have heard, know, or observe as trained officers."[29] Similarly, in *Ornelas v. United States*, 517 U.S. 690 (1996), Chief Justice Rehnquist noted that "our cases have recognized that a police officer may draw inferences based on his own experience in deciding whether probable cause exists."[30]

There are both direct and indirect sources of knowledge to support probable cause.

Examples of direct sources include

- Flight or hiding from officers (but this by itself is not sufficient)
- Furtive movements (interpreted based on the circumstances, and merely being nervous in the presence of police officers is not sufficient)
- False or improbable answers (typically provide a basis for further questioning)
- Presence at a crime scene or in a high-crime area (the crime scene standard is lower; for a high-crime area to be a justification, there must be other contributing factors such as a typical sequence of actions or events, flight or attempted flight, and furtive movements)
- Admitted ownership (usually of a container that is subsequently found to contain evidence)
- Association with known criminals (often identifying someone as a lookout, guard, courier, "mule," or a similar role based on police experience)
- Failure to protest (a definite gray area since being "too" nice or innocent may indicate deception as well)
- Past criminal conduct (only a contributing factor and usually requires personal knowledge of the individual on the officer's part)
- Observation of evidence (must be observable with the senses or sensory aids normally available—e.g., a pair of binoculars or a camera is acceptable, but not a microscope).[29]

The use of indirect (hearsay) evidence to support probable cause is subject to testing based on precedent. The *Aguilar* test of 1964 was replaced by the *Spinelli* test in 1969 and in turn by the *Gates* test of 1983. The *Gates* test is based on the totality of circumstances but incorporates both of the prior tests. *Aguilar* required the assessment of how the informant obtained the information provided as well as the informant's record of truthfulness. *Spinelli* added an assessment of how accurate the informant's information was likely to be from the standpoint of law enforcement—would it, for example, be in the informant's interest to provide the information in question to the police? Under *Gates*, police are required to test both subjectively (i.e., think like a criminal) and objectively (think like a reasonable person).[29]

The less stringent *Terry* stop can be based on reasonable suspicion. While the standards of reasonable suspicion are obviously lower than those of probable cause, the officer must be able to articulate or explain the basis of his suspicion that criminal activity has taken or is about to take place. A mere "hunch" or "feeling" is *not* sufficient. Because the *Terry* stop still qualifies as a seizure under the Fourth Amendment, it must be limited to a reasonable period of time.[31]

The conduct of a *Terry* stop does *not* automatically create justification for a *Terry* frisk.

The pat-down is justified by the officer's need for personal safety during the conduct of the interview, so there must be a reasonable belief that the suspect might be armed, and the search must be confined to the individual's outer (i.e., easily accessible) clothing. The search must be limited to hard objects, although not necessarily to purpose-designed weapons—a pen or set of keys can be used to injure, and in extreme cases, weapons can be concealed inside normal-looking objects like a lipstick tube. Hard objects may be manipulated through the fabric of the clothing as much as necessary in an attempt to identify them; soft objects may not be manipulated.[32]

As an adjunct to the *Terry* frisk, a container may also be "frisked" if (1) the circumstances already justify a *Terry* frisk, (2) the container could contain a weapon (based on the officer's training and experience), (3) the container is within reach (including lunging distance) of the suspect, and (4) the container is not locked.[33]

Reasonable Expectation of Privacy

Although privacy is not a concept explicitly described in the Constitution, the notion of the citizen's "reasonable expectation of privacy" arose from the concurring opinion of Justice John Harlan in *Katz v. United States*, 389 U.S. 347 (1967). Katz was a habitual gambler in Los Angeles who conducted his illegal activities from a bank of payphones. The FBI placed microphones atop the telephone booths and recorded Katz's conversations without obtaining a warrant, and the content of those conversations led to his conviction. SCOTUS ultimately overturned his conviction because even though the eavesdropping occurred in a public place—the phone booths— Katz had a right to justifiably rely on the privacy of those telephones, and moreover, the Fourth Amendment protects people, not places (except to the extent that they are associated with a person).[34]

Justice Harlan's concurrence stated in part:

> As the Court's opinion states, "the Fourth Amendment protects people, not places." The question, however, is what protection it affords to those people.
>
> Generally, as here, the answer to that question requires reference to a "place." My understanding of the rule that has emerged from prior decisions is that there is a twofold requirement, first that a person have exhibited an actual (subjective) expectation of privacy and, second, that the expectation be one that society is prepared to recognize as "reasonable." Thus, a man's home is, for most purposes, a place where he expects privacy, but objects, activities, or statements that he exposes to the "plain view" of outsiders are not "protected," because no intention to keep them to himself has been exhibited. On the other hand, conversations in the open would not be protected against being overheard, for the expectation of privacy under the circumstances would be unreasonable. *Cf. Hester v. United States, supra.*
>
> The critical fact in this case is that "[o]ne who occupies it [a telephone booth], shuts the door behind him, and pays the toll that permits him to place a call is surely entitled to assume" that his conversation is not being intercepted. *Ante at 352.* The point is not that the booth is "accessible to the public" at other times, *ante at 351*, but that it is a temporarily private place whose momentary occupants' expectations of freedom from intrusion are recognized as reasonable. *Cf. Rios v. United States, 364 U.S. 253.*[35]

Since *Katz*, this reasonable expectation of privacy standard has been adopted repeatedly by SCOTUS in Fourth Amendment cases.

Fourth Amendment and the Home

When it comes to an individual's home, the courts have applied the Fourth Amendment with a heavy hand—bear in mind the historical origins of the law and the high regard shown for the sanctity of the home. SCOTUS stated in *Payton v. New York*, 445 U.S. 573 (1980), that the "physical entry of the home is the chief evil against which the wording of the

Fourth Amendment is directed," and as such "searches and seizures inside a home without a warrant are *presumptively unreasonable* [emphasis added]."[36] Warrantless entry of a home is forbidden unless the officer has consent or valid exigent circumstances exist—and in many cases, the courts have been hard to convince that such was the case: space does not permit a discussion here, but read the background of *Michigan v. Fisher*, 130 S. Ct. 546 (2009).

Entry into a residence for the purpose of arrest requires an arrest warrant, absent consent, or exigent circumstances that justify entry and result in the officer's direct observation of a crime in progress. Moreover, even *with* an arrest warrant, an officer may not enter the residence of a third party to conduct an arrest without a *search* warrant, because the arrest warrant alone does not address—and therefore does not protect—the privacy expectations of the third party.[36]

The concept of curtilage was discussed briefly in the previous examination of the open-field doctrine. Warrantless entry into the curtilage is not permissible except for approaching a house by a common route such as a driveway or sidewalk with legitimate cause; the resident must reasonably expect use of these routes by the public and so has no reasonable expectation of privacy there.[36]

Nonresidential structures such as storage sheds and unattached garages still count as curtilage if they are fairly close to the dwelling and serve the daily needs of the resident.

However, the defendant in *United States v. Dunn*, 480 U.S. 294 (1987), argued that a barn similarly constituted curtilage, but SCOTUS disagreed. In this particular case, DEA agents had entered the fields of a ranch that was surrounded by a perimeter fence and crossed by several barbed wire fences, as well as a wooden fence that enclosed the front of the barn. The barn itself had locked, waist-high gates; the agents did not enter but shined a flashlight inside due to the smell of chemicals and the sound of a motor running and observed what appeared to be a drug laboratory. In this case, the barn was approximately 60 yards from the house and well outside (50 yards) a fence encircling the house. In addition, all of the fences were of the type used to corral livestock rather than designed for privacy.[15]

Aerial observation or photography of a home and its curtilage (so long as the cameras are of a common type and not highly sophisticated surveillance devices) conducted from lawfully navigable airspace *and at an altitude that is traveled with sufficient regularity*, even if the exterior spaces are enclosed by a privacy fence, does not represent a search under the Fourth Amendment. The courts' rationale has been that since overflight by virtually any member of the general public is a common possibility, the resident has no reasonable expectation of privacy for observation from this vantage point. Overflight of open fields regardless of altitude is permissible since there is already no expectation of privacy.[37]

Finally, garbage that has been set out for collection represents no reasonable expectation of privacy since the resident knows that any passerby or sanitation worker has access to pilfer through that trash at his or her leisure at any time. It is even permissible for law enforcement to make arrangements with sanitation workers to deliver all trash from a specific residence to them.[37]

Fourth Amendment and Motor Vehicles

As mentioned previously, the mobility of a motor vehicle and its resultant ability to move evidence beyond the reach of law enforcement before a warrant could be obtained has led the courts to grant wide latitude and a looser application of the Fourth Amendment to searches of motor vehicles. This rule dates from *Carroll v. United States*, 267 U.S. 132 (1925), and the principle holds even when a warrant could have been obtained without any risk to preserving the evidence.[38] Naturally, however, there are limits.

It is not permissible to stop a motor vehicle solely to examine the driver's license absent reasonable suspicion of any legal violation. However, it is acceptable to establish a checkpoint to do so, since all vehicles passing that location are treated equally; it is also acceptable to establish a similar checkpoint to screen for DUI violations. In both cases, the safety of the driving public is being enhanced. However, a checkpoint to search for illegal drugs is not permissible since highway safety is no longer the primary object, and allowing such a checkpoint would by extension make it acceptable to set up checkpoints to search for *any* criminal violation.[37]

Once a vehicle stop is conducted for a valid reason, officers are entitled to order the driver and any passengers to exit the vehicle, and need not provide a reason for doing so.

SCOTUS held in *Pennsylvania v. Mimms*, 434 U.S. 106 (1977), for drivers, and in *Maryland v. Wilson*, 518 U.S. 408 (1997), for passengers, that the officer has a legitimate interest in preventing an assault using weapons that might be present in the vehicle.[37]

If probable cause has been established, and assuming that the vehicle is in a public location (meaning the owner has no reasonable expectation of privacy) and is "readily mobile," the officer may permissibly seize the vehicle and may conduct a search, in both cases without obtaining a warrant. The search may be conducted on the spot, or the vehicle may be removed to a law enforcement facility or other location.[37] (As an extension of the "readily mobile" principle that underlies the looser rules for motor vehicles, motor homes are legally treated as vehicles, not dwellings, if they are immediately movable—i.e., being operated on a roadway as opposed to parked and hooked up in an RV park or similar setting.)[39]

Once probable cause has provided the basis for a vehicle search, the officer may search any and every part of the vehicle and its contents—including containers—that could reasonably contain evidence of the suspected offense. To explore two specific variations on this principle, the Ohio Supreme Court has held that the smell of *burned* marijuana emanating from the passenger compartment of a motor vehicle does not by itself create probable cause for a warrantless search of the *trunk*. However, the Ohio courts have ruled that the strong odor of unburned marijuana does provide grounds for a general search of the vehicle.[40] The distinction between a small, probably personal-use quantity of marijuana having recently been used and the likelihood of the transportation of a significant quantity of marijuana in justifying the search of the trunk should be evident.

As for searches of a vehicle incident to the arrest of an occupant, the Fourth Amendment is more stringent. There are two main justifications for a vehicle search: safety, which assumes that the arrestee is unsecured and within reaching or lunging distance of the passenger compartment, and evidence, which assumes it is reasonable to believe that the vehicle contains evidence of the crime in question. For example, in *United States v. Lopez*, 07-5768 (6th Cir. 2009), the defendant had been arrested for reckless driving and was handcuffed and secured in the backseat of a patrol car when the search was conducted. Although crack cocaine and a weapon were found, that evidence was excluded since neither of the aforementioned justifications for a search existed.[41]

It is permissible for an officer who is outside his normal jurisdiction to make a stop for a traffic violation he personally observes. However, all traffic stops are subject to limits (though not rigidly defined limits) if no other source of probable cause is noted. The duration of the stop must be reasonable given the "totality of the circumstances," and any questioning must be primarily focused on confirming the occurrence of the traffic violation and issuing a citation, although a *limited* amount of unrelated questioning intended to uncover possible criminal conduct is acceptable.[42]

Eavesdropping and Surveillance

Interestingly, there have been few Fourth Amendment court cases related to wiretaps and other forms of eavesdropping (primarily surreptitiously recording conversations) because both federal and state statutes are in general more restrictive than the Fourth Amendment might be. This should not be surprising considering that they involve technology that did not exist and was not contemplated by the framers. Consequently, it is these laws that will govern most eavesdropping and surveillance activities, and their discussion is not warranted here given the focus of this chapter.

The main exception is video surveillance that does not include audio recording. Such surveillance does not fall under federal or state statutes, and so Fourth Amendment standards apply. Once again, the reasonable expectation of privacy is the basis. Video recording of a street, sidewalk, storefront, or other public place is permissible. However, placing a camera to conduct video surveillance of an area where privacy is reasonably expected, such as a residential yard surrounded by a privacy fence, does require a warrant.[43]

The main Fourth Amendment issue for consideration in this section is the use of surveillance technology to determine what may be transpiring inside a premise. As we will see in section "Technology and the Fourth Amendment," initially the courts did not consider surveillance that did not include physical penetration of a protected space to constitute a search and therefore require a warrant. However, substantial improvements in technology (that particular ruling took place in 1942) changed the viewpoint of the courts.

Kyllo v. United States, 533 U.S. 27 (2001), arose after law enforcement officers used a thermal imaging scanner to examine Kyllo's home. Based on the heat patterns they detected and a comparison of Kyllo's home to nearby residences, they determined that he was likely using high-intensity heat lamps to cultivate marijuana indoors. This information formed a significant part of the affidavit they subsequently used to obtain a search warrant, and that search confirmed that Kyllo was indeed growing marijuana. The officers had not obtained a warrant for the initial thermal scan of the house, but they had merely parked on the street nearby and used the scanner from their vehicle.[44]

The rationale of the SCOTUS ruling in this case was that police used technology to obtain information about the interior of Kyllo's residence that could not have otherwise been obtained without a physical intrusion into a Fourth Amendment–protected space, and the evidence obtained was excluded. A key factor, however, as we will see in the next section was that the thermal imaging device was not something in common use by the general public.[45]

Technology and the Fourth Amendment

The framers had sufficient wisdom to understand that the U.S. Constitution would have to change with the times. That provision is built into it in Article V, which sets rules for amending the Constitution. As it turns out, the more significant mechanism has been judicial review in the various federal courts, up to and including SCOTUS, as was discussed previously in section "Evolution of Constitutional Law." Neither mechanism, however, is meant to engender fast or radical change—what was intended was evolution, not revolution.

Overall, most would say that this process has served us well. However, today's technology and the speed at which it changes have created some special challenges for the Fourth Amendment.

In his concurrence in *Katz v. United States*, 389 U.S. 347 (1967), Justice Harlan made reference to this changing technology. *Silverman v. United States*, 365 U.S. 505 (1961), had already established that "eavesdropping accomplished by means of an electronic device that penetrated the premises occupied by petitioner was a violation of the Fourth Amendment." While *Goldman v. United States*, 316 U.S. 129 (1942), had held that "electronic surveillance accomplished without the physical penetration of petitioner's premises by a tangible object did not violate the Fourth Amendment," Justice Harlan went on to opine, "This case [*Katz*] requires us to reconsider *Goldman*, and I agree that it should now be overruled. Its limitation on Fourth Amendment protection is, in the present day, bad physics as well as bad law, for reasonable expectations of privacy may be defeated by electronic as well as physical invasion."[35]

A standard often applied by the courts, such as in *Kyllo v. United States*, 533 U.S. 27 (2001), is whether a particular technology used for surveillance is in common use by the general public.[36] If it is, then law enforcement gains no particular advantage and the individual has no reasonable expectation of privacy in an area that can be observed with the use of such a device, since in essence anyone could make the same sort of observation. (Recall that in the discussion of the open-field doctrine in section "Exclusionary Rule and the Warrant Requirement," it was mentioned that the courts have ruled it permissible to observe into a protected area from an unprotected area with the aid of a flashlight—a technological aid to observation that is in common public use.)

A significant Fourth Amendment technology issue arose with the use of GPS tracking devices placed on vehicles. In January 2012, SCOTUS ruled in *United States v. Jones*, 132 S. Ct. 945 (2012), that placing a GPS tracker on a vehicle without a warrant was an impermissible search under the Fourth Amendment. (Ironically, police *had* obtained a warrant for the tracker, but failed to comply with two of the associated stipulations: a 10-day deadline and a requirement that the device be installed within the District of Columbia. The tracker was actually installed 11 days later and in Maryland.)[46] The ruling was once again based on the reasonable expectation of privacy. As Judge Douglas Ginsburg, who heard the case in the U.S. Court of Appeals for the District of Columbia, wrote, "A reasonable person does not expect anyone to monitor and retain a record of every time he drives his car, including his origin, route, destination, and each place he stops and how long he stays there; rather, he expects each of those movements to remain 'disconnected and anonymous.'"[47]

Shortly thereafter, however, on August 14, 2012, the Sixth Circuit Court of Appeals upheld the use of GPS location data from a mobile phone that police used to track Melvin Skinner during an investigation that ultimately led to the discovery of half a ton of marijuana in a motor home operated by Skinner and his son. The court relied on two key differences between the facts of the Skinner case and those of *Jones*, which the appellate panel actually mentioned in its ruling: the police did not emplace a tracking device but rather made use of an existing capability in Skinner's phone, and Skinner and his associates used prepaid phones based on the assumption that such phones could not be GPS-tracked. Apparently less than sympathetic, Judge Rogers noted in his ruling, "The Constitution…

does not protect their [Skinner and his associates'] erroneous expectations regarding the undetectability of their modern tools."[48] Mobile phone technologies change rapidly, of course, and the phone used by Skinner certainly had much less capability in virtually every regard than any of today's smartphones. In April 2014, SCOTUS heard two separate cases both involving warrantless searches of smartphones that took place incident to an arrest in one case and a traffic stop in another. The government has argued that mobile phones are no different from other personal property, which may be searched in such cases—purses, wallets, and so forth. The counter is that smartphones are capable of holding a tremendous amount of data potentially involving many aspects of a person's life, that there is no physical threat to be encountered by examining the data on such a phone, and that there are ways to preserve data until a warrant can be obtained.[49] The decisions in both cases are likely to have a significant impact unless the rulings are especially narrow.

It is worth noting that between *Skinner* and the current cases was *Ohio v. Smith*, 124 Ohio St. 3d 163 (2009-Ohio-6426), decided in December 2009. Smith was arrested after he answered a cell phone call made by an informant. During the search incident to his arrest, one officer placed Smith's phone in his pocket. Bags of crack cocaine were discovered at the scene, and police later searched the call records in the phone without a warrant. The evidence recovered from the phone was suppressed because the court held that there was no valid interest in officer safety or evidence preservation to justify the warrantless search. While this ruling serves as precedent only in Ohio, the appellate panel cited several federal cases in their opinion, and some of those cases may appear again when SCOTUS rules in these two matters.[50]

Conclusion

Attorneys and judges have the luxury of considering Fourth Amendment standards and precedent at their leisure and after the fact. Making an on-the-spot decision when confronted with a dynamic and potentially dangerous situation is another matter entirely. This discussion hopefully made clear two consistent points that can help guide those difficult decisions. One is the concept of the reasonable expectation of privacy and where that expectation applies and where it does not. The other is the notion of reasonableness and whether an action can be justified by articulable facts and/or questions of officer or public safety or the preservation of evidence. Some situations will tread close to the imprecise line that determines what degree of infringement on individual rights is justified in the name of law enforcement, but the best defense will always be a clear explanation of the facts that justified any actions taken.

References

1. Thomson, G.A. (June 1999). *The Demarcation Line of Liberty: The Decimation of the Fourth Amendment at the Border*. Nogales, AZ: Nogales Unified School District. Accessed online at http://web1.nusd.k12.az.us/schools/nhs/gthomson.class/pol699.paper/pol699.hist.overview.html. Accessed on May 16, 2014.
2. Seidel, D., Stewart, C., Nichols, J. Okane, M., and Rooney, T. (Fall 2010). *Background of the Fourth Amendment*. State College, PA: Pennsylvania State University, College of Information Sciences and Technology. Accessed online at https://wikispaces.psu.edu/display/IST43210/Background+of+the+Fourth+Amendment##. Accessed on May 16, 2014.

3. The 4th Amendment. (n.d.). Accessed online at http://www.revolutionary-war-and-beyond. com/4th-amendment.html. Accessed on May 16, 2014.

4. Harlan, J.M. (January 4, 1892). *Boyd et al. v. United States*. Ithaca, NY: Cornell Law School, Legal Information Institute. Accessed online at http://www.law.cornell.edu/supremecourt/ text/142/450. Accessed on May 16, 2014.

5. The Fourth Amendment: Origins, Text, and History. (2014). Accessed online at http://law.jrank. org/pages/2014/Search-Seizure-Fourth-Amendment-origins-text-history.html. Accessed on May 16, 2014.

6. Colonial History of the 4th Amendment. (n.d.). Accessed online at http://www.revolutionary-war-and-beyond.com/4th-amendment.html. Accessed on May 16, 2014.

7. Joint Resolution of Congress. (December 15, 1791). *Transcript of the Bill of Rights*. Washington, DC: National Archives. Accessed online at http://www.archives.gov/exhibits/charters/bill_of_ rights_transcript.html. Accessed on May 16, 2014.

8. Legal Information Institute. (n.d.). *Illinois v. Gates*. Ithaca, NY: Cornell University Law School. Accessed online at http://www.law.cornell.edu/supremecourt/text/462/213#writing-USSC_CR_ 0462_0213_ZO. Accessed on May 26, 2014.

9. Legal Information Institute. (n.d.). *United States v. Leon*. Ithaca, NY: Cornell University Law School. Accessed online at http://www.law.cornell.edu/supremecourt/text/468/897. Accessed on May 26, 2014.

10. Legal Information Institute. (n.d.). *Hudson v. Michigan*. Ithaca, NY: Cornell University Law School. Accessed online at http://www.law.cornell.edu/supct/html/04-1360.ZS.html. Accessed on May 26, 2014.

11. Legal Information Institute. (n.d.). *Fourth Amendment*. Ithaca, NY: Cornell University Law School. Accessed online at http://www.law.cornell.edu/wex/fourth_amendment. Accessed on May 26, 2014.

12. Legal Information Institute. (n.d.). *United States v. Grubbs*. Ithaca, NY: Cornell University Law School. Accessed online at http://www.law.cornell.edu/supct/html/04-1414.ZS.html. Accessed on May 26, 2014.

13. 4th Amendment in Everyday Life. (n.d.). Accessed online at http://www.revolutionary-war-and-beyond.com/4th-amendment.html. Accessed on May 27, 2014.

14. Legal Information Institute. (n.d.). *Curtilage*. Ithaca, NY: Cornell University Law School. Accessed online at http://www.law.cornell.edu/wex/curtilage.

15. Legal Information Institute. (n.d.). *United States v. Dunn*. Ithaca, NY: Cornell University Law School. Accessed online at http://www.law.cornell.edu/supremecourt/text/480/294. Accessed on May 26, 2014.

16. *Missouri v. McNeely*. (2013). Accessed online at http://www.scotusblog.com/case-files/cases/ missouri-v-mcneely/. Accessed on May 27, 2014.

17. Legal Information Institute. (n.d.). *Kentucky v. King*. Ithaca, NY: Cornell University Law School. Accessed online at http://www.law.cornell.edu/supct/cert/09-1272. Accessed on May 26, 2014.

18. Legal Information Institute. (n.d.). *Fourth Amendment: Exigent Circumstances*. Ithaca, NY: Cornell University Law School. Accessed online at http://www.law.cornell.edu/supct/cert/ case_summary/2011/fourth_amendment_exigent_circumstances. Accessed on May 26, 2014.

19. Pettry, M.T. The exigent circumstances exception after Kentucky v. King. *FBI Law Enforcement Bulletin*. Washington, DC: Federal Bureau of Investigation. Accessed online at http://www. fbi.gov/stats-services/publications/law-enforcement-bulletin/march-2012/the-exigent-circumstances-exception-after-kentucky-v.-king. Accessed on June 1, 2014.

20. *Commonwealth v. Duncan*. (2014). Accessed online at http://law.justia.com/cases/massa chusetts/supreme-court/2014/sjc-11373.html. Accessed on June 1, 2014.

21. Border Searches. (n.d.). Accessed online at http://law.justia.com/constitution/us/amendment-04/18-border-searches.html. Accessed on June 1, 2014.

22. Vehicular Searches. (n.d.). Accessed online at http://law.justia.com/constitution/us/ amendment-04/15-vehicular-searches.html. Accessed on June 1, 2014.

23. Vessel Searches. (n.d.). Accessed online at http://law.justia.com/constitution/us/amendment-04/16-vessel-searches.html. Accessed on June 1, 2014.

24. Neil, R. (n.d.). *Search & Seizure Law Update* [PowerPoint presentation]. Slide 85. Accessed online at http://www.leotrainer.com/pptsearchupdate.ppt. Accessed on June 3, 2014.

25. Neil, R. (n.d.). *Search & Seizure Law Update* [PowerPoint presentation]. Slides 6–9. Accessed online at http://www.leotrainer.com/pptsearchupdate.ppt. Accessed on June 3, 2014.

26. Legal Information Institute. (n.d.). *Terry v. Ohio*. Ithaca, NY: Cornell University Law School. Accessed online at http://www.law.cornell.edu/supremecourt/text/392/1. Accessed on June 3, 2014.

27. Bertomen, L. (n.d.). *Probable Cause* [PowerPoint presentation]. Slide 11. Accessed online at http://www.hartnell.edu/faculty/lbertomen/adj1/ADJ1onwebsite/ADJ1lec8/Probable Cause.ppt. Accessed on June 4, 2014.

28. Bertomen, L. (n.d.). *Probable Cause* [PowerPoint presentation]. Slide 12. Accessed online at http://www.hartnell.edu/faculty/lbertomen/adj1/ADJ1onwebsite/ADJ1lec8/Probable Cause.ppt. Accessed on June 4, 2014.

29. O'Connor, T. (August 18, 2010). *Probable Cause*. Accessed online at http://www.drtomoconnor.com/3000/3000lect03a.htm. Accessed on June 6, 2014.

30. Legal Information Institute. (n.d.). *Ornelas v. United States*. Ithaca, NY: Cornell University Law School. Accessed online at http://www.law.cornell.edu/supct/html/95-5257.ZO.html. Accessed on June 15, 2014.

31. Neil, R. (n.d.). *Search & Seizure Law Update* [PowerPoint presentation]. Slide 18. Accessed online at http://www.leotrainer.com/pptsearchupdate.ppt. Accessed on June 1, 2014.

32. Neil, R. (n.d.). *Search & Seizure Law Update* [PowerPoint presentation]. Slides 26–30. Accessed online at http://www.leotrainer.com/pptsearchupdate.ppt. Accessed on June 1, 2014.

33. Neil, R. (n.d.). *Search & Seizure Law Update* [PowerPoint presentation]. Slide 25. Accessed online at http://www.leotrainer.com/pptsearchupdate.ppt. Accessed on June 1, 2014.

34. Farb, R.L. (Spring 2002). *The Fourth Amendment, Privacy, and Law Enforcement. Popular Government*, p. 13. Chapel Hill, NC: University of North Carolina. Accessed online at http://sogpubs.unc.edu/electronicversions/pg/pgspr02/article2.pdf. Accessed on June 12, 2014.

35. Legal Information Institute. (n.d.). *Katz v. United States*. Ithaca, NY: Cornell University Law School. Accessed online at http://www.law.cornell.edu/supremecourt/text/389/347. Accessed on June 15, 2014.

36. Farb, R.L. (Spring 2002). *The Fourth Amendment, Privacy, and Law Enforcement. Popular Government*, p. 15. Chapel Hill, NC: University of North Carolina. Accessed online at http://sogpubs.unc.edu/electronicversions/pg/pgspr02/article2.pdf. Accessed on June 12, 2014.

37. Farb, R.L. (Spring 2002). *The Fourth Amendment, Privacy, and Law Enforcement. Popular Government*, p. 16. Chapel Hill, NC: University of North Carolina. Accessed online at http://sogpubs.unc.edu/electronicversions/pg/pgspr02/article2.pdf. Accessed on June 12, 2014.

38. Neil, R. (n.d.). *Search & Seizure Law Update* [PowerPoint presentation]. Slides 58–61. Accessed online at http://www.leotrainer.com/pptsearchupdate.ppt. Accessed on June 1, 2014.

39. Neil, R. (n.d.). *Search & Seizure Law Update* [PowerPoint presentation]. Slide 62. Accessed online at http://www.leotrainer.com/pptsearchupdate.ppt. Accessed on June 1, 2014.

40. Neil, R. (n.d.). *Search & Seizure Law Update* [PowerPoint presentation]. Slides 66–68. Accessed online at http://www.leotrainer.com/pptsearchupdate.ppt. Accessed on June 1, 2014.

41. Neil, R. (n.d.). *Search & Seizure Law Update* [PowerPoint presentation]. Slides 70–72. Accessed online at http://www.leotrainer.com/pptsearchupdate.ppt. Accessed on June 1, 2014.

42. Neil, R. (n.d.). *Search & Seizure Law Update* [PowerPoint presentation]. Slides 86–87. Accessed online at http://www.leotrainer.com/pptsearchupdate.ppt. Accessed on June 1, 2014.

43. Farb, R.L. (Spring 2002). *The Fourth Amendment, Privacy, and Law Enforcement. Popular Government*, p. 18. Chapel Hill, NC: University of North Carolina. Accessed online at http://sogpubs.unc.edu/electronicversions/pg/pgspr02/article2.pdf. Accessed on June 12, 2014.

44. Legal Information Institute. (n.d.). *Kyllo v. United States*. Ithaca, NY: Cornell University Law School. Accessed online at http://www.law.cornell.edu/supct/html/99-8508.ZS.html. Accessed on June 15, 2014.

45. Farb, R.L. (Spring 2002). *The Fourth Amendment, Privacy, and Law Enforcement. Popular Government*, pp. 15–16. Chapel Hill, NC: University of North Carolina. Accessed online at http://sogpubs.unc.edu/electronicversions/pg/pgspr02/article2.pdf. Accessed on June 12, 2014.

46. Legal Information Institute. (n.d.). *United States v. Jones*. Ithaca, NY: Cornell University Law School. Accessed online at http://www.law.cornell.edu/supremecourt/text/10-1259. Accessed on June 15, 2014.

47. Reisinger, D. (January 23, 2012). Police need warrant for GPS tracking, high court rules. CNET.com. Accessed online at http://www.cnet.com/news/police-need-warrant-for-gps-tracking-high-court-rules/. Accessed on June 23, 2014.

48. Reisinger, D. (August 15, 2012). Federal court OKs warrantless cell phone tracking by police. CNET.com. Accessed online at http://www.cnet.com/news/federal-court-oks-warrantless-cell-phone-tracking-by-police/. Accessed on June 23, 2014.

49. Editorial Board. (April 27, 2014). Smartphones and the 4th Amendment. *The New York Times*. Accessed online at http://www.nytimes.com/2014/04/28/opinion/smartphones-and-the-4th-amendment.html. Accessed on June 30, 2014.

50. Warrantless Search of Cell Phone Data Barred Unless Necessary for Officer's Safety or to Preserve Evidence. (December 15, 2009). The Supreme Court of Ohio & The Ohio Judicial System. Accessed online at https://www.sconet.state.oh.us/PIO/summaries/2009/1215/081781.asp. Accessed on July 2, 2014.

How to Get That Warrant Every Time

20

MATHEW O'DEANE

Contents

Chapter Objectives	338
Introduction	338
Totality of the Circumstances Test: *Illinois v. Gates* (1983) 462 U.S. 213	339
Good Faith Exception: *United States v. Leon* (1984) 468 U.S. 897	339
Traversal of Warrant: *Franks v. Delaware* (1978) 438 U.S. 154	339
Search Warrant	340
Warrants and the Law	341
Affidavit	341
What Property to Search?	342
What Property to Seize?	343
Prior Investigation	345
Relevant Experience and Training	345
Cause for Belief	345
Sample Probable Cause Statement: Gang Case Example	346
Night Service	347
Seal the Deal	348
General Search Warrant Tips	348
Jurisdiction	350
Knock and Notice	351
Conducting the Search	351
Supplies Needed	353
Receipt and Inventory	354
Releasing Property Seized Pursuant to a Search Warrant	354
Alternatives to a Search Warrant	355
Exigent Circumstances	355
Searching a Car	355
Search Incident to Arrest	356
Plain View	356
Conclusion	356
Questions for Discussion	356
Reference	356

Chapter Objectives

After reading this chapter you should be able to do the following:

1. Understand search warrants and arrest warrants, including the reasons why they are required. This chapter will serve as a guide for peace officers and prosecutors writing search warrants.
2. Understand what the elements of a warrant are.
3. Understand how search and arrest warrants are executed.
4. Understand some of the legal issues that are related to warrants including nighttime service, knock-and-notice requirements, and telephonic warrants.

Introduction

When you make the transition from patrol officer to detective, you will be writing a lot more search and arrest warrants, as such it is important to understand the key components a warrant. Regardless of where in the United States you work and despite formatting differences, search warrants are basically the same regardless of the crime you are investigating. The purpose of this chapter is to help investigators with a type of how to guide based on the best practices in the law enforcement industry, including practical information on related topics such as serving a search warrant, nighttime service, knock-and-notice law, conducting the search, informant disclosure motions, and telephonic warrants. This chapter also contains case law citations and statutory references that have a national impact.

Searches and seizures must be reasonable and based on probable cause. No warrants shall be issued without probable cause per the Fourth Amendment, which protects individual privacy and prevents arbitrary intrusions by the government. The Constitution provides a means for governmental agents and police officers to conduct a reasonable search. Not only it is in the law that you obtain a search warrant before you begin many criminal searches, it's also in your best interest much of the time. With probable cause and a warrant, the court will reward you by presuming your search is legal, and it will attempt to uphold your search at every level of appellate review. Even better, the burden of attacking the warrant is now on the defense.

For example, let's say two detectives go to the residence of the suspect they believed to be involved in the theft of car stereos in the neighborhood. They knock on the door and are met by their suspect who says he or she has no knowledge of the thefts. The detectives ask the suspect for consent to come in and look around, and he or she allows the officers to enter the house and conduct a search for the stereos. This may be fine in many cases, however at times issues can arise when the consent is challenged in court. The voluntariness of a consent search is often a question of fact; if the judge finds that the consent was not voluntary the evidence obtained may no longer be admissible. The inferences and conflicts of the evidence will be resolved against the people in support of the judge's ruling. In simple terms, this problem does not exist if detectives obtained a search warrant rather than asking for consent.

Another advantage in obtaining search warrants is that an officer serving a valid search warrant of an otherwise lawful manner is considered to be acting in the performance of his or her duties. This means an officer obtaining and serving a warrant is typically entitled to qualified immunity from civil damages in most cases.

Courts across the country have consistently emphasized their preference for searches made pursuant to a search warrant versus consent, for example, as judicial review has tremendous benefit. Warrants are normally drafted by nonlawyers, you the detective, often in the midst of a criminal investigation along with all of the stress and distractions that come along with it. By bringing a warrant to the magistrate for review, the underlying circumstances and details of the investigation to date can be validated, which helps the magistrate and the detective perform his or her duties.

Totality of the Circumstances Test: *Illinois v. Gates* (1983) 462 U.S. 213

The U.S. Supreme Court abandoned the old and highly technical "two-prong test" for determining whether an informant's information establishes probable cause. Instead, a "totality of the circumstances" approach was adopted. The *Gates* opinion is also important because it states that the standard for probable cause for the issuance of the warrant is a "fair probability" that contraband or evidence of a crime will be found in a particular place. The duty of a reviewing court is simply to ensure that the magistrate had a substantial basis for concluding that a probable cause existed.

Good Faith Exception: *United States v. Leon* (1984) 468 U.S. 897

The U.S. Supreme Court established a "good faith exception" to the exclusionary rule when a search warrant is obtained. The rule of the *Leon* case is that evidence seized pursuant to a search warrant will not be suppressed if officers obtained the warrant in good faith and acted in a reasonable reliance on a warrant issued by a neutral and detached magistrate. The evidence is admissible even if the search warrant is later found to be unsupported by probable cause, but this rule may not save the warrant if the affidavit contains substantial intentional misstatements, if the magistrate is not neutral and detached, or if the officer–affiant is not acting in good faith. *Leon* was a drastic departure from previous case law since this case allows the introduction of evidence seized pursuant to a search warrant, even if the search warrant is quashed for insufficient probable cause or is otherwise defective.

Traversal of Warrant: *Franks v. Delaware* (1978) 438 U.S. 154

The U.S. Supreme Court held that before a defendant can traverse a search warrant, the defendant must make a "substantial preliminary showing" with an offer of proof pointing out the specific areas of the affidavit claimed to be false, accompanied by supporting reasons. This means that only in rare cases can the affiant–officer be cross-examined about the information contained in the affidavit (i.e., a motion to traverse). The *Franks* decision is a compelling reason to use a search warrant when it is desirable to protect the identity of an informant. In nonwarrant situations in which an informant provides probable cause for an arrest or search, the police officer making the arrest or search can be cross-examined by the defense attorney about the informant. When a search warrant is obtained, however, the defense attorney is precluded from cross-examining the officer–affiant about the information contained in the affidavit (including information about the informant), except in rare situation where the defense can make a "substantial preliminary showing" as required by *Franks*. In short, the message delivered by the highest judicial authority is plain. The discharge, unpunished, of guilty defendants exact an enormous price from society. Consequently, the sanction of suppressing relevant evidence should be reserved for cases of the most serious misconduct committed by agents. With specific reference to facially sufficient warrants issued by neutral magistrates, it is rare when they can be successfully challenged.

Search Warrant

It is an order in writing, in the name of the people, signed by a magistrate, directed to a peace officer, commanding him or her to search for a person or persons, a thing or things, or personal property and, in the case of a thing or things or personal property, bring the same before the magistrate. This is the California definition as defined in Penal Code section 1523; however, many states have a very similar definition. In its most basic sense, a search warrant contains the following elements. It directs service to any peace officer; this of course can be federal state or local law enforcement officers. Every search warrant must also provide the statutory grounds or the reasons why it should be issued. There is no limit to the number of locations, vehicles, and persons that may be searched pursuant to a single warrant so long as the affidavit sets forth probable cause for each. A search warrant may be issued upon any of the following grounds:

1. When the property was stolen or embezzled
2. When the property or things were used as the means of committing a felony
3. When the property or things are in the possession of any person with the intent to use them as a means of committing a public offense or in the possession of another to whom he or she may have delivered them for the purpose of concealing them or preventing their being discovered
4. When the property or things to be seized consist of any item or constitute any evidence that tends to show a felony has been committed or tends to show that a particular person has committed a felony
5. When the property or things to be seized consist of evidence that tends to show that sexual exploitation of a child, in violation of Section 311.3, or possession of matter depicting sexual conduct of a person under the age of 18 years, in violation of Section 311.11, has occurred or is occurring
6. When there is a warrant to arrest a person
7. When a provider of electronic communication service or remote computing service has records or evidence, as specified in Section 1524.3, showing that property was stolen or embezzled constituting a misdemeanor or that property or things are in the possession of any person with the intent to use them as a means of committing a misdemeanor public offense or in the possession of another to whom he or she may have delivered them for the purpose of concealing them or preventing their discovery
8. When the property or things to be seized include an item or any evidence that tends to show a violation of Section 3700.5 of the Labor Code or tends to show that a particular person has violated Section 3700.5 of the Labor Code

9. When the property or things to be seized include a firearm or any other deadly weapon at the scene of or at the premises occupied or under the control of the person arrested in connection with a domestic violence incident involving a threat to human life or a physical assault as provided in subdivision (b) of Section 12028.5

10. When the property or things to be seized include a firearm or any other deadly weapon that is owned by, or in the possession of, or in the custody or control of, a person described in subdivision (a) of Section 8102 of the Welfare and Institutions Code

11. When the property or things to be seized include a firearm that is owned by, or in the possession of, or in the custody or control of, a person who is subject to the prohibitions regarding firearms pursuant to Section 6389 of the Family Code and if a prohibited firearm is possessed by, owned by, in the custody of, or controlled by a person against whom a protective order has been issued pursuant to Section 6218 of the Family Code, the person has been lawfully served with that order, and the person has failed to relinquish the firearm as required by law

Warrants and the Law

Decisions of the U.S. Supreme Court favor the use of search warrants. The current state of the law makes it extremely difficult for a defendant to prevent the admission of evidence seized pursuant to a search warrant. Three decisions, in particular, have had a tremendous impact on the law and litigation of search warrants. These cases are *Illinois v. Gates* (1983) 462 U.S. 213, *United States v. Leon* (1984) 468 U.S. 897, and *Franks v. Delaware* (1978) 438 U.S. 154.

Affidavit

A search warrant cannot be issued but upon probable cause, supported by affidavit, naming or describing the person being searched for and particularly describing the property, or things in the place to be searched. The affidavit must set forth the facts tending to establish the grounds for the application or probable cause for believing that they exist. The Fourth Amendment to the U.S. Constitution states in part that "no warrants shall issue, but upon probable cause, supported by Oath or affirmation...." It is recommended that the search warrant contain language that the affiant specifically swears that the facts set forth in the affidavit are true.

Again the format of affidavits varies depending on jurisdiction; however, all affidavits generally include the name of the affidavit; statutory grounds for issuance; a description with reasonable particularity of the persons, places, and vehicles to be searched; and a description with reasonable particularity of the property and or persons to be seized. The affidavit is essentially your report to the judge, detailing the facts of the case and why you believe you have probable cause to search the listed property and seize the listed items. In many states, the following six questions will need to be answered by the officer, regardless of the type of search warrant being requested:

1. What property do you wish to search?
2. What property do you wish to seize?
3. What investigation have you conducted regarding the listed property?
4. What training and experience do you have regarding this investigation?

5. Why do you believe the listed property will be at the listed address?
6. Is night service needed? And do you need to seal this warrant? Why?

In answering these questions in proper legal language, the law enforcement officer must convince the judge that all relevant concerns have been addressed.

The affiant must state facts establishing probable cause for the seizure of the described items at the described locations. The task of the issuing magistrate is simply to make a practical commonsense decision whether, given all the circumstances set forth in the affidavit before him or her, including the veracity and basis of knowledge of persons supplying hearsay information, there is a *fair probability* that contraband or evidence of a crime will be found in a particular place. This means as a detective, you need to make sure your affidavit is clear and easy to follow and articulates your probable cause to get the warrant issued.

It is recommended that the affidavit be in a chronological and narrative form. It should include all the information the affiant has, including what he or she has personally seen and heard and what has been stated by others. Simple, declarative sentences are best: "I saw X, I did X, The CI told me X, etc." Further, the affidavit should include a recitation of the affiant's training and experience and the affiant's conclusion, drawn from all the information in the affidavit that the items sought will be found at the locations to be searched. Documents such as police reports may be attached and incorporated by reference into the affidavit.

The affidavit must state the facts establishing probable cause for the seizure of the described items at the described location. The U.S. Supreme Court has expressed the standard of probable cause as follows: the task of the issuing magistrate is simply to make a practical commonsense decision whether, given all the circumstances set forth in the affidavit before him or her, including the veracity and basis of knowledge of the person supplying the information, there is a fair probability that contraband or evidence of a crime will be found at the location. The magistrate typically takes into account the totality of the circumstances as outlined in the affidavit in making their decision whether to issue or not issue the search warrant that is being requested by law enforcement.

Once the entire affidavit has been written and submitted to the magistrate, after the affidavit warrants have been reviewed, the affiant will swear to the contents of the affidavit under oath. Typically, the police officer will raise the right-hand swear under penalty of perjury that all of the contents included in the affidavit and warrants are true and accurate.

What Property to Search?

Generally, the description of a dwelling should include the complete address and a brief description of its outer appearance. A vehicle description should include the color, year, make, model, and license number. The description of a person should include a name (if known), physical appearance, and distinguishing marks, if any. It is also good practice to give the probable location of a vehicle or person to be searched, especially if either cannot otherwise be fully described. This adds "particularity" to the description. It is also desirable when describing structures such as houses, apartment units, and stores to include a phrase that makes clear that the search is to encompass the entire structure, its surrounding grounds, and any associated structures.

As a detective, you must ensure that the location you intend to search has been properly investigated and a visual has been made by the investigator. There must be no mistake about the location, and the location must be described in detail. If you're going to search a residence, for example, what kind of residence is it? Is it a single- or multistory building? Is it a single-family-style house or a duplex, condominium, town house, or apartment building?

Further, what does the residence look like? Describe the building color and composition. Include any identifying features, including where the address is on the residence. If it's a vehicle, describe all the containers therein. Include the color, make, model, and license plate number. Always include the name of your target as well as all pertinent information on your target. The more detail, the better. If you know your gang member's social security number, driver's license, and/or immigration number, include these.

The use of the word "premises" in the description of a location to be searched provides a broad scope of the search to be conducted. A warrant to search "premises" located at a particular address is sufficient to support the search of outbuildings. For this reason, it is critical to add language to include all rooms, attics, basements, and other parts therein and the surrounding grounds and any garages, storage areas, trash containers, and outbuildings of any kind located therein. Also, if there are any places of special interest at the location to be searched such as a safe, or wall compartment, or underground bunker in the backyard, that place should be specifically described, especially if it is believed the items sought will be found within that particular place.

In giving a street address, it is important to specify "North," "South," "East," or "West," if that is part of the address. Also, it is important to specify "Street," "Avenue," "Boulevard," "Way," etc. This avoids any ambiguity as to the address. When requesting a warrant for an apartment or condo, be certain to limit the description to the apartment or condo unit in question and not the entire apartment building, unless the affidavit justifies a search of the entire building. Thus, include the apartment number or its location within the building or complex. For a store or business, the name of the business, the address, and a brief description of its outer appearance should be stated. If a vehicle is included in your warrant, generally the color, year, make, model, and license number of the vehicle to be searched will constitute an adequate description.

What Property to Seize?

The property you wish to seize must relate to your investigation. This prevents an unnecessary seizure of items not related to a case. A good test of "reasonable particularity" is whether or not an officer with no knowledge of the facts underlying the warrant and looking only at the description of the property on the face of the warrant would be able to recognize and select the items described while conducting the search. Descriptions should be as specific and complete as possible. Model numbers and serial numbers should be included, if known. Warrants that fail to describe property with reasonable particularity are considered "general exploratory warrants" and are forbidden by both the U.S. and California Constitutions. When officers, in the course of a bona fide effort to execute a valid search warrant, discover articles which, although not included in the warrant, are reasonably identifiable as contraband, they may seize them whether they are initially in plain sight or come into plain sight subsequently, as a result of the officers' efforts.

In a drug case, for example, the description should specify the type of controlled substance to be seized, such as heroin, cocaine, marijuana, and amphetamines. The use of the general terms "controlled substances," "narcotics," or "dangerous drugs" without further description might be held by a reviewing court to be too indefinite, inasmuch as there are many types of controlled substances, narcotics, and dangerous drugs. The description of items to be seized should also include paraphernalia that is commonly associated with the sale, storage, possession, and use of the controlled substance, for example, "heroin and paraphernalia related to the use and sale of heroin, including hypodermic syringes, hypodermic needles, eye droppers, spoons, cotton, milk sugar, scales and other weighing devices, balloons, condoms, paper bindles, and measuring devices." The affidavit should contain the opinion of a narcotics expert (usually the officer–affiant) that such paraphernalia will be found on the premises. Case law has held that where drugs are possessed for use or sale, it is reasonable to infer that paraphernalia for their use or sale will also be present.

In a gang case, for example, some of the items you may add to your warrant to be seized if located could include:

- Firearms, including ammunition, casings, holsters, targets, and cleaning equipment
- Evidence of street gang membership or affiliation with any street gang
- Paraphernalia to include any reference to the gang, including any drawings, writings, objects, or graffiti depicting gang members' names, initials, logos, monikers, slogans, or mention of street gang membership or affiliation, activity, or identity
- Any paintings, drawings, photographs, photograph albums, photographic negatives, undeveloped film, or homemade videotapes, depicting persons, vehicles, weapons, or locations that appear upon observation to be relevant to gang membership or association or depicting items believed to be evidence in the case being investigated with this warrant or depicting evidence of any criminal activity
- Any newspaper clippings relating details of or referring to any crime or crimes of violence
- Any address books, lists of, or single references to addresses or telephone numbers of persons who are determined to belong to or to be affiliated with any street gangs
- Papers, documents, and effects tending to show dominion and control over said premises, including keys, fingerprints, clothing, photographs, photographic negatives, undeveloped film, homemade videotapes, and any other noncommercially manufactured video/audio recordings, handwritings, documents, and effects bearing a form of identification such as a person's name, photograph, social security number, or driver's license number

You may also have to answer incoming phone calls, either landline or cellular, during execution of the warrant, to view any videotapes seized pursuant to the warrant, and to open or download and forensically examine all computer software and programs seized pursuant to the warrant.

Computers have become a principal means of storing both personal and business information for many people. For criminals, computers provide an excellent means of collecting and storing information that pertains to the criminal's unlawful activities. A criminal's computer may contain items such as a drug dealer's list of suppliers and/or customers, a bookmaker's records of gambling transactions and moneys owed, a street gang's membership roster, child pornography, financial records supporting a fraud scheme, and identity theft software.

For law enforcement officers, if you feel the suspect may be using a computer to commit a crime, put in your warrant that you would like to seize and forensically examine the computers, and articulate your probable cause; this way, the computer evidence will be admissible in court. If there is probable cause to believe a computer or computers within premises were used in the commission of a crime and/or contain evidence of criminal activity, all computers within the premises can be seized and their electronic contents searched pursuant to a search warrant. It is not necessary to show that a named suspect owned or used a particular computer. Computer records are extremely susceptible to tampering, hiding, or destruction, whether deliberate or inadvertent. Images can be hidden in all manner of files, even word processing documents and spreadsheets. Criminals will do all they can to conceal contraband, including the simple expedient of changing the names and extensions of files to disguise their content from the casual observer.

When confronted with a computer at a search scene, officers have several options as to how to conduct the search. One option is a search of the computer at the scene. A second option is to remove the computer to another location where the search of the computer can be conducted. Often it is simply impractical to search a computer at the search site because of the time and expertise required to unlock all sources of information. The third option involves a forensically trained expert making an exact duplicate of the hard drive's contents, commonly known as a "clone" or "bit-image copy", and then search the clone. If option two or three is used, officers should include language in the search warrant authorizing the removal of the computer for an off-site search and/or the making of a cloned copy.

Prior Investigation

What investigations have you conducted to lead you to request this warrant? This outlines the who, what, when, where, why, and how—probably the largest portion of your search warrant affidavit. Nonetheless, this section should be simple to complete, because this is basically the follow-up report of your investigation. What did you do or what did you see that you feel gives you probable cause to search?

Most warrants start off with a statement by the officer, who requests the warrant with substantial probable cause to search the premises and all parts therein, including all rooms, attics, basements, cellars, crawl spaces, safes, mail receptacles, storage areas, containers, surrounding grounds, trash areas, garages, and outbuildings assigned to or part of the residence located at [address] of [city] and [county]. What are the facts of your case?

Relevant Experience and Training

Simply describe your experience as a law enforcement officer, an investigator, and a gang investigator. How many search warrants have you been involved in? what is your training? and so on. *The bottom line* is who are you and what are your qualifications.

Cause for Belief

Why do you believe the property you're looking for is at this location? You must also establish that this property is relevant to the case being investigated. You must show up-to-date facts regarding the presence of items in the house and connection of a suspect to the residence. See sidebar later.

Sample Probable Cause Statement: Gang Case Example

Based on my training and experience, I know that people in general and street gang members in particular commonly hide the weapons used in violent crimes. They hide other evidences associated with crimes, such as clothing and other paraphernalia, in their homes, the homes of coparticipants, and the homes of fellow gang members or in their vehicles. Further, my experience indicates that most street gang members are known by street names or monikers to their fellow gang members and that they frequently write their gang name, their street name or moniker, and the street names or monikers of their associates on walls, furniture, miscellaneous items, or papers, both in residences and vehicles.

I know that gang members frequently adorn their bodies with tattoos, many of which declare their gang affiliation. Most gang members keep photographs and photograph albums in which the following are depicted: (1) themselves and fellow gang members who are posing and displaying hand gang signs, which indicate gang identity or affiliation; (2) gang members or associates posing with weapons, which are often used for criminal activities; (3) gang members or associates posing beside vehicles, which are occasionally used during the commission of crimes; and (4) gang members or associates posing at locations, which are known to be specific gang hangouts.

Gang members occasionally maintain scrapbooks or newspaper articles describing acts of aggression committed by or against their gang. They also frequently maintain the current phone numbers or addresses of fellow gang members or associates. It's also my experience that gang paraphernalia (described earlier in detail) is frequently maintained. Therefore, it's necessary and incident to the possession and use of such weapons. Furthermore, such evidence of gang membership and clothing aren't normally dispose of and, therefore, are likely to be found at the location to be searched.

It's also my opinion that evidence of gang membership or affiliation with any street gang is important, as it may suggest motive for the commission of the crimes in the instant case and it may provide evidence identifying other persons who have knowledge of, or who are involved in, the commission of the crimes in the instant case. It may also corroborate information given by other witnesses.

Furthermore, my training and experience indicates persons in control of premises leave evidence of their identification, such as fingerprints and handwritings, which are subject to expert identification, routinely in the normal course of living within their premises. Also, clothing, photographs, canceled mail, and the like are routinely maintained in a person's premises as necessary and incident to maintaining such premises. In addition, by intercepting phone calls at the premises while the search warrant is being executed, I expect to talk with persons who are familiar with the persons in control of the premises and will so testify. Such callers and described dominion-and-control evidence is vital to proving control over the described property to be seized.

Therefore, based on my training, experience, and the aforementioned facts, which I believe to be true, I believe I have substantial cause to believe the previously described property or a portion thereof will be at the described premises when the warrant is served.

Based on the aforementioned information and investigation, I believe grounds for the issuance of a search warrant exist as set forth in the penal code [insert relevant penal code numbers for your jurisdiction].

I, the affiant, hereby pray a search warrant be issued for the seizure of said property, or any part thereof, from said premises at any time of the day, good cause being shown therefore and the same be brought before this magistrate or retained subject to the order of this Court.

Night Service

For search warrant purposes, nighttime is defined as those hours between 10:00 PM and 7:00 AM. Before a warrant may be served at night, it must contain a statement or "direction" that it can be served at night, and its supporting affidavit must set forth facts and circumstances establishing good cause for a nighttime search. Regardless of the state you work in, officers must bear in mind the added dangers a nighttime service might engender. In some states, search warrants are executed during the day and early evening hours—unless a warrant is *endorsed* for night service.

There's good reason for this. Imagine how a law enforcement officer would react if someone pounded on his or her front door in the middle of the night and claimed to be the police. As a person with easy access to firearms, the law enforcement officer's natural reaction would be to reach for a weapon. Criminals and citizens in general have easy access to firearms too. The risk factors for both citizens and law enforcement may increase at night. These are particulars the officer must overcome if confronted with them by a magistrate. Therefore, a nighttime service endorsement is not granted easily.

Question: "Officer, why do you want a nighttime service endorsement?" Officers may want to execute the search at a period when those inside are most likely to be asleep, thereby lessening the risk to officers and citizens alike. The nighttime endorsement request may be for reasons of evidence (i.e., the suspects deal in controlled substances only in specific nighttime hours, or evidence is known to be at a particular location only at specific nighttime hours). Perhaps witness or informant information is such that the investigator knows evidence is present, and such evidence will likely be disposed of or removed if there is further delay in executing the warrant. Reasons for a nighttime endorsement request may be predicated on information found in police records, investigation, or observations. For example, if your officers have found that a wanted suspect resides at the target residence, but efforts to find the subject during daylight hours have proven ineffective and his or her successful evading of law enforcement jeopardizes the safety of citizens in the community, then the investigator needs only to articulate his or her reasons for requesting the nighttime service endorsement. This is done in a brief paragraph outlining the request.

Upon a showing of good cause, the magistrate may, in his or her discretion, insert a direction in a search warrant that it may be served at any time of the day or night. In the absence of such a direction, the warrant shall be served only between the hours of 7 AM and 10 PM. When establishing "good cause" under this section, the magistrate shall consider the safety of the peace officers serving the warrant and the safety of the public as a valid basis for nighttime endorsements. Also, nighttime warrants should be served promptly. It tends to cast doubt on the affiant's veracity if the statement requesting a nighttime search stresses the necessity for an immediate search and then three days pass before the warrant is served.

Seal the Deal

All documents relating to a search warrant become open to the public as judicial records following execution and return of the warrant. However, all or part of the search warrant documents may be sealed pursuant to a court order under certain limited circumstances. Such an order can be requested at any time, but it is most often sought at the time of the issuance of the warrant. The California Supreme Court case people V Hobbs held that all or part of the information in a search warrant affidavit provided by an informant may be sealed to protect the informant's identity. For example, in gang cases, the issue of victim or witness intimidation in gang-related cases is very real. Even if a culprit is arrested, gang associates will often threaten, terrorize, or target victims and witnesses to dissuade or prevent testimony. Furthermore, effective gang investigators often deal with paid informants or individuals who provide information on condition of anonymity. In such cases, "sealing" the warrant may save an ongoing case or prevent an informant from being killed.

Unless the informer is a percipient witness (i.e., a material witness to the guilt or innocence of the accused of the offense charged), investigators have the privilege and an obligation to prevent disclosure of this person's name if information is provided in confidence. If this informer's name is used in an affidavit in support of a search warrant, his or her name in some states will be in the public record for a given period. This means any defense investigator or attorney, as well as the defendant, will have access to it. Especially in gang cases, this may be a critical and life-threatening issue. Furthermore, any intimidation or violence aimed at witnesses who provide information in confidence will undermine the investigator's credibility in future investigations and likely ruin the current case. More importantly, it may mean the injury or death of an innocent citizen who expected to remain anonymous.

Sometimes, it may be desirable to seal all the search warrant documents to protect the integrity of an ongoing investigation. Such a sealing order goes well beyond what is authorized by *People v. Hobbs*, earlier, which authorizes sealing only to protect the identity of an informant. Such a sealing order, to protect an ongoing investigation, may be appropriate if there are no court proceedings and pending case has been filed, but arrest warrants remain outstanding. However, once arrests are made and/or the investigation has concluded, the search warrant documents will likely be unsealed so that a public return can be filed and discovery provided to the defense.

General Search Warrant Tips

1. Prepare a neat, concise, and businesslike affidavit. You are preparing a legal document for submission to the court. It also reflects on your professionalism. If you haven't already done so, you may want to review "AAA Formatting Tips."
2. Be judge friendly. Eliminate anything that is not pertinent to helping the judge understand the probable cause that connects the place to be searched to the items to be seized. Do *not* simply copy and paste your arrest reports or surveillance logs into the affidavit.
3. Paragraph often, especially in your probable cause statement. It makes long sections of a narrative easier to read. Start a new paragraph every time there is a change in time, for example, another hour and another day.

4. Tell the narrative in chronological form, that is, the order in which the events happened. Don't jump back and forth in time, if you can help it. Give time references to help the judge understand the chronology, for example,
   a. Shortly thereafter, …
   b. Later that afternoon, …
   c. About 5 min later, …
   d. In late August, …
   e. Sometime in the summer of 2005, …
   f. After the CI arrived, …
5. Provide the basis of all information. From whom did you get the info? (The dispatcher issued an APB for…; my partner radioed me and said…; the CI told me…; etc.) Likewise, explain how you or someone else knew or came to know certain information. For example, do not say, "The car is registered to Smith," without explaining how you know that. Instead, say, "A check with the Department of Motor Vehicles shows the car is registered to …." Similarly, don't say, "The CI went into the apartment and met with Jimmy…," without explaining how the CI knew his name was Jimmy. (Had they been previously introduced? Did he or she hear everyone else in the apartment calling him Jimmy? Had they interacted at anytime in the past, legally or illegally?)
6. It is acceptable to use acronyms, but don't assume all readers know what they mean. Acronyms make reading easier and save time; thus you are being "judge friendly" by using them. Just be sure to spell out the complete name the first time it is used, followed by the acronym in parentheses, for example, cooperating individual (CI), Oceanside Police Department (OPD), methylenedioxymethamphetamine (MDMA), Department of Motor Vehicles (DMV), and San Diego Gas & Electric (SDG&E).
7. Stay away from Sally LNU, José LNU, etc., meaning last name unknown. Instead, say, "I was contacted by a tipster who only identified herself as Sally," or "After entering the apartment, the UC was introduced to a man only referred to as José."
8. Don't burn your CI. Eliminate references to sex. If possible, give time and date ranges rather than specific times or dates, for example, within the past 10 days and sometime after sundown. If possible, don't give the exact amount of money paid for contraband, the amount of contraband provided, or how it was packaged, regardless whether it's stolen property, drugs, child pornography, or whatever.
9. Don't give up your good meeting locations. Say "a strip mall parking lot in San Diego" instead of "the Wal-Mart parking lot on Murphy Canyon Road" or "a coffee shop in Chula Vista" rather than "the Starbucks at 4th and C in Chula Vista."
10. Never give officers' badge or ID numbers. There is no legal reason to do so, and it just makes it easier for the defense attorneys to track that person in their databases.
11. In your list of items to be seized, have you included "…to seize, view, and forensically examine all computer hardware and software and all other devices capable of digitally or electronically storing information, including such devices as cellular phones, Blackberries, and personal data assistants (PDAs)…?" Can you think of a crime in which computers, PDAs, cell phones, etc., are not or could not be used? Could/did your suspect likely conspire, plan, or brag about the crime to others via e-mail? Could/did your suspect try to sell, swap, or ship drugs, stolen property, or child pornography on eBay, Craigslist, or other websites?

12. Include a summary paragraph in your OPINONS AND CONCLUSIONS section. After you have finished your investigative narrative, include *one* final paragraph that summarizes the primary pieces of evidence pointing to the likelihood that the stuff you want to seize is currently at the place you want to search.

13. It is almost impossible to proofread one's own material. After you have spell-checked the entire affidavit, have a colleague proofread it for accuracy (if he or she knows the facts of the case), spelling (remember, spell-check won't fix homonyms: to, two, too; there, they're, their; etc.), and grammar (is the tense consistent? are pronouns used correctly? "its" is not the same as "it is," and "myself" is *not* the equivalent of "I" or "me"). Accuracy is important. An incorrect address or mistaken description may invalidate a search warrant. Reference to sources such as the U.S. Post Office website, road maps, and telephone books may help determine a correct address and avoid the misspelling of a street name. Old police reports may be used to obtain or verify an address, license number, vehicle description, name, and physical description. DMV records and documents are also helpful. If problems in surveillance make it difficult to obtain a complete description, explain this difficulty in the body of the affidavit. In the event a description is found to be incorrect after the warrant has been signed but before it has been served, it must not be served without first being corrected and signed again by both the magistrate and the affiant. Every effort should be made to ensure accuracy during the preparation of the warrant. Proofreading is essential.

14. Be mindful of PC964. Do not include confidential personal information of *victims* or *witnesses* in your affidavit. This includes an address, telephone number, CDL or CID number, Social Security number, date of birth, place of employment, and bank or credit card number.

15. Check for or provide attachments. Depending upon where you work, it may be acceptable to attach police reports to support your probable cause: most jurisdictions prefer for the affidavit to be a self-contained document that has all of the support needed to obtain the warrant without the need to attach police reports to affidavits. It is typically not being judge friendly to have numerous attachments. As a detective, you should condense the information you need from the report and include it in the narrative of the affidavit. On the other hand, it is totally acceptable to attach photos, county assessor maps, graphs, and timelines when they help the judge understand the location of the place to be searched or help illustrate information contained in your probable cause narrative.

Jurisdiction

A magistrate can't issue a search warrant for any location within the county in which he or she sits. For example, superior court judge in San Francisco issues a warrant for location in San Diego and vice versa. Magistrate may issue a search warrant for a location outside of his or her county but within the state as long as it relates to an offense that can be prosecuted in that magistrate's county. The California magistrate can also issue a search warrant for a location in his or her county to search for evidence of crimes committed in another state even in the absence of a request from law enforcement authorities. In that state, its search warrant statutes contain no language suggesting the things to be seized must relate to the crime committed within this state.

Knock and Notice

The officer may break open any outer or inner door or window of a house, or any part of a house, or anything therein, to execute the warrant, if, after the notice of his or her authority and purpose, he or she is refused to admittance. Laws regarding knock and notice vary from state to state. Boiled down, knock and notice are required for two reasons: privacy and safety. In state statutes, the word *break* doesn't necessarily mean smash, knockdown, or dismantle. Even peaceable entry might be construed as "breaking," if doing so causes the officers to incur undue risk. There are cases where breaking the door down is warranted, for example, when knock and notice will cause suspects to flee or for evidence to be destroyed or tampered with, but before you commit your officers to taking such actions, ensure you've weighed the potential consequences of not waiting (legal and otherwise).

In the usual case, officers should simply go to the front door of the premises described on the warrant and knock on the door. If an occupant opens the door or states "Who is it?," the officer should state "Police officers with a search warrant demanding entry" or "We have a search warrant. Let us in." Officers must wait a reasonable time to allow any occupants within to come to the door before forcing entry. A 30–60 s wait is recommended in most situations, minus exigent circumstances.

In order to justify a "no-knock" entry, the police must have a reasonable suspicion that knocking and announcing their presence, under the particular circumstances, would be dangerous or futile or that it would inhibit the effective investigation of the crime by, for example, allowing the destruction of evidence. Compliance with knock and notice will be excused if the items sought are capable of swift destruction and the officers have a reasonable belief the occupants, upon hearing knock and notice, will destroy or dispose of the items. This belief requires specific facts, not mere speculation. Several other cases hold that if officers knock and give notice or even just knock and then hear running footsteps away from the door, they may then force entry. In such cases, officers have a reasonable basis for a belief that the suspect is going to destroy or dispose of the items sought (*People v. McCarthy* [1978] 79 Cal.App.3d 547, 550–551, *People v. Watson* [1979] 89 Cal.App.3d 376, and *Brown v. Superior Court* [1973] 34 Cal.App.3d 539, 544).

After entry is made, the officer should show the original search warrant to the occupant and give him a copy of the warrant. Occupants should be treated in a courteous and professional manner. If no one is present at the premises being searched, a copy of the face sheet(s) of the warrant should be left in a conspicuous place within the location.

Conducting the Search

The officers should conduct an unhurried, thorough, and systematic search. Each officer searching must know what items are listed on the warrant and can search for those items only. Generally, all containers within the described premises may be searched pursuant to the warrant. The police may ordinarily assume that all personal property which they find while executing a search warrant is the property of a resident of the premises subject to search. It is recommended that at least one officer (and preferably two) be designated "evidence collectors" and be able to testify to observing each seized item before it is moved. The evidence collector(s) should also be able to testify to the recovery, packaging, and marking of all seized items. Documentation of the exact place from which each item is recovered is important and is best done during the search. Consideration should also be given to the use of videotapes, photographs, a fingerprint kit, and scientific analysis at the scene of the search. This may prove extremely helpful in later court proceedings. Also, it is important to maintain the chain of custody and the integrity and security of the items seized.

The search must be terminated when all the described items have been found or it is clear they are not on the premises, vehicle, person, or other things to be searched.

Briefing of a search warrant action should be held prior to the search. Copies of the operational plan, search warrant, and affidavit should also be made available. A tactical entry plan, a summary of the case and information on suspects or subjects found at the location, and any safety issues will be discussed.

A staging area should be selected to meet on the day of the search with all assigned personnel and local law enforcement agency near the location, that is, the residence to be searched. Consider surveillance for any changes of the location. Paralegals (civilian personnel) will be transported to the staging location by a detective.

- Secure the location of the search warrant utilizing the team listed in the OPS plan and execution of the tactical entry plan.
- Only after the location has been secured, civilian personnel (paralegals) can be transported to the search warrant location.
- Mark general areas and locations (rooms, closets, etc.) to be searched with alphabetical letters A, B, C, etc.
- Take a *photograph* of a label marked "Entry Photographs."
- Take *entry photographs* or video of the interior of the location prior to the search documenting the condition of the location and the labeled areas A, B, C, etc.
- Take *photographs* of the front, back, sides, and any significant areas of the search warrant location, that is, the residence.
- Identify a work area for the paralegal to be stationed where labeling and marking evidence can be documented on the receipt and inventory (R&I). Paralegals will assign and mark item numbers/box numbers on labeled items of evidence and on boxes or similar container. Paralegals should complete all pertinent information on labels presented to them.
- *Investigators* will fill out information listed on labels placed in the evidence; this information will include the room and area where the evidence is found, description of the contents of the item, who found the item, the date, and location.
- Once *photographs* have been taken, mark areas within locations or areas A, B, etc., to be searched with numbers (A-1, 2, 3, etc.), marking areas where potential evidence will be found.
- A continuous numbering system for all found evidence items 1, 2, 3, 4, etc., will be used until the last piece of evidence is marked. Numbered items will be placed in numbered boxes. Original packaging taken from the defendant's residence to the evidence room of the police facility is strongly discouraged. These containers carry nests of spiders, cockroaches, etc., requiring fumigation, for example.

- When taking *photographs* of specific evidence, in an area (room, garage, etc.), rephotograph the room/location *letter* A, B, C, etc., before taking the photograph of the item.
- Complete a *diagram* of the location, that is, the residence. The diagram needs to reflect the location/area markers designated for the search. Show relationships between items of evidence if needed.
- Remove all stickers (location/area markers) and throw away all trash prior to taking exit photographs. Take a photograph of the *exit photograph* sign, and proceed with taking photographs of the interior of the location searched.
- Computers, money, jewelry, cell phones, guns, and other electronic devices are logged at the end of the receipt and inventory and will receive item numbers.
- Items taken from the location (i.e., computer, money, weapons, drugs, electronic equipment) and transported to another storage facility (RCFL, evidence room safe, other law enforcement agency) require a notation on the master R&I before removing the item from the evidence. *Note* the investigator's name (or agency) and location where the evidence is to be transported and stored.
- Envelopes are prestamped with evidence labels to document the items contained within. *Finders need only to record* the room, area, description, date, and items found by fields. The R&I paralegal will complete all remaining fields.
- Box labels/item labels are preprinted onto adhesive paper in groups of four and are removed and placed on boxes or items of evidence capturing certain information recorded on the R&I and as an identifier.

Supplies Needed

Detectives will generally monitor necessary contents needed in a search warrant kit. See the following list:

1. Plastic bags for evidence and trash
2. Rubber gloves
3. Dust masks
4. Black markers
5. Post-its/evidence markers (large and small)
6. Diagram paper
7. Measuring tape
8. Black permanent markers small and large
9. Note paper
10. Camera, batteries, lenses, video camera, charging cords, battery, cards
11. Evidence stamp (for envelopes)
12. Box and item labels
13. Envelopes various sizes
14. Brown bags
15. Scissors
16. Tape
17. Stapler

Receipt and Inventory

The officer must give an inventory of the property seized to the person from whom it was taken, or in the absence of any person, the officer must leave the inventory list at the place where the property was found.

The return to the search warrant consists of an inventory or list of all the property seized during service of the warrant including unlisted items seized during the search. Ordinarily, a copy of a recovered property report attached to the return form is sufficient. (See Penal Code section 1537 and see Appendix H for a sample return.) The return may be prepared and filed by any officer who participated in the search. It need not be done by the search warrant affiant. If money is seized in the service of the search warrant, it must be listed on the inventory along with the other seized items and stored in a secure manner. If the seized bills do not have any unique evidentiary value in and of themselves, the money may be deposited into a bank account or checking account for safekeeping. This may be done by the use of an addendum to the search warrant return. Such an addendum appears in this manual as Appendix I and is entitled "Request and Order for Deposit of Seized Funds into Bank Account." This addendum is easily prepared by inserting the search warrant number, the amount of money seized, and the name of the agency that executed the warrant, for example, Los Angeles Sheriff's Department. The original warrant and affidavit, as well as the return to the search warrant, should be delivered forthwith to the magistrate or to his or her court after the search has been conducted and not later than 10 days after issuance of the warrant.

Releasing Property Seized Pursuant to a Search Warrant

All property or things taken on a warrant must be retained by the officer in his or her custody, subject to the order of the court to which he or she is required to return the proceedings before him or her or of any other court in which the offense in respect to which the property or things taken are triable. An officer should not release property seized pursuant to a search warrant unless a valid court order, either oral or written, authorizes him or her to do so. Sometimes, an investigator obtains a search warrant in which it is anticipated that a large amount of stolen property will be recovered. Release of the property to their rightful owners may require multiple court orders. Under these circumstances, the affiant/investigator may desire to seek in the search warrant authority to release recovered property to its rightful owner without having to obtain an additional court order. Such language in the search warrant might be phrased as follows: "Officers involved in this investigation are authorized to release property seized pursuant to this search warrant to its rightful owner without a special court order to that effect. Such release shall only be made if the owner of the property is clearly identified and the release of the property is well documented, such as a photograph of the owner with the released property." There have been isolated instances of attorneys obtaining ex parte court orders for the return of property prior to the disposition of the case and without any legal authority to do so. If there is any doubt regarding the validity of such an order, particularly if the case has not yet been filed or is still pending, the property should not be returned until the legality of the court order is thoroughly reviewed.

Alternatives to a Search Warrant

Generally, when there is time to obtain a search warrant, one should be sought. However, sometimes, there is insufficient probable cause for search warrant or other reasons exist making it impractical or impossible to obtain in these cases. Detectives should be aware of some of the alternatives in conducting a search pursuant to the search warrant.

For example, a probation search may be a viable alternative. The suspect may be on probation, and a check of the court files is called. The probation department may reveal that a condition of the suspect's probation is that he or she submits to a search by a peace officer at anytime of the day or night with or without a warrant. Such a condition of probation permits a search of the suspect's person or property without a warrant and without the suspect's consent. A search may be conducted without any probable cause at all; however, probation searches may not be undertaken for harassment arbitrary or capricious reasons.

The same may be true if your suspect is on parole. Officers may search of the parolee in his or her residence and any property under his or her control without a warrant. This gives a parolee a reduced expectation of privacy, but such a search is reasonable within the meaning of the Fourth Amendment as long as it is not arbitrary, capricious, or harassing. In all cases, officers may obtain consent to search.

Exigent Circumstances

The existence of emergency or other action circumstances makes entry justifiable, at least a partial search without a search warrant. For example, detectives receive a call that a residence appears to have been ransacked through the front door that is left open upon their arrival. The officers can make entry to discharge the community caretaker functions to make sure there's no one inside for emergency assistance. The U.S. Supreme Court recognized emergency aid as an exception to the warrant requirement. Warrantless entry into a residence by peace officers is justified by the need to protect and preserve life or avoid serious injury.

Searching a Car

The U.S. Supreme Court has set forth basic rules for searching a car. The court can order the police to search a vehicle incident to a recent occupant's arrest only if the arrestee is within reaching distance from the passenger compartment at the time of the search word, which is reasonable to believe that the vehicle contains evidence of the offense related to the arrest. The Supreme Court can also act as the police officers who can lawfully stop an automobile and have probable cause to believe that contraband is located somewhere therein and may conduct warrantless search of the vehicle, which can be assisted by a magistrate who could authorize a search warrant. The contraband includes closed containers within the vehicle. Additionally, when officers impound a vehicle, inventories pursuant to standard police procedures are reasonable, and any contraband or other evidence of a crime discovered during the search may be seized.

Search Incident to Arrest

Federal law permits a full search of any arrestee, regardless of the offense for which the arrest was made. The U.S. Supreme Court held that a custodial arrest is justified if an officer has probable cause to believe that an individual has committed even a very minor criminal offense in his or her presence, such as a fine-only offense. California appellate decisions follow federal law and hold that officers in California may conduct full searches (including into pockets) following a lawful arrest.

Plain View

An officer may seize items that appear contraband and are in plain view. Also an officer may, without a warrant, see the container in plain view where the officer has probable cause to believe the container holds a legal substance; however, if an officer sees contraband through a window while standing on the suspects property the officer may need to obtain a search warrant or have legal justification, such as consent, to make entry. When in doubt, it is always advisable for a police detective to contact their local prosecutor and see counsel as each situation may have slightly different facts and different procedures.

Conclusion

Gangs are organized and constantly evolving, but it's our duty to protect our citizens from their depredations. Search warrants will allow your patrol officers to seek out the evidence they need to prove what the gang members don't want them to prove—namely, the criminal nature of their activities.

Remember: The search is only as good as the search warrant that precedes it. Evidence thrown out of court serves no purpose, other than allowing the gang to adapt their strategy and further evade justice. So it's imperative that supervisors work with their officers to ensure that the details that might come back to bite them are addressed with professional awareness of potential pitfalls.

Questions for Discussion

(Example)

20.1 Discuss the most common situations in which a search warrant would be required and what exceptions exist.

20.2 Discuss what the first responding officer(s) should do when they obtain a warrant and are in the planning stage to execute the warrant.

Reference

Illinois v. Gates (1983) 462 U.S. 213, 238.

Index

A

Access control list (ACL) system, 82
ACFE, *see* Association of Certified Fraud
       Examiners (ACFE)
Administrative and operational analysis, 165–166
Administrative warrant, 54, 56, 106
Affidavit, 341–342
American Hospital Association (AHA), 103
American Medical Association (AMA), 103
Amphetamines, 343
Antistatic bags, 144–145
Arizona v. Gant (2009), 54
Arson investigation
    definition, 52–53
    fifth amendment, 54–55
    fire scene documentation
        accelerant residue, 60
        burn patterns, 60–61
        collection process, 60–61
        detectors, 61–62
        fire safety equipment, 59
        forensic television program, 58
        glass breakage, 61
        incendiary device, 61
        information notes, 59
        oxidation, 61
        photographs, 59–60
        sketches, 60
        spalling, 61
        videotaping, 59
        volatile evidence, 61
    follow-up investigation, 62–63
    fourth amendment, 53–54
    preliminary investigation
        administrative warrant, 56
        criminal search warrant, 56
        failure analysis, 58
        human actions, 57
        incendiary fire, 57–58
        natural fire, causes, 57
        NFPA, 56–58
        point of origin, 56–57
        property damage/fire spread, 55
    prosecution, 63
    sixth amendment, 55
    substantial risk, 53
Association of Austrian Insurance Companies,
    71, 77–78
Association of Certified Fraud Examiners (ACFE),
    82–83, 114–115
Austrian insurance companies, 71–72
Autism spectrum disorder (ASD), 306–308
Automated teller machine (ATM), 47, 95
Autopsy, 12–13, 16, 168

B

Botnet, 157
Bounty hunter, 185, 199
Brown v. Superior Court [1973] 34 Cal.App.3d 539,
    544, 351
Burglary
    definition, 88
    investigative techniques
        commercial burglaries, 94–95
        evidence collection, 93–94
        point of entry, 92–93
        residential properties, 92
        vehicle burglary, 95–96
    proactive preventative measures
        CCTV, 90–91
        Operation ID, 91
        patrol checks, 91
        police agencies, 91–92
    theft/felony crime, 88
    types, 88–89
    UCR, 89–90

C

CAD system, *see* Computer-aided dispatch
        (CAD) system
Canada's confidential informant privilege, 206–207
Carroll v. United States, 267 U.S. 132 (1925), 54, 330
CART, *see* Computer Analysis Response Team
        (CART)
CCTV surveillance, *see* Closed-circuit television
        (CCTV) surveillance
Centers for Disease Control and Prevention (CDC)
    reports, 308–309
Centers for Medicare and Medicaid Services (CMS),
    101, 103–104, 107, 109, 113
Central information system (ZIS–Austria), 77–78

357

Certified fraud examiner (CFE), 111
Child advocacy centers (CACs), 38
Child grooming, 21–22
Closed-circuit television (CCTV) surveillance,
    90–91, 95–96, 220
CMS, see Centers for Medicare and Medicaid
    Services (CMS)
Cocaine, 72, 188, 215, 343
Coin-operated machines, 89, 95
Community Resources Against Street Hoodlums
    (CRASH), 183
Computer-aided dispatch (CAD) system, 166–167
Computer Analysis Response Team (CART),
    129–130
Concealment, 118, 120–122
Connecticut case, 107
Coroners and Justice Act 2009 (UK), 205–206
Corrections department, 189
Corroboration
    DNA evidence, 42–43, 48–49
    resources, 42
    subpoenas, 44
    warrants, 43–44
Court testimony, 189
CRASH, see Community Resources Against Street
    Hoodlums (CRASH)
Crime analysis
    administrative and operational analysis,
        165–166
    clear cold/unsolved cases, 174–175
    criminal investigative analysis, 168–169
    definition, 165
    generating leads, 174
    IACA crime pattern, 171–173
    induction and deduction, 173
    intelligence analysis, 167
    key cases, 174
    principle case, 173
    related cases, 174
    strategic crime analysis, 166–167
    TCA, 169–171
Crime scene investigation (CSI), 31, 234, 240, 283
Crime scene unit (CSU), 10, 279
Criminal investigation process
    case file folder, 280
    crime scene, 279–280
    defense counsel
        constitutional rights, 285, 292–294
        fourth amendment, 289–290
        prosecute Staci, 288–289
        Rosario disclosure, 286–287
        testimony, 290–291
    evidence
        bloodstain patterns, 282
        chain of custody, 282–283
        circumstantial evidence, 280

direct evidence, 280
        fact-finding, 280–281
        fingerprints, 281–282
        warrants, 281
    judges, 287–288
    lead detective, 278–279, 285
    police misconduct
        brutality, 291–292
        planting evidence, 292
        profiling, 291
    private investigators, 288
    prosecutors
        blue wall of silence, 284–285
        Drug Treatment Court, 284
        exculpatory evidence, 284
        former prosecutor, 284
        fourth amendment, 289–290
        photo lineups, 283
        prosecute Staci, 288–289
        prosecutorial obligations, 283–284
        testimony, 290–291
Criminal investigative analysis, 168–169
Criminalistics, 76
Criminal profiling, see Criminal investigative
    analysis
Criminal's computer, 344–345
CSI, see Crime scene investigation (CSI)
CSU, see Crime scene unit (CSU)
Cybercrime investigation
    affliction, 149
    challenges, 159–160
    Convention on Cybercrime
        (Council of Europe), 154
    crackers, 153–154
    deception, 149
    destruction, 149
    exchange illegal materials, 154
    financial motives, 151–153
    INTERPOL definition, 148
    money tracing, 157–158
    motive, means, and opportunity, 150
    perpetrator
        botnet, 157
        IPv4 addresses, 155–156
        opportunity, 155
        scam e-mail, 153–154
    political motives, 150–152
    spam e-mails, 158–159
    stealth, 148–149
    transaction, 149
    victimology, 159

D

Deaf community, 302–303
Deductive reasoning, 173

Defense attorney, *see* Defense counsel
Defense counsel
    constitutional rights, 285, 292–294
    fourth amendment, 289–290
    prosecute Staci, 288–289
    Rosario disclosure, 286–287
    testimony, 290–291
Deoxyribonucleic acid (DNA) evidence, 29–30,
        42–43, 48–49
Digital evidence, 31
    antistatic bags, 145
    cloud services and internet providers, 138
    definition, 138
    digital media, 138
    digital storage devices, 138
    documentation, 144
    legal issues, 138–139
    packaging and transportation, 144
    seizure of cell phone/mobile devices, 144
    seizure of computer, 142–143
    sources of, 138
    U.S. Department of Homeland Security (2007)
        diagram, 136–137
    U.S. Department of Homeland Security (2007)
        questions
        e-mails crimes, 141–142
        general investigative questions, 140
        identity theft/financial crimes, 140
        instant messaging/internet relay chat
            crimes, 142
        internet crimes against children, 140–141
        intrusion/hacking (network), 141
Digital media, 31, 138–139, 144
Digital storage devices, 138
District Attorney's Office, 189, 284, 286, 289, 292
DNA evidence, *see* Deoxyribonucleic acid (DNA)
        evidence
Documentary evidence, 8, 10, 128
Dying declaration, 7, 279–280

E

ECtHR, *see* European Court of Human Rights
        (ECtHR)
Electronic surveillance, 190, 332
Entrapment, 28
European Court of Human Rights (ECtHR), 195
Evidence technician (ET), 30–31
Exclusionary rule
    anticipatory warrant, 322
    consent search, 325
    emergency entry, 324
    exigent circumstances, 323–324
    Illinois v. Gates, 462 U.S. 213 (1983), 321
    knock-and-announce warrant, 321–322
    lawful arrest, 323

motor vehicles, 324–325, 329–331
national border, 324
no-knock warrant, 322
open-field doctrine, 322–323
plain view doctrine, 322
United States v. Leon, 468 U.S. 897 (1984), 321
vessel search, 325

F

Facebook, 160, 191
Federal Bureau of Investigation (FBI), 118
    burglary, 89
    CART, 129
    Financial Intelligence Center, 124
    gang members threat, 182
    HC fraud, 100–101, 107
    homicides, 5
    Innocent Images National Initiative program, 28
    insurance fraud, costs
        Austrian insurance companies, 71–72
        Europe, 71
        United States, 71
    money laundering, 125
    privacy, 328
    property crime offense, 90
    UCR program, 52–53
    white-collar crime, 118
Federal law enforcement agencies, 189
Federal Trade Commission (FTC), 129
Field interviews (FIs)
    biographical information, 268
    detectives, 266–267
    documentation criteria, 271–273
    law enforcement, 269
    minimize role, 266
    officers, 268
    phone numbers, 269
    photographs, 269–271
    pocket litter, 269
    police contact, documentation, 266
    potential criminal activity, 266
    psychological advantages, 267
    time and location, 268
    vehicle information, 271
Fifth amendment
    defendant's constitutional rights, 293
    rights of criminal defendants, 293
    "right to remain silent," 265–266
    self-incrimination and guarantees, 54–55
Financial Crimes Enforcement Network
        (FinCEN), 126
Financial fraud investigations
    badges of fraud, 121–122
    bank robberies, 120–121
    defendants, 121–122

detectives, 121
  financial investigations, 121
  perpetrator identity, 121
  U.S. Department of Justice (*see* U.S. Department
       of Justice)
Financial Intelligence Center, FBI, 124
Financial motives, 151–153
Fire and police investigation, *see* Arson
       investigation
Fire scene documentation
  accelerant residue, 60
  burn patterns, 60–61
  collection process, 60–61
  detectors, 61–62
  fire safety equipment, 59
  forensic television program, 58
  glass breakage, 61
  incendiary device, 61
  information notes, 59
  oxidation, 61
  photographs, 59–60
  sketches, 60
  spalling, 61
  videotaping, 59
  volatile evidence, 61
Forensic analysis, 30–31
Fourth amendment
  vs. administrative warrant, 54
  automobile exception, 54
  consent, 53–54
  constitutional law, 320–321
  eavesdropping and surveillance, 331
  exclusionary rule
    anticipatory warrant, 322
    consent search, 325
    emergency entry, 324
    exigent circumstances, 323–324
    Illinois v. Gates, 462 U.S. 213 (1983), 321
    knock-and-announce warrant, 321–322
    lawful arrest, 323
    motor vehicle searches, 324–325, 329–331
    national border, 324
    no-knock warrant, 322
    open-field doctrine, 322–323
    plain view doctrine, 322
    United States v. Leon, 468 U.S. 897 (1984), 321
    vessel search, 325
  fire investigators, 54
  history, 316–317
  home searches, 328–329
  lawful arrest, 54
  legal aspects, 317–320
  probable cause
    Cleveland Police Department, 326
    direct and indirect sources, 326–327
    reasonable and prudent person, 325–326
    reasonable suspicion, *Terry* stop, 325–327

  stops and frisks, 325
  Terry frisk, 328
  prosecutors, 289–290
  reasonable expectation of privacy, 328
  seizures, 54
  technology, 331–333
Franks v. Delaware (1978) 438 U.S. 154, 339–341
FTC, *see* Federal Trade Commission (FTC)

G

Gang graffitti, 184–185
Gang investigations
  definition, 181
  electronic surveillance, 190
  gang members in law enforcement, 183
  gang populations, 182
  gangs in military, 182–183
  impact on society
    clothing, 185
    gang art and violence relationship, 184–185
    numerology, 185–186
    shaking down pedestrians, 183
    stealing from bodegas, 183
  investigative information and procedure
    broken promise, 190
    court testimony, 189
    cross-agency sharing, 188–189
    gangs and drugs relationship, 188
    informants, 187–188
  reasons, 182
  social media, 191
  U.S. News World News report, 180
  WASP ethnicities, 182
Geographic profiling, 168–170, 173

H

Handling informants
  casual observer, 200
  in criminal investigations, 194
  ethical handling, 200–201
  evidence
    prosecution immunity, 204–205
    sentence reduction, 204–205
    witness anonymity, 205–207
  law/policy
    in Australia, 195–197
    United Kingdom's RIPA, 195
    in United States, 197–199
  motives and incentives
    bounty hunter, 199
    legal duress, 199
    money, 199–200
    police buff, 199
    protect corrupt officers, 199–200
    vengeful informants, 199

one-off accomplice witness, 200
    recruiting, 202–203
    supergrass, 200
    unethical police handling, 201–202
HCFAC program, *see* Health Care Fraud and Abuse
        Control (HCFAC) program
Health Care Finance Administration (HCFA),
        103, 113
Health-care (HC) fraud
    AHA, 103
    AMA, 103
    big data, 108
    billings and payment, 101
    cataract surgery, 107–108
    CMS, 101, 104
    credit card companies, 101
    cyclical audits/surveys, 101
    drug-related crimes, 108–109
    FBI, 100
    federal law enforcement, 105
    Fraud Prevention System, 104
    HCFA, 103
    insurance business, 101
    licensing board, 108
    local police, 106–107
    NHCAA, 101–102
    nursing homes, 105–106
    patient/elder harm, 106
    pay-and-chase model, 104–105
    pharmaceutical fraud, 108
    quality of care, 109
    surveillance and detection, 103–104
    transportation fraud
        cybercrime unit, 111
        exclusion/sanction action, 111
        hotline, 109
        medical identity theft, 114
        medical providers, 111
        organized crime groups, 109–111
        SIUs (*see* Special investigative units (SIUs))
Health Care Fraud and Abuse Control (HCFAC)
        program, 113
Health Care Fraud Prevention and Enforcement
        Action Team (HEAT), 105
Health Insurance Privacy and Portability Act
        (HIPPA), 105
Heroin, 72, 188, 343–344
Homicide investigations
    anthrax poisonings, 15
    autopsy, 13
    bullet wounds, 12
    court law, 13–14
    crime scene, 7–8
    defensive wounds, 12–13
    definition, 4–5
    documentary evidence, 10
    dying declaration, 7

guns and violence, 5–6
homicide detectives, 15–17
identifications, 14
incision, 12
lacerations, 12
lineups, 14
motive, method, and opportunity, 14
patrol officer, 6–7
physical evidence, 10–11
puncture wounds, 12
rivalry, 14
seasoned detectives, 6
strangulation/stabbing, 6
testimonial evidence, 8–10
time of death, estimation, 11–12

I

Illinois v. Gates (1983) 462 U.S. 213, 339, 341
Inductive reasoning, 173
International Association of Crime Analysts
        (IACA), 171–173
Instagram, 191
Insurance fraud
    advantages, 69
    Austrian insurance companies, 71–72
    automobile property, 70
    criminal acts, 74
    criminal investigation, 76
    elements, 69
    enterprise development, 68–69
    Europe, 71
    hard and soft fraud, 69–70
    health insurance, 70
    indicators, 76–78
    initial investigation, 75–76
    insurance agencies/agents, 70
    Insurance Information Institute, 74
    investigation positions, 78–79
    national and international investigation,
            cooperation, 81–83
    natural disasters, 70
    personal profile information, 78
    police strategies, 80–81
    prevention, 83
    psychological aspects, 73–74
    United States, 71
    white-collar criminals, 74–75
    workman compensation, 79–80
Insurance Information Institute, 69, 71, 74–76
Insurance policyholders, 69, 72–74, 77–78, 82
Intellectual disability (ID), 300, 305–306
Intelligence analysis, 167
Internal affairs investigation
    administrative investigations, 220–221
    apathy, 217
    criminal investigations, 220–221

effectiveness, 224–225
evidence assessment, 223
external sources, 220–221
findings determination, 223–224
gluttony, 217
greed, 217
intake process, 219–220
internal sources, 220–221
interrogation, 222
interviews, 222
lust, 217
pride, 217
report preparation, 223–224
resentment, 217–218
root causes, 218–219
wrath, 217–218
Internal Revenue Service (IRS), 126
International Criminal Police Organization
        (INTERPOL), 80, 148, 158
Interview and interrogation
    anger and fear, 260
    behavior analysis, 260–261
    court of law, 262–264
    deception, 260
    decision to prosecute, 273–274
    eye contact, 261
    facial expressions, 261
    false confession, 258
    gang members
        avoider, 260
        denier, 259
        minimizer, 259–260
    hands watching, 261–262
    lawful exceptions
        anticipatory invocation, 266
        custody release, 265
        field interviews (see Field interviews (FIs))
        public safety exception, 264–265
        reinitiating questioning, 265
        rescue doctrine, 265
        right to remain silent, 265–266
    open-ended questions, 258
    physical evidences, 258
    recanting witness, 257
    recording, 257
    reluctant witness, 257
    signs of stress, 259
    sitting position, 262
    slam dunk, 258
    technique, 256–257
    testimonial evidence, 8–10
Invisible disability, 301–303
IRS, see Internal Revenue Service (IRS)

J

Judicial review, 317, 320–321, 339

L

Law Enforcement Information Technology
        Standards Council (LEITSC), 166, 197
Lead detective, 278–280, 285

M

Marbury v. Madison, 5 U.S. 137 (1803), 321
Marijuana, 188–189, 330, 332, 343
Medicaid Fraud Control Units (MFCU), 104,
        107–109, 112, 115
Medical examiner (ME), 7–8, 221
Michigan v. Fisher, 130 S. Ct. 546 (2009), 329
Miranda admonishment, 262–264
Miranda v. Arizona (1966), 55
Mobility/communication disability
    ASD, 306–308
    cognitive impairment, 304–305
    implementation, 299–300
    intellectual disability, 305–306
    invisible, 301–303
    TBI
        CDC reports, 308–309
        mental illness, 310–313
        recommendations, 310
        SAMHSA, 309
        severity, 308
        training methods, 309–310
    visible, 300–301

N

Narcotics investigations, 188
Nassau County Police Department, 181–182
National Fire Protection Association (NFPA),
        56–58, 61
National Health Care Anti-Fraud Association
        (NHCAA), 101–102, 114–115
National Institute of Mental Health (NIMH)
        reports, 310–311
National Sex Offender Public Website (NSOPW),
        32–33
National Sex Offender Registry, 32–33
New York City police department (NYPD)
    "The Dirty Thirty," 213
    Frank Serpico's testimony, 213
    internal affairs, 224
    Knapp Commission, 213
    lessons learned, 215–216
    Milton Mollen's 1994 report, 214
    police culture, 214–215
NFPA, see National Fire Protection Association
        (NFPA)
NHCAA, see National Health Care Anti-Fraud
        Association (NHCAA)
Night service, 347

NSOPW, *see* National Sex Offender Public Website
  (NSOPW)
NYPD, *see* New York City police department
  (NYPD)

O

Occult groups investigation
  alternative-belief-related crimes, 235
  barriers, 247–248
  contributing factor, 229
  crimes
    animal sacrifice, 236
    arson, 236
    graffiti, 236
    kidnapping, 237
    murder, 237
    suicide, 237
    thefts, 236
    trespassing, 236
    vandalism, 236
  crime scene identifiers, 242–243
  crime scene investigation, 240–241
  CSI effect, 234–235
  cult cops, 231–232
  factors, 240
  first amendment protections, 230–231
  ghostbusters, 231–232
  indicators, 244–245
  individuals involved types
    dabblers, 237
    levels of involvement, 238–239
    ritualism, 237
    true believers, 237–238
    true criminals, 238
  labels, 230
  lack of education, 229–230
  legend tripping, 239
  occult holidays, 243–244
  occult-related crime, 235
  police training and education impact, 231–232
    cause-effect relationships, 232
    cult crime experts, 232
    cult crime theories, 233
    Satanic connection, 233
  Satanic panic, 233–234
  Satanic-related crime, 235
  Satanic tourism, 239
  search warrant, 246–247
  symbols and rituals, 241–242, 245–246
  terminologies, 230
  titles, 230
Office of Inspector General (OIG), 104–105, 107,
  109, 114
Office of Investigations (OI), 105
Operation Night Watch, 189
OxyContin, 108–109

P

Patrol force, 188
Payton v. New York, 445 U.S. 573 (1980), 328
People v. Hobbs, 347
People v. McCarthy [1978] 79 Cal.App.3d 547,
  550–551, 351
People v. Watson [1979] 89 Cal.App.3d 376, 351
Physical evidence, 10–11, 58, 258
Police buff, 199
Police investigations
  bootleggers, 212
  internal affairs investigation
    administrative investigations, 220–221
    apathy, 217
    criminal investigations, 220–221
    effectiveness, 224–225
    evidence assessment, 223
    external sources, 220–221
    findings determination, 223–224
    gluttony, 217
    greed, 217
    intake process, 219–220
    internal sources, 220–221
    interrogation, 222
    interviews, 222
    lust, 217
    pride, 217
    report preparation, 223–224
    resentment, 217–218
    root causes, 218–219
    wrath, 217–218
  NYPD
    "The Dirty Thirty", 213
    Frank Serpico's testimony, 213
    lessons learned, 215–216
    police culture, 214–215
  police corruption issues, 212
  rampant police misconduct, 212
Political motives, 150–152
Ponzi scheme, 118, 124
Posttraumatic stress disorder (PTSD), 310–313
Procedural law, 320

R

Record management system (RMS), 166–167
Rights of criminal defendants, 292–294

S

Search warrant kit, 353
Search warrants
  vs. administrative warrant, 54
  affidavit, 341–342
  alternatives, 355
  automobile exception, 54

California, definition, 340
car search, 355
conduct search, 351–353
consent, 53–54
custodial arrest, 356
documents sealing, 348
exigent circumstances, 355
experience and training, 345
fire investigators, 54
Franks v. Delaware (1978) 438 U.S. 154, 339–340
general tips, 348–350
"good faith exception," 339
Illinois v. Gates (1983) 462 U.S. 213, 339
jurisdiction, 350–351
knock and notice, 351
lawful arrest, 54
night service, 347
plain view, 356
prior investigation, 345
probable cause statement, 346–347
property searching, 342–343
receipt and inventory, 354
release property, 354
search warrant kit, 353
seize property, 343–345
seizures, 54
statutory grounds, 340–341
"totality of the circumstances" approach, 339
United States v. Leon (1984) 468 U.S. 897, 339
Seasoned detectives, 6, 17
Self-incrimination, 54–55, 128
Serious Organised Crime and Police Act (SOCPA),
  204–205
Sex crime investigations
  acquaintance case, 40–41
  canvass, 41–42
  false reporting, 41
  strange case, 40–41
  witnesses, 41
Sexual assault response team (SART) nurses, 43
Sexual offenders, *see* Sexual predators
Sexual offense evidence collection kit (SOECK), 43
Sexual predators
  characteristics and patterns, 21
  child grooming, 21–22
  child sexual abuse, interviews, 29
  crime scene processing, 29–30
  CSI, 31
  digital evidence, 31
  entrapment defense, 28
  evidence technician, 31
  forensic analysis, 30–31
  fourth amendment, 30
  Internet, 27–29
  law enforcement, 27–29
  National Sex Offender Registry, 32–33
  patience, 24–25

persuasion, 25–26
planning, 24
power, 26
praise, 25
preference, 23
privacy, 26
proficiency, 22–23
puberty, 23–24
SVUs, 31–32
SIUs, *see* Special investigative units (SIUs)
Sixth amendment
  arson investigation, 53
  defendant's constitutional rights, 293–294
  guarantees, 55
Social media, 187, 191, 229
SOCPA, *see* Serious Organised Crime and Police
  Act (SOCPA)
SOECK, *see* Sexual offense evidence collection kit
  (SOECK)
Special investigative units (SIUs)
  access to information, 113
  certifications, 114–115
  CFE, 111
  employee complaints, 113
  enforcement actions, 114
  genesis, 112
  HIPAA, 114
  labor records, 113
  MFCU, 112
  qui tam, 112–113
  research fraud, 113
Special victims
  child victim interview, 38
  confessions, 40
  corroboration
    DNA evidence, 42–43, 48–49
    resources, 42
    subpoenas, 44
    warrants, 43–44
  forensic interview, 38–39, 47–48
  identification process, 44–45
  indicated criminal sexual act, 46–47
  indicated robbery act, 46–47
  investigations
    acquaintance case, 40–41
    canvass, 41–42
    false reporting, 41
    strange case, 40–41
    witnesses, 41
  subject interview, 39–40
  trainings and conferences, 36–37
  victim interview, 37–38
Special victims units (SVUs), 31–32
Strategic crime analysis, 166–167
Substance Abuse and Mental Health Services
  Administration (SAMHSA), 309, 311
Suspicious activity reports (SARs), 125–127

T

Tactical crime analysis (TCA), 169–171, 174
TBI, *see* Traumatic brain injury (TBI)
Testimonial evidence
   cybercrime investigations, 161
   reliability/credibility, 305
   suspects, 8–10
   witnesses, 8–9
Transactional analysis, 82
Transportation fraud
   cybercrime unit, 111
   exclusion/sanction action, 111
   hotline, 109
   medical identity theft, 114
   medical providers, 111
   organized crime groups, 109–111
   SIUs (*see* Special investigative units (SIUs))
Traumatic brain injury (TBI)
   CDC reports, 308–309
   mental illness, 310–313
   recommendations, 310
   SAMHSA, 309
   severity, 308
   training methods, 309–310
Twitter, 191

U

Uniform Crime Report (UCR)
   burglaries, 89
   program, 52–53
   property crime offense, 90
United States v. Dunn, 480 U.S. 294 (1987), 322, 329
United States v. Leon (1984) 468 U.S. 897, 321, 339, 341
U.S. Department of Health and Human Services
   (DHHS), 105, 107, 111–113
U.S. Department of Homeland Security (2007)
   diagram, 136–137
   investigative questions
      e-mails crimes, 141–142
      general investigative questions, 140
      identity theft/financial crimes, 140
      instant messaging/internet relay chat
         crimes, 142
      internet crimes against children, 140–141
      intrusion/hacking (network), 141
U.S. Department of Justice (DOJ), 181
   actual/potential victim, 126
   commercial databases, 127
   definition, 124–125
   FinCEN, 126
   IRS, 126
   law enforcement, 127
   money laundering, 126
   Postal Service, 126
   regulatory databases, 127

   SARs, 125–126
   structuring, 126
U.S. New Jersey Brimage guidelines, 205
U.S. Postal Service, 126

V

Vengeful informants, 199
Victimology, 14, 37, 159

W

White-collar crime
   accounting fraud, 130
   American households, 129
   baby boomer population, 130
   Bitcoin, 130
   consumer payments, 129–130
   cornerstone, 119
   e-mails and text messages, 131
   embezzlement, 119–120
   FBI, 118, 124
   financial institution fraud crimes
      badges of fraud, 121–122
      bank robberies, 120–121
      defendants, 121–122
      detectives, 121
      financial investigations, 121
      perpetrator identity, 121
   FTC, 129
   immunity, 128
   information collection, 128–129
   initial investigation, 122–124
   insurance fraud, 74–75
   investment fraud, 130
   mortgages, 130
   nonprosecution agreement, 128
   Ponzi scheme, 118
   subpoena duces tecum, 128
   substantial monetary resources, 127–128
   Sutherland, 118
   U.S. Department of Justice
      actual/potential victim, 126
      commercial databases, 127
      definition, 124–125
      FinCEN, 126
      IRS, 126
      law enforcement, 127
      money laundering, 126
      Postal Service, 126
      regulatory databases, 127
      SARs, 125–126
      structuring, 126

Y

YouTube, 191